# ROPE WALKER

# ROPE WALKER

## A Texas Jewish History Mystery

# Jim Yarin

248 Ancestors

Acton, Massachusetts

In Memory of "Rope Walker"

*All the past is somehow grown dim*

Herman Melville, "The Chase—
Third Day," *Moby Dick*

# CONTENTS

# EXTRACTS

Copious extracts from a variety of sources appear in this volume as block text rendered in bold italics. Like the graphics of readable text found in this book, errors in sources materials are copied and transcribed without correction so that misspellings, grammatical issues, and factual mistakes are carried over without emendation. The reader should feel confident that errors appearing in such quotations are also found in the original sources, and by Grace and diligent labor the author has been etymologically true to those sources, neither correcting such errors nor introducing new ones of his own making.

All epigraphs in this volume, except for the epigraph above, are from Herman Melville, *Moby Dick, or The Whale* (Indianapolis: Bobbs-Merrill Educational Publishing, 1964. First publ., 1851). Chapter citations for the epigraphs are listed in the table below. These extracts reflect and illuminate the vastness of human expression which Melville captured, but never subdued, in *Moby Dick*. Like the notorious Captain Ahab, Rope Walker was a one-legged risk taker who challenged fate with a rope. Ahab is a fictional character and Rope Walker is not. The former had no last name and for all of Melville's persnicketies, he never indicated which of Ahab's legs was amputated. Rope Walker, on the other hand, will be named, first, last, and then some, and which leg he was missing will be discovered in due course. Ahab's character, his personality that is, even unto his very soul, is brilliantly examined with a complexity and thoroughness unrivaled in most of literature, while the inner thoughts, motivations, the essence of Rope Walker the human being will never be known, simply because he was never a historical figure in whom anyone had ever taken a biographical interest, but especially because he was real.

Melville in *Moby Dick* warns against putting too much faith in compiled facts, even as an exhausted, over-labored scholar at the start of the book collects his data for the benefit of future readers, information which this "sub-sub" describes as no more than "random allusions:"

**As touching the ancient authors generally, as well as the poets here appearing, these extracts are solely valuable or entertaining, as affording a glancing bird's eye view of what has been promiscuously said, thought, fancied, and sung ...**

## Citations for Epigraphs

| _Rope Walker_ Chapter | _Moby Dick_ Chapter |
|---|---|
| Intrologue | XVI. The Ship |
| 1 | VI. The Street |
| 2 | CXXXII. The Symphony |
| 3 | LX. The Line |
| 4 | LXXXIX. Fast-Fish and Loose-Fish |
| 5 | CXII. The Blacksmith |
| 6 | LXIII. The Crotch |
| 7 | CXII. The Blacksmith |
| 8 | XIV. Nantucket |
| 9 | XIX. The Prophet |
| 10 | CXIV. The Gilder |
| 11 | XCIX. The Doubloon |
| 12 | CXXIV. The Needle |
| 13 | LIV. The Town-Ho's Story |
| 14 | XXXII. Cetology |
| 15 | CI. The Decanter |
| 16 | LXXXV. The Fountain |
| 17 | CIV. The Fossil Whale |
| 18 | XVI. The Ship |
| 19 | XLV. The Affidavit |
| 20 | XLV. The Affidavit |
| 21 | XXV. Postscript |
| 22 | XLI. Moby Dick |
| 23 | XXIII. The Lee Shore |
| 24 | XIII. Wheelbarrow |
| 25 | VII. The Chapel |
| 26 | CXXVI. The Life-Buoy |
| 27 | CX. Queequeg in His Coffin |
| 28 | XLVII. The Mat-Maker |
| 29 | C. Leg and Arm: The Pequod, of Nantucket, Meets the Samuel Enderby, of London |
| 30 | CII. A Bower in the Arsacides |
| 31 | LXXXVI. The Tail |
| Supp. I | XVIII. His Mark |
| Supp. II | XCVI. The Try-Works |
| Supp. III | CI. The Decanter |

# Key to Corsicana, Texas Map

A. Hebrew Cemetery

B. Navarro College/Pearce Museum

C. Oakwood Cemetery

D. Jester Park

E. Pioneer Village/Lefty Frizzel Museum

F. Agudas Achim Synagogue* (Senior Center)

G. First Public (Townsend's) School* (Early Education Building)

H. Temple Beth El* (Community Center)

I. H-E-B

J. Collin Street Bakery, downtown shop

K. First Brick Building in Corsicana*/First Newspaper*

L. Court House

M. Firefighters Monument

N. Third Ward School* (location of Donohoo killing)

O. Fox's First Store*

P. First Agudas Achim Synagogue*

Q. London Residence*

R. IOOF Hall* (Marks Residence*/100W Arts Collaborative)

S. First State Bank*/Jester Building

T. 125 N. Beaton St. (Across the Street Diner/Hashop's*)

U. NW Corner of Collin and Beaton Streets

V. State National Bank Building

W. SE Corner of Collin and Beaton Streets

X. Molloy Hotel* (Napoli Restaurant)

Y. Goldsmith Bros. Store*

Z. Visitor Center (H&CT Depot*/Union Station*)

*Building no longer exists or no longer functions as described

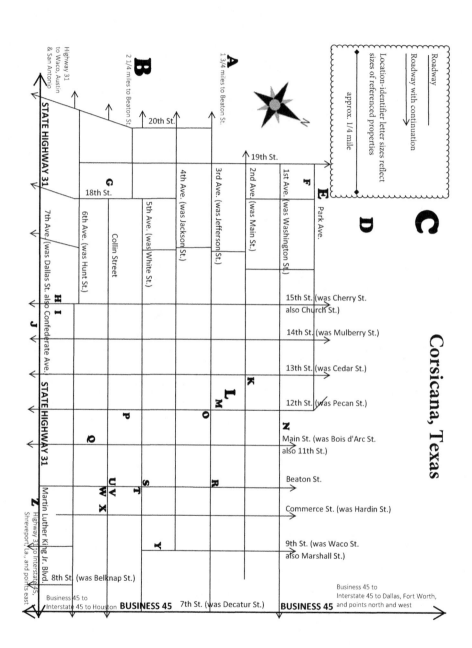

Corsicana, Texas

Roadway
Roadway with continuation
Location-identifier letter sizes reflect sizes of referenced properties

approx. 1/4 mile

N

**A** 1 3/4 miles to Beaton St.

**B** 2 1/4 miles to Beaton St.

Highway 31 to Waco, Austin & San Antonio

**STATE HIGHWAY 31**

20th St.

18th St.

**G**

19th St.

1st Ave. (was Washington St.)

2nd Ave. (was Main St.)

3rd Ave. (was Jefferson St.)

4th Ave. (was Jackson St.)

5th Ave. (was White St.)

6th Ave. (was Hunt St.)

Collin Street

7th Ave. (was Dallas St. also Confederate Ave.)

Park Ave.

**E** **F** **C** **D**

15th St. (was Cherry St. also Church St.)

14th St. (was Mulberry St.)

13th St. (was Cedar St.)

12th St. (was Pecan St.)

Main St. (was Bois d'Arc St. also 11th St.)

Beaton St.

Commerce St. (was Hardin St.)

9th St. (was Waco St. also Marshall St.)

8th St. (was Belknap St.)

7th St. (was Decatur St.)

**H** **I** **J** **K** **L** **M** **N** **O** **P** **Q** **R** **S** **T** **U** **V** **W** **X** **Y** **Z**

**STATE HIGHWAY 31**

Martin Luther King Jr. Blvd.

Highway 31 to Interstate 45, Shreveport, La., and points east

Business 45 to Interstate 45 to Houston **BUSINESS 45**

Business 45 to Interstate 45 to Dallas, Fort Worth, and points north and west **BUSINESS 45**

# Location of Corsicana in Context

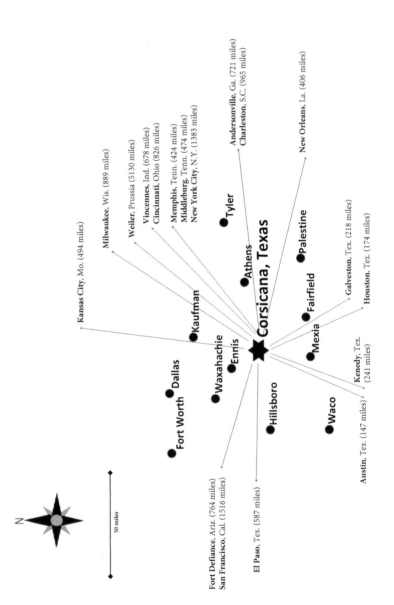

Kansas City, Mo. (494 miles)

Milwaukee, Wis. (889 miles)

Weiler, Prussia (5130 miles)

Vincennes, Ind. (678 miles)
Cincinnati, Ohio (826 miles)

Memphis, Tenn. (424 miles)
Middleburg, Tenn. (474 miles)
New York City, N.Y. (1383 miles)

Andersonville, Ga. (721 miles)
Charleston, S.C. (965 miles)

New Orleans, La. (406 miles)

**Tyler**

**Athens**

**Corsicana, Texas**

**Kaufman**

**Palestine**

**Waxahachie**
**Ennis**

**Fairfield**

Galveston, Tex. (218 miles)

Houston, Tex. (174 miles)

**Fort Worth** **Dallas**

**Mexia**

**Hillsboro**

Kenedy, Tex. (241 miles)

**Waco**

Austin, Tex. (147 miles)

Fort Defiance, Ariz. (764 miles)
San Francisco, Cal. (1516 miles)

El Paso, Tex. (587 miles)

50 miles

N

# PREFACE

Here is a work of nonfiction. Filled with many fictions, none are of my own making. Accounts of the Rope Walker legend have been retold so often, no version accurately describes what truly happened. The basics of the story have long been accepted as true, even without any solid underlying factual evidence to support it except one thing: a small, time-worn gravestone in a Texas Jewish cemetery.

The unproven facts and flimsy corroborations of the Rope Walker legend will be stamped for what they are: the untested bolts and braces of a shaky house, maybe true, maybe false. Under the least bit of serious inquiry, the entire thing collapses. To solve the Rope Walker mystery, each key facet of the legend will be tested to distinguish truth from fiction and reality from fantasy. In the end there will be a fit and sturdy structure, albeit less capacious.

I had already caught the genealogy bug for at least ten years when, in 2004, I first encountered the Rope Walker story. I was then building family trees for families with the Jewish surname "Effron" (and spelling variations), "collect–ing Effrons" from the past in the same way other hobbyists collect coins or stamps. It all began when I learned that my grandmother had cousins with that surname in Chattanooga. Nana's family emigrated from Eastern Europe in 1904 and settled in Boston, a metropolis with a large Jewish population, and the idea that Jews lived in Chattanooga, a southern city—my relatives no less—was not only surprising but intriguing. As I soon discovered, to my amazement, there were additional Effron relatives who had emigrated to Georgia, Kentucky, and even West Virginia—hardly the urban, cosmo–politan communities one usually imagines for American Jews! I began to build up a robust collection of Effrons. One family, who spelled their name with only one "f" and apparently unrelated to my Effron family, were early Jewish residents of Waco, Texas, with kin in other Texas towns, including Corsicana. That's when, in 2004, I first learned there was a peg-legged tightrope walker buried in Corsicana's Hebrew cemetery.

The mystery central to the "Rope Walker" legend presented a compelling challenge—no one knew his name. So, I did some research. I couldn't solve the riddle, and that made sense: there was a reason why no one had figured it out for well over a century! I dreamed that someday I would be the person to finally discover his name and solve this bizarre, seemingly unsolvable puzzle. And I did.

More than ten years after that initial effort, during the final week of 2015, I was doing genealogical research for a client whose family briefly lived near Corsicana, and there he was again. I had not forgotten about him in the least.

I made another effort to discover the man's name, and, in short, this time I succeeded and solved the mystery.

I knew immediately I wanted to tell his story. In due course I realized I had an opportunity to tell another story, the story of an early Texas Jewish community. And then I found myself delving into questions about historical fact finding, and this too became a major theme woven into the Rope Walker saga. Lastly, the memorialization and remembrance of the dead became a topic which also deserved inclusion in this book.

Keeping to verifiable facts means I often resort to hazy qualifications and disclaimers: *it seems, evidence suggests, it is likely, if/then,* and *perhaps.* I chose not to make assumptions, make stuff up, or insert fanciful descriptions and dialogue. Instead, I have tried to present only facts. I've opted to say, for example, "it took between one and two seconds for him to fall" instead of the more eloquent, but unprovable, "he fell in a second."

The discovery of Rope Walker's identity is told within the context of the history of the Jews of Corsicana, their leaders in commerce, community, and faith, their prominent families, Jewish institutions, and interactions with their Gentile neighbors. Unlike most other American Jewish community histories, this book also includes in-depth profiles of non-leaders and ordinary families. A thorough review of the town's synagogues, its rabbis, and its earliest Jewish burials is included in three appendixes following the last chapter, supplements which may be read in part, or in their entirety, at any time.

This book possesses an unusual duality not found in history books: a real-life mystery, several generations old, that is thoroughly analyzed—a micro–history or "anatomy", if you will, and a definitive solution to that mystery. Writing a "history mystery" with an indisputable solution presented several special challenges. What if someone independently discovers the same thing I discovered, or borrows my ingenuity, and beats me to the book shelf? Luckily, no one has. Will social media or book reviews publish spoilers, and give away the recipe to the special sauce, blurt out the identity of Rose Bud? I hope not.

I could not have wished for a richer array of threads, even had I created them purely from my own imagination: pioneer Jews in Texas, a crippled acrobat, and a mysterious death. To braid these threads into one narrative presented quite a challenge in and of itself. I took on that risk, as a first-time author, and hope I have successfully traversed the line.

Jim Yarin
Acton, Mass.
November 8, 2020

# ROPE WALKER

Intrologue

# AN EXCITEMENT
# NOT ON THE BILLS

*It might be thought that this was a poor way to accumulate a princely fortune—and so it was, a very poor way indeed.*

**An Exciting Time – Visitors to the Milwaukee Garden yesterday were treated to an excitement not on the bills. A one-legged acrobat—or rather with one real and one wooden leg—was giving exhibitions in rope walking. His wire was suspended some thirty feet in height and over this the sound leg and the wooden leg gaily went much to the delight of all. In the midst of the scene, he was seen to drop his pole and to stand for a few seconds trembling and then to fall upon the rope. This was supposed for a few seconds to be a part of the play, but it was not. The daring acrobat had overtaxed his strength and was in great danger of falling to the ground. In coming down he managed to get his wooden leg twisted about the rope and for some seconds this alone kept him from falling. The crowd, now realizing the state of affairs, stood spell-bound, expecting every moment to see the reckless man dashed to his death below, but that wooden leg was true to the last. He twisted and worked carefully and cautiously, clinging the while with his leg to the rope, until he succeeded in reaching it with his hands, and then pulled himself up. When firmly on the rope his strength was gone, and he said to those about that it was the closest fall he had ever had. When he was in safety the crowd yelled their joy loudly, and he came down from his rope to rest.**

This mid-summer, 1869 item from a Wisconsin newspaper should have included a more robust description of the performer. It failed to mention his white, form-fitting bodysuit, a recent invention by "the daring young man on the flying trapeze," Jules Léotard, how it reached down to the rope walker's right ankle but only to the top of the tapered dowel, carved from oak, attached to his amputated left leg. Just below the left knee the stocking ended with a ruffle of flowery lace, and then: a peg leg. Black leather straps with brass buckles secured the artificial limb to his thigh. A pair of colorfully embroidered silk trunks with wide, vertical, red and yellow stripes billowed in the gentle breeze. A sleeveless, open, matching vest rested loosely on his shoulders, revealing two medals pinned to his Herculean chest.

The body stocking emphasized his tremendous physique. From his neck, shoulders, and bulging arms to his trim torso and his leg-and-a-half he was one rolling landscape of muscle. Happy hazel eyes pleased a large, oval face and a tallyho pursuit of side whiskers gracing florid cheeks stopped just short of a Spartacus chin. His nose—it was unremarkable, except that it was the only modest feature of his physical self. Age? Somewhere in his thirties—give or take a few years. His hair was wavy brown, neatly trimmed.

Smiling Milwaukeeans ambled aimlessly over the park's yellowy-orange brick paths past patiently manicured greenery, arm-in-arm toward the promised coolness of the setting sun. The lamps were already lit. Giggling and shouting youngsters scurried about in every direction.

The wooden-legged acrobat tossed one end of a heavy coil of quarter-inch rope over the branch of a pine tree, about thirty feet high. He used the end that came back down to tie a slip knot around the rope and pulled so the knot slid up the rope, closing the loop snuggly around the branch. He tested it, tugging on the rope with his entire body to pull it tight. Several people stopped to watch. He smiled, nodded, and with his crutch under his left arm swiftly skipped over to an elm a hundred feet away. With careful aim he tossed the remainder of the rope into the elm, looping it over a branch at roughly the same height as the first end and climbed up. Astraddle the branch, he pulled the rope taut from the pine tree and tied it off. He climbed down the remainder of the rope, which hung loosely off the branch, grabbed another lengthy piece of rope, and tossed the second rope over the first piece, midway between the two trees. He selected two men from the crowd and instructed them to securely hold the ends of the second piece of rope, pulling just tight enough to increase the tension of the rope strung between the trees. Back to the elm, the rope walker attached a long wooden pole to the loose end of the rope hanging from the branch, climbed up the rope, and then pulled up the balancing pole after him up to the branch.

Dozens of adults and scores of children by now had gathered around, knowing they would be treated to a free performance. If he was any good, maybe they would give him a few cents, a nickel, maybe more if they could afford it, and if he earned it, once he came around with a bowl or hat or box or open hands. He stood up and gingerly placed his wooden leg at the start of the rope. He waved for people to approach, drawing them in with one hand as the other held the pole against his waist. Like magic, hundreds of people converged to the area around him, and conversations trailed off to whispers. He took his free hand, turned it toward his face as if he was checking his own fortune in the hardened carved creases of his palm, stretched it straight up above his head, lifted his face skyward, closed his eyes, and held this reverent attitude for a lengthy ten seconds.

He opened his eyes and scanned the crowd. He spoke, loud and slow, carefully enunciating each word, speaking at first in German and then in a deeply accented English: "Meine Damen und Herren! As you know from the preface, just a few pages back, this is a nonfiction story. In truth, no one knows what I wore, how I secured the rope, or what I said to you. But fear not, you will learn many things about me, starting with my name, hitherto unknown. You will learn in detail the unusual circumstances of my death, something about my background, my unusual occupation, and how I lost my leg. Be forewarned: this book is not a biography, even though it is about me. It is not a *yizkor* book—a memorial to a Jewish community—although one can be constructed within these pages. There is also a fair accounting inside here of a certain Texas town's history, but this is not a local history. Rest assured; every fact presented in the following pages is true. Where there is uncertainty, it is admitted to, and you can judge for yourself. Some things will be left for speculation—that's the reality of a history written about an unknown man who lived so many years ago.

"The news item transcribed above, about my performance at the Milwaukee Garden on Tuesday, July 13, 1869, that report is genuine; but everything that followed, up to this point—all made up."

Ω

Many a member of Corsicana's once-vibrant Jewish community, now mostly in the town's Hebrew cemetery, will be brought back to life in the following chapters and the supplements which follow them. The rope walker was one of them, if only for a brief moment.

Discovering the truth behind the tragic story of a tightrope walker's accidental death will require a lot of construction and deconstruction. This knotty problem is first worked at by picking and pulling at any loose thread in a tangled lump of compressed, crisscrossed loops. Unwinding the Rope Walker story starts at the beginning, which, in this case, was the end of a crippled acrobat.

# Chapter 1

## A ROPE WALKER
## STOPPED IN CORSICANA

*It is a land of oil, true enough: but not like Canaan*

The beginning and end of the Rope Walker legend takes place in Corsicana, a Texas city of nearly twenty-five thousand less than an hour south of Dallas along Interstate 45, one quarter of the way to Houston. Quite a bit of time will be spent there—or, more accurately, in the Corsicana of long ago.

While travelling from Dallas to Corsicana along Route 45, following directions which say to take Exit 231, suddenly, out of nowhere, appears a sign that says instead that Route 45 to Corsicana is Exit 235B. Take it, or don't take it?

**A sign**

The journey has hardly started, and already—confusion! It's a sign of the many ambiguities and uncertainties to be encountered on the way to learning the truth behind the Rope Walker legend. Even if destinations will not always be reached as planned, they will be reached; however, the traveler must be prepared and flexible because the next time, though travelling the same route, the signs will be different and the off-ramp completely reconfigured.

Exit 235B leads to downtown Corsicana, putting drivers on 7th Street, a street that does indeed mean business. Nothing much to see, coming this way. Exit 231, further on, instead, is more scenic. Take it. It leads to Route 31W, aka Martin Luther King Jr. Boulevard. Passing numbered streets and rumbling over a set of railroad crossings, a large cylindrical structure, which could be an alien invader from *War of the Worlds*, arises suddenly on the left.

It would be a great place for an advertisement or a "Welcome to Corsicana" banner. Route 31 at this point is called 7th Avenue, its original name (it was also once called Confederate Avenue). On the other side of the tracks, on the right, is Beaton Street, the gateway to downtown; on the left, a handsome railcar is on display.

Behind the railcar is the Corsicana Visitor Center, set back from 7th Avenue, allowing travelers to pull off the road and get their bearings. This cheery stop immediately refocuses wayfarers' senses to the quaint history of this onetime oil boomtown, now a blooming olio town. Inside the center, a replica railway ticketing office, is a large collection of brochures, books, refrigerator magnets, and the other touristy items that are the blood and guts of visitor centers from coast to coast. Museums, shopping, and an assortment of interesting and sometimes unusual attractions—here can be found brochures for them all.

Only a few short blocks down Beaton Street is the historic town center, where Rope Walker descended into Corsicana history. Note: in Corsicana, "Rope Walker" is not simply the nineteenth century term for a tightrope performer. It's a name. The words are capitalized and an introductory "the" is not used, as if he were a member of the Walker family, first name "Rope," brother perhaps of Rice and Rock.

Beaton Street, Corsicana's historic boulevard with its temples of commerce, is the stage where the curtain is raised on the first scene of the funambulist tragedy, a turn off of 7th Ave. directly opposite the front door of the Visitor Center. Curiously, the center's address is 301 South Beaton, even though it fronts on 7th Ave., and Beaton Street does not continue across 7th Avenue. If Beaton did cross over 7th Ave. it would go right through the Center's front door, out the back, across a train yard and skirt along various commercial buildings. A half-mile from the Visitor Center the roadway does reappear and is once again called Beaton Street.

Before crossing 7th Ave. to walk down the historic part of Beaton Street, the heart and soul of Corsicana, a visitor might take inventory of the historic markers, interpretative placards and other information planted around the Visitor Center. These are a few of the many remembrances spread throughout a town proud of its past. Tourists don't need to read and meditate on every marker and plaque; after a while there's a need to skip ahead to the peculiar incident that is the purpose of this trip.

Next to train car 305 is a glass-covered sheet explaining that the Texas Interurban Electric Railway operated from 1913 to 1941, shuttling between Dallas and Corsicana, and terminating at this very spot. In front of the Center is an official Texas Historical Marker for Capt. Charles Henry Allyn, a New York native who was a leading merchant of Corsicana and mayor from 1888-1890. The land where the center is situated is called Allyn Park. A cement fountain adorns the small plaza in front of the Center, bearing a cryptic inscription, "PHIFE." Along the base are the only other words engraved in the fountain: "Memory" and "C.P. Pinkston." A Google search reports it was created by Lucian A. Pinkston, Sr. in memory of his brother, Phife, created as a watering station for horses. The automobile made it obsolete by the time it was completed, so it's now a planter. Poking around in Ancestry.com and FindAGrave.com reveals that Lucian was a railroad man, and Caleb Phifer Pinkston, an insurance man, Lucian's brother, lived from 1862-1914. Nearby, a placard mounted on a short post dictates that a slight, wispy tree there is to be decorated for Christmases future, in memory of Mack Cooper.

A recently erected black, wrought iron arch over the start of Beaton Street, across from the Visitor Center, makes clear this is the entrance to "HISTORIC CORSICANA." A walk along Beaton, past antique shops, boutiques, and cafes, buildings which still have their nineteenth century facades and many with lively decorated display windows, is a pleasant stroll and an interesting lesson in local history. Two brochures plucked from the pamphlet rack in the Visitor Center summarize.

The town's official "Visitor & Relocation Guide" has this introduction:

> **Corsicana was established in 1848 to serve as the seat of government for Navarro County, which the first Texas Legislature created two years earlier. When asked what the new town should be called, Texas Patriot and county namesake Jose Antonio Navarro replied, "Call it Corsicana after the island of Corsica, the birthplace of my father."**
>
> **In 1894, oil was discovered by accident only blocks from Corsicana's business district as drillers were completing an artesian well to expand the city's water supply. Within six years, 500 wells operating within the city limits were producing 800,000 barrels of crude annually, making Corsicana the site of the first commercial oil field in Texas. Today the 25,000 residents of Corsicana take great pride in their rich history.**

The other brochure is "Walking Tour of Historic Downtown Corsicana." It has pretty much the same introduction. The quote from José Antonio Navarro is not identical, but then again, maybe he spoke in Spanish, and both are English translations.

And here is Rope Walker. Unlike most of the walking tour's features, he did not get one of the twenty-seven enumerated stops. Those attract–

ions are commemorated with diamond-shaped markers affixed to buildings and mounted on posts dotting Beaton Street and vicinity, each bearing a number corresponding to the walking tour. A well-placed example, stop twelve, is attached near a mural painted on an exterior wall of 125 N. Beaton Street.

**Historic walking tour stop twelve plaque, next to a wall mural on the side of 125 North Beaton Street, celebrates Wolf Brand Chili**

Rope Walker falls between stops four and five. Four is the landmark 1926 State National Bank Building, now occupied by Chase Bank, at the inter–section of Beaton and Collin Streets—just a few blocks from the Visitor Center. Built in the Gothic Revival style, its eight floors make it one of the tallest buildings in the county. From this historic center of Corsicana streets are divided north and south and avenues east and west.

Following stop four, the pamphlet says:

### Downtown Corsicana and the "Rope Walker"

*Before you move on, look from the NW corner of the intersection to the SE corner, transport yourself back to 1884, and imagine the crowd gathering to watch an event destined to become a tragic mystery of downtown Corsicana history. An itinerant rope walker with a peg-leg strapped an iron stove to his back, picked up a long balancing pole and began walking a rope stretched high across the intersection as a stunt. Halfway across, the Rope Walker fell and lay in the street mortally wounded. The unnamed performer was able to whisper to those gathered to comfort him that he was a dying Jew. A Jewish merchant rushed to his side and shared a prayer with him as he lay dying. The townspeople were never able to determine his identity and he was buried in the Jewish Cemetery with a tombstone reading simply 'Rope Walker'.*

Ω

Here's a good jumping-off point. Continuing north on Beaton, turn left on 3rd Ave. and continue just past 31st Street. Here the tombstone tourist arrives at Corsicana's Hebrew Cemetery, the final resting place of Rope Walker.

# Chapter 2

## WRITTEN IN STONE

*toil we how we may, we all sleep at last on the field*

**Original Rope Walker gravestone and recently installed granite marker**

If not for that gravestone, the Rope Walker legend would have died out long ago. But there it is, a steadfast reminder of an unusual tragedy from a long time ago—and a persistent mystery ever since.

If there were a name on the stone, things might have been different. If the stone said Abe Weiss, instead of Rope Walker, there would be no legend of a stove-wielding, one-legged Jewish tightrope walker.[1] People might know of Abe, that he was once a tightrope walker, but for the most part he would have been long-forgotten. Even if "rope walker" were added below Abe's name, designating his profession, it wouldn't garner the heightened intrigue generated by the Rope Walker stone. It is this audacious absence of information that reminds each new generation of local residents about this man, how he died, and the attendant mystery of that death. A little marble tombstone, with its peculiar inscription and no name, has kept Rope Walker's memory alive all these years.

The drive to the cemetery from Beaton Street up 2nd Ave., instead of 3rd, has far fewer stop signs, a higher speed limit, and a much smoother roadway, but 3rd Ave. has the charm of a pleasant Corsicana residential neighborhood and better parking at the end. Visitors, no matter how they get there, are cautioned not to go on Saturdays, the Jewish Sabbath, or after dark. Police take notice!

The Hebrew Cemetery covers five and a half acres, roughly square, with gates on 2nd and 3rd Avenues. On the east side it shares a fence with Corsicana's Catholic Calvary Cemetery, which is roughly the same size.

Sometime in the 1960s, Rope Walker's tombstone was placed in a horizontal bed of concrete.[2] Later, around 2004, a granite headstone was added, inscribed with the same two words plus his date of death, 1884.[3] Care for this unusual internment—actually, for the entire Hebrew Cemetery—had been for decades and until just recently the responsibility of Babbette Samuels, a beloved and respected Corsicanan, last of the once-thriving Jewish community who still lives in town. Other Corsicana Jews moved to Dallas, Houston, and elsewhere. Many of them who passed away outside of Corsicana were brought back to the Hebrew Cemetery where they could be remembered alongside lifelong friends and family.

Babbette has reached her tenth decade, and despite some health setbacks she still has incredible energy and a sharp mind. Confident and active, her devotion to the care of the cemetery is evident in the immaculately maintained grounds. Babbette was born in the Texas gulf town of Port Arthur, long after Rope Walker died, but she looks after his grave as if it were yesterday. She came to Corsicana in 1951 when she married Irvin Samuels, a native Corsicanan, and together they made their home and raised a family in Corsicana. Irvin passed away in 2003, his final resting place in the Hebrew Cemetery, lovingly cared for by Babbette.

The Samuels family was a typical Corsicana Jewish family. Fully integrated into the social fabric of the town, Irvin's father, Philip Samuels, was a clothier on Beaton Street, starting in 1897.[4] Young Irvin would post himself on the store's steps, offering free lemonade to entice customers to come inside and have a look. The shop was eventually taken over by Irvin, who ran it until it closed in 1990. "P. Samuels" was a fixture in town for close to a century.

The neatly laid-out grounds are divided into quadrants with a fountain and circular path in the center. The fountain, built in 1905, was paid for by brothers Joseph and Kal Shwarts in memory of their parents, Aaron Shwarts, a longtime town grocer, and Caroline (Zander) Shwarts, a mother of eleven children, all born after the couple arrived in Texas. The Shwarts family was one of the Jewish families living in Corsicana when Rope Walker died. Several members of the family likely witnessed his death.

At the 3rd Ave. entrance is a Historic Texas Cemetery marker, erected in 2008. The first half gives an overview of the cemetery's history and the history of the Jews of Corsicana. The second half identifies Rope Walker and four other individuals whose mortal remains are interred there. If dead men could talk, what would these four say about Rope Walker? All of them appear in later chapters, so only a brief look suffices for now, taken in the order in which they appear on the plaque.

**The Shwarts Fountain in the Hebrew Cemetery**

# CORSICANA HEBREW CEMETERY

THIS BURIAL GROUND HAS SERVED THE JEWISH RESIDENTS IN CORSICANA SINCE THE LATE 1800s. THE FIRST JEWISH SETTLERS IN THE COMMUNITY CAME HERE IN 1871, WHEN THE HOUSTON AND TEXAS CENTRAL RAILROAD EXTENDED ITS LINE FROM HOUSTON TO CORSICANA EN ROUTE TO DALLAS. THE FIRST JEWISH SETTLERS, MANY OF WHOM TRACED THEIR ORIGINS TO EASTERN EUROPE OR TO ALSACE LORRAINE, WERE MERCHANTS WHO MADE USE OF THE RAILROADS. SOON, THE JEWISH POPULATION WAS WELL ESTABLISHED IN CORSICANA AND NEEDED A CEMETERY. IN 1881, THE HEBREW CEMETERY ASSOCIATION PURCHASED THIS PROPERTY FOR USE AS A BURIAL GROUND. HOWEVER, THE LAND HAD BEEN USED FOR JEWISH INTERMENTS PRIOR TO THIS TIME; THE EARLIEST KNOWN BURIAL DATES TO 1877. IN 1887, THE LADIES HEBREW CEMETERY ASSOCIATION FORMED TO RAISE FUNDS FOR CEMETERY UPKEEP. IN 1951, ADDITIONAL PROPERTY WAS PURCHASED.

CEMETERY FEATURES INCLUDE OBELISKS, STATUARY AND CURBING. NOTED INDIVIDUALS INTERRED HERE INCLUDE CIVIC LEADER, BUSINESSMAN AND 14-TERM PRESIDENT OF TEMPLE BETH EL, SIDNEY MARKS; ENTREPRENEUR AND PHILANTHROPIST, KALMAN WOLENS; CIVIL WAR VETERAN MAX LONDON; AN ANONYMOUS ROPE WALKER, WHO IN 1884 FATALLY FELL FROM A TIGHTROPE, LEADING TO A SEARCH FOR HIS IDENTITY WHICH GRIPPED THE COMMUNITY; AND ERNEST JOSEPH, WHO SERVED AS RABBI FOR BOTH THE REFORM AND ORTHODOX CONGREGATIONS UNTIL HIS DEATH IN 1999. TODAY, THERE ARE OVER 400 INDIVIDUALS BURIED HERE. CORSICANA HEBREW CEMETERY REMAINS A HALLOWED GROUND WHICH CHRONICLES THE HISTORY OF CORSICANA'S JEWISH RESIDENTS, WHO SINCE THE 1800s HAVE PLAYED A VITAL ROLE IN THE COMMUNITY'S CIVIC, CULTURAL AND ECONOMIC DEVELOPMENT.

HISTORIC TEXAS CEMETERY - 2008
MARKER IS PROPERTY OF THE STATE OF TEXAS

Texas Historical Marker at the Corsicana Hebrew Cemetery

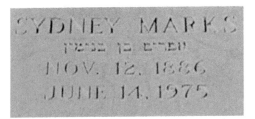

# SIDNEY MARKS

**"Civic Leader, Businessman and 14-Term President of Temple Beth El"**

His longtime service to Temple Beth El was one of many ways Sydney Marks served Corsicana and its Jewish community. His involvement can be traced to the first decades of the temple. During rabbi-less periods he conducted religious services. He was president of the Crippled Children's Society and the Navarro Community Foundation and a board member of the city's public library. He was a founding board member of the Drane Foundation, a charity serving Navarro County's poor. Marks took his philosophy of life from the Bible: "What doth the Lord require of thee but to do justice, and to love mercy, and to walk humbly before thy God?"[5]

Sydney was born in Corsicana. By 1910 he had joined his father's dry goods business, helping with his brothers to build it into one of the leading department stores in Corsicana. He later opened and ran a successful advertising agency.[6] His father, Benjamin Marks, a native of Russia, was an energetic and early supporter of the town's orthodox synagogue, Agudas Achim, which was founded when the elder Marks was sixty-five.[7]

# KALMAN WOLENS

**"Entrepreneur and Philanthropist"**

K. Wolens, as he was known, emigrated from Poland in 1893 and settled in Chicago. A year later he came to Corsicana with his brothers, Nathan and Jack. In 1898 he borrowed fifty dollars to open a stand on a Beaton Street corner and sold glasses. He next opened a menswear store behind Louis Levine's Iron Front Saloon,[8] on N. Beaton St., near 5th Ave., which later became the Wolens Department Store. The Wolens brothers opened additional stores, in Wortham and Waxahachie.[9] In 1926, after oil was discovered on his farm, K. Wolens expanded his chain of stores, eventually numbering sixty-three. He gave generously to charity, including a $50,000 gift to help establish Navarro Memorial Hospital.[10]

Wolens was an Orthodox Jew. He and his family ate only kosher food and obeyed the commandment to keep the Sabbath holy by abstaining from all work from sundown Friday to sundown Saturday. In 1914 he bought some land and opened a small store outside of town. He raised cattle to be slaughtered according to Jewish law so he could sell kosher meat to other religious Jews in the region. He and his wife helped establish Congregation Agudas Achim, in 1915.

### "Civil War Veteran"

When Rope Walker fell, Sydney Marks was not yet born and K. Wolens was years away from leaving Poland. Max London, however, was an established resident of Corsicana and could have been on Beaton Street and saw the accident.

During Corsicana's April 26, 1918 Confederate Memorial Day lecture, Mrs. J.A. Townsend informed the audience that the Jewish Cemetery held two Daughters of the Confederacy, Mrs. A. Fox and Mrs. Max London, and three veterans:[11] Joseph Levy,[12] Louis Niveth,[13] and Moises Hirsch.[14] Max London was not included because he was still very much alive. London served for the entirety of the Civil War.[15]

London came from London to Texas in 1855, landing at Galveston. By 1920 the retired insurance man had lived in Corsicana since 1877 and believed himself to be the only then-living Jew who had lived in Galveston before the Civil War.[16] He claimed that a man should be measured not by his years, but by his deeds.

He initially settled his family in a house at the location where the town's newspaper, the *Corsicana Daily Sun*, was once situated, 106 S. 11th Street,[17] next to the current location of the post office. In 1880 he moved to 316 W. 6th Street. It was there that Max, his wife Bertha, and his two unmarried daughters lived out their days.

Longevity ran in the London family. His brother Elkan died in 1922, at the age of ninety-two,[18] and their father was eighty-three when he died.[19] In an eighty-second birthday tribute Max London had the local paper reprint a *Louisville Evening Post* article about the accomplishments and contributions of Jews. The quoted article listed numerous famous Jewish men in diverse fields, such as drama, mathematics, and medicine. It closed with general comments about the positive characteristics of the typical Jew, including an account of their contributions to government and military service in the United States. The article is reminiscent of Simon Wolf's 1895 book, *The American Jew as Patriot, Soldier and Citizen*, written to rebut allegations that Jews were unpatriotic.[20] Wolf attempted to list all Jews who served in the U.S. military, but only one Corsicana name shows up in his short list of Confederate Texas Jews, and it's not London. It's A. (Alexander) Fox, a soldier in Waul's Legion. Like London, Fox was also still living in 1918 when Corsicana's Jewish Confederate burials were remembered.[21] Max London was a thirty-second degree Mason.

# AN ANONYMOUS ROPE WALKER

**"In 1884 Fatally Fell from a Tightrope, Leading to a Search for his Identity which Gripped the Community"**

The plaque does not say anything about a peg leg or stove, mentioned in the walking tour pamphlet, but does add that there was a *gripping* search for his identity. The only evidence of any such search having ever taken place is this *gripping* statement itself. But, one step at a time.

# ERNEST JOSEPH

**"Served as Rabbi for both the Reform and Orthodox Congregations until his Death in 1999"**

Rabbi Ernest Joseph was born in Halle an der Saale, Germany. In 1947, at the age of sixteen, he and his parents arrived in San Francisco after having lived in Shanghai during the war. His family settled in Dallas.

Rabbi Joseph was the beloved leader of Corsicana's Jewish community for decades. He arrived in 1956 to work for K. Wolens and later became an assistant to the rabbi of the orthodox synagogue. The Wolens family paid for his rabbinic training, and after two years away he returned to Corsicana as the syn—agogue's newest rabbi.[22] Three years later he also assumed the pulpit of the town's reform congregation, Temple Beth El, simultaneously leading both synagogues.

Rabbi Joseph's son, Frank Joseph, carries on his father's legacy, holding bimonthly services in the building formerly used as Temple Beth El.

♎

The Corsicana Jews singled out for mention on the historical plaque are only some of the exceptional Jewish men and women who contributed to the vitality, character, and success of Corsicana as builders of the town's commercial and social institutions. Three of the five, Marks, Wolens, and Joseph, were very religious—the two most religious Jews who made Corsicana their permanent home plus the town's last rabbi. They are not representative of the typical Corsicana Jew's adherence to Jewish tradition. The other two, Rope Walker and Max London, are each in a category of his very own. It's not easy to categorize anyone, even those collectively called "the Jews of Corsicana"; each left his own, distinctive mark, as future chapters will bear out.

# Chapter 3

## CERFS

*All men live enveloped in whale-lines. All are born with halters round their necks; but it is only when caught in the swift, sudden turn of death, that mortals realize the silent, subtle, ever-present perils of life. And if you be a philosopher, though seated in the whale-boat, you would not at heart feel one whit more of terror, than so seated before your evening fire with a poker, and not a harpoon, by your side.*

Louis Cerf family monument, Hebrew Cemetery

Two notable individuals buried in the Hebrew Cemetery but not named on the historical plaque are Louis Cerf and his son, I.N. Cerf. They were two of the earliest Jews in Corsicana, arriving in 1871 when the Houston & Texas Central (H&TC) railroad line was extended to Corsicana on its march north to Sherman, via Dallas. Louis Cerf and his brother, Dave, were two of the seven founders of the Hebrew Cemetery. Louis also helped establish Corsicana's first Jewish house of worship, Temple Beth El. Dave Cerf moved from Corsicana while still a young man, established himself and a family in Indiana, and died in New Orleans, where he was buried.

Louis and Dave Cerf came from Mittelbronn, a French town near the German border. Mittelbronn is in Lorraine, which in turn is part of Alsace-Lorraine, an area long subject to cultural and political divisions between France and Germany. Those from the region were referred to as *Alsatians*. Louis, Dave, and five other Cerf brothers and sisters—seven out of a total of ten siblings—were Alsatian emigrants who came to Texas in the 1860s or thereabouts.

Inquiry into the origins of Corsicana's Jewish tightrope performer begins with an inquiry into nineteenth-century Jewish circus performers in general, an inquiry that immediately turns up an internet reference to the founder of the Blumenfeld Circus, Maurice Levi Cerf, who, like the Corsicana Cerfs, was an Alsatian Jew. Is this coincidence, or was there some connection between the Corsicana Cerfs and this circus Cerf which might explain why Rope Walker came to Corsicana? A detailed examination, laying out details on both families, might reveal a link that leads to Rope Walker's identity.

## Maurice Levi Cerf and His Blumenfeld Circus

**Maurice Levi Cerf (1783-1867).** No Jewish-run show was as celebrated as his Blumenfeld Circus,[23] a German troupe which performed for nearly one and a half centuries. Cerf's family was operating travelling menageries, featuring birds and apes, at the time he married **Yetta Blumenfeld**, in 1811. Yetta came from a family of acrobats and rope dancers who had already been performing for more than a century. Their nuptials also wedded the two productions to create the Blumenfeld Circus. Maurice Levi Cerf adopted his wife's surname, Blumenfeld.

Maurice and Yetta had nine children, nearly all of them circus performers or in the business, including some who started their own shows, all in Europe. There is no evidence, however, that any of them had a connection to Texas. The Blumenfeld Circus temporarily closed their show in 1933, because of the Nuremburg Laws, the Nazis' exclusion of Jews from many professions. After the war the circus resumed, but it permanently folded its tents in the 1950s.[24]

Finding historical records for Maurice Levi (Cerf) Blumenfeld, like an entry in a birth, marriage, or death register, one which might connect him to the Corsicana Cerfs, first requires an analysis of his name since he may have been documented under some variation of the names by which history now remembers him. Parsing out his original name, **Maurice Levi Cerf**, which also appeared as **Moritz Hirsch Levy**,[25] it can be presumed that Maurice/Moritz was a variation of a Hebrew given name, likely Moises (Moses) or Mordecai. Moses and Mordecai are common formal Hebrew names, the type traditionally given to Jewish boys soon after birth, the form that might be found on a historical document. Culturally acceptable, everyday names, like Maurice or Moritz, would be derived from the more formal, sacred Hebrew name, like Moses or Mordecai.

Hirsch and Cerf are German and French words, respectively, both translating to "deer."[26] Cerf/Hirsch was also a common given name. Its position as the second name in one case and third name in the other case complicates the analysis because it may be a given name, in this case, and not a surname.[27] The same is true for Levi/Levy. It could either be a given name or a surname.[28] Further difficulties arise because Maurice/Moritz's surname was changed to Blumenfeld.[29] All permutations of these names were considered in a search for records about him, but none were found.[30]

## Cerf Links?

The parents of the several Texas Cerf siblings were **Moise** (Moses) and **Jeannette** (**Kahn**) **Cerf**. Moise was born in Mittelbronn in 1803 and died there seventy-one years later. Jeannette was born around 1816 and died in France on Feb. 4, 1911, at the age of ninety-four.[31] Moise's parents were **Lazare** and **Gittel** (**May**) **Cerf**, and Lazare's father was also named **Moise**.

Maurice Levi (Cerf) Blumenfeld, circus founder, and Moise Cerf, father of the Texas Cerfs, had different children, therefore they were not the same person. Maurice Levi (Cerf) Blumenfeld, who was twenty years older than Moise Cerf, was not Moise's father because Moise's father's name was Lazare. It is possible they were uncle and nephew, brothers, cousins, or something else, but this couldn't be ascertained because Maurice's parents' names could not be learned.

Approached differently, if Louis, Dave, or one of the other Texas Cerfs had a connection to the circus world, that would suggest a connection to the Blumenfeld Circus, and therefore possibly lead to the Rope Walker's identity. There were at least ten Cerf children of Moises and Jeannette Cerf of Mittelbronn, a typical[32] French-German-Texan-Jewish family. In order by birth date, they were:

**Henry (ca. 1840-1911)** arrived at New Orleans in 1855.[33] He was in the wholesale grocery business there for several years, then moved to Galveston, and later was a merchant in Waxahachie, not far from Corsicana. Around 1906, Henry and his family moved to New York City.[34] He and his wife Sarah had seven children who reached adulthood.[35] None of them were in the circus or a similar profession.

**Dave (ca. 1841-May 12, 1881),** the next oldest, married Sophia Meyer and had a large family. He was a merchant. His story is told further below.

**Sophie Levy (Oct. 8, 1844-Dec. 16, 1920)** was the wife of Uriah P. Levy. She came to the U.S. in 1865. Her husband, a jeweler in Texarkana, died on the young side. They had nine children.[36] No circus performers there.

**Esther Raphael (1846-1916)** was the wife of Moises Raphael. They didn't emigrate to the U.S.[37] Their two known children were Leonie "Nonnie" (Raphael) Levine of Corsicana[38] and David A. Raphael of Ferris, a small town three quarters of the way from Corsicana to Dallas.[39] Neither child was in the circus.

Louis Cerf

**Louis (Feb. 7, 1846-Mar. 12, 1917)** married in Corsicana to Rachel Flonacher of Louisiana. They had one child, Isaac Newburgh "I.N." Cerf. Louis was born in Mittelbronn and left for the U.S. on January 1, 1867.[40] He was one of Navarro County's "leading capitalists."[41] In remarks at a "Zionist Celebration," a year after Cerf's death, Mayor Halbert lauded Louis Cerf as an ideal citizen and decried depictions of Jews as a "commercial race."[42] No circus connection.

I.N. Cerf (Dec. 23, 1873-June 21, 1935),[43] Louis's son, was born in Corsicana and lived his whole life there. He married his cousin, Eugenia Levy.[44] He was the State National Bank President when it erected its new building, in 1926, at the corner of Collin and Beaton Streets, stop four on the Walking Tour of Historic Downtown Cor-sicana. He was a director of Corsicana's Chamber of Commerce, president of Temple Beth El, a

I.N. Cerf

Mason, and a leader of many other community organizations, and none of
them affiliated with the circus.

**Minna Raphael (Dec. 15, 1850-Mar. 27, 1921)**[45] married Edmond
Raphael (Jun. 6, 1851-Aug. 24, 1927). They lived in Corsicana. They had
two daughters: Sophie, who married Kalman "Kal" Shwarts, a member of
another early and prominent Corsicana Jewish family, and Lena, who
married Ike Jolesch.[46] Edmond and his sons-in-laws were all merchants.

There were no contortionists in the Raphael family, but family inter-
relationships were certainly convoluted, starting with a second Edmond
Raphael, no ascertainable blood relation, who lived in nearby Ennis. Both
Edmond Raphaels died in the summer of 1927. The elder one, of Corsicana,
outlived the younger by twenty-nine days.[47] Edmond Raphael of Ennis,
born in 1866, married Fannie Jolesch.[48] She was a sister of Ike Jolesch, who
was the son-in-law of Corsicana's Edmond Raphael. Another Jolesch
sibling, Joseph, married Mamie Cerf, daughter of Leon Cerf (below). Both
Edmond Raphaels were Alsatian Jews.[49] Furthermore, no connection was
found between either of the two Edmonds and Moises Raphael, husband
of Esther Cerf (above).

**Isidore (Apr. 11, 1851-Oct. 9, 1923)**[50] married Julia Shwarts, daughter
of Aaron Shwarts. Isidore was a longtime, prominent merchant in Ennis.
They had one child, Louis, not to be confused with his uncle, also named
Louis Cerf. Julia died in 1897. In 1899 Isidore married again, to Julia's sister,
Mamie Shwarts.[51] Julia and Mamie were sisters of Kal Shwarts, a son-in-law
of Minna Raphael (above). Isidore came to the U.S. in 1869, landing at New
Orleans, sold general merchandise at Calvert, Texas, later went to Corsicana,
and lastly went into business with his brother Leon, in Ennis, in 1877. Their
dry goods shop grew into a major department store.[52] Isidore turned profits,
not somersaults.

**Leon (Sept. 5, 1852-Aug. 13, 1932)** married Leonie Dreyfus.[53] They
lived in Ennis and had five children.[54] He arrived in the U.S. in 1872.[55] He
and his brother Isidore, as mentioned, ran a store in Ennis. Like the others,
he was not an entertainer.

**Sara Behr (1858-Mar. 12, 1910)** was the first wife of Edouard Behr. She
did not emigrate.[56]

**Rosalie Wahl** married a man name Wahl and lived in Luxeville, France, near Mittelbronn. She did not emigrate.[57]

In conclusion, no connection could be made between the Texas Cerfs and Maurice Levi Cerf, Maurice Levi Cerf's Circus Blumenfeld, or anything remotely related to the circus. Therefore, there is no discernable connection between the Corsicana Cerf family and Rope Walker.[58] Cerf, it turns out, was a common Jewish surname in Alsace-Lorraine.[59]

♎

The Cerf clan of Texas was financially successful, as the foregoing shows, but they also suffered the heartaches and pain that visited all families, tragedies like infant mortality, which was as common in their family as it was in other nineteenth-century Texas families. A more unusual crisis was the December 10, 1930 kidnapping of Robert Cerf. He was held for twenty-four hours before his father, banker I.N. Cerf, paid a $15,000 ransom.[60] Perhaps the stress of the ordeal hastened the community leader's death at the age of sixty-one.

## Dave Cerf

Louis and nearly all of his siblings, those just listed, lived into their seventies. A notable exception was Dave Cerf, who died at the age of forty-two. Dave arrived in the U.S. around 1854 and first lived in New Orleans. From at least 1874 thru 1878 he resided in Corsicana, where two of his children were born[61] and where he helped establish the Hebrew Cemetery. After Corsicana, he and his wife Sophie and their seven children[62] lived in Evansville, Indiana.

Dave and Sophie's oldest, Louis Amadee Cerf, was an insurance executive in New York. He was born Nov. 30, 1863, in Jackson, Louisiana, and died in 1959 at the age of ninety-five. He was one of two Jews, both from Corsicana, who graduated from the inaugural class of Texas A&M.[63] Louis A. Cerf's enrollment in 1876, at the age of twelve, required a special meeting of the school's directors. For several years he was the school's oldest living alumni.[64]

David Cerf's life ended tragically on May 12, 1881, in a New Orleans boarding house. After waking that morning and going about his morning routine, he asked his assistant to deliver a letter to a business associate. Due to financial problems, the letter said, he intended to take his life. Before anyone could reach him he shot himself in the heart. His family at the time was living in Evansville. He was buried in the Hebrew Rest Cemetery in New Orleans.[65]

In 1902, Dave's son Louis and his wife, Camille, donated $50,000 to the New Orleans Public Library, made possible following the 1898 death of her father, Simon Hernsheim, a wealthy New Orleans cigar manufacturer. Hernsheim died of heartache after the quick successive deaths of his wife and sister. The official cause was self-administration of potassium cyanide.[66]

♎

Steinbeck said, "I see too many men delay their exits with a sickly, slow reluctance to leave the stage. It's bad theater as well as bad living."[67] With apologies to Mr. Shakespeare, all the world's more a circus than a stage, and life more a series of derring-do stunts than scenes: high-flying spectacle, a passion to scamper up to the edge, occasional missteps, adulation, and tragedy. For some, simply the looming dawn requires courage. But the show, like life, must go on. Every living soul deserves applause, an appreciation for every step forward along their own taut, braided cord. Too often the act is over while the canvas is yet pitched, before the triumphant salute of a slowly sweeping, outstretched arm, and so it was for Dave Cerf, Simon Hernsheim, and Rope Walker.

**Detail from the Isidore Cerf monument, Hebrew Cemetery**

## Chapter 4

# HISTORIES OF THE JEWS
# OF CORSICANA–TEXANS

*What to that apostolic lancer, Brother Jonathan* [the United States], *is Texas but a Fast-Fish? … What to the ostentatious smuggling verbalists are the thoughts of thinkers but Loose-Fish? What is the great globe itself but a Loose-Fish? And what are you, reader, but a Loose-Fish and a Fast-Fish, too?*

How to solve the mystery of the one-legged acrobat? It might help to know something about the other Jews who lived in Corsicana when he fell, besides the Cerfs. It's plausible that when he arrived in town the first thing he did was seek out his fellow Jews. Maybe one of them, like Max London, the Civil War veteran buried in the Hebrew Cemetery, knew something about him and left some record which, if discovered, could lead to his identification. Did he gather the Israelites, like Moses at Sinai, to see his performance? Did he bid them to bring their Gentile friends and neighbors, to increase the multitudes who would watch him pass over Beaton Street on a tightrope with just one leg, while carrying a stove, and perform other minor miracles?

That he was somehow connected to some of the town's Jews is only speculation, but speculation can lead to verified factual information, and if this mystery is to be solved, once and for all, it will require facts. Like a street performer draws in spectators, the historical investigator collects facts. It can't be said which factual nugget will lead to discovery of Rope Walker's identity, but the more information collected the better the chances for the big payoff. And the place to start is with the little information already known, that the man who died without a name was a Jew in Texas.

## Ride 'Em Jewboy[68]

Jews in Texas in the 1880s? Texas had several Jewish communities then, and earlier—some small, like Corsicana, and some sizeable. Following the Civil War, Jewish communities sprang up along the American frontier like bluebonnets on a West Texas prairie. Here comes a town, growth and promise, and here comes the peddler and merchant, frequently Israelites. The typical Jewish merchant had crossed an ocean to escape an inhospitable homeland, to find greater opportunity. Thousands of years of abuse, displacement, and trade made the descendants of Abraham, Isaac, and Jacob well-adapted for migration and commerce.

Corsicana had at least a dozen Jewish families in 1884 and the Hebrew Cemetery already had sixteen burials. Some families, like the Cerfs, were from Alsace-Lorraine. *Oy! Très exotique, pardner!* Others were from Prussia, Bavaria, or Poland. They were not easy to pick out of a crowd. They had European accents, but so did many non-Jews on the western frontier. A Jew encountered on a Corsicana street back then would appear no different than any other Texan with a foreign accent. These Corsicana pioneers are identifiable as Jews now because they were buried in the Hebrew Cemetery or were listed as members of a synagogue or other Jewish institution.

Texans in 1884 were independent-minded individualists. Almost every–one was an immigrant from another state or country. Texas pioneers were judged on character, not characteristics.[69] As one Texas booster put it,

**There is something special and different about Texas and Texans, just as there is something special about Israel and Jews, or France and Frenchmen.**[70]

Being a Texan is

**a state of heart and mind. This may not be an entirely rational state – but then there is not much rational about being French or Jewish, or having powerful notions of blood and soil. Such things spring from the chemistry of history and culture.**[71]

No matter what the background, blood or soil, a Texan *is* special, and is a Texan regardless of any other heritage he or she happens to possess. In the soul of all Texans, whether Jewish, French, or otherwise; whether born in the Lone Star State, abroad, or in some other state,

**there is a true Texan ethnicity, American to the core, American in its origins, American in its intense patriotism ...**[72]

Of all the superlatives attached to Texas (Texas has more superlatives than anywhere!), it's safe to say, it's true: Texas history is more interesting than the history of any other state. It was once a country! It fought its own revolution! Reduce that "American to the core" individuality to just those folks of Hebrew stock, add to a Corsicana consommé, and *bon appétit!*

Spoiler alert: if Rope Walker had a personal connection to some of Corsicana's Jewish citizens and that leads to the discovery of his identity, it won't be revealed in this chapter. And, acknowledging that not everyone can stomach 22 pages filled with names and dates, readers may, therefore, select *a la carte* from the following menu and enjoy a repast according to their own curiosity and intellectual tastes. Recommended, however, is Jay Silverberg's history of Jewish Corsicanans (section VI) and his oral history (section VIII)—both add to the Rope Walker *tzimmes*, a savory Jewish stew.

**I. Conversos and Crypto-Jews.** The earliest Jews in Texas had to hide their Jewish identity. No mention of Jean Lafitte or other Jewish pirates.

**II. Mexican Rule and Texas Independence.** Judaism and Jews were legally permitted for the first time.

**III. The Republic of Texas, Statehood, Castro, and De Cordova.** The creation of Texas and some Jews who were instrumental in its early growth.

**IV. "A Brief History of the Corsicana Jewish Community."** A 1920 article about Corsicana's Jewish institutions and institutional leaders.

**V. Jews in Corsicana When Rope Walker Fell.** Identifying Jewish Corsicanans in 1884.

**VI. Jay Silverberg's History of Jewish Corsicanans.** A 1977 paper about some pioneer Jewish families.

**VII. "Corsicana, Texas: An Unlikely Promised Land."** A 1990 social history of Corsicana's Jews written by a local historian, Professor Tommy Stringer.

**VIII. Oral Histories.** Several Jewish residents recorded oral histories in 1978 and 1979.

**IX. Corsicana's Earliest Jews.**

**X. Other Notes on Early Corsicana Jews.**

A more extensive summary of Texas-Jewish history can be found at the website of the Texas State Historical Association,[73] and a broader study of the Jews of Texas can be found in books specifically dedicated to the subject.[74]

## I. Conversos and Crypto-Jews

Most of what is now Texas was, prior to Mexican Independence, a part of vast territories claimed by Spanish conquistadors who exercised domin-ion over native peoples by force and conversion. The spread of diseases brought by the Europeans contributed to the devastation of aboriginal populations. Spain's Mexican territories extended northward from present-day Mexico into a good bit of the American Southwest and Pacific Coast. Judaism was strictly forbidden under Spanish law. Jews were persecuted, expelled, tortured, burned at the stake, and forced to convert for centuries under the Spanish Inquisition, which Spain exported to its New World empire.

The expulsion of Jews from Spain and Portugal in the late fifteenth century coincided with Spain's exploration of the Americas. Many Sephardic Jews—the Jews of Spain and Portugal—converted, and some of those *New Christians* made their way across the Atlantic Ocean. They were also called *Conversos*, and less politely, *Maranos* (pigs).[75] They were often suspected of and sometimes caught backsliding into their old, Israelite ways. Those who secretly practiced Judaism were *Crypto-Jews*. Historians have determined that many early travelers from Europe to the Americas were Conversos, including some of the men who travelled with Columbus. There has even been speculation that Columbus himself had Jewish origins.[76] Crypto-Jews in Spain's New World territories were sought out and forced to either truly convert or suffer deadly consequences.[77] Efforts to avoid discovery pushed them into northern parts of Spanish Mexico, what is now the southwestern U.S., including what are now areas of Texas.[78]

There are numerous stories today about Jewish ancestry being rediscovered after five centuries of hiding, denial, and abandonment. DNA tests have confirmed Converso roots, making sense of what seemed like odd family traditions, like covering a mirror after a person's death or lighting candles on Friday nights.[79] Many Catholic *Tejano* (Texans with Spanish roots) families today are unaware they are partly Jewish—of *sangre Ebreo*. Just how many is not known, but a lot of ethnic identity can disappear in five hundred years, especially considering that the truth, at one time, was a death sentence.[80]

## II. Mexican Rule and Texas Independence

Jewish worship was legally permitted in Mexico after it gained independence from Spain, in 1821, but there were few identifiable Jews in the Texas territory at the time.[81]

Mexico promoted colonization of its Texas-area territory to assert ownership of the land against a quickly expanding United States and the protestations of indigenous populations. It used empresarios—immigration promoters and agents—of whom Stephen Austin was the earliest and best-known. These efforts to populate the land were so successful that the Mexican government feared it was losing control to the *Anglo* (non-Hispanic, European) settlers. In 1830 a law was passed to limit immigration to the area and rein in any notions of self-government. General Antonio López de Santa Anna, "Santa Anna," who first came to power in 1833, established policies which centralized the Mexican government, thereby curbing independence sentiments in Mexico's Texas territory.

The Mexican government's distrust of Texas settlers, who were arming themselves—not so much against Mexican authority as against Indians—prompted Santa Anna in 1835 to send reinforcement troops to Texas military posts. The unwelcomed show of force prompted William B. Travis and a band of upstarts to take control of one of the posts, Anahuac. The objective was to prepare the Texans, led by Travis, to oppose any military action initiated by Santa Anna. No fighting occurred, but the government viewed the takeover as a rebellion. Distrust and animosity reached a peak on October 2, 1835, when armed conflict broke out at Gonzales. The Texas Revolution had begun. After a few additional, minor battles, a large force led by Santa Anna marched to Texas. This caused the sentiments of the Anglos in Texas to consolidate, and a Declaration of Independence was made on March 2, 1836. Fifty-nine men signed it, of which three were Tejanos, one of them Jose Antonio Navarro, for whom Navarro County was named, and who gave Corsicana its name, as previously related in Chapter 1.

Four days later, Santa Anna's forces lay siege to the Alamo, a fortified mission in San Antonio. Far outnumbering the defenders, the Mexican troops nevertheless took thirteen days to defeat the fort's gallant defenders, killing or executing all of them, including the legendary David Crockett, a Tennessee congressman; James Bowie, a fearless frontiersman; and William Travis. The Mexicans also took substantial losses. Historians conjecture that as many as four Jews died defending the Alamo, but their Jewishness has not been verified.[82] The Mexican victory served to rally the *Texians* (Texas Anglos). Fighting continued until Sam Houston's forces met Santa Anna's troops at San Jacinto on April 21. Houston's forces attacked first, routing the enemy. Santa Anna was captured and the fighting ended.[83] On May 14, 1836, peace terms were signed and the Republic of Texas was born.

Not much is known about the Jews from this early period. One famous Jewish Texian was Adolphus Sterne, of Nacogdoches, who was there from 1826. Albert Moses Levy was surgeon-in-chief of the Texians in their fight for independence.[84] There were maybe one or two dozen identifiable Jews in Texas before Texas Independence, total, but no historian has attempted to catalogue them.[85]

### III. The Republic of Texas, Statehood, Castro, and De Cordova

The Republic of Texas was not a possession, territory, or state—it was an independent country. One Jew who played a major role at the time was empresario Henri Castro. Born at Landes, France, in 1786, the descendant of Portuguese Jews became a U.S. citizen in 1827. Texas President Sam Houston appointed him Consul General to France. He promoted emigration to Texas along the French banks of the Rhine and elsewhere in Europe. Between 1843 and 1847 he brought to Texas 485 families plus 457 single men. At least a few of those new arrivals, presumably, were Jewish. With the help of other empresarios, word of mouth, and generous incentives of free land, Texas's population continued to grow.

Another Jewish promoter was Jacob Raphael De Cordova (1808-1868). He was born in Jamaica and grew up in England. His father, Raphael J. De Cordova, moved from Jamaica to Philadelphia, where, in 1820, he was president of Congregation Mikveh Israel. Jacob, meanwhile, returned to Jamaica where he published a newspaper, and later, in New Orleans, shipped goods to Texas during its fight for independence. Arriving in Texas in 1839, Jacob bought and sold huge tracts of land, at one time acquiring as many as a million acres. He travelled to northeastern U.S. cities and England to encourage the adventurous and ambitious to emigrate to Texas for free land and economic opportunity.

De Cordova laid out the town of Waco and was instrumental in the creation of a well-received "Map of the State of Texas," published in 1849. He wrote *The Texas Immigrant and Traveller's Guide Book* (1856) and *Texas, Her Resources and Her Public Men* (1858), "the first attempt at an encyclopedia of Texas."[86] He was a representative to the second Texas legislature in 1847. De Cordova established Odd Fellows lodges in the Republic of Texas, the first established outside of the U.S.

The United States considered annexation of Texas as early as 1803, at the time of the Louisiana Purchase. In 1836, just months after Texas gained independence, the people of the republic voted in favor of joining the Union. The U.S., however, opposed it, believing the move would provoke a war with Mexico (it did). There were also concerns from U.S. anti-slavery factions because slavery was legal—and thriving—in Texas. The following year, Texas President Mirabeau B. Lamar withdrew the offer. Annexation was raised again in 1841, by Sam Houston, but the U.S. remained uninterested. In 1843, when Great Britain expressed a desire to partner with Texas, the U.S. was concerned enough that it reassessed its position. Following additional negotiations, an annexation resolution was passed by the U.S. Congress on Feb. 28, 1845, and later that year the Republic's congress and its citizens overwhelmingly approved annexation. Texas officially became a state on Dec. 29, 1845, when the Texas State Constitution was accepted by the United States. A ceremony handing over governance from the president of the Republic to its new governor, James Pinckney Henderson, took place on Feb. 19, 1846.[87] Navarro County was founded two months later and Corsicana two years after that.

Corsicana's population was sparse up until the Civil War, and even in 1870 it was nothing more than a village. All that changed with the arrival of the H&TC railroad, celebrated on November 15, 1871. The population quickly grew to more than three thousand, and by 1890 it was the sixteenth largest city in Texas with more than six thousand residents.[88]

## IV. "A Brief History of the Corsicana Jewish Community"

This was an article appearing in the Dec. 17, 1920 issue of *The Jewish Monitor*, a Dallas weekly.[89] Corsicana's sizeable Jewish population in the 1890s, it said, made little effort to have an organized Jewish community because they came from countries where religious practice was greatly diminished.[90] There were, it noted,

*cold indifferences to affairs of a religious nature ... petty jealousies to business and social affairs rendered cohesion impossible. For several years organization for holiday purposes only existed. No effort was made to secure the services of a rabbi, even for holidays, and on numerous occasions when services were held they were conducted by laymen.*

They did finally build themselves a synagogue, at the turn of the century, but nevertheless religious commitment soon faded. At an October 26, 1913 meeting to reorganize Temple Beth El, Kal **Shwarts** was temporary chairman and Moise **Hirsch** temporary secretary. A plan was made to bring a rabbi to Corsicana, which had been without one for several years. Officers were elected, with I.N. **Cerf** as president.[91] "Rabbi David Goldberg, of Fort Worth, accepted the call to Temple Beth-El. He arrived January 1st, 1914, to take active charge."[92] Over the years the temple continued to suffer periods without a rabbi; at the time the article was written, in 1920, was one such time. Layman Sydney **Marks** was once again conducting services.[93]

A Brief History of the Corsicana Jewish Community

The International Order of B'nai B'rith, IOBB Lodge No. 275, the article states, was organized in 1915[94] with Sydney

**Marks** its first president.[95] The Council of Jewish Women, formed in 1918, was led by Mrs. **Harris** and was very active; within two years the council had set up a religious school for the children.

The orthodox congregation, Agudas Achim, was organized in 1916, the article continues, and its synagogue was built in September, 1917. Orthodox services before then were held in the large Odd Fellows Hall.[96] J.G. **Goldman**, the congregation's president in 1920, was active in the building's construction. Several men participated in fundraising for the synagogue, foremost E. **Golden**, its first president,[97] and Benjamin **Marks**, Sydney's father. A Ladies Auxiliary for AA was organized in 1917 with Mrs. Harry (Sadie **Schloss**) **Miller** as president and Mrs. Mose (Josephine **Bloomberg**) **Blumrosen** as vice president.

## V. Jews in Corsicana When Rope Walker Fell

The walking tour booklet says Rope Walker prayed with a Jewish merchant just before he died. While there's a chance that this merchant, or, as stated at the outset of this chapter, some Jewish member of the community knew Rope Walker's identity before he died, it can't be said for sure who that was. Maybe someone had invited the aerialist to come to Corsicana to perform. Learning something about the Jews who lived in Corsicana in 1884, not just the Cerfs, could, potentially, lead to the discovery of Rope Walker's identity.

Among the earliest Jewish arrivals were Philip and Alex **Sanger**, two of eight brothers who operated Sanger Bros., an extensive and highly successful Texas mercantile. Family members at one time were vintners and weavers in their native Obernbreit, Germany, close to the River Rhine where De Cordova once trolled for Texas converts. Sanger Bros. stores opened along the H&TC line as its tracks extended northward. Philip and Alex arrived on the first train to reach Corsicana, the latest terminus, in 1871, when the town was twenty-three years old. Philip was a personable and popular Confederate veteran, and Alex, his younger brother, was learning the business. The younger Sanger quickly moved on, but Philip did business in Corsicana for several years before he left. By 1876, all but two of the Sanger Brothers stores, in Waco and Dallas, had closed, and Philip had left Corsicana.[98] Other Jewish merchants came to Corsicana when the railroad arrived there and similarly left as the line continued its progress toward Dallas.[99] But many stayed and were there when Rope Walker fell.

The 1880 census recorded eighty-five Corsicana residents whose Jewish ethnicity or Jewish affiliation can be confirmed, most of them still there in 1884. There were others in the census whose Jewishness is questionable, and others still who were Jewish, but their residence in Corsicana four years later could not be verified. Jews who arrived after the 1880 census but before Rope Walker are not easily identified. Nearly all of the Jewish residents of 1880 Corsicana remained in town for a substantial number of years, if not the remainder of their lives.

Jews in Corsicana in 1880 were: William & Mary (**Buford**) **Wolf** with four children;[100] Aaron & Caroline (**Zander**) **Shwarts** with nine children;[101] David & Cecelia (**Joachim**) **Deutschner** with five children;[102] Louis & Rosa (**Samuels**) **Cohen** with four children and two nieces;[103] Louis & Rachel (**Flonacher**) **Cerf** with one child; Rachel's sister and brother, Henrietta **Newburg**[104] & Henry C. **Flonacher**;[105] Adolph & Mary (**Mindek**) **Cahn** with one daughter;[106] Isaac **Baum**;[107] the **Zadek** family of Adolph, sister Bertha **Casper**, their mother Rosalie (maiden name unknown), and Bertha's son;[108] Max & Bertha (**Simon**) **London** with four children;[109] Alex & Bertha (**Solomon**) **Fox** with four children; Bertha's sister and brother, Lena[110] & Abe **Solomon**;[111] Solomon Sampson & Carrie (**Frank**) **Freedman** with two children; Solomon Sampson's brother, **Ruben Freedman**;[112] brothers Isaac & August **Levy**;[113] Edmond & Mina (**Cerf**) **Raphael** and two children; Michael & Josephine (**Aaron**) **Obright** with four children;[114] Morris **Sterne**;[115] and lastly, Isaac and Harriett (**Hart**) **Rich**, living just outside of Corsicana, with six children.[116]

A few of those eighty-five did not stay long in Corsicana. The **Obright** family moved on fairly soon, eventually settling in Hot Springs, Arkansas. Henry Clay **Flonacher** was a native of Louisiana who lived at various places around the country. The **Wolf** family likewise was not long in Corsicana.[117]

People listed in the 1880 census had Jewish-sounding names and came from Prussia, Bavaria, France, etc., but there is no other evidence that they considered themselves Jewish. Foremost in this category are Charles and "Lou" (Louella) **Blum**.[118] Also, two young women who boarded together just outside of Corsicana, Lizie **Freeman** and Corine **Levy**, have Jewish sounding surnames and Corine's parents, it says, were born in Prussia.[119] One Benjamin **Myers**, born in Germany, enumerated near Morris Sterne, similarly could not be verified as a member of the Hebrew people, despite his commonly (but not exclusively) Jewish surname and the given names of his family members—quite fitting had they been found speaking Yiddish on Hester Street in New York's Lower East Side: Benjamin, Fannie, Harry, and Ethel.[120] Another twenty or so individuals listed in the census were born in Prussia or Germany, many of them railroad workers, but none had Jewish-sounding names.

It is not known exactly when Corsicana's Jewish residents first arrived, but two sources, the 1870 federal census and *Logan's Railway Directory*, an 1873 catalog listing commercial establishments at stations along numerous rail lines, should help.[121] Also, any document that identifies someone's birthplace as Corsicana is proof the family lived there at that time.

Commercial Restaurant, J. P. Lasserre, Proprietor.
Cooper & Fletcher, Saloon.
Damon & Bro., Dry Goods and Notions.
Denman, F. G., Crockery, Queensware, etc.
Deutschner & Cohen, General Dry Goods.
Edwards & Kerr, Druggists.
Eika, Charles, Saloon.
Eliot, J. M., Land Agent.
Fewell, C. S., Tinsmith.
Fonche, A., Saloon.
Fox, A. & Bro., Dry Goods, Notions, etc.
Froman, R. D., Physician.
Fryan, J. T., Billiard Saloon.
Furche, August, Saloon.
**Garitty, Huey & Co.**, Bankers and Brokers.
Goodman, K. P. & Bro., Groceries and Produce.
Gowan & Robinson, Dentists.
Gulick, J. W., Physician.
Hamm, F. H., Merchant Tailor.
Hutchison, G. H., Agricultural Implements.
Hord, W. S., Dry Goods and Notions.
Harberson, George, Livery Stable.
Huey, J., Stoves and Tinware.
Jester, C. W., Harness-maker.
**Jones, Jno. B. & Co.**, Commission Merchants and Bankers.
Kerr, C. P., Commission Merchant.
Kerr & Hayes, General Merchandise.
Kerr & Roberts, General Merchandise.
Kerr, W. J. W., Physician.
Kindon & Adams, Bakery.
Knoth, William, Barber.
**Knox, William**, Agent Texas Express Company, at Depot.
Krohn, E., Groceries and Produce.
Kuska & Martens, Bakers.
Learmonth, James, Wagon-maker.
Lebermann, F. E. J., Wines and Liquors.
Lee, U. M. & Co., Dry Goods and Notions.
Ligon & Walkins, Carpenters.
Lindly, J. M., Groceries and Produce.
Littlefield, G. M., Furniture.
Littlefield, J. H. & Co., Commission Merchants.
Love, W. J., Physician.
McAfee, D. M., Groceries and Produce.
MacCulloch, Route Agent Texas Express Company.
McElwee, W. H., General Merchandise.
Mann, J. M., Agent Weed Sewing Machines.
Martin & Son, Shoemakers.
Mills, R. Q., Attorney-at-law.
Molloy House, H. S. Molloy, Prop., N. E. cor. Square.

*Logan's Railway Business Directory*

A close examination of the 1870 census finds no one in Corsicana who appears to be Jewish, but the *Logan Directory* shows several were there by 1873. Charles **Blum**, a saloon keeper, is an unconfirmed Hebrew. Louis **Cerf** is listed, selling groceries and produce at "S. S. Square."[122] **Deutschner**

& **Cohen** ran a general dry goods store. A. **Fox** & Bro. sold "dry goods, notions, etc."[123] E. **Raphael** had a shop selling groceries and produce and Abe **Shwarts** (i.e., Aaron Shwarts[124]) sold general merchandise. Adolph **Zadek**, Sr. also sold groceries and produce.[125] There was a T.D. **Solomon** who sold groceries and produce, possibly related to the Jewish Solomon family in Corsicana (see above), although nothing ties T.D. to that clan.[126]

Many of the Jewish people in Corsicana in 1880, it turns out, had been there since at least 1873. One Jewish resident, according to the legend, the one who prayed with Rope Walker in 1884, was very likely in town for at least ten years, and likely would have learned something about the Jewish acrobat's identity. But which one?

## VI. Jay Silverberg's History of Jewish Corsicanans

"Corsicana's Early Jewish Community," a lecture delivered by Jay **Silverberg** (1901-1998) to the Corsicana Historical Society on Oct. 17, 1977, was summarized in the local paper and subsequently published in the local historical society's *Navarro County Scroll*.[127] The talk focused on people and families, unlike the *Jewish Monitor*'s 1920 focus on Jewish institutions. Silverberg probably gathered his information by speaking with his fellow Jewish Corsicanans, relying on their recollections to prepare his talk. It's unlikely he had access to any documentation such as immigration, naturalization, or census records. As a result, much of Silverberg's infor—mation cannot be verified, and some of what can be checked into, it can be shown, was incorrect.

He discussed several pioneer families: Golden & Goldman; Cerf, Raphael & Levy; Shwarts & Raphael; Freedman; Rosenberg; Marks; and Wolens. Several have already been mentioned as early Corsicana residents, while others arrived later, long after Rope Walker's fall.

> *E. Golden settled here about 1870, because of that early date, Corsicana was a Jewish center and all the Jewish peddlers congregated here. Corsicana had a synagogue, not as we know it now, but a place to worship, whether it was in a store, or a room over a store for the more than 100 years up to the present time. There were a few Jewish women who prepared strict kosher meals and these peddlers would stay here and pray. When the selling season was over they would go north or to some other towns.*

This is a stark difference from *The Jewish Monitor*'s 1920 history, lamenting the town's early Jews' "cold indifferences to affairs of a religious nature."

As for E. **Golden**, census records say he came to the U.S. in 1881 or 1882, not 1870.[128] Born in 1862, he was only eight in 1870.[129] His oldest child, Lizzie, was born in Texas (town not known) in December, 1883, so he and his family might have been in Corsicana when Rope Walker fell. Silverberg talked about E. Golden's children: Lizzie and twin sons, Labe and Mace. He did not mention the events of August 1890—within the course of three days Golden's wife Sarah died and his store burned down.[130]

About the **Goldman** brothers, Silverberg said Jake arrived first, around 1870 or 1871, Jake brought over Sam, and then Will arrived around 1880. Census records again tell a different story: Jake, born about 1864, arrived in 1885,[131] Sam was born in 1870 and arrived around 1886,[132] and Will, born in 1873, arrived in 1890.[133] Their mother, Rosa, was buried in Corsicana. It is not known if their father, Labe Hirsch Goldman, made it to the U.S.[134]

Will Goldman married Lizzie Golden, Silverberg's reason for discussing the two families together. Silverberg didn't mention another link: E. Golden's second wife, Lizzie's stepmother, was Sarah Ida Goldman, a sister of the three Goldman brothers. Put another way, Lizzie Golden was her husband's step-niece—if there is such a thing. Will was ten years older than Lizzie and had become her uncle seven years before they married. Silverberg said Will Goldman "always looked upon [Lizzie, his wife] as a little girl,"[135] but didn't explain why.

Of the **Cerf**, **Levy**, & **Raphael**[136] families, Silverberg explained, Louis **Cerf** and his four brothers came from Alsace-Lorraine, landed at Galveston in 1885, and then worked their way up toward Corsicana. One went to Waxahachie, two went to Ennis, and one eventually settled in New York City. The Silverberg history got the towns mostly correct, except it was a son of one of the brothers (Louis Amadee Cerf, son of David) who went to New York. Also, the Cerfs arrived much earlier than 1885.[137] It's as if the immigration dates for the Goldmans and Cerfs were switched by mistake.

About Louis and Rachel **Cerf**, Silverberg said,

> **They had one son, Isaac Newberg Cerf, named after his uncle who was a colonel in the Civil War.**

Indeed, records show that Rachel's sister, Henrietta (**Flonacher**) **New-burg**, a longtime Corsicana resident, was the widow of Lewis Newburg,[138] but no record confirms Newburg's service in the Civil War, as a colonel or otherwise.

Silverberg explained how some grocers and dry goods merchants, like the Cerfs, became bankers. Farmers pledged their future crops (cotton, typically) as security to make purchases on credit and they would borrow money in the same way. There were few banks back then, so merchants became de facto bankers.[139]

Silverberg praised "Ike" (I.N.) Cerf for his philanthropy, adding that he was a volunteer fireman under Chief Rube **Freedman**, and a close friend of Judge Charles "Lee" **Jester**. Around 1924, said Silverberg, I.N. Cerf

> *went to the State National Bank as vice president and two years later became its president, and built the present building which was completed in April 1926.*

The lecture included the story of Uriah P. **Levy**. At the age of twelve he was studying to be a rabbi but ran away. He later joined the U.S. Navy and rose to the rank of commodore. In a duel, he killed a British naval captain who had spoken ill of Thomas Jefferson, a great hero to Levy.

> *He was a batchelor and owned the home that Thomas Jefferson lived in and later gave it to the government. This home, called Monticello, has its picture on the back of our nickle.*

Silverberg furthermore assured his audience, "All this was written in the *Congressional Record*." The *Scroll* 's transcription of the lecture includes an essential detail missing from the version appearing in the newspaper, an explanation that Commodore Uriah P. Levy was the great uncle of Eugenia (Levy) Cerf and thereby removing the implication that at some point he lived in Corsicana. All the same, the *Scroll* added something that was *not* in the newspaper version, that Commodore Levy was buried in Corsicana's Hebrew Cemetery—which is entirely incorrect. Commodore Levy, an American hero of the War of 1812, famous for having abolished corporal punishment in the navy, died in 1862 and was buried in New York City, many years before the Hebrew Cemetery existed.[140] The confusion probably stems from Eugenia's father and her great uncle having the exact same name. Eugenia, her mother, and some of her siblings are indeed buried in Corsicana's Hebrew Cemetery, but not her father. *That* Uriah P. Levy was buried in 1891 in Texarkana, Texas where he once ran a jewelry store.[141] *That* Uriah P. Levy's family, including I.N. Cerf's mother, Eugenia, initially lived in Texarkana and nearby Jefferson.[142]

Silverberg said that Aaron **Shwarts** brought his family to Corsicana from Galveston in 1880. As shown earlier, the Shwartses were in Corsicana from at least 1873 because Aaron ("Abe") Shwarts was listed in the *Logan Directory* of that year. Silverberg's article noted that "E. Rayfield" (**Raphael**) and

Louis **Cerf** were in-laws and opened a business together, and the "Rayfields" were among the first stockholders in the First National Bank.

Rube **Freedman** (or "Freidman," as it is misspelled in the lecture transcript), Silverberg noted, was friends with very influential people in the Republican Party and was a compassionate, community-oriented person.

> ***A monument has been erected on the courthouse lawn in memory of fire chief Rube Freidman.***[143]

Ben **Rosenberg** came to Corsicana in 1890 via Waco, eight years after arriving in the U.S., noted Silverberg. He sold liquor and was later in the implements business. He was an Odd Fellow and active in B'nai B'rith and Corsicana's Temple Beth El. His son, Ivan, was in business with his father and a lifelong resident of Corsicana. Ivan was a longtime member of the Masons, B'nai B'rith, and Temple Beth El. Ivan and his wife, Adelle (**Shwarts**),[144] donated a new pediatric ward for the Navarro Memorial Hospital, financed by the sale of property they owned on Beaton Street. Archival records agree with Silverberg's info on the Rosenberg family.

Jay Silverberg said:

> ***I was told that Ben Marks was the last person to talk to the Rope Walker before he died and was buried in the Hebrew Cemetery.***

Benjamin **Marks** came to the US from Russia in 1867, married Jenny **Levy** of New York, in 1872, and came to Corsicana in 1880, according to Silverberg.[145] They had five sons and two daughters. The sons had a store called "Marks Brothers." Silverberg spoke extensively about Ben's son Sydney's community involvement in both Jewish and non-Jewish groups. "Sydney was one of Corsicana's most beloved and respected citizens."[146] Sydney has already been a subject of interest in Chapter 2 and in the 1920 *Jewish Monitor* article, above. Other sons of Ben Marks, Alexander and Abe, managed a branch store in Sherman. Mendel, a fourth son, managed the Corsicana store with Sydney.[147] The original Marks house was at the corner of W. 3rd Ave. and Beaton where later the IOOF building was built.[148]

Silverberg's information about the Marks family agrees with available historical records, so his assertion that Ben Marks was the last person to talk to Rope Walker might be correct. But if anyone in the Marks family knew something about Rope Walker's identity, certainly it would have come out at some point. Nothing did come out, and the man remained unknown.

Ben, Jennie, and their four children born before 1884 can be added to the list of Jews who lived in Corsicana when Rope Walker died.[149]

Silverberg gave a detailed and knowledgeable account of Kalman **Wolens**, a successful merchant, philanthropist, and active member of the Jewish community. He too was already mentioned in Chapter 2. **Silverberg** married Wolens's daughter, Daisy. "K." Wolens was not there when Rope Walker fell and therefore has little bearing on the legend from which this chapter has temporarily detoured, but no history of Corsicana's Jews would be complete without him. As Silverberg tells it, K. borrowed fifty dollars from Mr. and Mrs. **Hayman** to open a stand where he sold spectacles, on the corner where **Hashop**'s Drug Store stood. He then opened a menswear store behind the old **Levine** store, and later moved to a larger store, directly on Beaton Street.

> *When the oil boom hit Powell Field, Mr. K who had previously purchased a farm in Navarro on the strength of a dream he had that a cow was delivering black milk to him, interpreted that to mean that he would received black gold or oil. .... As it turned out, he was right.*

With newfound money, Wolens expanded. His brothers, who initially came with him to Corsicana but then returned to Chicago, once again came to Corsicana to help with the business.

Silverberg said that K. and Ida Wolens founded Corsicana's Agudas Achim synagogue, and K. was its leader as he had studied to be a rabbi in Poland before he emigrated. The Wolens were generous philanthropists. A floor of Navarro Memorial Hospital was dedicated to the family in gratitude for a $50,000 donation which helped to get the hospital built.[150]

## VII. "Corsicana, Texas: An Unlikely Promised Land"

This brief, 1990 history of Corsicana's Jewish community was written by Dr. Tommy Stringer, History Department Chair at Corsicana's Navarro College.[151] Unlike the histories previously discussed, about institutions and people, this one had a decidedly sociological approach. The paper emphasized how the Jews of Corsicana were well-integrated with the town's Christian majority. The town's Jews maintained their own cultural and religious institutions, but there was an extraordinary amount of acceptance between Jew and Christian. Stringer discussed the histories of the two synagogues and gave a good, concise overview of other Jewish institutions. He also presented profiles of Sydney **Marks** and Kalman **Wolens**.

## VIII. Oral Histories

Professor Stringer conducted several interviews of Jewish residents prior to writing his monograph.[152]

Morris **Evans** spoke of boom times in Corsicana around the time he arrived there, in 1923, and the many business establishments run by the Jews. "It seemed the Jews pretty well controlled the business in town. ... When we closed up for the High Holy Days, there wasn't much business transacted in Corsicana."[153]

The oral history of Rabbi Ernest **Joseph**,[154] another subject from Chapter 2, laid out detailed information about his family's time in China after escaping Nazi Germany, how he was brought to Corsicana by K. Wolens, and how he became a rabbi in Corsicana. He explained to Stringer the major tenets of Judaism, including liturgy, holidays, b'nai mitzvah,[155] and the three schools of Jewish practice: Reform, Conservative, and Orthodox. The Jews who belonged to Agudas Achim, he said, "would tell you they are Orthodox," but weren't really. They didn't follow the rules for Sabbath, even though they may have eaten only kosher food. The lengthy interview covered everything from sacrificial lambs to Jewish evangelism, from heaven to Jesus-the-Jew, interfaith marriage, and so on. Twenty-nine pages (as transcribed) into the interview, Stringer asked about the history of Corsicana's Jews, to which Joseph replied he had researched their history: the first Jews came in 1871 and the Cemetery Association was organized in 1887.[156] "The first burial took place on March 19, 1877, which was ten years before the cemetery was officially organized. This is from the cemetery records."[157] Joseph recounted the establishment of the synagogues and places where Jewish communal observances took place before the synagogues were built. Appended to the interview is a three-page history, "The Jewish Community of Corsicana, Texas," unattributed but obviously written by Joseph. It repeats historical facts found in the interview and ends with a list of sources.[158]

Irvin **Samuels**, husband of Babbette Samuels, the cemetery admin–istrator first met in Chapter 2, gave an oral history, mostly about his father's clothing store. Samuels confirmed that only **Wolens** could afford to not work on Saturdays. His was the only authentic orthodox family in town. Samuels recounted that once, in the twenties, Klan members put KKK stickers on the windows of all the town's businesses and told people to only shop at stores with stickers, knowing the Jewish merchants would scrape them off. But Samuels believed it didn't make any difference to people. His view was that the large membership of the local Klan was a way to make sure they wouldn't harm anyone—people joined, including prominent citizens, to keep an eye on things and to vote against any violent or de–structive proposals.

The oral history given by Louis **Wolens**, son of K., had many interesting anecdotes about his youth as a troublemaker and how he tried to make amends in later years. He gave a detailed account of his family's business accomplishments, in much greater detail than in Silverberg's lecture. He described how his father and uncles created an empire of forty-eight "K. Wolens" stores, all in Texas, before they sold out. Louis Wolens demonstrated an exceptional memory for details and a keen sense of pathos in his many recollections.

Stringer's interview of Jay **Silverberg** also covered a lot of the Wolens family's story. Jay met his future wife, Daisy Wolens, at the University of Chicago. After living in Chicago for five years they came to Corsicana. He bought into the Wolens business and opened up the first branch store, in Wortham. His details are a bit at odds with the corporate history told by his brother-in-law, Louis.[159] Most of the transcript of Silverberg's oral history, a half-year after his talk to the local historical society (Section VI, above), is a verbatim copy of the lecture as it was printed in the *Scroll*. A difference, though, is whereas the *Scroll* transcript briefly touched on the Rope Walker legend, Silverberg's oral history gave a much more detailed account:

> *The Ropewalker was with a firm that was selling stoves and appliances. He had a peg leg. He would string a rope across a street from one building to another. With an iron stove strapped to his back, he would walk on that rope. It was a publicity stunt to attract attention. He was doing this here in Corsicana when something happened. He tripped or something and fell to the ground. The stove crushed his back. When the people started to gather around him, he first said that he wanted a priest. The priest came, and then he said that he wanted a rabbi. We didn't have a rabbi at that time, so they called Benjamin Marks and Ben Rosenberg, who were both Orthodox. The man asked them to say a prayer for him. When they began to say the prayer in Hebrew, he immediately picked it up and repeated it after them in very good Hebrew. Before they could find out who he was, he died. Since he had asked for a rabbi and he knew Hebrew, they assumed that he was Jewish. So the Jewish people took him and buried him in the Hebrew cemetery. They erected a little marker with the inscription, "the Ropewalker." They never found out his name, never knew whether he had any relatives or anything. That happened shortly before the turn of the century.[160]*

Silverberg's story adds many new details. How much is accurate and how much is just the most recent variation of a story which had been told and retold, even at that point, for nearly a century? To be determined. As already demonstrated, some of Jay Silverberg's historical pronouncements were inaccurate.

Dr. Stringer probed each interviewee about anti-Semitic experiences, and everyone responded the same—there were none. Even the KKK, they said, which existed in Corsicana, had no effect on its Jewish population.

## IX. Corsicana's Earliest Jews

Corsicana histories say its first Jewish settlers arrived there in 1871, when the tracks of the H&TC reached town. Some Jewish families that ended up in Corsicana had lived elsewhere in Texas before then and found their way to Corsicana later. The Max **London** and Alex **Fox** families, for example, in 1870 lived in Eutaw, now a ghost town in neighboring Limestone County.

When Mary (McKinney) Miller, one of Corsicana's very first settlers, arrived in Corsicana, in 1847, at the age of eight, she was seven years older than the State of Texas. In a 1921 sworn statement[161] she spoke about, among other things, businesses near the courthouse "before the war":

### *there was a Jew named Michael had a grocery store*

This would appear to be Michael H. **Solomon** (1805-1889), whose gravestone is in the Hebrew Cemetery, but no census or other records could be found to support or refute that theory. A search of the 1860 census of Navarro County for residents who were foreign-born with the first name "Michael" came up empty, and of those men who were U.S.-born and named Michael, none had particularly Jewish-sounding surnames.

A search of early Corsicana newspapers for the text "Michael"—there are some extant issues of newspapers from the 1850s and early 1860s— found an 1859 advertisement in the *Navarro Express* for "A. Michael & Co.," a dry goods store. Further review[162] revealed that "Alex. Michael" was the owner of a large dry goods and hardware store. Promotion of his extensive line of goods filled an entire newspaper column, labeled, appropriately, "Michael Column." As of Sept. 12, 1859, his business was renamed "A. Michael & Bro.,"[163] reflecting his brother Jacob's contribution to the business and possibly the dissolution of a partnership with some other person, probably one "Roller" (see below).[164]

Annie Carpenter Love's 1933 *History of Navarro County* ("*Love*") identified many early merchants of Corsicana.[165]

> **As was usual with the frontier town the greater portion of the business activities centered around court house square and on the Northwest corner of the old Corsicana business district Alex Michael built a two-story brick store building which was the first brick edifice in Corsicana. Michael's store was a forerunner of the present department store, judging from the sign which read "Dry Goods, Groceries, Hardware and Drugs." The second story of Mr. Michael's building was a newspaper office and both the store and the newspaper changed hands from time to time, through the years.**[166]

Back to the 1860 census, now looking for the *surname* **Michael**, finds A. Michael, age 24, merchant, born in Germany. On a different page, J. Michael, age 26, and Henry Michael, age 18, also merchants, also born in Germany, were listed next to each other.[167] Jacob Michael, age 27, also a merchant from Germany, is another entry in that census, and quite likely a duplicate enumeration of "J. Michael."[168] The earliest mention of the surname Michael in Corsicana is an 1855 "Michael & Roller" advertisement in the *Prairie Blade*, the town's first newspaper.[169]

In September 1860, Alex Michael re—turned to Corsicana from a New York buying trip. The *Express* welcomed back its "friend and neighbor" who brought news of the political winds up North. If Texas factions could unite, opined Michael, then they could defeat Lincoln.[170]

There is no sign of the Michael family in Corsicana after the 1850s. On November 15, 1860, Alexander Michael married Helen **Oppenheimer** in Palestine, Texas.[171] Their family later appeared in some records as "**Michel**," but also with the usual spel—ling.[172] The Michaels/Michels had several children and were longtime residents

*New and Cheap !*

THE undersigned have just received a large and well selected assortment of **Staple and Fancy Dry Goods,** Hats,
  Caps,
    Bonnets,
      Mantles,
        Jewelry,
          Silk Dress Goods,
            Embroidery,
              Ribbons
                etc.,
              Nails,
            Castings,
          Cutlery,
        Cigars and Tobacco,
      Plantation Supplies,
    Books and Stationery,
  Yankee Notions,
Shirts and Shirt Bosoms,
  Mens' and Boys' Clothing,
    Brooms, Stoves, Carpeting,
      Wood and Willow ware,
        China, Glass, and
          Earthenware,
            Cordage,
              Pails,
                Mats,
and a great variety of other Goods too nu-merous to mention, all of which we will sell at low rates.

We return our thanks to our old custom-ers, and the public generally, for their lib-eral patronage heretofore, and respectfully solicit a continuance of the same, promis-ing our very best endeavors to please.
n2          A. MICHAEL & CO.

*Navarro Express*, **December 17, 1859**

*Prairie Blade*, November 17, 1855

of San Antonio. Alexander died in 1885[173] and Helen in 1909. Mrs. Michael was the daughter of Julius Oppenheimer, a suc–cessful merchant from Germany who brought his wife and two children to Texas after previously living in New York, Maine, and Pennsylvania. Following his marriage, Alex worked in the San Antonio banking house of D & A Oppenheimer, run by Helen's uncles, Daniel and Anton.

At the start of the war, Jacob Michael was dispatched to New Orleans to pick up arms purchased for Corsicana soldiers heading to Virginia. Travelling via the Red River, he brought back fifty-three Minie muskets with bayonets and one hundred musketoons.[174] CSA muster rolls for Navarro County include three soldiers surnamed Michael: Jacob, A. [Alexander], and Henry.[175]

♎

The earliest Jews in Corsicana were not necessarily the Michaels:

*A. Fox & Brothers had a store on the square until the coming of the railroad after which this was moved to Beaton Street. Mr. Fox was widely respected for his business ethics and he was given not only the patronage but also the friendship of the inhabitants of Navarro County.*[176]

*A. Fox had a dry goods store here before the war. His store was on the east side of the square, north of the Stell property.*[177]

Alexander Fox (1838-1922), a Jewish citizen of Corsicana for several decades, certainly had a shop on Beaton Street, but other than the above two references, there is no evidence he was in Corsicana before 1873, the year his name appeared in the *Logan Directory*, as previously shown. Other Foxes, however, were there before 1873. In October 1855, the "Fox & Jacobs" merchantry of Henry Fox and Manheim Jacobs started doing business in the Wybrants and Ransom building on the east side of the public (courthouse) square, next to the drug store.[178] The Nov. 17, 1855 issue of the *Prairie Blade*, the same issue with the above Michael & Roller advertisement, had a large ad for Fox & Jacobs, noting they also a store in Wheelock.[179] Although still operating in Corsicana in early 1856, by the end of 1858 Fox & Jacobs had moved to Waco.[180] Later still it was in Houston, where it operated from 1860 until January 1863, when Henry Fox turned over the firm to partners Manheim Jacobs and S. Meyer.[181]

The aforementioned November 1855 issue of the *Blade* also had a lengthy political notice, calling on Democrats to organize and appoint delegates to the Democratic convention in Austin. "All persons opposed to Know Noth-[Nothing] heresy, are invited to attend."[182] The item was endorsed by about a hundred men, including Henry Fox, Morris Fox,[183] J. Michael, and A. Michael. Judge C.L. Jester's Corsicana history, printed serially in the *Corsicana Daily Sun* in 1922, said Morris and Alex Fox had a store on the public square before the train line reached Corsicana.[184] Although Alex Fox may have *operated* a store in Corsicana in the late 1850s, there's no confirmation that he lived in town at that time. Records show he was living in Navasota in 1860, where he was enumerated in that year's census with Morris. His son Robert was born in Louisiana in 1863 (or '64), and he and his family in 1870 lived in Limestone County, according to that year's census. Nevertheless, so far as Alexander is concerned, here is no doubt that he and his brother, Abraham L. Fox, operated a store styled as "A. Fox & Bro." on Beaton Street from as early as 1873 until at least 1897.[185]

In the 1920s and 30s, Mary Miller, Lee Jester, and Annie Carpenter Love all said that Alex Fox, a central figure in Corsicana Jewish activities until his death in 1922, had been a part of the community since before the war. It's possible that Mary Miller, the only one of them who was actually alive in antebellum Corsicana, may have misremembered, and the others were repeating what she had told them. Apparently, Henry and Morris Fox were there, at that early date, and Alex came later, after the war.

## X. Other Notes on Early Corsicana Jews

Alexander Michael was Secretary, Corsicana Lodge No. 174, Grand Lodge of Texas Masons, in 1857.[186] The seven other officers of the lodge are names at the forefront of Corsicana's well-established early history, including Senior Warden C.M. **Winkler**, Junior Warden Samuel H. **Kerr**, and Treasurer Alexander **Beaton**. Among the seventeen Master Masons at the time were Hampton **McKinney** and Messrs. **Loughridge**, **Donaldson**, **White**, and **Henderson**—the top echelon of Corsicana's founding fathers—and Henry **Fox**.[187]

In the 1860 census, Sol **Weil**, thirty-nine, was living near the Richland Crossing Post Office, Navarro County,[188] twelve miles south of Corsicana. He was a "stock raiser" with personal property worth $640 and real estate valued at $1000. He is presumed Jewish based on his name and his Bavarian nativity.[189] Weil was a private in Co. I of the 4th Tex. Infantry, as shown on a Nov. 18, 1863 "Certificate for Disability for Discharge." He was enlisted in Corsicana by Capt. C.M. **Winkler** on July 17, 1861, served under Capt. J.R. **Loughridge**,[190] and was discharged on Nov. 11, 1863 from the Empire Hospital in Atlanta having been "unfit for duty" for six months due to insanity. "His captain and the surgeon of his regiment strongly recommend his discharge."[191] A "Parole of Honor," the acknowledgement by Confed–erate soldiers of defeat and agreement to cease fighting was signed by Sol Weil at Houston on June 18, 1865.[192]

The *Logan Directory* of 1873 includes a listing for "**Block** Bros. & Co., Groceries and Produce." The Jewish-owned firm, based in New Orleans, owned the building diagonally across from what is now the "Across the Street Diner," but only for a short time.[193]

♎

Most of the eighty to ninety Jews living in Corsicana in 1884 probably knew about Rope Walker's fall, and a fair number of them probably witnessed it. Some Corsicanan from that period, Jewish or otherwise, Ben Marks or Ben Rosenberg according to one recollection, surely knew something about his identity. But those individuals are long, long gone, and if they knew something, they never passed that information along to someone who fixed the gravestone. Surely someone left something, a document or handwritten note perhaps, identifying him. But nothing has ever been found.

# Chapter 5

# WALK INTO OBLIVION

*Come hither! bury thyself in a life which, to your now equally abhorred and abhorring, landed world, is more oblivious than death. Come hither! put up thy grave-stone, too*

There are four sources, so far, for the Rope Walker story:

- Walking Tour Booklet

- Historic Texas Cemetery marker

- Jay Silverberg's history of Jewish Corsicana

- Jay Silverberg's oral history

Another source is Babbette Samuels. No one in Corsicana knows more about Rope Walker than Babbette, the recently retired manager of the Hebrew Cemetery and last of the town's once-thriving Jewish community. Babbette has been the subject of several magazine articles about Jewish Corsicana, often focusing on its ebbing population, restoration of Temple Beth El, and care of the cemetery. Babbette, Beth El, the cemetery, Rope Walker—this is the natural progression of an interview with Babbette Samuels.[194]

Until recently, Babbette was in charge of the alphabetical register which records burials in the cemetery. The first page under R, for example, lists Herriett Rich and her son, Charles:

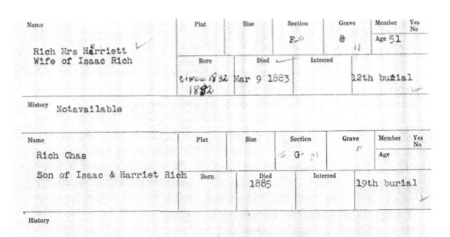

Cemetery record book

Information includes the grave location (for those not buried in one of the many large family plots), birth and death dates, and age at time of death. One box is used to record the order of burials. Herriett and Charles Rich were the twelfth and nineteenth internments, respectively. Additional infor–mation, if any, appears in the "history" area.

Attached to and between the pages are newspaper clippings, mostly obituaries. The ledger is, in effect, a record of the passing of a vibrant Jewish community, a memorial to a 150-year-old Jewish community.

Babbette took over responsibility for the register from Ivan Rosenberg, who created it in 1951.[195] (Ivan's father, Ben, according to Jay Silverberg, prayed with Rope Walker before he died.) She was also given a long list of burials which were not yet entered. It took several years of visiting and revisiting the cemetery for Babbette to bring the register up to date and make sure it was complete and accurate. Record keeping was complicated by old and faded gravestones and some that had no dates at all. She also compiled two spreadsheets of the burials—one by date and one alphabetical—and com–pared them to the register.

The page for Rope Walker, typed up by Ivan Rosenberg, describes what happened and is the main source of Babbette's information.

### ROPE WALKER
### Section K
### Grave 1
### Died 1884
### 17th Burial

*This being such an unusual name on Grave Head stone You may be interested in the History–In 1884 one day a stranger arrived, he stretched a wire across Beaton St from the SE Corner of Collins St, to the opposite NW Corner of the street–The unusual part this Wire Walker had a Peg Wood leg. He attempted to cross this wire on one leg and a wood peg leg with a cook stoved tied on this back-he had a long bar in his hand to help balance himself-when just about half way across he lost his balance and fell to the street-he was badly crushed by the weight of the stove on his back-He was immediately picked up and carried to a near by hotel where Dr. J.T. Gulick a pioneer physician attended him-When he first fell he said that he was a Methodist and would like to see a preacher, Abe Mulkey a famous Evangelist was called and prayed. when asked his name he turned his head and did not answer-they asked about his relatives and home and again he did not answer-Finally the injured pain whipped man realized the time had come to walk a strange rope and that he was not going to finish the act, he looked to those around him and then to the Doctor and said. "Doc" I wish to talk with a Jew, "I am a dying Jew"*

*The startled Protestant withdrew from the hotel room and they quickly rejoined the crowds on the streets and soon the strange story spred around that this man who had denied his religion to who in the face of death had deserted*

*his teachings and barley snatched them back in time A Jewish merchants was called, (there being no Rabbi here then) and he requested the dying man to repeat a Certain prayer, which he did in excellent Hebrew and there was no doubt that he was a Jew.*

*In 1949 Robt C Campbell a reporter from the Daily Sun gathered lots of facts and wrote a feature story on this-it was later reproduced Denver Post Rock Mountain Empire Magazine Section Sunday Dec 11 1949*

*In years to come some of the new generations may be interested in this story. –see picture on back of this page*

*Ivan Rosenberg.*

Attached to the back of the page are two clippings from the referenced article. One is an ink drawing of a peg-legged man walking a tightrope with a stove strapped to his back above a gaping crowd,[196] captioned with a quote from the story: "There he was, a lone man with a wooden leg on a tight wire, a cookstove on his back and a block to go. The crowd was stunned. Slowly the man came with a stride born of endless practice." The other clipping, a photograph, is "Rope Walker's tombstone, Corsicana, Tex." The article itself is not attached, but a copy was obtained from the Denver Public Library.

*No one knew who he was or from whence he came. They knew only that a man of courage was taking a*

## Walk into Oblivion

### By ROBERT C. CAMPBELL

*I STOOD in the soft rain, the first of early fall, and looked down on the little upright slab. I kneeled, and with a fingernail scratched away a part of the lichens which long ago—so very long ago—had started their parasitic taking over. It was a neat tombstone, white and cold.*

*I stood looking down upon it, and I thought: No, neither graves nor tombstones reveal the enigmas they cover. No, you cannot look at a marker and solve a puzzle: you can't sit by a grave and pull out the secrets as if they were dandelions.*

*I wished then—and I wish now—it were possible. For I wanted desperately to know the truth about Rope Walker, the only wording found on the tombstone. No date, no little inscription, not even a name.*

*You see, the "Rope Walker" chiseled beautifully across the face of the marble wasn't put there as a name. It is an occupational title. It might as well have been Truck Driver, or Dish Washer, or Café Owner. That's the kind of a gravestone it is.*

*It has been there 65 years.*

*IT WAS hot and dusty that summer day of 1884 in Corsicana, Tex., cradle of the mid-continent oil field.*

*The sun beamed down with frying intentions. It beat down on famous Beaton Street, paved with tough old bois d' arc bricks. Farmers' wagons cornered the available hitching places. The walks were crowded with men and women who had driven far to see the free show.*

*Driven far, they had to see the beginning of the story of Rope Walker, although, of course, they had no way of knowing this.*

*They had come to see a tight-rope-walking act, and they had responded nobly to the colored dodgers announcing this stupendous event. Schools had been dismissed for the occasion. It was a gala day with the promise of thrills.*

*They stood solid-massed on Beaton street looking upward at a tight line that extended thirty feet or more overhead. It angled across, corner to corner, connecting the roofs at the* two tallest buildings in town. It was a block long, that tight line.

The tight rope walking should be a fine sight, and worth putting up with all the dust the horses were stirring. The people waited anxiously, chatted nervously, then fell silent as they saw a figure high above approach the south end of the wire and prepare to make his crossing.

The daredevil, they saw immediately, wasn't cut from common cloth. He had come prepared to reward the crowd for its trouble. Any fool might walk a tight wire, but it took an artist to step onto the taut line with a heavy cook stove strapped to his back.

The Act Begins ...

This was an added attraction, and the spectators gasped. They had never seen THAT done. Yes, this was really an event, and surely worth all the trouble coming to town.

The performer, confident and smiling, paused just long enough to gain the applause of the crowd. He smiled for only the fraction of a second. He tested his delicate balance on the rope, looked straight ahead, slid one foot forward.

The crowd was stunned into an eerie silence.

One foot was gone!

The man had a wooden leg. There he was, a lone man with a wooden leg on a tight wire up there with an iron cookstove on his back and a block to go.

"Look!" the crowd shouted. "One leg!"

"He's gotta wooden leg!"

"Oh, look, up there on a peggie!"

Up and down the filled avenue went the chant. This rope walker was giving them something they had never seen before, did not dare hope to see again.

Slowly he came in perfect cadence, using a stride born of endless practice. He made a balance shift to counteract a treacherous little gust, the same tight smile flashing to the corners of his mouth. The peg leg was notched on the end, and he would fit the rope into the slot, put forward his good leg, drag the artificial one back to his body and thrust it forward again. He was good, there was no doubt about his being good.

Suddenly there were horrified screams. Terror had chased wonder off the street.

It was hushed, the cold, quiet hush that comes with tragedy.

For a second the body flashed in midair, the sun bouncing

its rays off the shiny cookstove. Then the body hit the wooden street with a terrible clank and thud.

### ... And the Act Concludes

He fell on his front side, and the heavy stove crushed him into the street. One of the stove lids rolled aimlessly along the hard earth and came to rest against the board walk.

The act was over. That part of it, anyway.

The still-conscious man was taken, as gently as men can carry another, to a nearby hotel. Emergency treatment was given; the man was made somewhat comfortable in a cool, clean bed in the best room the inn had to offer.

Dr. J T Gulick, a pioneer physician, stood over him. He knew death when he saw it coming, and he knew it was on its way. He couldn't do much for the aerialist, but perhaps he could ease him spiritually.

"I'm afraid you're done in," he told the stranger. "Perhaps a preacher ...?"

The man spoke then for the first time since his footing had failed him.

"Yes," he said, "I am a Methodist. I would like to see a Methodist preacher."

There was in the crowd that day a young Corsicana minister who was destined to become one of the greatest evangelists in the United States—the famous Abe Mulkey. Summoned, he gathered members of his congregation around him and they went to the bedside of the broken, dying man.

They talked with him about death, the mysteries of life in the hereafter. They prayed. And then they asked him his name.

He did not answer.

They asked him about his relatives, about his home, about his past.

He turned his head away.

Death tightened the ring.

Finally, the injured, pain-whipped man realized the time had come to walk a strange rope. He wasn't going to finish this act at all.

He looked at those around him, and he looked at the doctor.

"Doc," he said, slowly, deliberately, as a man would who knows he has but few words to say and doesn't dare risk dropping any of them, "Doc, I wish to talk with a Jew."

"I'm a dying Jew, Doc."

*The Prayers Spoken ...*

*The startled Protestants withdrew from the hotel room. They rejoined the crowd, quickly spread the story, wondering of the strangeness of this—this man who had denied his religion, this man who even in the face of death had deserted his teachings and barely snatched them back in time.*

*A Jewish merchant (there was no rabbi) was summoned hastily. The dying man told the merchant he was an Orthodox Jew.*

*It is not easy to fool a Jew about his religion. He asked the dying man to repeat certain prayers. He did, readily, in excellent Hebrew.*

*He was a Jew all right, the merchant said.*

*The man smiled then, first at the merchant, and then at the doctor, and then at something removed, utterly remote. He died, taking his identity with him.*

*Corsicana's little Jewish congregation buried him. It never occurred to them that the man would not be identified within a few months. They logically thought it out: he was a skilled performer, marked because he used only one leg in his act. A one-legged rope walker, they felt sure, just couldn't escape quick identification.*

*... For the Fallen Unknown*

*They tried, these friendly Jews. They gave the information to every vaudeville troupe that crossed Texas. They wrote letters to newspapers in the east and south and west. They sent notices to theaters. They did it for weeks, then months, then years.*

*"Did you ever know or hear of a one-legged rope walker? Surely in vaudeville or the circus, perhaps, a one-legged performer ..."*

*No. None had ever heard of one before.*

*In the old burial record book that records the history of the Hebrew cemetery a queer entry was made. It was short.*

*There was no name, so the space allotted to it was left blank. Only this inaccuracy was written there: "Fell from a trapeze, 1884."*

*That is all. Not since that day has another scrap of information been written.*

*The Jews bought a headstone and sank it.*

*They had no name to put there, and it didn't look right to leave it blank, an anonymous stone among the identified ones.*

*So they had chiseled in all they knew:*

*"Rope Walker"*

*Someday, they say, somebody may recall an old trouper who had lost a leg and disappeared. A man, they say, who was good in his act.*[197]

## "The Act Begins ... And the Act Concludes"

Campbell's story is a wonderful piece of writing, but mostly fiction. The gravestone photo plants the story in reality, but like the gravestone, there's no foundation. As a bit of writing for popular readership, one doesn't expect footnotes or a bibliography, but there isn't even an introductory "so and so told me," or, "it has been said." The only sources mentioned are the grave-stone and an "old burial record book." The rest is derived from some unidentified source(s) and/or the author's fanciful imagination. All of the minutiae and dialogue must have been made up; how could anyone in 1949 know that someone in 1884 said: *He's gotta wooden leg!; Oh, look, up there on a peggie!;* that there was a *clank and thud;* or that he was put *in a cool, clean bed* ? Most of the story describes exactly what would be found in 1884 on a Corsicana street with a crowd gathered to watch a street performer. It is historical fiction, with no way to distinguish the historical from the fiction.

Rosenberg's write-up in the record book says the article was "repro-duced" from an article published earlier that year in the *Corsicana Daily Sun,* but no such article could be found.[198] Campbell was a reporter for the *Sun,* 1946 to 1953, writing under the byline, "Bob Campbell, Daily Sun Staff."[199] His writing was free-flowing, imaginative, lyrical. His epic poem written for Corsicana's centennial, in 1948, covering the better part of two full pages, was so beloved it was republished in 1976 for the paper's bicentennial edition.[200]

Campbell published another piece in the *Rocky Mountain Empire Magazine* in 1949, before "Walk into Oblivion." In three installments, in January, March, and April, he told the story of the Springtown massacre, another historical-but-hazy Texas tale. Like the Rope Walker story, over time it had evolved into a local legend.

Historian Helen McLure analyzed the historical facts behind the Springtown massacre in an article in the 2001 issue of *The Southwestern Historical Quarterly.*[201] In 1873, a Springtown mother and her five daughters, ages sixteen to twenty-five, were killed, three of them shot and the other three hung. Others also lost their lives. A profusion of questions arose over the years about motive: was it a justified, extrajudicial, vigilante execution? Was it a witch hunt? A combination of both? Were they a family of outlaws and whores? Were they defiant, Union-sympathizing non-conformists? Again—both?

John Nix presented a version of the murders in his 1945 book, *History of Springtown, Parker County, and The Tale of Two Schools.* Nix found some just-ification for the Hill family killings and it sparked renewed interest in the story. Four years later, Campbell wrote his version.

Professor McLure analyzed the story's transformation following the publication of Nix's local history:[202]

> From this point forward, the legend of the Hill family began to blos-som. Robert C. Campbell's 1949 story "When Death Danced With Eleven" spun a marvelous Wild West tale. Paragraphs of invented dia-logue, a "tall, striking, vivacious" Nance Hill, a gunfight between Allen Hill Sr. and a Confederate, and the Hill home as a place of "sweet music and shuffling feet and gay laughter" where "strange men" came every night to dance with the daughters are only a few of the imaginative ele-ments of this piece. Campbell names Nance's boyfriend "Henry" Porter and details a confrontation between Porter and "Charlie" Laird in which Laird chides the young man for the bad company he is keeping. A shot rings out, Laird slumps, murmuring, "His folks raised him better," and loses consciousness, although he does not actually expire for five weeks. The five men and Nance flee into the brush. Their bodies are later dis-covered in a grotesque tableau—Nance hanging from a tree limb and the five dead men arranged as if kneeling beneath her. Campbell described the killing of Dusky and the rest of her girls in similarly vivid detail but of-fered no real explanation for any of the carnage except Dusky's despair-ing "statement" to her children that "they've hated us ever since we came here."[23]

**Critical analysis of Robert Campbell's "When Death Danced with Eleven"**

Campbell's version assigned incorrect given names to Porter and Laird, the reason McLure put them in quotes. He claimed he was told the story by an old man, who, at the age of ten, was an eyewitness to the Laird murder and whose identity Campbell had pledged to keep secret.[203] McLure never located any further mention of Campbell's supposed percipient witness in her detailed investigations, and she doubted such a witness ever existed.[204] Campbell peppered his Springtown story with an incredible amount of previously unknown details. He was either a phenomenal investigative reporter or an out-and-out fabricator. The cumulative evidence suggests the latter.

## "The Prayers Spoken ... For the Fallen Unknown"

Campbell's publishing career started as early as 1923, when he was editor in chief of the *Weatherford Melon Vine*, his high school yearbook. Sixteen years later he was forty-four when he wrote "Walk into Oblivion." He had been a newspaperman for more than thirty-six years when he died in Dallas on May 12, 1965.[205] His earthly departure at the age of sixty followed a severe drinking binge and a week of the DTs, a nightcap to decades of chronic alcoholism.[206] A proximate cause of death, not entered on his death certificate, was heartbreak: his mother, Rena Bonner Campbell, had died only two months earlier and they were very close. In the 1920s and 30s they

Robert Campbell

were both editors of the *Ranger Times* and the *Mineral Springs Index*[207] and he lived with her for much of his adult life.[208] She divorced her first husband when "Bobby" and his sister were young children, then remarried in 1928 to Arthur Conway, a local oilfield worker. Conway died in 1933.[209]

Before Campbell was born, his mother wrote several lengthy, fictional, slice-of-life pieces for the *Dallas Daily News*. In the fashion of the day, her stories were placed amidst news items, even though they were obviously made-up, with dialogue and fanciful descriptions. The apple didn't fall far from the tree.

Rena Bonner's first marriage, in 1901, to Claude S. Campbell, Robert's father,[210] coincided with the end of her romantic, homey fiction in the Dallas paper, and perhaps her romantic view of life. Claude was a pathetic drunkard who died in a Dallas jail when Robert was twelve.[211] Robert was briefly married, and divorced, in the 1930s.[212] The apple, fermented, didn't fall far from the tree.

♎

Rosenberg's write-up in the record book mentions Campbell's "Walk into Oblivion" and includes the same unique phrasing Campbell used in the article, so it was written based on Campbell's article. Rosenberg does include one fact that is not in the article: the rope went "across Beaton St. from the SE Corner of Collins St, to the opposite NW Corner of the street." Campbell only said that the rope over Beaton Street "angled across, corner to corner, connecting the roofs at the two tallest buildings in town. It was a block long, that tight line." He didn't specify which block on Beaton Street or which corners.

The record book referred to in the article is not the current record book because the one kept by Babbette does not include the "Fell from a trapeze, 1884" notation mentioned by Campbell. It makes no sense that Campbell would make up a detail so incongruous with the rest of the story. There must have been another, earlier record book.

Campbell's only sources, the gravestone and the "queer entry" in the cemetery record book, say nothing about a peg leg, a stove, Mulkey, or Gulick. It's not at all apparent where Campbell found his information. It's conjecture, but it seems likely Campbell got much of his information from Rosenberg, and maybe others who had heard the story, to write his article. Rosenberg then used Campbell's article to create the record book's narrative, adding that one detail Campbell had left out (or got wrong)—the intersection where the accident occurred. It is unknown how much of Campbell's version is from what people like Rosenberg told him versus what he simply made up, and at this point it's not even possible to estimate.

☊

One virtue of Campbell's story is its graphics. The photo of Rope Walker's gravestone in the article shows Herriet Rich's gravestone in the background. She is geographically and alphabetically (in the record book) close to Rope Walker, and her death, Mar. 9, 1883, was not much earlier than Rope Walker's death, which, according to a "queer entry" in the old record book, was in 1884. The drawing of a tightrope walker holding a balancing pole with a stove strapped to his back has the virtue of accurately depicting which leg was amputated, a fact which the artist, Herbert Levene, had a 50 percent chance of getting right. Proof left for a later chapter.

Hebrew-text side of Herriet Rich's
gravestone, still standing;
Rope Walker's gravestone, in the
background, in repose

# Chapter 6

## A BETTER MEMORIAL

*Out of the trunk, the branches grow; out of them, the twigs. So, in productive subjects, grow the chapters.*

**Clipping in the cemetery record book**

Another clipping in the cemetery record book is a Tolbert's Texas column, dated Feb. 26, 1968, one of hundreds Frank X. Tolbert (1912-1984) wrote over the course of his forty-two years at the *Dallas Morning News*.[213] "A Better Memorial for 'Rope Walker'?" concerns itself with the fading inscription on the gravestone. Referring to the photo accompanying the article, Tolbert concedes, "the letters have been accent–ed on the picture, not on the stone, by an artist's brush." Tolbert asked Jay Silverberg if the "almost incredible" story could be added to the gravestone or put on a historical marker at the gravesite. Silverberg, Tolbert tells us, is secretary of the Jewish Cemetery Association, a fact that gives Silverberg's version of the Rope Walker tale, a few chapters back, a lot more weight.

The article launches right into the story: "The Rope Walker was a stove salesman who came to Corsicana in 1884 on a 'Trade's Day.'" Where did Tolbert get this stove salesman idea? From Silverberg, who also included that detail, ten years later, in his 1978 interview with Tommy Stringer? Or did Silverberg get it from Tolbert? The "stove salesman" idea is not in the cemetery record book and not in Campbell's 1949 article.

Before continuing, Tolbert cites his source:

> **Some years ago Ivan Rosenberg of Corsicana supplied me with some information on the Rope Walker from "The Perpetual Record Book of the Jewish Cemetery, Corsicana."**

Tolbert then quotes extensively from the record book, repeating close to what is now written there. He says it "reads, in part" and adds ellipses for omitted text. There is one big difference, though, between Tolbert's quotes and the record book itself. Tolbert writes:

***The man died after saying the prayer. And according to the Perpetual Record Book, "the Jewish people of Corsicana made up a purse and buried him with this simple marking on his tomb, 'Rope Walker.'"***

This part about raising money for Rope Walker's burial is not in the record book. It could be that the page now in the book is not the same page Tolbert saw—maybe it was copied over at some point and that sentence was mistakenly left out.

Ω

That exhausts everything about Rope Walker in the record book. The newspaper clippings there suggest another approach to solving the mystery: newspaper articles written about the one-legged tightrope walker. Online historical newspaper databases contain images of millions of newspaper pages (some instead contain images for each article), from all over the world, going back hundreds of years.

Nothing turns up with a search for the word *Corsicana* plus either *tight rope* or *rope walker* in 1884 newspapers. Variations were tried, without success. For example, broadening the search by removing the requirement for *Corsicana* should generate results, which can then be read to see if they have the information being sought, which in this case is a story about a rope walker who fell in Texas with some details in common with the Rope Walker legend. An article about Rope Walker's fall would probably mention Corsicana, but this strategy makes sense because it reduces the effects of errors which frequently occur during the process of converting images of newsprint into computer-readable text. Removing *Corsicana* would now yield articles where that word was "misread" by the computer as *Corslcana*, *Cersicana*, *Corsicaua*, etc. This change to the search query also means that many more images from the database would be selected, not just those where *Corsicana* was "misread"; now, <u>anything</u> which includes either of the two phrases, *rope walker* or *tight rope*, from 1884 papers, would be found.

Indeed, the revised query, executed in www.Newspapers.com, a robust subscription-based newspaper database, returned 129 hits, that is, 129 images of pages from 1884 newspapers, each with the found text (*tight rope* or *rope walker*) electronically highlighted in yellow. Every article was reviewed, but none of them mentioned a fall in Corsicana, a peg leg, or a stove. Of the three from Texas newspapers, one was for a rope walker named "Savir" who performed (successfully) in the town of Belton. Anoth–

er opined that a performer named "Butler" may attract a lot of attention. The third was about the wonders of a new medicinal formulation:

> *With a little of the hydrochlorate of cocaine a man could be run over by a train of cars and not feel it. A rope walker could dance over Niagara Falls all day without fear, and a man with chronic neuralgia could have all his teeth drawn for pastime.*

Interesting, but not remotely close to what is being sought—something about the tragic fall of a tightrope walker in Corsicana.

## Corsicana's Newspapers

A close examination was made of Corsicana's newspapers, seeking further enlightenment about Rope Walker. Corsicana had no shortage of newspapers, starting in 1855 with the *Prairie Blade*, printed a floor above A. Michael & Co.'s store at the northwest corner of the town's public square.[214] In the following fifty years there were no fewer than nine additional papers.[215] Near the end of 1884, an astonished Dallas reporter observed,

> *Corsicana has five newspapers and possibly four more will be started here on the 1st of January. A newspaper man arrives on almost every train.*[216]

Today, Corsicana reads the *Corsicana Daily Sun*, published on Tuesdays and Saturdays.[217] Started in 1897, it traces its lineage, more or less, back to the *Prairie Blade*, first published in 1855.

Despite all of those old Corsicana newspapers, virtually none can be

found today. An early morning inferno on April 18, 1911, is considered the reason why no early issues of the *Sun* still exist.[218] It started in the Steam Bakery, on W. Collin Street, and spread to the Sun-Light Publishing Co., the paper's publisher. The report of the fire doesn't mention the loss of old issues, but that's what presumably happened. The earliest extant issue of the *Corsicana Daily Sun*, viewable at www.Newspapers.com, is dated Apr. 1, 1909, about two years before the fire.[219] The fire, however, doesn't explain why newspapers other than Sun-Light papers are missing.[220]

Earliest available issue of the *Corsicana Daily Sun*, April 1, 1909

A search of the Library of Congress's "US Newspaper Directory, 1690-Present," an inventory of historic newspapers at ChroniclingAmerica-.loc.gov, shows that only a smattering of issues of old Corsicana newspapers still exist. A few issues of the *Observer*, for example, it says, are at the San Jacinto museum, in La Porte, Texas.[221] Online newspaper databases were also checked to see if their inventories included Corsicana or Navarro County newspapers from 1884, databases like ChroniclingAmerica.com, which in addition to its newspaper directory hosts the largest free online database of newspapers. Most states have free databases of their own historic papers, often duplicating what is found at Chronicling America. Texas has an excellent database at its Portal to Texas History at texashistory.unt.edu. Newspapers.com and GenealogyBank.com are two very large, fee-based newspaper databases, and there are several others, some free, some not.[222]

Extensive searching turned up only one issue of one 1884 Corsicana newspaper. The Portal to Texas History website has the Dec. 15, 1884 issue of *The Semi-Occasional Advertiser*, a tabloid-formatted paper. A careful reading of the entire paper, all four pages, found no mention of Rope Walker. Corsicana's Public Library and the library at Corsicana's Navarro College were also consulted for 1884 newspapers, all to no avail.

In downtown Corsicana or some tiny Navarro County hamlet, in a musty, cobwebbed basement of an old building that once was, or still is, a library, courthouse, church, town hall, or Masonic Hall, are boxes filled with stacks of rodent-gnawed, moldering 1884 issues of the *Observer*, the *Daily Courier*, *The Semi-Occasional Advertiser*, the *Messenger*, or the *Journal*. Somewhere there is a detailed account of the fall and death of Rope Walker on a balled-up page of newsprint inside some living room wall, helping to insulate someone's Central Texas home.

Articles about the Rope Walker *legend* did occasionally appear in the *Sun* family of papers, usually on dates celebrating historic anniversaries like Corsicana's founding, Texas Independence, or American Independence—times when Corsicana took stock of its history. Nothing promotes history better than recounting the momentous events and larger-than-life characters of bygone days. The June 29, 1976 issue of the *Corsicana Daily Sun*, for example, had a good review of the saga, sticking to known facts without adding too much conjecture. It hit on key elements seen so far, like the peg leg and Abe Mulkey, although nothing about Dr. Gulick.[223]

## Casting a Wider Net for Rope Walker

All published versions of the Rope Walker legend were reviewed in case some fact or hint in one of them might lead to an answer, perhaps in some strange, alternate version of the story. Books about tightrope walking and books about Corsicana were reviewed and the internet was thoroughly examined.[224] Local history materials were reviewed at the Richard M. Sanchez Library at Corsicana's Navarro College, at Corsicana's Public Library, and at the Navarro County Historical Society's office at the city's Pioneer Village museum. The *Corsicana Daily Sun*, available online, was extensively queried.[225] From all the stories about the legend, four stand out because they have unique, substantive material not derived from an earlier source. All other instances, most of them of recent vintage, can be traced back to one of these four. One of the four sources is "Walk into Oblivion," previously analyzed and discredited as fictionalized, lacking credibility, and failing to identify its sources. On the other hand, "Oblivion" was endorsed by Ivan Rosenberg in his cemetery record book write-up, which does gives it some credibility, coming from a member of the Hebrew Cemetery Association. Silverberg's version is not much different from the "Oblivion"/record book version, and though it does have some unique factual elements, it is only a partial telling of the legend.

The four foundational sources of the legend are:

- "Walk into Oblivion," from 1949, and the cemetery record book write-up, done in 1951. They are counted as one version because of their many similarities

- Tolbert's Texas columns, including the one at the start of this chapter

- "Identity of 'Rope Walker' Killed Here 52 Years Ago Remains Unsolved Mystery," a 1936 article printed in the *Corsicana Daily Sun*;

- "Rope Walker—True Story from Jewish American History," a 2003 internet article from *Jewish Magazine*

The first-listed of these and one Tolbert's Texas column have already been examined. The remainder are taken up in the next three chapters.

# Chapter 7

# THE WONDERFUL COUNTRY

*Death seems the only desirable sequel for a career like this*

Frank Tolbert was the best-known writer of what were deemed, at the close of the previous chapter, four foundational versions of the Rope Walker legend. His widely read column on Texas history in the *Dallas Morning News* brought him celebrity and credibility. He wrote five of his Tolbert's Texas columns about Rope Walker and put the tale in his book, *An Informal History of Texas*. His version of the Rope Walker story for the most part repeated what Ivan Rosenberg had set down in the cemetery record book, except for two key differences: one is Tolbert's idea that Rope Walker was a stove salesman; the other is a theory he presented about Rope Walker's identity.

## 1958 – "Tragic Saga"

Tolbert's earliest piece about the legend was "Tragic Saga of a Rope Walker,"[226] written ten years before he wrote the "Better Memorial" article, the clipping found in the cemetery record book just examined. His source of the "Tragic Saga" story, he says, was Robert Monaghan Cooksey, a well-known citizen of Corsicana, and he had verified the story with "leading Corsicana citizens" Ivan Rosenberg and Wally Levy—all within a week of writing the article. He starts out with a brief summary, not at odds with other versions seen so far, except for one minor detail: the cook stove, he says, was *small*. This sounds reasonable; carrying a normal-sized cook stove would be like carrying a full-grown ox.

> **We think the best way to tell this almost incredible-sounding story is to repeat the wording on it from "The Perpetual Record Book of the Jewish Cemetery, Corsicana." This was furnished by Mr. Levy.**[227]

Tolbert then quotes virtually the identical material he did ten years later, in the "Better Memorial" piece, but with fewer omissions. When he says he will "repeat the wording" from the record book "furnished by Mr. Levy," does he mean the *wording* or the *book* was "furnished?" If Tolbert did not copy from the book itself, but instead was informed of its contents by letter or telephone, it would explain why the quoted material is not perfectly identical to what is in the record book. It would also explain why the last portion, where Tolbert says the Jews of Corsicana "made up a purse," was included as quoted matter in the article although it is not in the record book: it might have been communicated to Tolbert, perhaps over the telephone, at the same time as verbatim text from the record book was communicated, and Tolbert mistakenly thought the "purse" part also came from the record book.

The 1958 article makes no mention of the "stove salesman" or "Trade's Day" scenario found in the "Better Memorial" article ten years later.

## 1959 – "Mesmeriser and Other Screwballs"

Tolbert's second mention of Rope Walker is about a year and a half later. It is nothing more than a brief aside as he introduces a story about a different local legend in a column titled, "'The Mesmeriser' Named a Creek."[228]

> *My favorite in the Navarro County screwball gallery is the poor fellow buried in a Corsicana cemetery with only the words, "Rope Walker" on his gravestone. ... He fell to his death before the eyes of a "First Monday" crowd.*

A "First Monday crowd" is the mass of people who came to town for "Trade's Day," as he called it in a later piece, the market day held on the first Monday of each month. This is the earliest mention of a Trade's Day/First Monday as part of the Rope Walker legend. This detail may have come to Tolbert from someone claiming knowledge of the incident, perhaps someone spurred to send him information after reading the 1958 "Tragic Saga" article.

## 1961 – An Informal History of Texas

Tolbert told a slightly different version of the tale in his 1961 book, *An Informal History of Texas*, an anthology of his best Tolbert's Texas columns. This iteration of the story was the first time Tolbert described Rope Walker as a stove salesman:

> *In 1884 a one-legged stove peddler, a complete stranger, arrived in Corsicana. To call attention to his business he volunteered to walk a tightrope stretched two stories up over Corsicana's main street. ... He tried this stunt on a First Monday (the first Monday of each month when Texas*

*farmers traditionally come to town and do most of their shopping and trading).*
*The one-legged stove peddler didn't make it.*

## February 1968 – "A Better Memorial"

This is the clipping found in the cemetery record book, discussed in the previous chapter.

## May 1968 – "Theory"

Tolbert wrote a second article in 1968, "Theory on 1-Legged Rope Walker," just months after "A Better Memorial." An extended discussion of this theory is presented further below.

## 1973 – "Gravestone Restored"

"Gravestone Restored for Rope Walker"[229] was a follow-up to his February 1968 article advocating for "A Better Memorial." It was the last column Tolbert wrote about Rope Walker. The words "Rope Walker," he tells readers, have been re-etched into the stone. Once again, Tolbert refers to Rope Walker as a "stove salesman." Is this simply a case of stereotyping: if he was a Jew, he must have been a merchant, because all Jews are merchants? He had a stove, it was Trade's Day, ergo, he must have been a stove salesman. There is no explanation why Tolbert came up with the Trade's Day/stove salesman notion. It is not in the record book or any—where else.

## Tolbert's Theory about Rope Walker

In his May 1968 article, "Theory on 1-Legged Rope Walker," following only a few months after his previous Rope Walker column, Tolbert presents a well-reasoned hypothesis about Rope Walker's identity:

> *In El Paso Tom Lea was telling me about "The Great Professor Berg," a 1-legged tight rope walker. Professor Berg was a real life character of frontier days in the El Paso country, said Tom.*[230]

Lea had come across the Berg story while doing research for his novel, *The Wonderful Country*, explains Tolbert. Lea had found an article "in either an 1878 or 1879 edition of a Mesilla, N.M., newspaper, Mesilla being a colorful town just north of El Paso," writes Tolbert.

*In the Mesilla newspaper of the late 1870's there was an account of how Professor Berg walked a tight rope, actually a lariat rope, stretched between Hogan's Saloon and the roof of a barber shop. He did this despite several handicaps. One being that the professor had only one leg, and wore a peg leg. And another being the fact that some of the uncouth onlookers had been expressing applause by firing their 6-shooters into the air.*

Tolbert then presents a very short version of the legend, again citing the burial register of the Hebrew Cemetery as his source. Tolbert adds, parenthetically, "Apparently he was trying to promote the sales of iron stoves."

*Tom Lea and I were wondering whether The Great Professor Berg and the nameless fellow buried in Corsicana were the same man. Certainly it's unlikely there could have been two peg-legged tight rope walkers performing in Texas in the 1870's and 1880's. (Samuel F. Tulhill of Dallas had suggested in a letter to me that the Mesilla and Corsicana 1-legged rope walkers might be the same man.)*

Tolbert continues,

*"Professor Berg, according to the Mesilla newspaper, had quite a troupe of performers, including a yellow-haired show girl type," said Tom Lea. "It could have been that between the late 1870's and 1884 he had some bad luck, lost his wagon show, and wound up doing that solo show in Corsicana."*

*Certainly 1878 or '79 was a dangerous time for a wagon show to be traveling around in the El Paso country. Wild Apaches were on the prowl. And white outlaws who could be just as brutal.*

*So it may be that The Great Professor Berg is the fellow buried in the Corsicana graveyard under the laconic gravestone, "Rope Walker."*

Curiously, five years later, in his final Rope Walker column, "Gravestone Restored," Tolbert doesn't mention the Berg theory. There is no sign of any follow-up at all on this revelation—not by Tolbert nor anyone else, until here, now.

## Tom Lea

Tom Lea was a native of the Mexican border city of El Paso, Texas, where his father at one time was mayor. A prolific painter and occasional author, Lea's affection for his city's culture and history inspired *The Wonderful Country*.[231]

The 1952 novel follows hero Martin Brady after the Civil War as he straddles the American-Mexican border and balances allegiances on both sides, all the time in conflict with the Apaches. A border town, modeled on El Paso, is visited by a troupe of travelling entertainers made up of a one-legged rope walker, Professor Berg, two banjo-playing men in blackface (the ubiquitous minstrels of that era), and a plump, red-headed girl in a colorful costume. Lea described Prof. Berg as tall, "in yellow tights, silk hat and Spanish cape."

The book says the rope was stretched from Hogan's Saloon to a barbershop called "Peeble's." After the performance the professor announces there will be another show in the evening, and he will pass around a hat for donations. The book's hero, Brady, after the rope walker's successful crossing, declares to his buddy, "He sure did [it]" and makes a generous donation of all the money he has left to his name, four pesos and three reales, into the professor's hat. The reader understands that Brady, who is nursing a broken leg, is uplifted by the courage and resilience of the peg-legged man.

The novel was made into a 1959 movie starring macho screen idol Robert Mitchum, as Martin Brady, and sultry Julie London, as his love interest. Critical review of the movie was mixed, due in part to the complicated plot in which some of the political intricacies were difficult to follow. In other respects the movie was celebrated for its thorough inclusion of historical and cultural details. The peg-legged rope walker was left out of the movie, but there was a big scene with the showgirl doing a saucy dance to "Where'd You Get That Hat," a silly old English show tune, a scene right out of the book.

Ω

Tom Lea and Frank Tolbert were highly respected in their respective fields. There is no reason to doubt their credibility, as there was for Campbell and his story. The existence of the real-life one-legged rope walker used by Lea as a model for his fictional Professor Berg could be confirmed if the Mesilla newspaper article Lea referred to, where he said he read about the professor, could be located. Online searches in available issues of the *Mesilla Valley Independent* and *Mesilla News*, newspapers published in 1878 and

1879, turned up nothing about a Professor Berg.[232] There was an article in one paper about Professor *Bergh*, a widely known animal rights proponent from New York City,[233] but he was not in Mesilla during that time and there is no mention of him ever walking a tightrope. Not all issues of the Mesilla papers from that period could be searched and there is a lot of distorted, illegible text in those which are available. It's possible Lea misremembered the town or time period of the article; it was at least sixteen years after Lea had found the article when Tolbert spoke to him about it.

Lea might have told someone where he had found the Mesilla article— at some local library or archive—if someone had asked, or maybe he had clipped the article, and it was somewhere among his personal papers, but Lea left this world in 2001, at the age of ninety-three, and no research notes for *The Wonderful Country* have been found. The Tom Lea Institute[234] could not provide further insight. The Lea Collection at the Harry Ransom Center, UT, Austin, likewise does not have a file about Lea's research for the book.

The Professor Berg theory has a lot of potential. Following up on this lead would require manually reading all of those Mesilla newspapers, front to back. Electronic searching is not feasible because of the poor condition of the text. There are other avenues to pursue, happily, so it won't be necessary to read all those pages of newspaper to discover Rope Walker's identity.

# Chapter 8

## IDENTITY OF "ROPE WALKER" REMAINS
## UNSOLVED MYSTERY

*Thus goes the legend.*

**John Sam Haslam**

John Sam Haslam was born Sept. 16, 1908, in Corsicana.[235] In 1936, at the age of twenty-seven, he wrote the article "Identity of 'Rope Walker' Killed Here 52 Years Ago Remains Unsolved Mystery" for the *Corsicana Daily Sun*. It is the earliest-known telling of the story,[236] predating Campbell's "Walk into Oblivion" (and Ivan Rosenberg's write-up in the cemetery record book) by almost fourteen years, Tolbert's first article by more than twenty years, and Silverberg's 1978 oral history by more than forty years. Haslam's version earns credence simply for being the earliest, the closest in time to the actual events he wrote about.

No better-qualified person could have undertaken the task. Haslam was a detail-oriented reporter who brought out the interesting and pertinent dimensions of subjects without straying from the focus of his examinations. He had a knack for relating a story with intelligence and integrity. He also had an ease with language, creating short, pointed descriptions which somehow fully illuminated the object of his reporting, an efficiency reflected in his very name: neither John nor Sam was a shortened version of his given names. He was always *John Sam Haslam*, never *John S.*, never *John Samuel*, and never simply *John* or *Jonathan*.

At the age of fourteen he was nearly killed in a car collision. A *Sun* reporter visiting his home described him as "an exceptionally gentlemanly little fellow, bright at school and popular with all who know him."[237] His reporting was an outlet for his intellect, his curiosity to know how things worked, to get into the very details of a thing. When a child, for example, he learned how a Model T worked, and many decades later he could still recall every detail.[238] At the age of fifteen he won second prize in a worldwide contest for the best hand-built radio set, sponsored by *Boy's Life* magazine. At the time, he was described as "a genius along scientific lines."[239]

He was a scorekeeper for Corsicana's high school sports teams, which led to writing sports stories for the *Sun*, and later, feature stories. His first major story was about a speech by the school superintendent of Corsicana schools in October, 1929.[240] For a period of time, around 1931, he was working in the East Texas oil fields but returned home periodically to visit family, attend a Corsicana Tigers football game,[241] and occasionally keep score for high school teams.[242] He gave tours of the *Sun*'s newspaper works, describing in great detail the mechanics of the teletype, presses, and other machinery.[243]

Haslam wrote for the *Sun* until he left for college in 1938.[244] After he earned a journalism degree at UT and started on a masters he headed off to the working world. He was a reporter at the *Tampa Times* and then took a position with the newswire service UP, United Press (later United Press International), in Dallas, in 1944. He next worked in Jefferson City, Mo., and following that took a position as manager of UP's Little Rock office.[245]

In 1959 he reported on the turmoil of court-ordered desegregation, when Little Rock was in the national spotlight as the center of opposition. His radio copy of the Apollo moon landing and the funeral of President Kennedy, two seminal historic events, are preserved at the Smithsonian Institute's Newseum.[246]

Haslam was a dedicated worker. One day, in 1954, after finishing a story about a fire at a Little Rock office building, he had to run up to his building's rooftop to be airlifted by a helicopter's aerial ladder.[247]

♎

The February 25, 1936 article begins by identifying Haslam's research strategy and disclosing how much time he spent investigating the story:

> *Late Monday afternoon more than a dozen persons were visited and interviewed before the following story could be pieced out.*

That's a frank admission that while some effort went into this, it was not a major undertaking. It was investigated for a few hours, and for that matter, only a day before publication—the story ran on a Tuesday.

At the article's conclusion he names only one of the "more than a dozen persons" he says he interviewed: Miss Rachel Mae London. Accordingly, it is safe to say this is largely the story told by Mary (the given name she commonly used) London, one of the children of Max London, the Civil War veteran introduced in Chapter 2.

## IDENTITY OF "ROPE WALKER" KILLED HERE 52 YEARS AGO REMAINS UNSOLVED MYSTERY

### By JOHN SAM HASLAM

IDENTITY OF "ROPE WALKER"
KILLED HERE 52 YEARS AGO
REMAINS UNSOLVED MYSTERY

John Sam Haslam's
Rope Walker article

*On a little lichen and moss covered marble tombstone in the Hebrew cemetery here are two simple words— "Rope Walker."*

*There is no other information—no identity of the person buried under that brick surrounded mound—no date of that person's birth,—or even death.*

*Down on Commerce street, in the safe of the Goldsmith Brothers dry goods store is a somewhat ancient volume of Hebrew burial records and on the yellowed pages of the book is the only clue to the identity of that person: "———Fell from Trapeze—1884."*

*The space allotted to names is blank, and the succinct statement of how he met his end is contained in the next space, and is followed by the year. The records now are kept by Ben Goldsmith, secretary of the Hebrew Cemetery Association, but at that time, by Max London.*

*Late Monday afternoon more than a dozen persons were visited and interviewed before the following story could be pieced out:*

### Happened 52 Years Ago.

*One afternoon 52 years ago, after children had been dismissed from Capt. J. A. Townsend's school, a rope had been stretched from the roof of an old frame building which later was the site of the First State bank building, to a similarly constructed building now housing the Louis Hashop Confectionary. In the first named building was Bernard Simon's grocery store, while the present Hashop location was the "Blue Front" drug store, operated by one Dr. Carter.*

*Tied from roof-top to roof-top, the rope was about 20 feet from the ground, and ranged "catty-cornered" across Beaton street and Fifth avenue.*

*At that time in Corsicana the opportunity of seeing a daredevil walk a tight rope was a carnival occasion, and practically everybody in town had come from near and far over the dusty, unpaved streets and board sidewalks to see the event.*

*As eyes were focused on the Simon building, a medium-sized man appearing to be about 40 years of age, climbed to the roof; fastened a wood-stove on his back, to begin his perilous trip across the rope.*

*To the surprise of the villagers, the man had but one leg, the other being a wooden limb. The bottom end of the false leg was notched to fit the rope.*

### Fell To Ground.

*As the rope-walker reached the middle of the street intersection, sliding his notched wooden leg along the rope and cautiously pulling the other after, he became over–balanced and fell to the ground, landing on his frontsides, with the stove crushing on top of his body.*

*Women and children screamed and fainted. Some of the older men surged forward in a body to where the man had fallen. Some fathers and brothers took their daughters and sisters inside nearby stores "for protection" and then joined the other men to give what assistance they could.*

*The man was taken to the Molloy hotel, around the corner, where Dr. Gulick was summoned, and performed what first aid treatment was available at that time.*

*The broken man told some of the bedside attendants that he was a member of a Methodist church, and asked for a minister of that denomination. Rev. Abe Mulkey came and talked for some time to the man.*

*Later in the evening, Dr. Gulick reported the man was dying, and that he wanted to talk to "a Jew man." Mr. Simon, owner of one of the stores, was summoned, and with the dying man, repeated the Jewish prayers in Hebrew.*

### Refused Information.

*The rope-walker told Mr. Simon that he had been "joking" when he said he was a Methodist, but really was an Orthodox Jew, which was proven to Mr. Simon's satisfaction when he repeated his prayers in Hebrew. During his several interviews he refused to divulge his name or residence, or any information concerning his identity.*

*The broken body was laid to rest in the Jewish cemetery here through the benevolence of a number of Corsicana Hebrews.*

*Not a word was ever learned of the man's identity, and it was some time later before the little marble tombstone was put at the head of the grave, which now may be seen near the Third avenue entrance to the cemetery.*

———

*Most of the details of this story were related by Miss Rachel Mae London, 316 West Sixth avenue, daughter of the late Max London, the record keeper, who as a girl, was an eye-witness to the tragedy.*

This is the first version of the legend found that identifies a reliable source—an eyewitness! For that reason alone it is probably more accurate than other sources. Even Ivan Rosenberg's typewritten page in the cemetery book is a little suspect since it seems to have been derived in large part from Campbell's article, which itself is quite suspect. A point-by-point comparison of Campbell's and Haslam's articles, with a few exceptions, suggests Campbell copied Haslam and then added an array of fictional flourishes.

Four sources are referenced in Haslam's story: 1. a "little lichen and moss covered marble tombstone"; 2. an "ancient volume of Hebrew burial records"; 3. "more than a dozen persons … interviewed"; and 4. "details … related by Miss Rachel Mae London."

### *a little lichen and moss covered marble tombstone*

This poor, pampered tombstone is touchstone to a legend and lodestone to a Texas town's Jewish history. It was Robert Campbell's Blarney Stone and *tabula rasa* for inspiration and introspection. It is no Rosetta Stone. It is no Holy Tablet for the prophet who, by God's edict at Moab, could not cross over into Canaan.[248]

### *ancient volume of Hebrew burial records*

Instead of Campbell's passing reference to an "old burial record book," Haslam tells us the *who, what,* and *where* of the death ledger. It's obviously a predecessor to the current record book, until recently kept by Babbette Samuels. Its present whereabouts is unknown. Haslam, like Campbell, does not speculate why the entry says "Fell from trapeze" despite a gravestone that says "Rope Walker." Haslam does not speculate that

- Perhaps the record keeper who made that entry did not understand the difference between a tightrope and a trapeze

- Perhaps the entry was made long after the actual event, and was based on a mistaken memory

- Perhaps it *was* a fall from a trapeze, and the inscription on the gravestone should say "Trapezist"

- Perhaps it was a fall from a trapeze, which was part of a tightrope walking act. The gravestone inscription is correct, and though it would be assumed he fell from the tightrope, he actually fell during the trapeze part of his performance

It seems impossible for a trapeze performer to carry a stove on his back—a notion even more absurd than a one-legged man carrying a stove across a rope. For the time being the trapeze ropes are untied, and dropped, while the stove, which appears in every version of the story, is held fast. All the same, this trapeze business has thrown us for a loop, a full-twisting double-back somersault of perhapses.

*more than a dozen persons … interviewed*

Haslam does not say whom he spoke with, or what he learned from his interviewees, except to single out Mary London. In 1884 there were four thousand or so residents in Corsicana and thousands more in the surrounding towns and farms. Hundreds would have witnessed the performance; as Haslam said, it was an exciting town event. If there were four hundred spectators, how many were old enough at the time to understand what had happened, i.e. ten years old or older, who were still alive fifty years later, in 1936? Ten percent, or forty people, seems quite plausible. If roughly half of those people still resided in Corsicana when Haslam was looking for information, that would yield an estimated twenty eyewitnesses who could tell Haslam what happened. In the course of a few hours, "late Monday afternoon," Haslam was able to find at least one of those twenty people. Others who were not eyewitnesses may have heard the story and could recount the story as they knew it, but Haslam found someone who was actually there.

*details related by Miss Rachel Mae London*

And that person was Mary London, age sixty-six.[249] If Haslam had not already identified her as a town resident who was old enough in 1884 to have witnessed the event, no doubt others told him about her, that she was a good source of information. After all, her father was the cemetery's records keeper.

Haslam's story has many facets of the legend found in later versions, while some of his details never show up again. Still other elements are at odds with later versions. Unique information in the article not found elsewhere includes his description of the grave as a mound surrounded by bricks. Bois d 'arc bricks were very popular at the time, and the better streets at one time were paved with them. Haslam's story describes in detail, presumably from information provided by Mary London, the buildings to which the ends of the rope were tied, important details which did not make it into other versions. The performance took place at Beaton Street and 5th Ave., says Haslam, one block from Beaton and Collin, the intersection where Ivan Rosenberg, in the cemetery record book, said he fell.

This is the only source that says Rope Walker was brought to the Molloy Hotel. This suggests that later stories, like Campbell's, did <u>not</u> copy Haslam. In the Campbell/Rosenberg version the fallen acrobat is brought to an unnamed hotel, and later versions usually have him dying in the street, right after he fell. Then again, if Campbell copied all of Haslam's details there would be no doubt that Campbell plagiarized Haslam's article.

After Rope Walker died, says Haslam,

**it was some time later before the little marble tombstone was put at the head of the grave.**

This makes sense. The delay was to give people time to learn his name before putting up a gravestone. One might suppose Haslam wrote "it was some time later" for dramatic effect only, or because it was a nice turn of phrase, but he was not that kind of reporter.

**Ben Goldsmith**

Haslam not only explains that the Hebrew Cemetery Association record keeper in 1884 was Max London, but also that Ben Goldsmith was in charge in 1936. Goldsmith, a native of Clinton, Mo.,[250] was secretary-treasurer of the Corsicana Hebrew Cemetery Association continuously from 1914 until his death, in 1946. "It may be said that he guarded with jealous envy the duties he performed... He would in no way consider voluntary retirement from his office."[251] He served Temple Beth El and Corsicana's B'nai B'rith lodge with the same dogged devotion.[252]

# Chapter 9

## TRUE STORY

*I know all about the loss of his leg ... Look here, friend, said I, if you have anything important to tell us, out with it; but if you are only trying to bamboozle us, you are mistaken in your game*

The fourth and final foundational story comes from the internet. "Rope Walker" is a June 2003 posting on the *Jewish Magazine* website.[253]

Donate
to the
Jewish Magazine

*The Jewish Magazine*
Always Great!

 CLICK
THROUGH

parsha
of the
week

Tombstone of the "Rope Walker"

"Rope Walker"

As told to Jerry Klinger

My great grandfather, Hyman Tikvah Rabinowitz plodded the towns

*Jewish Magazine* article, top

The story was related by William Rabinowitz of Boynton Beach, Florida. His great-grandfather, Hyman Tikvah "Manny" Rabin (formerly Rabinowitz), "Gramps," was an eyewitness to Rope Walker's fall. The article is Rabinowitz's a recollection of Gramps's marvelous stories:

> **Gramps was blessed by a long life, well into his nineties, with a sharp clarity of mind and flair for storytelling. My sister and I would sit with Gramps for hours deeply absorbed, frequently with our mouths hanging open, while he would share with us story after story about his life. But mostly, he shared stories of the Jews in the small towns of the South and the Midwest he had come to know...**

*There are many stories that Gramps shared with us. One of my favorites was about a man who, when he died, no one knew his name. On his tombstone was carved only "Rope Walker."*

Rabinowitz retells the story Gramps had told him, starting with the discovery of oil in Corsicana. Following a short, unrelated discourse on Albert Moses Levy's service at the Alamo and three or more pages of additional narration, Gramps returns to Corsicana:

*"Corsicana had its Jewish community too. They were building their new synagogue, Temple Beth El. It was something from out of my past with two large onion domed cupolas, on either side of the grand two story façade, rising forty feet into the sky. It had stained glass windows from the famous glassmaker Tiffany. It wasn't fancy. It was grand. It wasn't just that it was a new building, it was unlike anything Corsicana or East Texas had ever seen architecturally. It was a statement that the Jews are here and we were welcome. ...*

*"Like everything else in Corsicana it was still being built when I was there that hot July day in 1898. It was July 28, I remember it well because of what happened.*

*"Corsicana was celebrating something new being built or something new being dedicated all the time. It was growing so fast that just opening a new store and hanging out a huge banner with the grand opening announcement was not enough. You had to do something that would attract attention. The biggest dry goods store ever was opening that day, Meyers and Henning Dry Goods Emporium. M&H, it was called for short. 'The Biggest Shovels to the Biggest Bodices, We Have It', was their motto.*

*"They needed something to get people into town and into the store. They did not have radio – they had word of mouth and gimmicks. Bands worked sometimes, even marching bands but what worked best to get folks into town to see what was what, was something new, something that had never been seen before.*

*"M&H came up with a brilliant gimmick. They had a band playing and they even got the mayor to stand in front of the store and cut a grand opening bright scarlet ribbon. What really got the people to come outside M&H was the special traveling, astounding, astonishing, amazing, unbelievable, never seen before or probably never again, act of strength, gravity and common sense defying stunt. They had hired a 69 year old one legged, the other was a peg leg—like a*

*pirate—man to tight walk across a rope strung across Beaton street, from the second story of M&H to Jackson's Saloon and Gentlemen's Relaxation Salon.*

*"The rope was drawn taught between the two buildings twenty maybe it was thirty feet in the air. I am not sure anymore. What was even more amazing is that the ancient one legged tight rope walker was going to do this amazing feat carrying a full sized stove on his bare back. Can you imagine carrying a stove on your back—that is very hard. Now try this walking a rope high in the air and with only one leg.*

*"M&H gathered quite a crowd for the noon event. The band struck up a high note and the people grew silent. Sam Hennings proclaimed to all that the "rope walker" would be performing but he needed absolute silence to perform his dangerous act. He had done it many times in the past. But he had to concentrate and silence was called for. The street grew quiet even two barking dogs were grabbed and thrown into a shed in back to shut up their yapping. It was so exciting as Rope Walker appeared in a sky blue outfit and bowed to the assembled throng. Every eye was upon him as two strong young men hefted a stove on his shoulders and then stepped back. Rope Walker adjusted the weight and with his good leg tested the rope gently then with his full weight. He edged out little by little, the awkward sight transfixing every tongue in every mouth. My own mouth turned dry one wrong step and.... Rope Walker edged out, his good leg leading and feeling the rope, his peg leg stabilizing him from behind. Slowly he edged out foot by foot until he stood in the middle of the rope high between the two buildings in the middle of Beaton Street and smiled a semi-toothless smile to the crowd. He was an amazing sight of courage and strength. My heart was beating very fast with excitement and amazement.*

*"From the far side of the street it happened. The rope across from M&H had not been tied securely enough. The rope started to sag and then suddenly I saw that Rope Walker knew he was going to fall. It was terrible. The people screamed as he fell to the ground with the stove crashing down and crushing his chest. We all surged forward but there was nothing to do. A priest rushed up and offered him a chance at confession and last rites before he died. He only managed to look up into the priest's face and say, 'I am* **Jewish. Please bury me with my people'.**

managed to look up into the priest's face and say, '*I am Jewish. Please bury me with my people*'.

"The funeral was the next day at the Hebrew Cemetery in Corsicana. Everyone attended. We never did learn his name. Rumor was that he came from Princeton, N.J. but we were never sure. When he was buried a tombstone was erected over his grave. It said simply – "Rope Walker". You can go to Corisicana someday and you will find this unknown Jew resting amongst our people in the Jewish cemetery to this very day."

Gramps died about a year after he told me this story. But then he told me many other stories about his life and the Jews of the South and the Midwest. That will be for another time.

I am getting older myself and I decided to write down the stories for my own grandchildren so they will know who they are. Someday they will wonder about Manny Rabin and why I changed our name back to Rabinowitz.

As told by William Rabinowitz, of Boynton Beach, Florida.

Jerry Klinger is President of the Jewish American Society for Historic Preservation www.Jashp.org

~~~~~~~

from the June 2003 Edition of the Jewish Magazine

E-mail This Page to a Friend

*Jewish Magazine* article, bottom

**"The funeral was the next day at the Hebrew Cemetery in Corsicana. Everyone attended. We never did learn his name. Rumor was that he came from Princeton, N.J. but we were never sure. When he was buried a tombstone was erected over his grave. It said simply – "Rope Walker". You can go to Corisicana someday and you will find this unknown Jew resting amongst our people in the Jewish cemetery to this very day."**

**Gramps died about a year after he told me this story. But then he told me many other stories about his life and the Jews of the South and the Midwest. That will be for another time.**

**I am getting older myself and I decided to write down the stories for my own grandchildren so they will know who they are. Someday they will wonder about Manny Rabin and why I changed our name back to Rabinowitz.**

**As told by William Rabinowitz, of Boynton Beach, Florida.**[254]

This detailed account has none of the invented dialogue which helped brand Campbell's story as a fraud. It identifies the source of the information, an eyewitness, just like in Haslam's story, thereby giving it credibility. William Rabinowitz, great-grandson of the eyewitness, narrated Gramps's story to Jerry Klinger, president of the Jewish American Society for Historic Preservation (JASHP) and sponsor of the website. A check on JASHP shows it is a longtime, reputable, nonprofit organization dedicated to pre–serving Jewish history.

There are many new and important clues here. Rope Walker was possibly born in Princeton. He was sixty-nine. The date of the tragedy was July 28, 1898, fourteen years later than the date found in nearly every other story, including Haslam's "somewhat ancient volume" of cemetery records. Jay Silverberg's 1978 oral history, in Chapter 4, on the other hand, agrees, saying it "happened shortly before the turn of the century."

A search was made of nineteenth-century Princeton records for a Jewish or immigrant family where a member of the family was in a profession akin to tightrope walking. Nothing was found. Further investigations to locate any circus performer or acrobat who may have lived in Princeton with a birth date of approximately 1829 also came up empty.

The www.CircusHistory.org website has an extensive message board. The following message was posted in September, 2006, three years after the JASHP magazine piece came out:[255]

> **Are any of the Jewish Circus performers in the United States by 1830? Am looking for the name of rope walker died unnamed in Corsicana, Texas, 1898, of Jewish descent. Possibly born in Princeton, New Jersey, USA in 1829.**

There were no responses.

Tracking down William Rabinowitz of Boynton Beach, narrator of the story, was difficult, as were attempts to locate more information about Manny "Gramps" Rabin, a traveling shoe salesman from Altoona, Pennsyl–vania according to the story. Those efforts, in 2006, produced no answers and the search was abandoned. Ten years later, when the effort was renewed, an email was sent to Jerry Klinger to get contact information for William Rabinowitz:[256]

> **I'm trying to verify research about the Rope Walker story and found your retelling by William Rabinowitz. Unfortunately, I could not verify anything to give veracity to that particular retelling of the story. I have no doubt that you**

*recorded the info as William told it to you, but I could not verify that William's great-grandfather could have witnessed the event. ... What do you think – are there additional details not included in your write up that might help me, here?*

Klinger replied the same afternoon:

*Thanks for writing. Unfortunately for historical accuracy, the stories are part of a series of stories that eventually became social commentary on Jewish life in Boynton Beach. The stories are largely fiction.*

*The Institute of Southern Jewish Life authenticated that Rope Walker was a real Jewish personality. The balance was creative storytelling.*

Creative indeed! The heading of the webpage, "True Story from Jewish American History," and Gramps's homey, conversational tone fooled many people.

Jerry Klinger, creator of *Jewish Magazine*, on the internet since 1997, and the source of more than 2,500 articles on all manner of Jewish culture and history, is the founder of JASHP, which he still heads after more than twenty-five years. He *is* JASHP. Its laudable mission is to remember places of Jewish historical importance by erecting historical markers. Klinger and JASHP are responsible for placing dozens of these markers in more than twenty-five states and even in other countries.[257] Klinger does good, bringing American Jewish history to a wide audience. He is a skilled writer— no doubt—but in this one instance his misstep damaged the historical record of Rope Walker. To his credit, he readily acknowledged that the story is fiction. The search continues.

An interesting coda to William Rabinowitz's oral history is that the birth and death dates and birth location invented for Rope Walker are the actual birth and death data for Dr. Gulick, the doctor mentioned in the Rope Walker legend. Gulick will be properly introduced soon enough, but why were his vital record dates applied to Rope Walker? According to a certain Princeton University professor, Richard Pierson, in 1938,

*I can give you no authoritative information – either as to their nature, their origin, or their purposes here on earth.*[258]

# Chapter 10

## DESCENDED FROM A LEGEND

*And all this mixes with your most mystic mood; so that fact and fancy, half-way meeting, interpenetrate, and form one seamless whole.*

Corsicana's elusive Rope Walker has made several appearances over the years. A recap of versions of the story presented so far:

- Walking Tour Booklet

- Historic Texas Cemetery Marker

- Jay Silverberg's history of Jewish Corsicana

- Jay Silverberg's oral history

- Ivan Rosenberg's write-up in the cemetery record book

- Campbell's "Walk into Oblivion"

- Five Tolbert's Texas columns and Tolbert's book

- Haslam's "Identity of 'Rope Walker' Killed Here 52 Years Ago Remains Unsolved Mystery"

- Klinger's "True Story from Jewish American History"

### Foundational Stories About Rope Walker—A Summary

The legend has been retold numerous times. All versions are based on one or more of the four basic sources, even though two of them have been exposed as fanciful historical fiction, chock-full of fabrications. Again:

- *Walk into Oblivion.* Imaginative, with no identified sources. Possibly based on information supplied by Ivan Rosenberg and/or copied from John Sam Haslam's article. Rosenberg's write-up in the record book of the Hebrew Cemetery was largely copied from "Walk into Oblivion."

- *Rope Walker—True Story from Jewish American History* (Manny Rabin's story). Wonderfully crafted historical fiction.

- *Theory on 1-legged Tight Rope Walker* and other Tolbert's Texas columns. One column says Professor Berg, a character in Tom

Lea's book, *The Wonderful Country*, was based on a real-life peg-legged rope walker. There is no confirmation that such a person existed. Tolbert claims Rope Walker was a stove salesman.

- *Identity of "Rope Walker" Killed Here 52 Years Ago Remains Unsolved Mystery.* John Sam Haslam's 1936 story from the *Sun* is the earliest known telling of the legend. A trustworthy journalist interviewed an eyewitness and others.

Ω

This chapter presents additional appearances of the story that have shown up over the years but is not intended to be exhaustive. There are few new facts here; no effort to take a new crack at solving the mystery, just riffs on the foundational stories. Hard boiled readers will want to read each and every one of them while others are welcome to scramble through them or look them over easy-paced.[259]

## Rootsweb

Rootsweb is a vast online collection of historical information mined from local sources and organized by county for genealogical researchers. Navarro County local history researchers and family historians have an extensive, robust set of Rootsweb web pages.

At the top of the Rope Walker page[260] is a summary, "Rope Walker— The Short Version." A single paragraph, it includes this information, ostensibly from William Rabinowitz's account: "On July 28, 1898, the 69-year-old man, who claimed to have been born in Princeton, New Jersey, on February 6, 1829…"[261] It asserts that no one *could remember if* he gave his name. That his name was <u>forgotten</u> is at odds with all other renditions of the story, which say he <u>refused</u> to give his name. If he had given his date and place of birth, it doesn't make sense that he would not give his name, so naturally it makes sense that he <u>did</u> give his name, at some point.

The Rootsweb page also has a transcription of John Sam Haslam's article and reproductions of Tolbert's Rope Walker articles. The last item is a transcription of a Sept. 13, 1998 *Sun* article, part of the paper's celebration of Corsicana's sesquicentennial. The article points out the uncertainty in the Rope Walker story, recognizing that different versions set forth contra-dictory facts, repeats details from the cemetery record book version, and summarizes Tolbert's article about Tom Lea's Professor Berg.

## Find A Grave

A very useful and popular website for family historians, Find A Grave's (FAG)[262] goal is to record every existing gravesite. With nearly two hundred million names from over 250,000 cemeteries it is well on its way.[263] Each documented gravestone has its own internet page listing information found on the gravestone and frequently a photo of the stone. Information is contributed by volunteers who often add additional photos, documents, and links to FAG pages of immediate family members.

FAG has 420 web pages for the Hebrew Cemetery in Corsicana, nearly all of the burials, and virtually every one of them includes a photograph of the gravestone. Many have supplemental biographical information such as the obituaries found on the Navarro County Rootsweb site and attached to the pages in the Hebrew Cemetery record book.

Rope Walker's FAG page has his first name, *Rope*; last name, *Walker*; birth, *Feb. 6, 1829, Princeton, N.J.*, and death, *July 28, 1898, Corsicana, Tex.* The page includes an old photograph of Beaton Street and Haslam's article. It has three photos of his gravestone and three lengthy write-ups that are the same as, or nearly the same as, the articles on Rootsweb.

## JewishGen

The www.JewishGen.org website, operated by New York's Museum of Jewish Heritage, has more than thirty million historical records and other resources and utilities for people who are researching Jewish ancestry. Discussion-list subscribers post questions or respond to others' questions covering a wide variety of topics, mostly geographically focused but also regarding particular families, and methods, such as DNA research. Older messages are archived and searchable. The following archived message was posted on Oct. 6, 2008; predictably, nothing came of it:[264]

*NJ Vital Records Question: 1829 Princeton, Mercer Co. - A friend who oversees maintenance of the Corsicana, TX Hebrew Cemetery asked me to help. There was a man who was a "rope walker" who died in 1898 in an accident. On his death bed he stated he was Jewish & recited Hebrew prayers with those called to his bedside. He was buried in Jewish cemetery & his identity is still unknown. Does anyone know if it is possible to get birth records for 6 Feb 1829 in Princeton, Mercer Co, NJ? Likely there would only have been one Jewish birth on that date, possible name - Berg.*

## Blogs and Serials on the Internet

Many bloggers have recited the Rope Walker's tale, usually a variation on the most easily accessible version, Rabinowitz's fabulous "True Story."

D.W. Short related the story in a post on *Texas Escapes*, a travel blog, with this addendum: "I compiled information from William Rabinowitz's 2003 re-telling of the words of his grandfather Hyman Tikvah Rabinowitz. Hyman was a traveling salesman who was there that day. Additionally, from a 1936 Corsicana Daily Sun interview with Rachael Mae London, who as a child was also an eyewitness to the tragedy, although many details in the two stories differ."[265]

Another blogger, in 2013, tells how he learned about the legend from a religious Jew, like himself, who officiated at a funeral at Corsicana's Hebrew Cemetery. After hearing the sad story of the forgotten Jew, the writer felt compelled to visit the grave. He said *Kaddish*, the mourner's prayer, and lamented that he would never learn this fellow Jew's name.[266]

The Goldring/Woldenberg Institute of Southern Jewish Life's online "Encyclopedia of Southern Jewish Communities" includes the Rope Walker story as part of its history of the Jews of Corsicana.[267]

Ernest Joseph, Corsicana's last full-time rabbi, wrote a summary of the story, not unlike the cemetery record book version, for the January 1989 newsletter of the Texas Jewish Historical Society. It is brief, but has all the requisite, basic elements.[268]

*Now Magazine*'s April 2012 issue, focusing on Corsicana, has a feature article by Virginia Riddle, "L'chayim: To Life!," about Babbette Samuels, with a goodly mention of Rope Walker.[269]

The Jewish Federation of Tulsa's magazine, February 2013 issue, has a feature story by Louis Davidson, "The Last Jew and the Rope Walker,"[270] about Temple Beth El, Babbette Samuels, and Rope Walker. It has the Shoe Salesman's Tale, but also includes "Bernard Simon," so the author must have also come across Haslam's article.

Author and amateur historian Melody Amsel-Arieli took some creative liberties with her 2005 "A Custodian of Memories," published at www.TheForward.com,"[271] about Babbette, Corsicana's declining Jewish community, and Rope Walker:

*A priest administered the last rites, then leaned down to catch the man's dying words. The acrobat gasped, "But I'm Jewish." No Joke. He was.*

## Books

David Searcy, a writer-in-residence at 100West, Corsicana's artist collaborative on Beaton Street, featured the Rope Walker tale in "Nameless," one of several essays in his 2016 collection, *Shame and Wonder*.[272] The legend is an emotional catalyst for mournful musings on the meaningfulness/meaninglessness of endeavor and how experiences are interpreted.

Deeanne Gist's 2011 novel, *The Trouble with Brides*, which takes place in Corsicana, includes this author's note: "The peg-legged rope walker was true, but I found conflicting dates for the actual event, some saying 1884 and some saying 1898." Gist's story is set in 1894. It includes Dr. Gulick, but not the part where Rope Walker pretends to be a Methodist. The story says there is only one Jew in town. The rope walker says a Hebrew prayer, then dies. "His Hebrew. It was perfect," says Mr. Baumgartner.[273]

Corsicana, Navarro County, and Jewish-Texas histories that include the story typically give a straightforward version with no surprises, like the brief version found in *Brick Streets and Back Roads*, a colorful, glossy history of Corsicana published in 2000.[274]

Dr. Tommy Stringer's 2010 history, *Corsicana*, part of Arcadia Publishing's ubiquitous "Images of America" series, has a version based on the professor's 1978 interview of Jay Silverberg. Rope Walker was "a travelling salesman with a peg leg hoping to promote his wares."

*Deep in the Heart: The Lives and Legends of Texas Jews*,[275] a 1990 historical survey of accomplished Texas Jews, says: "In 1884, a circus came through town. One of the performers was an acrobat … The rope failed, and the man plunged to the ground." This is the only version that says Rope Walker was part of a circus and the first one to say that the rope broke.[276] The authors cite as their source a paper given by Rabbi Joseph at the Kallah (convocation) of Texas Rabbis in Galveston, in 1976, titled "Rope Walker's Tombstone." No copy of that paper could be found. It seems unlikely Rabbi Joseph's paper had contributed those two novel facts—the 1989 newsletter article Joseph wrote[277] makes no mention of them.

In *The Chosen Folks: Jews on the Frontiers of Texas*,[278] author Professor Bryan Stone uses the Rope Walker story as an allegory for his book's thesis, that Jews in early Texas precariously balanced two cultural identities, Jew and Texan. The prologue, "Rope Walker, A True Story," like Campbell's story, includes invented dialogue and imagined details, but with a significant and meaningful difference—in an endnote, Stone cites his sources. He references an Oct. 30, 1988 *Corsicana Daily Sun* article, "Tombstone Seals Secret of Peg-Leg Ropewalker" (which itself presents nothing new); Campbell's "Walk into Oblivion"; Rabbi Joseph's paper published in the

Texas Jewish Historical Society's newsletter; and Tolbert's "A Better Me—
morial for 'Rope Walker'?" He acknowledges the discrepancies found in his
sources:

> **Later tellers of the story disagree on whether he was
> working for someone wishing to make a lasting advertising
> impression or had dreamed up the stunt on his own. Some
> have suggested that he was a former circus performer plying
> the only trade he knew for scattered nickels and dimes from
> the crowd.**[279]

Stone injected several new and creative elements not found in any of his
cited sources, or elsewhere, details of no consequence to his sociological
arguments but make for a more exciting opening for his book, i.e.,

> **Struggling only a little under the weight of the stove, the
> stranger stepped to the end of the roof, the balancing pole
> stretched out away from him on either side. He had his
> trouser legs over his knees, revealing the wooden leg, which
> he slid carefully out onto the line.**[280]

Stone added not only embellishments, but also consequential facts made
out of whole cloth. For example, he says it was "a warm, still afternoon."[281]
Campbell said it was a hot and dusty summer day (Haslam declined to
comment on atmospheric conditions). At least one of them got it wrong.
Stone, it turns out, was closer to the truth, as will be shown soon enough,
but both were guessing.[282] Stone describes baked, fried, and barbequed
foods sold along Beaton Street. That's new. Rope Walker uses a "heavy
rope," and the peg was "where his right foot and calf used to be."[283] While
all these inventions make the prologue more fun to read, they also have the
potential to throw off future historical investigations. Just as Klinger's story
had researchers landing at Grover's Mill, N.J. (Chapter 9), so too Stone's
made-up facts, like the weather and which foot was missing, could trip up
efforts to discover and authenticate this hidden history. A researcher with
access to Trade's Day records might not examine rainy or cold days as
potential dates when Rope Walker fell. A reviewer of records of men with
missing limbs might only look at those with a missing right limb (*The Chosen
Folks* says it was the right leg, which is wrong). Stone's thesis advisors—the
book, including the Rope Walker device, was created from his doctoral
dissertation—were not concerned with the fictionalization of an historical
event about which there was no reliable historical documentation, perhaps
because there were source citations.[284]

Stone returned to Rope Walker at the close of the book:

> *The Rope Walker's story, while true, is also a fable about the fluidity of identity, about the impossibility in any frontier of being all one thing or the other.*

If anyone had a fluid identity it's a stove salesman who walks a tightrope; a disabled man who performs acrobatics; a Jew who seeks deliverance from a Methodist; a protagonist in so many stories who is still, up to this point, unknown.

After a chorus or two of the Rope Walker ballad and a short diver–tissement provided by Corsicana's most-celebrated family, in Chapter 10, back to business: the real, true, actual, honest, verified, proven identity of the Rope Walker of Corsicana.

## The Ballad of Rope Walker[285]

*Rope Walker, Rope Walker, what was your name?*
*Did you defy death in search of your fame?*
*Or did you need money to take you back home*
*Had you decided that no more you'd roam?*
*'Twas Autumn and we had a circus in town*
*The people had gathered from parts all around*
*A special attraction, one ne'er seen before*
*Was thrilling, stupendous, was free, furthermore.*
*You stretched a rope high across South Beaton Street*
*You said you'd walk it, a dare devil feat*
*Long pole in your hand and an iron stove on your back*
*You bravely stepped out on that wobbly track.*
*Oh somebody stop him, he's got a peg leg*
*He'll surely fall down and be crushed like an egg*
*But nobody did and we all held our breath*
*Strangely enchanted, we knew we watched death.*
*Half way across, can he go all the way?*
*"No," that slack rope is beginning to sway*
*Down falls the Rope Walker, we stand transfixed*
*Watching his blood flow across the red bricks.*
*Oh the Rope Walker's Dying, no name he has said*
*But, he wants a Methodist prayer to be read*
*Then at the last, he reveals he's a Jew*

*And uttering words that were plainly Hebrew.*
*Rope Walker, Rope Walker, why did you roam?*
*Were you rejected in your native home?*
*Why deny heritage centuries proud?*
*Say your Hebrew and say it out loud.*
*Rope Walker, Rope Walker, you won your fame*
*Even tho still we do not know your name*
*You are at home in Abraham's ground*
*Return to your father in Abraham's ground.*

# Chapter 11

## JESTERS

*some certain significance lurks in all things, else all things are little worth*

Rodeo clowns convert themselves into targets for charging bulls when a fallen rider needs to escape the arena. Circus clowns get sent into the ring to distract the crowd when an aerialist plunges to the ground. After ten chapters filled with lots of bull and quick letdowns, the protagonist of this true-life narrative is still unnamed. Bring on the Corsicana Jesters.

Jesters were the leading citizens of Corsicana when Rope Walker fell, industrious community leaders still celebrated today for their deep commitment to Corsicana and Texas civic affairs. They were not the first settlers in town, but they were first in the sense of preeminence. Corsicana's first permanent residents were Reverend Hampton McKinney, his wife, Mary (Banes) McKinney, and their children, except for their eldest daughter, Diadema (McKinney) Jester, matriarch of the Jesters, who arrived a bit later. The McKinneys, without Diadema, arrived in Dresden, Texas, from Illinois in 1847. Rev. McKinney soon found the perfect location for a homestead in what would shortly become the Navarro County seat. He bought a log cabin and moved it to a spot which later became Corsicana's public square, where the courthouse would be built. At the time there were a few other cabins scattered about on area farms, but McKinney's Inn, as it was called, was the first permanent dwelling in Corsicana.

In return for settling on the Texas frontier, Hampton McKinney received a headright certificate from the state entitling him to 640 acres (one square mile), and his sons, John and Thomas, each received 320 acres, the allocation for unmarried men.[286] The McKinney grant was patented (attained full legal status) by the family's settlement and development of the land, a requirement to receive the patent. When Corsicana was legally designated a town, McKinney traded in much of the land claimed by certificate in exchange for land in Johnson County and thus the town of Corsicana was able to grow.[287]

In 1858, when Diadema (McKinney) Jester's husband Levi had been dead for seven years, she and her six children traveled by covered wagon to join the rest of her McKinney family in Corsicana.[288] Her older sons, C.W. (Charles Wesley)[289] and G.T. (George Taylor) Jester,[290] were prominent Corsicana bankers and the best known of her children. The other four also lived in or near Corsicana.[291] Those six children raised up twenty-four of their own offspring to create the next generation of Jesters.[292] Members of the McKinney and Jester families likely watched, along with their neighbors, as Rope Walker fell to the ground on Beaton Street.

**C.W. Jester** was a leader in the business and religious life of Corsicana and instrumental in building its first Methodist Church, in 1871. One of his sons, C.L. (Charles "Lee") Jester, was a local judge who wrote a history of Corsicana.[293]

George Taylor Jester

**G.T. Jester** joined Hood's 4th Tex. Reg., but General Lee surrendered before he saw battle. After the war he worked in the hide trade, clerked in a dry goods store, and for ten years was a cotton broker. He started a bank with his two brothers, C.W. and Levi, which in 1887 became the Corsicana National Bank. He served one term each as a Texas State Representative and Senator and was elected as the state's Lieutenant Governor, serving in that position from 1894-1898.

Beauford Halbert Jester

**Beauford Jester** (1893-1949), G.T.'s son, was Corsicana's most revered native son, a governor of Texas from 1947 until his untimely death, while still in office.[294] A twenty-four-acre park named for him includes Pioneer Village, a museum of historical buildings fully outfitted with frontier-life arti–facts.[295] Across Park Ave. from Pioneer Village is Corsicana's Senior Center, formerly the Agudas Achim Synagogue.

Ω

As is the case for many surnames, "Jester" might be based on the occupation of a distant family ancestor. This would be no slight on the distinguished Corsicana Jesters, or for that matter, any other Jester family.[296] In the eighteenth century and earlier the court jester was more than a silly clown; he sang songs, told stories, performed acrobatics, and even did magic tricks. He had to have a sharp wit to entertain the court and the wherewithal to know how far he could go with his parodies of the royals. The jester was a confidant, even an intimate of the king, and was richly rewarded.[297] So respected was his role at court that a recurring theme over the centuries, in diverse cultures, is the playful idea of the fool as king and the king as fool.[298]

The unique status of the fool may explain why some jesters came from the well-educated Jewish population:

> *Russian czar Peter the Great (r. 1696-1725) [had] his jester Lacosta, a Portuguese Jew who spoke several languages and was well versed in Scripture, [who] became known as King of the Samoyeds after Peter gave him the island of Sommer in the Gulf of Finland. Zuniga, the most famous Spanish jester, called himself the Duke of Jerusalem, perhaps because he was a Jewish convert, and was also known as King of the Jesters (Rey de los Bufones)* [299]

As these examples illustrate, at least a few Jews made a living as jesters, centuries ago. In modern times, examples are numerous. Some of the best known are the Three Stooges, the Marx brothers (no known relation to the Marks brothers of Corsicana), Jerry Lewis, Sarah Silverman, Ben Stiller, Adam Sandler, and Jerry Seinfeld. Jewish comedian and actor, Danny Kaye, played the title role in the 1954 musical comedy, *The Court Jester.*[300]

Ω

In 1921, thirty-six years after Diadema Jester's death, her sisters Jane Beaton and Mary Miller were interviewed by Diadema's grandson, Lee Jester. The fifty-year-old judge was seeking documentation to qualify himself as a Son of the American Revolution via one of his McKinney ancestors, but the interviews also covered his Jester roots.[301] Diadema, he learned, was born in 1821, married Levi Jester in 1839,[302] and then moved with Levi to a farm in Macoupin County, Ill. According to her sister, Jane,

> *Father and mother were very much opposed to her marrying him and they ran away and married. ... The reason Father didn't want her to marry Levi Jester was because he didn't know anything about him. He just drifted in there from Delaware. He said he was a young man out there away from his folks and nobody knew anything about him and he had nothing but he was an energetic industrious little fellow and was always working at something. He came out there to make a living at anything that came up, there was nothing against him except that he was a stranger and nothing was known of him or his family. I never heard that he was a Jew, if there had been any talk of that kind we would have heard*

*of it at the time he ran away with my sister. ... He lived in Edwardsville ... He was a little bit of a fellow, a small man, very small, a great deal smaller than any member of our family. ... Your father, Charlie Jester, favored him more than any of the boys but Levi [Jr.] has a prominent nose like his.*[303]

Judge Lee Jester's questions, which prompted Mrs. Beaton's statements, have not been preserved, but based on her reply one of them must have been, "Did your parents disapprove of the marriage because he was Jewish?" Whether the judge knew something that Great Aunt Jane didn't, or whether the question was only based on a hunch, is not known. Maybe the idea was encouraged by, informed by, or suggested by one of Judge Jester's close Jewish friends.

As for the statement that Levi Jester was extraordinarily short, that is some modest evidence that he was indeed a descendant of court jesters. It is well documented that court jesters were often very short, even dwarfs.[304] Short stature was not a trait passed down to Levi Jester's children and grandchildren.[305]

There are few historical records related to Levi Jester besides his gravestone.[306] In 1850 he was a peddler, the only substantial information about him found in any census record.[307] That he came from Delaware, as stated by his sister-in-law, Jane Beaton, is confirmed by census entries for his children, where one of the questions asked is the birthplace of parents.[308]

There were numerous Jester families in Delaware. Runk's *History of the State of Delaware, Vol. II*, says the Jesters of Delaware trace their roots back to Abraham, Isaac, and Jacob—brothers who came from Scotland in the late eighteenth century, each settling in a different Delaware county—not the biblical patriarchs.[309] There is no solid evidence that Levi Jester was Jewish, only some hints of it, including the fact that one of Levi and Diadema's grandchildren was haberdasher to Moses and the Israelites.[310]

The only certain way to determine the ancestral origins of Levi Jester would be through DNA testing, commonly done to verify family relationships between individuals or to ascertain ethnic heritage. Heritage schmeritage—the origins of the Jester family and their family name are not important. Only the deeds and accomplishments of the Jesters matter, and in that respect, the Jesters were Corsicana royalty.

Enough clowning around. What news of Rope Walker?

Chapter 12

## CORSICANA NEWS

*its very blinding palpableness must have been the cause*

"A search for his identity which gripped the community" says the cemetery's historical plaque. Campbell said efforts to identify him stretched into years. The earliest evidence of any investigation was Haslam talking to more than a dozen local citizens, in 1936, but even that wasn't really an effort to learn his identity; it was only to tell the story, fifty-two years after the fact. It seems unlikely, after another eighty-three years—a total of one-hundred, thirty-five years after his death—that there could be any greater likelihood of discovering anything about that poor, nameless soul.

Just the same, in 2016, an inquiry was sent to the Circus World Museum, in Baraboo, Wisconsin.[311] Likewise, the online archives of the Johnson-Blalock Education Center at the Circus Museum of The Ringling's, in Sarasota, Florida, were scoured for answers.[312] Not one iota in Sarasota nor boo from Baraboo about a one-legged tightrope performer.

Were inquiries ever placed in newspapers, seeking information about the unidentified one-legged aerialist? None were found. Campbell was right: "A one-legged rope walker [should not] escape quick identification." Or so one would think. Somewhere, at some time, something must have been written about him, something beyond the searches made in Chapter 6, something other than what has been found about the legend in Corsicana's newspapers and histories.

The phrase "one-legged rope walker," entered into the Library of Congress's newspapers database, Chronicling America, without any date or place restrictions, did turn up fourteen "hits," but nothing from 1884.

### STATE AND COAST ITEMS.

They have a one legged rope walker at Reno. He's the "stump" walker of the coast.

*Morning Appeal* (Carson City, Nev.), August 20, 1879

Clicking on the first of the fourteen entries in the list brings up an image of the page with the requested phrase highlighted. (Highlighting has been removed from the graphics reproduced here.) Under the heading "State and Coast Items" is a lame pun on "stump," reflecting the article's 1879 date— high political season, just ahead of elections.

The fourteen articles are listed in order by the quality of the search results, that is, based on how many times the requested words/phrases appear and their proximity to each other on the page. That is the default order. When re-sorted, by date, the earliest hit is a Dec. 3, 1869 article.

> A one-legged rope-walker, performing at Vincennes, Indiana, fell from the tight-rope, last Wednesday of last week, breaking one of his wrists, knocking one of his eyes out of the socket, and injuring himself so internally that recovery is doubtful.

*Tiffin* (Ohio) *Tribune*, December 3, 1869

The one-legged rope walker injured at Vincennes likely did not survive his fall, let alone live for another fifteen years to perform again in Texas in 1884.

> A one-legged rope-walker is another Kansas freak, who does not, however, threaten Llewellyn's supremacy.—New York Recorder.

*Grand Rapids* (Mich.) *Herald*, July 20, 1892

The most recent article, from 1892, eight years after most sources say Rope Walker died, is good evidence that there were more than one one-legged rope walkers. Or, maybe as Jay Silverberg said, Rope Walker died near the end of the century. It's impossible to know, without a name, if the articles are about one, two, or three different people—let alone whether any of them is the same as Corsicana's rope walker.

Four of the articles are from 1883. Two are from Texas papers, describing a one-legged man who fell and had to have his remaining leg amputated. They give his name but not the location of the fall.

> Prof. DeHuone, the one-legged rope walker who broke his remaining limb, by falling from his rope Saturday, had it amputated about the knee to-day, as it was found impossible to save it.

*Weekly Democratic Statesman* (Austin, Tex.), March 8, 1883

> Professor D. E. Huone, the one-legged rope-walker who fell Saturday and broke his leg, had it amputated to-day, and is now without legs.

*Dallas Daily Herald,* March 7, 1883

And then, there it is, in the *Wheeling Daily Intelligencer* : Corsicana!

> Prof. De Huon, the one-legged rope walker who fell a few days ago and broke his leg at Corsicana, Texas, has had it amputated, and he is now legless.

*Wheeling* (W.Va.) *Daily Intelligencer,* March 15, 1883

Proof, finally, proof that this entire business was not some elaborate hoax!!! Several articles name the rope walker, all using different spellings: D.E. Huone, DeHuone, and De Huon, but still, that's better than no name! None of the articles call him "Professor Berg," Tom Lea's one-legged rope walker from *The Wonderful Country.*

> —A one-legged rope-walker broke his remaining leg in Texas the other day, by the breaking of the rope during a performance. It is to be hoped that he is satisfied now.—*Boston Post.*

*Wellington* (Ohio) *Enterprise,* April 25, 1883

None mention his death. Is it possible the gravestone at the Hebrew Cemetery marks only the grave of the (second) amputated leg, which, according to Jewish law, would have required burial? Is this why no one at the time, nor subsequently, ever bothered to add the man's name? What is certain, though, now, is that the fall happened in 1883, not 1884, a curious development which needs to be addressed; that, and a lot of other newly discovered information from several newspaper articles.

As shown, the story appeared not only in Texas papers but also in distant Boston and Wheeling. Intensive searching in other online databases uncovered an additional eighteen articles. The odd news item appeared in papers far and wide, including some of the country's largest dailies in New York, Chicago, St. Louis, Cincinnati, and New Orleans.

Back in 1883, stories were sent via telegraph across the country, the original "wire services," but for whatever reason they didn't print the exact same story. Three of the earliest appearances of the story were in the March 4 issues of newspapers in Waco, Dallas, and Fort Worth, the three cities closest to Corsicana.

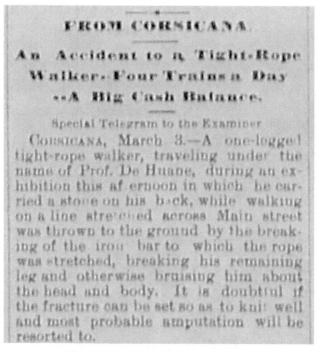

*Waco Daily Examiner*, March 4, 1883

The *Waco Daily Examiner* shoots down the standard account in the legend of how he fell, that he lost his balance. An iron bar, securing one end of the rope, it says, failed. Other articles say the same thing. The *Examiner* confirms Rope Walker was indeed carrying a stove, but doesn't say he was crushed by it, as is often repeated in the legend. Instead, his injury was not much more than a broken leg, albeit a badly broken leg. Some articles differ on the injuries suffered, but none of them say he was "crushed," or, for that matter, that the stove played any role in his injuries.

The *Examiner* mistakenly reported that he was performing on "Main street." Corsicana's "Main Street," in those early years, intersected Beaton Street and ran up past the courthouse. Renamed, today it is 2nd Ave., while today what is called Main Street is located one block west of, and parallel to, Beaton. Back then, Beaton was *the* main (lower case "m") street in Corsicana, as it still is today. Other papers at the time said the accident happened on Beaton Street, which agrees with Mary London's eyewitness's account. None of the news articles specify where on Beaton Street he fell.

## CORSICANA.

### TheO–ne Legged Rope Walker Breaks His Other Leg.

Special to the Gazette.

Corsicana, March 3.—A one-legged tight rope walker traveling under the name of Prof. DeHuone during an exhibition this afternoon in which he carried a stove on his back, while walking on a line stretched across the main street, was thrown to the ground by the breaking of the iron bar to which the rope was attached, breaking his remaining leg and otherwise bruising him about the head and body. It is doubtful if the fracture can be set so as to knit well and most probably amputation will be resorted to.

*Fort Worth Daily Gazette*, **March 4, 1883**

The story in the *Fort Worth Daily Gazette*, also published the day after the fall, is very similar to the *Examiner* account, but accurately says "the main street," with a lower case "m." The stories are otherwise identical, except for the spelling of the rope walker's name.

**Corsicana.**

CORSICANA, March 3.—[Special.]—A one-legged man, traveling under the name of Professor D. E. Huone, has been giving rope-walking entertainments here the past few days. This evening, while the professor was performing the feat of carrying a stove on his back across the rope one of the fastenings by which the rope was held broke, precipitating the professor to the ground, breaking his remaining leg and bruising him up generally. The professor has a mother, wife and sister dependent on him for support. The doctors think they may save his leg.

*Dallas Daily Herald,* March 4, 1883

*The Dallas Daily Herald*'s story on the 4th adds additional information. D.E. Huone "has been giving rope-walking entertainments here the past few days," *here* meaning Corsicana, as indicated by the article's dateline. The *Herald* says it happened in the evening, not in the afternoon, as stated in other March 4 articles.[313] The *Herald* adds: he "has a mother, wife and sister dependent on him for support" and "the doctors think they may save his leg," a better prognosis than found in the Waco and Fort Worth pieces, but based on later accounts, unduly optimistic. One thing all the articles have in common is that the accident occurred on Saturday, March 3, 1883.[314]

**CORSICANA, TEX.**

**A One-Legged Rope Walker.**

Special to The Times-Democrat.

CORSICANA, March 3.—Prof. D. E. Huon, a one-legged rope walker, while giving a performance this evening, fell to the ground, a distance of 30 feet, breaking his leg below the knee and fracturing the right arm. He will probably recover.

*Times-Democrat* (New Orleans), March 4, 1883

Another paper able to publish the story the next day was the *Times-Democrat* of New Orleans. It says he fell thirty feet and in addition to a broken leg he broke an arm, and "he will probably recover."

*Cincinnati Enquirer,* March 5, 1883

The *Cincinnati Enquirer* published the story with additional information not found in the other articles, with yet another spelling of his name. "Prof. Dehnon," it says, "is an Alsatian, and came from New York." On the 6th, an article identical to the one in the *Enquirer* was published in the *Chicago Daily Tribune* (not shown).

*Times-Democrat* (New Orleans), March 7, 1883

The March 7th New Orleans *Times-Democrat* reported events of the previous day at Corsicana, Texas. Top story: General Fitzhugh Lee will appear in town at a banquet. Both Confederate and Federal veterans will attend. Second: three train carloads of cotton went up in flames the previous day in Athens, a nearby town. Third: Prof. DeHuon had his leg amputated, "and now is legless."

**Corsicana.**

CORSICANA, March 14.—[Special.]—A young man named J. B. Upton, until lately employed as book-keeper in a cotton-broker's office here, fell dead last night on the depot platform at Houston. He came to Texas several months ago, for his health, but becoming worse, decided to return to his home at Sweetwater, Tennessee. He left here at noon yesterday, feeling somewhat feeble, and it is supposed the rough ride caused an internal hemorrhage. Dr. Blair, his uncle, left to-day for Houston, and will return with the remains to-morrow.

The much talked of cotton suit was decided to-day in Justice Walton's court. Two weeks ago a farmer named Owens sent two bales of cotton to town in charge of a a man named Sneed, with instructions to get the receipts and leave them at the cotton-yard, to be called for by him. Instead of doing as directed Sneed sold the cotton, turning the receipts over to the buyer and decamped with the proceeds. Owens brought suit to recover the cotton, as the receipts are all made to bearer any innocent person might have been taken in. Walton decided it was merely a breach of trust, as the buyer could not be proven a party to the fraud.

Fifty new post-office boxes arrived a day or so ago, and will be placed in position as soon as painted.

Professor DeHume, the rope-walker, was buried yesterday.

The Texas Express mule ran about two blocks this evening without a driver. No one hurt.

*Dallas Daily Herald*, March 15, 1883

Nine days after the amputation, the *Dallas Morning News* reported recent news from Corsicana. Top story: Dr. Blair's nephew dropped dead the night of the 13th on a Houston train platform while heading back to Tennessee. Second: a "much talked about" suit over a few bales of cotton. Third: fifty new postal boxes. Fourth: "Professor DeHume, the rope-walker, was bur–

ied yesterday." This briefest of the five reported items was at least deemed more important than the runaway Texas Express mule, the <u>Fifth</u> item—but probably because "No one hurt."

> The one-legged acrobat, who walked a rope here some weeks ago, and fell at Corsicana breaking his other leg, is dead.

*Fort Worth Daily Gazette*, **March 18, 1883**

On March 18, the *Daily Gazette* reported Rope Walker's death. Lest there be any confusion, it came out three days <u>after</u> the *Daily Herald* reported his burial.

Undoubtedly most, if not all of Corsicana's newspapers from that time—the *Observer*, the *Courier*, the *Journal*, and the *Messenger*—ran stories about the accident, stories repeated in the newspapers displayed here. There may have been additional stories in the Corsicana papers, following up about the accident and the dead man, which were <u>not</u> republished in other, non-local, papers. There is not even one surviving issue of any Corsicana newspaper from 1883, but, as previously stated when the year was believed to be 1884, something might turn up, maybe, someday.

Rope Walker's name was well known, it seems, even if it was seldom spelled the same way twice. Might this be the reason for its absence from his gravestone—were people trying to determine the correct spelling of his name, and, following an extended delay, when it was finally time to put up a stone, the only thing anyone could remember was his occupation, that he was a rope walker, even though his name had been printed in major newspapers in Corsicana, throughout Texas, and across the country?

Ω

Let there be light! Copious sunlight, in fact, was the weather reported in Dallas, a little north of Corsicana on the day he fell.

> The beautiful sunshiny weather of yesterday and the balmy, spring-like air set the birds to warbling, and the streets throughout the day were thronged with ladies, busy shopping.

*Dallas Daily Herald*, **March 4, 1883**

A little to the south, in Waco, the report was the same.

**Waco.**

Again we are blest with fine weather after the dreary rain which has continued so persistently for the past month or two. Everything wears a more smiling aspect, and doubtless

*Fort Worth Daily Gazette*, **March 4, 1883**

# Chapter 13

## PROFESSORS

*tell me if to the best of your own convictions, this your story is in substance really true? It is so passing wonderful! Did you get it from an unquestionable source?*

First mentioned in Chapter 6, millions of historical newspaper pages are freely and immediately accessible via the internet. Include fee-based sites and the number jumps to hundreds of millions. Newspapers from every U.S. state and worldwide, spanning centuries, can be searched to find any word/phrase combination using just a few keystrokes and in the comfort of one's own living room. Queries can be fine-tuned by filtering by pub–lication title, location, date, and in some databases, by newspaper type, such as ethnicity or religion.[315] Articles appear in seconds. This is the miracle of OCR—Optical Character Recognition. OCR converts computer images of newspaper pages into computer-readable—and searchable—text. OCR has given superpowers to scholar and dabbler alike—to anyone curious about the world before them.[316]

An online search of historical newspapers is only as good as the OCR process performed on the original images, which is determined in large part by the condition of the original newspaper pages. Blurred, dark, or damaged originals create gibberish, not computer-readable text; the OCR-generating software is unable to correctly recognize letters. A common example is that the lower case "e" is frequently misread as a lower case "c" because the horizontal bar is faint or missing.

*New York Sun*, April 25, 1873

By way of illustration, the above *New York Sun* article would not be found using a query that requires the phrase "tight rope," even though the phrase is there in the second line, because "tight" was incorrectly OCR'd, as shown in the OCR-generated text file linked to the image:

Yeaterdty aflenioiin Prof. Dehouue, tho ,

wiKi.len legged tnbt rope walker, whllu psrforuuas lo

"asl I ( bsrir. ton. H. C, li-ll a instance of tiny irrt.snd aia

( duiiKi-riiUBli bun Hi the head autl leg. The fall wtsi itaH

caused ny the break up of Hie rope,[317]

The *Galveston Daily News* was not one of the papers found to carry the story about a rope walker's fall at Corsicana, even when querying was restricted, by date, to only those issues of the paper published during the week after the accident, when the story should have appeared. This is odd because the *Galveston Daily News* of that era was very good at reporting local stories from towns and cities throughout Texas. The entire March 4th issue was read, one little news item at a time, and sure enough, the article was in there. The print quality was so poor that no query, no matter how clever, could have matched the OCR gibberish generated from it.

*Galveston Daily News*, March 4, 1883

The story, transcribed:

**CORSICANA, March 3 – A one-legged man named Professor DeHuone, met with a serious accident to-day. He was walk-ing a rope suspended across Beaton street and had on his shoulder a stove, when the rope broke and he fell, breaking his sole remaining leg and also his right arm.**[318]

Additional searches, using query syntax more creative than "one-legged rope walker," identified additional relevant articles, a number of them about a man named "Prof. Berg." Two of Berg's performances, in nearby Fort Worth and Dallas, were merely days before the Corsicana accident, conclusive proof that Tom Lea's "Prof. Berg," from Chapter 7, was indeed another name for the man who fell in Corsicana.

**Tight Rope Walking.**

of. Berg will entertain the citizens ort Worth at half-past two this noon by walking a tight rope as Houston street, from Lake's ware store to Warner & Samuels'. f. Berg has but one leg, being a sol- in the late war, one who received pension. The professor will bake cakes on the rope, give a trapeze ormance and perform other astoun- ng feats. All are invited. Half t two this afternoon.

*Fort Worth Daily Gazette*, February 16, 1883

In Fort Worth he was walking a tightrope, swinging on a trapeze, and cooking "pan-cakes."[319] Revelations! The comment in the original cemetery record book, "Fell from Trapeze," may be accurate after all! The stove *was* part of his act! He was a Civil War veteran who lost his leg in the war!

M. Berg a trapeze performer who lost one of his legs in the "las. cause," gave an exhibition on Main street yesterday and will again this 2 p. m.

*Dallas Daily Herald*, February 27, 1883

In Dallas, four days before his fall in Corsicana, the *Daily Herald* published a brief notice about a true American original: a crowd-pleasing wounded veteran; a paragon of grit, ingenuity, and courage; a trapezist and rope walker who performed astonishing feats: Professor De Houne; Monsieur Professor Berg. For a man who supposedly refused to divulge his name—so says the legend—he sure had his name, his names, spread all over the press. De Houne, Berg, or both? The man with no name, now has two.[320]

Perhaps what happened back in 1883 is that Max London and the other Hebrew Cemetery administrators were not sure which was his real name and which was his stage name, so they delayed the erection of his tombstone until they could figure it out. They put up a temporary gravestone and simply called him "Rope Walker," believing the confusion would be resolved. But it wasn't resolved, time went by, and nothing further was done to figure out his real name.

Much progress has been made, but there are still many unanswered questions, and not just about his names. None of the contemporaneous newspaper accounts reported anything about his religion, about a doctor, or any of the other various details found in Haslam's and Campbell/Rosenberg's accounts. The next three chapters examine several salient details that Haslam and later writers included in their recounting of the legend, size up those details against facts—to the extent facts can be found—and attempt to reach the truth about what really happened on Beaton Street on the otherwise delightful Saturday in 1883.

# Chapter 14

## ROPE WALKER SLIPPED HERE

*small erections may be finished by their first architects; grand ones, true ones, ever leave the copestone to posterity*

Where Rope Walker fell—the location of one of the most unusual events in Corsicana history—is in dispute. In the near future a historical plaque, or at least a numbered stop on Corsicana's walking tour, could be installed there to commemorate his final performance. But where? Haslam stretched the fateful line diagonally across the intersection of Beaton Street and 5th Avenue. Ivan Rosenberg placed it one block away, at Beaton and Collin. Either intersection could be considered the center of town activity in early Corsicana. Collin Street, as the dividing line for South and North street designations, has a legitimate right to that claim, but 5th Ave. at Beaton was arguably the center of commercial activity.

## Beaton Street at Collin Street

Ivan Rosenberg's entry in the cemetery record book says:

> the History—In 1884 one day a stranger arrived, he stretched a wire across Beaton St from the SE Corner of Collins St, to the opposite NW Corner of the street—The unusual part this Wire Walker had a Peg

**Cemetery record book entry for Rope Walker (excerpt)**

**he stretched a wire across Beaton St from the SE Corner of Collins St, to the opposite NW Corner of the street**

**Southeast corner, Beaton and Collin Streets**

The southeast corner of Beaton and Collin Streets, numbered 101, 103 & 105 South Beaton Street, houses the Turquoise Pistol Rustic Boutique, Interiors by Design, and the Vintage Farmhouse—fun things people want.

**Northwest corner, Beaton and Collin Streets**

The northwest corner is occupied by a law office, a finance company, and an auto parts store—practical things people need.

On the northeast corner, where spectators would have watched Rope Walker in awe—and then shock—stands the State National Bank Building, a Corsicana landmark already mentioned in Chapters 1, 3 & 4. Its current occupant is Chase Bank.

Affixed to the exterior is a Texas Historical Commission plaque which says, among other things, that the State National Bank's founding president, B.B. Munsey, was succeeded in 1926 by

**State National Bank Building, northeast corner, Beaton and Collin Streets**

*Isaac N. Cerf, a prominent Corsicana businessman and civic leader. The bank moved to this site in 1926, and in 1933 the accounts and loans of First State Bank of Corsicana were merged with those of State National Bank.*

On the sidewalk at the same corner stands the KAND statue, a radio announcer speaking into a microphone, with a plaque which reads:

*Radio station KAND began broadcasting in 1937, originally from the basement of the State National Bank building and later from the mezzanine. The license was granted to the WEST Family, owners of WOLF Brand Chili. The call letters signified "Canned" chili meat. After a change in ownership when Richard C. Parker came to Corsicana to manage and later own KAND, he changed the image from "Canned" to "Candy" with red and white striped outfits for the disc jockeys and highway billboards proclaiming "Welcome to KAN-D Land"!*

## Beaton Street at 5<sup>th</sup> Avenue

One block north of Collin Street is the intersection where Haslam pinpointed the accident according to information he likely learned from his interview with Mary London:

> *... "catty-cornered" across Beaton street and Fifth Avenue ... A rope had been stretched from the roof of an old frame building which later was the site of the First State bank building, to a similarly constructed building now housing the Louis Hashop Confectionery. In the first named building was Bernard Simon's grocery store, while the present Hashop location was the "Blue Front" drug store, operated by one Dr. Carter.*

Notwithstanding what it says in the cemetery record book, the walking tour brochure, and elsewhere, Haslam's convincing investigation says <u>this</u> is where Rope Walker fell. If Haslam's detailed description of the intersection agrees with historical records, surely that would argue that he had correctly identified the location of the fall.

Walking tour stop seven plaque

Coincidentally, and confusingly, the First State Bank, located at the intersection with 5<sup>th</sup> Ave according to Haslam, was one block away from the State National Bank which has a his—torical plaque that mentions the First State Bank. *Love* explains the mergers of banks but doesn't say on which corner the First State Bank was located.[321] No building at Beaton and 5<sup>th</sup> Avenue has a sign that indicates it was once the First State Bank.

Actually, it is far easier to identify the corner at the other end of the rope, which, based on Haslam's 1936 description, was the Louis Hashop Confectionary. A plaque, walking tour stop seven, affixed to the building on the southeast corner, identifies it as Hashop's Drug Store. The same building, 125 N. Beaton Street, is also stop twelve, as shown in Chapter 1, and also where K. Wolens got his start, according to Chapter 4.

Louis Hashop, a native of Syria, longed to come to America. He stowed away on a ship that landed at Galveston, made his way to Houston, and, as the story goes, bought an old mule named Jack, and a wagon, and set about

**Across the Street
Diner and Bistro**

peddling fruit. "He was credited as the first man to bring grapefruit to the area. People were leery of buying the unfamiliar fruit, so Mr. Hashop started selling them as large oranges." In 1905 he decided to relocate to Mexia. At a certain fork in the road Jack decided to go in a different direction and that brought them to Cor–sicana. That same year he established his first shop. He moved a few times before reaching this final location, in 1927, at the southeast corner of Beaton and 5th Avenue.[322]

The building later became Dee's Place, a restaurant,[323] and after Dee's closed, Corsicanan Jimmy Hale renovated the building and opened the Across the Street restaurant, in 2014.[324] "Across the Street" sounds like a virtual chalk outline of a peg-legged man, smack-dab in the middle of the intersection, but the moniker has nothing to do with the fabled aerialist. Hale created the name because he already owned businesses on the other side of Beaton. The building's facade still bears the name of an earlier owner, Isaac Baum, a member of Corsicana's Jewish community at the time Rope Walker fell.[325]

Hashop's was indeed the Blue Corner Drug Store, previously, what Haslam called the Blue Front Drug Store.

> Sol Gottlieb, proprietor of the Blue Corner Drug Store, will move soon from the corner of Fifth avenue and Beaton street to the corner of Fifth avenue and Commerce street. Louis Hashop will move from South Beaton street to the former Blue Corner store, it is stated.

*Corsicana Daily Sun,* **September 2, 1927**

Sol Gottlieb, a popular Jewish local, operated a shop there from 1917 until Hashop took it over, ten years later.[326]

**We wish to notify our patrons and the general public that we have moved from our old location on S. Beaton Street to the corner building on Beaton Street and 5th Avenue, formerly occupied by the Blue Corner Drug Store.**
**We are now ready to serve you in our new home**
**—Call and see us.**

## *Louis Hashop*

*Corsicana Daily Sun,* **October 22, 1927**

**Entrance to the Jester Building, aka the First State Bank Building**

Now that Hashop's/Blue Front is identified,[327] the First State Bank building can be found, diagonally across the street on the northwest corner. The only sign on the nondescript building is on the building's 5th Avenue side, where a marquee says it is the "JESTER BLDG." Further research shows George T. Jester and his nephew, George E. Jester, bought control of the two-year-old First State Bank in 1909.[328] A 1915 article about the remodeling of the large, brick building reports it was then owned by George T.[329]

Nothing verifies Haslam's (i.e., Mary London's) claim that in 1884—actually, 1883—before the current First State Bank/Jester building was built on the corner, there was an "old frame building" containing Bernard Simon's grocery store. An 1885 Sanborn Insurance Company map[330] shows a brick, not wood-framed building there,[331] although it does have a grocery and provisions store on the first floor, according to the map, consistent with what Haslam said. The map is shown below. The corner in question is near the bottom, just left of center. Note that 5th Avenue at the time was called White Street.

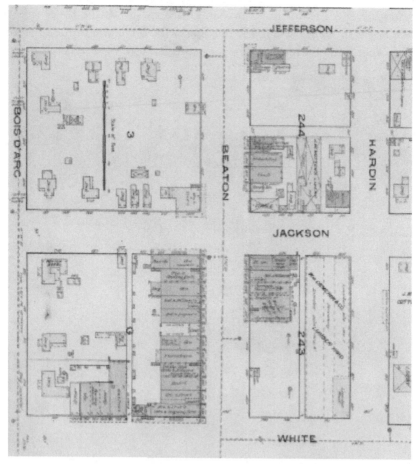

Part of sheet 3, 1885 Sanborn map of Corsicana. North is on top.

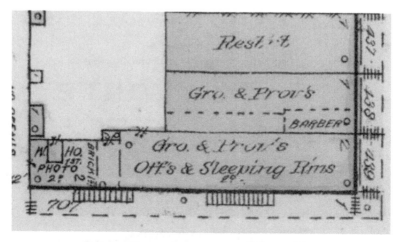

Detail of the northwest corner of Beaton Street
and White Street (5th Ave.). North is on top.

Another sheet from the same Sanborn map shows the other side of White Street (5th Ave.), where the building at the other end of the rope, the Blue Corner Drug Store, would be located at the top, right of center.

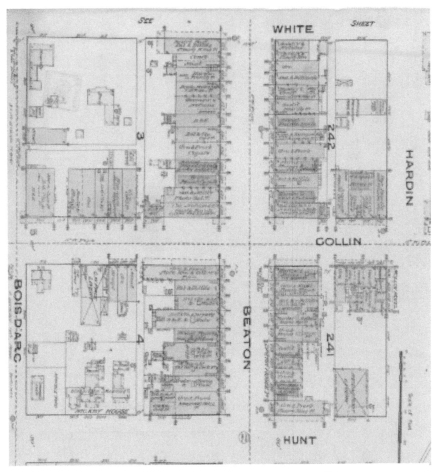

Part of sheet 2, 1885 Sanborn map of Corsicana. North is on top.

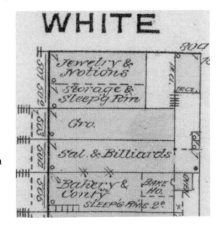

Detail of the southeast corner of Beaton Street and White Street (5th Ave.). North is on top.

The building on this corner is brick, also, instead of the wood-framed building Haslam said was there when Rope Walker fell.

It may be that the brick buildings the map says were at this intersection, in 1885, were built after Rope Walker's fall but before the map was made, sometime within those two years. Very possible—during those years there was an ongoing effort to get rid of wooden buildings and replace them with brick. Reducing the number of destructive fires was the main reason why new, block-long brick buildings were going up. In fact, the last of the wooden structures on the commercial stretch of Beaton Street burned down in October, 1883.[332]

Blue Corner, according to the map, had a jewelry & notions shop, not the drug store Haslam said was there just two years earlier. This may also be understood without too much difficulty—businesses and commercial tenants moved around frequently.

If the 1885 Sanborn map agreed with Haslam's detailed description of where Rope Walker performed it would securely validate Haslam's identification of where the accident happened, but unfortunately there are several differences. There is another map which may help. The 1886 bird's-eye view map below identifies the locations of several early Corsicana businesses.[333] The reproduction which follows on the next page has been cropped to remove the less built-up areas on the outskirts of town, thereby allowing for a more magnified view of downtown Corsicana. The courthouse is the large building along the top edge, right of center. Beaton Street starts near the train junction, a little to the right of bottom-center, and extends diagonally up into the top-right corner. A more magnified view appears on the page after.

Detail of 1886 bird's-eye view map showing the built-up portion of Corsicana

At the bottom of the map is a numbered list of sixty-two buildings, corresponding to numbers on the map.

Index to bird's-eye view map

Preceding the "B" in "Beaton," at the top right of the map enlargement on the next page, is the intersection of Beaton and White Street (5th Ave.). Blue Corner is marked by what looks like "48." In the index, 48 is "W. Caston & Co., Drugs, Medicines and Toilet Articles." According to Haslam, in 1883 it was the Blue Front drug store, operated by Dr. Carter.[334] A drug store run by W. Caston is a better match to Haslam's description than a jewelry & notions shop, shown on that corner on the 1885 Sanborn map previously discussed, but still not the exact match that would deliver certainty that this was in fact where Rope Walker fell.

Bird's-eye view map. Close-up of Beaton Street

A source to check to see if it was actually Dr. Caston who ran the Blue Corner Drug Store, on the chance that Haslam (or one of his interviewees) said "Carter" in error, is *Logan's Railway Business Directory*, from 1873.[335]

"Carter, T.N. & Co., General Druggists" is listed, not Caston, but like most others listed in the directory, no location is given for his business.

## CORSICANA, TEXAS.

This town of 1,500 inhabitants, 117 miles south of Sherman, 747 miles from St. Louis, and 261 miles from Galveston, is well situated, and has a fair trade; but its business men do not appreciate it, principally because they are men of small means and little enterprise, who are in need of some live additions to their number. See names below.

Aldrich & Allyn, Groceries and Produce.
**Arto House,** A. E. Quinn, Proprietor, near Depot.
Baker, I. W. & Co., General Druggists.
Beall Bros., Druggists.
Becker, Mrs. B., Restaurant.
Black, J. E., Livery Stable.
Block Bros. & Co., Groceries and Produce.
Blum, Charles, Saloon.
Braswell, S. N., General Merchandise.
Broadway, —— Photographer.
Burck, George & Co., Books and Stationery.
Burns, D., Groceries and Produce.
Campbell, J. G., Druggist.
Caplen & Bro., Dry Goods and Notions.
Carruthers, F. W., Lumber Merchant.
Carter, T. N. & Co., General Druggists.
Cerf, I., Groceries and Produce, S. S. Square.
Cheek, H., Physician and Surgeon.
**City Hotel,** J. H. Neims, Proprietor.

*Logan's Railway Business Directory*

The *Navarro Express* advertised Dr. Carter's business as early as 1860, but like most businesses at the time he was probably located at the public square.[336] His drug store might have been located at Blue Corner in 1883, but Dr. Carter was not; he died on Aug. 27, 1882.[337] Maybe it was Dr. Caston's Drug Store, after all.

♎︎

Haslam's locus for Rope Walker's fall is far better substantiated than the location identified by Ivan Rosenberg, even though some of Haslam's details can't be validated by available documentary evidence. Haslam had an eyewitness, whereas Rosenberg wasn't even born until 1895, long after Rope Walker fell. Rosenberg may have heard the story from his father, Ben Rosenberg, but Ben hadn't moved to Corsicana until 1889, at the earliest.[338]

Haslam's very qualified eyewitness, Mary London, was the daughter of the secretary of the Hebrew Cemetery Association and at one time helped to care for the cemetery.[339] The best conclusion is that Rope Walker attempted to cross the street at the Across the Street Diner. Excellent burgers *and* an excellent name.

It's also possible Rope Walker performed at <u>both</u> locations. According to the *Dallas Daily Herald* article, in Chapter 12, D.E. Huone had been putting on exhibitions for a few days in Corsicana when he fell. Nothing dictates that he performed at the same place each time. It's also possible that instead of walking across an intersection, the rope stretched diagonally across an entire block, thus giving partial credence to both versions. Not that Campbell is a reliable source, but he did say, "it was a block long."

Blue Corner (nearer corner) and the mule-powered
"Texas Express," east side of Beaton at White Street, 1895

# Chapter 15

## MOLLOY, GULICK, AND MULKEY

*I devoted three days to the studious digesting of all this beer, beef, and bread, during which many profound thoughts were incidentally suggested to me, capable of a transcendental and Platonic application*

Haslam said Rope Walker was brought to the Molloy Hotel, while Campbell/Rosenberg only said a "nearby" hotel. Both versions agree that Dr. Gulick and Rev. Mulkey attended to Rope Walker, one for his medical needs and one for his spiritual needs. The core story, first written in 1936, has remained fairly consistent over the years: a one-legged man, with a stove on his back, fell from a tightrope on Beaton Street and was brought to a hotel; he initially told Rev. Mulkey he was Methodist, but later said he was Jewish; he was brought to a hotel and treated by Dr. Gulick; he refused to identify himself before he died; he said a Hebrew prayer with a local Jewish merchant.

Molloy, Gulick, and Mulkey were well-known Corsicana names on the day Rope Walker attempted to cross Beaton Street. This chapter resurrects their memory and amplifies the brief mention of them by Haslam, Campbell, and Rosenberg. The true extent of their roles may never be known, but just the same, they get bold-faced billing in the *Tragedy of Rope Walker*.

## Ghostly Guests: The Molloy Hotel

The Molloy Hotel was a block away from where Rope Walker fell; "around the corner," according to Haslam. The building has been there since the mid-1870s, a Corsicana landmark. The injured man would have been conveyed—he wouldn't have been able to move on his own—one block south along Beaton Street, then left (east) on Collin where the hotel sits, on Collin at Hardin.[340] The hotel is building 30 on the 1886 bird's-eye view map, "Molloy House, A. Adams, Prop."

In the magnified detail on the next page, the location of Rope Walker's fall is where the first few letters of "BEATON" are printed, near the top-right corner, and building 30, Molloy House, is near the bottom-right corner.

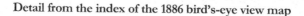

Detail from the index of the 1886 bird's-eye view map

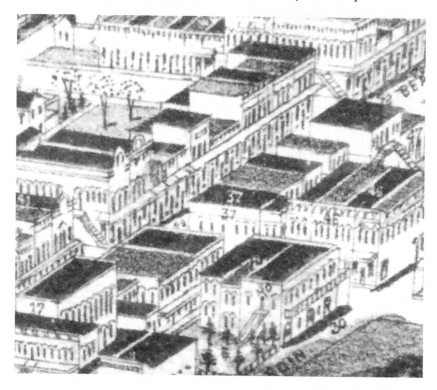

Detail from bird's-eye view map, showing the Molloy House (30)

**Napoli's Italian Restaurant & Bar,
formerly the Molloy Hotel, Collin Street**

The Texas Historical Commission plaque on the building[341] says it was built by lawyer Henry Molloy in 1874, with a second story added in 1881. In 1880, the *American Sketch Book* noted that Corsicana had three hotels, "of which the Mallory [sic] house stands pre-eminent and first, and for courtesy, attention, cleanliness, it is utterly impossible to find its superior."[342] The hotel ceased operations in 1975. Today, the ground floor is Napoli's Italian Restaurant and the second floor has rental apartments.

A pallid lady sits by an upstairs window, gazing out into eternity. Mack Cooper recounted Sally's sad story.[343] A "working girl," she transacted bus–iness at the Molloy Hotel during the oil boom at the turn of the century.

She met an oil worker, fell in love, and decided to marry and disengage from commerce. Once, however, when Sally was alone at the hotel, a man mistakenly knocked on her door.

Sally, permanent resident
of the Molloy Hotel

"Our lady of the night took the knock as opportunity," writes Cooper. As she was getting busy, says Mack, her fiancé returned and shot (or stabbed) her dead. Many years later, after the hotel became a restaurant, strange noises were heard and things mysteriously moved around on their own. Mack experienced her pres– ence himself when he once (and only once!) visited there—the light switch in the room clicked off twice, all on its own.

The origin of this little local legend has been long forgotten, but after digging into old newspapers its basis in reality seems fairly obvious. Late on a Sunday night, Nov. 8, 1890, in Room 6 of the Molloy Hotel, William Vallie shot his wife, Laura, and then killed himself.[344] Was it De Houne's ghost, by then a six-year resident of the Molloy, who came gently rapping at her chamber door?

♎

Henry L. Molloy, the original hotel owner and manager,[345] was the second oldest son of David (1801-1870) and Mary (Thompson) Molloy (1804-1881).[346] David and Mary were born in North Carolina, died in Corsicana, and had a family of seven children.[347] Henry, born about 1829, came to Corsicana in the early 1870s from Vineyard, Arkansas, took over the McKinney Inn at the public (courthouse) square, and named it the Molloy House. Around 1874 he built a brick hotel at the corner of East Collin and Hardin (later 10th, aka Commerce) Streets, in what was then the newer commercial center of town. That too was called the Molloy House, and later, the Molloy Hotel. It was sold out of the family in 1916 by Henry's son, Will Molloy, to C.C. Walton.[348]

Henry's brother, John Thompson Molloy, the oldest Molloy son, was born in 1824 in Alabama. He was murdered in 1862 at Dutch Mills, Arkansas, by "bushwhackers." In this context that term appears to mean highwaymen, although it could also mean guerrilla fighters on either side of the War of Secession. He was returning home to his pregnant wife and two young sons in nearby Vineyard when he was attacked. Discovered a few days later, he was buried where found, in a field, beneath a pile of stones.

The body was initially misidentified, but later a slab was placed there and a gravestone put up. Today, it is still a cemetery of one.[349] Three months following his murder his wife gave birth to a third son, Robert Bates Molloy, who grew up to became a well-known, highly respected Corsicana attorney, "Dean of the Navarro County Bar Association."[350] R.B. Molloy, as he was known, was a close friend to Corsicana's Jews. He was a pall bearer at Jewish funerals, including Max London's, and did legal work for several Jewish Corsicanans.[351]

The third oldest was Dr. H.H. (Hartwell Horace) Molloy, Henry's younger brother, one of the first teachers in Corsicana. He ran the Female Institute and Male Seminary, both operating from at least 1859. On July 18, 1861, three months after the assault on Fort Sumter and two days before First Manassas, the first major battle of the Civil War, he and Roger Mills[352] travelled to the headquarters of Gen. Ben McCulloch to "procure definite and reliable information of the state of affairs."[353] A year later, H.H. Molloy was elected captain of a company of Navarro men,[354] and a year after that, on July 17, 1863, he was killed at the Battle of Honey Springs.[355]

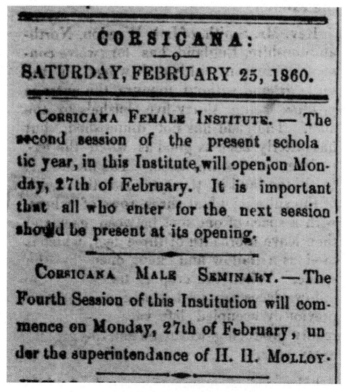

## CORSICANA:

### SATURDAY, FEBRUARY 25, 1860.

CORSICANA FEMALE INSTITUTE. — The second session of the present schola tic year, in this Institute, will open on Monday, 27th of February. It is important that all who enter for the next session should be present at its opening.

CORSICANA MALE SEMINARY. — The Fourth Session of this Institution will commence on Monday, 27th of February, under the superintendance of H. H. MOLLOY.

H.H. Molloy, an early Corsicana educator

## Doctor John Wiley Gulick

Dr. Gulick is mentioned in all foundational versions of the legend. In Haslam's article he is simply "Dr. Gulick." In Campbell's article, and consequently in the cemetery record book, he is "Dr. J.T. Gulick a pioneer physician." The historical Dr. Gulick was indeed a prominent Corsicana doctor. His full name was John Wiley Gulick, but he used only his first two initials, as was common in those days, "J.W. Gulick"—not "J.T. Gulick."

Gulick's biography appeared in the 1893 history of Navarro County.[356] He was born near Princeton, N.J., Feb. 6, 1829, and died in Corsicana in 1898 at the age of sixty-nine. In "True Story of the Rope Walker," the fictionalized story which frustrated efforts to identity the fallen acrobat, Gulick's birth and death data were inexplicably assigned to Rope Walker.

Gulick's family roots go back to seventeenth-century Princeton, and before that, to Holland.[357] His early education was by private tutor, after which he studied at Princeton University. At the age of fifteen his father suffered a "financial embarrassment" and his mother died, suddenly ending his privileged life. In Cheraw, S.C., he worked for Dr. Archibald Malloy (also spelled Molloy), a druggist. With his newly acquired interest in medicine he completed his general studies and continued his education under Dr. Malloy. When he had saved enough money, he enrolled at U. Penn, and earned a medical degree there in 1855. He practiced medicine at Cheraw for four years, married Margaret J. Sutherland, and together they left for the Texas frontier. Doctor and Mrs. Gulick arrived in 1859, initially making their home at Gay Hill, about twelve miles northwest of Brenham.

In April 1862, Gulick enlisted in Co. B of Terry's Rangers and was made regiment surgeon. Five months later he became senior surgeon in General Forrest's first brigade. He took a leave, in Texas, in November 1864, and was then reassigned to serve under General Buckner.[358] Before returning to the war he was discharged, despite his desire to serve at the front, and returned to Texas.

Gulick is a man who has always enjoyed the unbounded confidence of those among whom he has practiced and is highly esteemed also by his medical brethren. He has always made it a point to be honest with himself and with his patients, not pretending to do more than he could do nor assuming to know more than he really knew. He is a great stickler for the ethics of his profession, being always courteous to his medical brethren and especially considerate toward the younger members

**Biography of John Wiley Gulick (excerpt)**

Gulick gallantly battled the yellow fever outbreak of 1867. His courageous and tireless efforts nearly killed him after he himself contracted the deadly disease. In 1870 the Gulicks had four children and he was practicing medicine in Brenham. Soon after, they moved to Corsicana.

The first Mrs. Gulick died in Corsicana on June 3, 1879. She raised five children and all of them married. The second Mrs. Gulick, born Lizzie Talley, daughter of a Savannah Methodist preacher, operated "Mrs. Gulick's Select School" for girls in Corsicana between 1879 and 1887.[359]

In the bird's-eye view map of Corsicana, index entries 49, "Dr. W.J.W. Kerr," and 50, "Dr. J. W. Gullick" (sic), are identically listed as "Physician & Surgeon, Office at Revares Drug Store":

49  Dr. W. J. W. Kerr, Physician & Surgeon, Office at Revares Drug Sto-
50  Dr. J. W. Gullick,         "         "         "         "

Detail from the 1886 bird's-eye view map

Location "50" could not be found on the map, but "49" is near the intersection of Beaton and 5th Ave. (visible in the enlargement detail of the map shown near the start of this chapter, just above the "ea" in "Beaton," along the right edge, near the top). Since both doctors had their office at the same location, 50 is as good as 49. No source shows an address from that time for either doctor or Revares Drug, but "49" is at the same location where one end of the rope, according to Haslam's article, was tied to "Mr. Simon's Grocery," where the First State Bank/Jester Building now stands. Dr. Gulick (and Dr. Kerr) probably had an excellent view from their offices, and seeing the fall came rushing down to the street to help. The location of Gulick's office is good evidence that he did in fact take care of Rope Walker.

Gulick had a connection to the Molloy family, which might explain why Rope Walker was brought to the Molloy Hotel. Gulick's mentor in Cheraw, Dr. Archibald Malloy/Molloy, was a first cousin to David Molloy of Corsicana, whose son Henry owned the hotel.[360] Gulick, quite possibly, ended up in Corsicana because of that connection.

Dr. Gulick suffered a stroke on Nov. 2, 1890, leaving him partially paralyzed, and he gradually withdrew from practice. He died in 1898[361] and was buried in Corsicana's Oakwood Cemetery, next to his first wife.[362] The second Mrs. Gulick died in 1927.[363]

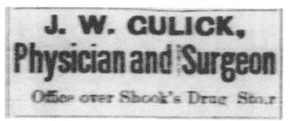

Advertisement by
Dr. Gulick, 1888

## Reverend Abe Mulkey

Abe Mulkey, to put it in today's parlance, was in your face. He had an overabundance of confidence and humility, but his humility was for God, and God alone. He had a charming, straight-shooting personality which

made him beloved and respected by thousands. To the extent he was lacking in some of the more refined ways of society and education, his smart and adored wife, Louisa Pratt (Kerr) Mulkey, "Sister Mulkey," took up the slack. Abe was a man of God and faith who brought religion down to earth and delivered it up in everyday language and experience, drawing parallels to commerce, clothes shopping, eating, and so forth.

His appeals for faith, devotion, right-living, and charity were emotional and dramatic. One writer compared his exhortations to a pneumatic drill,

**Rev. Abe Mulkey**

typical of the fire and brimstone revivals of the era.[364] In the words of Reverend E.L. Armstrong, who knew Mulkey's itinerant preacher father and knew Abe from birth, "If Abe is eccentric, he came by it honestly, for his father was both eccentric and original."[365]

*Abe Mulkey not only brought many thousands to declare their faith in Christianity, but was also able to raise large sums of money for many churches in Texas and other states, as well as to be the man who dreamed of a great orphanage for Texas Methodism and help this dream come true.*[366]

Abram Mulkey was born in Center Point, Howard County, Arkansas, on Apr. 15, 1850,[367] to Annis (neé Pinkerton[368]) and William Aken Mulkey, a minister in the Methodist Episcopal Church South. William Mulkey did missionary work with the Choctaw Indians, and in his earlier years wrote books on orthoepy (the study of proper pronunciation) which devised phonetic systems for teaching literacy. At one point, in an effort to get his work published, the elder Mulkey moved his young family to Nashville.[369]

At a young age, Abe was a Nashville newsboy helping to support his family and therefore his formal education was limited. At the close of the war, at age sixteen, the family moved to Waxahachie. Abe used money earned from various jobs to buy a wagon and team and began trading in hides and cotton. A year later, he started a grocery there, but it was destroyed by fire in 1871. With losses totaling $5,500 and no insurance, Mulkey went bankrupt. A plan of repayment at twenty-five cents on the dollar was not accepted by his creditors so he opted, upon legal advice, to hold on to his remaining assets, which he subsequently used to buy a house.[370]

Louisa, daughter of Judge S.H. Kerr of Corsicana, married Abe on Dec. 13, 1869, when he was nineteen and she was seventeen. Abe and Louisa moved to Corsicana, around 1873, where he worked as a clerk at various places, including F.L. Fewell's hardware store and U.M. Lee's clothing store. Earlier in life he had fallen away from religion, but sometime in the early '80s he returned. When Called, he had been operating a successful grocery for seven years. He had a Divine Revelation about his Waxahachie debts. Determined to make things right, by God and man, he sold everything he owned to pay off his creditors, including his home. He raised $5,500, which was not enough, but he kept at it and eventually paid off the remainder.[371] Repayment of debt represented Salvation to him and formed the crux of his popular "Restitution" sermon. Fully out of debt, in 1894, he bought the corner lot at 3rd Ave. and 12th Street from his father-in-law, paying $900 and giving a note for $800. Across from the courthouse, it was once the site of Judge Kerr's wagon, buggy, and furniture shop.[372]

In 1889 Mulkey became a Sunday school superintendent for the First Methodist Church of Corsicana. Two years later he received his license to

**Louisa Pratt (Kerr) Mulkey**

exhort, the Methodist Episcopal Church South's authorization for him to minister as a lay preacher. A year after that he held his first meeting, at Tyler, and in another few years he received his full preacher's license. Mulkey held revival meetings throughout Texas and around the South. He was a phenomenal fundraiser, at one point raising $4,000 during the dedication of a new church for the First Methodist Church of Corsicana, admonishing the congregation that it was improper to establish a church which was not fully funded. Mulkey raised funds and saved souls with a sacred shtick. He amused his audiences to get their interest, got them hooked, and reeled them in.

Abe and Louisa published two books, *Abe Mulkey's Budget* (No. 1), in 1897, and *Abe Mulkey's Budget* (No. 2), in 1909. They are filled with sincere, unabashed stories about Abe and Louisa, Abe's career, Abe's relationship with God, and God's expectations for Mulkey and others. The introduction to *Budget No. 2* says Mulkey conducted 526 revival meetings and converted 53,654 souls, plus the "reclamation of another 860 lapsed Methodists brought back to the faith." He raised $36,000 for the orphanage in Waco, $6,000 of which came from the Mulkeys' personal funds.

*Dallas News.*

He is here. Abe Mulkey, the great evangelist has arrived. He preached an introductory sermon at the Mulkey tabernacle last night and it was a stunner. Mulkey made himself known before he said a half dozen words and he did it in a way that knocked conventionalism silly. He talks with his head, feet, mouth and hands; he is sharp; has a big mouth and can say more funny things than any man in Texas.

I went out to hear him last night and promised myself not to laugh at what he said; I didn't listen but ten minutes when I broke the covenant and fell all over myself in laughter. I straightened my face, upbraided myself only to break out in a new place.

"Mulkey has got 'em on the run," I said to myself, as he pranced up and down the plank resting on a lot of beer kegs. A long face could no more stand before Mulkey unmelted than a stick of molases candy could in the broiling hot sun.

*The Texas Star, Decatur, Texas.*

Abe Mulkey, the acrobatic, double back-action pulpit wind-spouter, has arrived in Decatur,. He and Louisa came to aid in a united church revival. He is as ugly as sin—a cross between Doc Wilson and Clyde Emerson—but we are glad to have him with us.

P. S.—(Put Sooner.) The above is a mistake. Since setting up the above notice we have heard Mr. Mulkey preach, and he is a Jim dandy. We rendered our verdict too soon. He is not a windspouter, but he is a regular Devil fighter, and he gets better looking every time we see him. Go out and hear him. We hope he may accomplish much good.

There is no mention of Rope Walker in Mulkey's books, and yet, they had so much in common. They were both entertainers. One used his entire body to get a message across about faith and morality. He got his congregants to open their purses to support his causes—the building of a church, an orphanage, an old-age home for ministers. The other used his body to get *himself* across, preaching from a lofty position down to the congregation below about the ties that bind each to each, as the rope must be securely attached at both ends—or maybe he delivered a message of faith—faith that he would make it to the other side.

Abe and Louisa's one child, Royal Rex "Roy" Mulkey, graduated Vanderbilt University in 1898 and returned to Corsicana as a dentist.[373] In January 1904, at his parents' home, he died from tuberculosis. He was twenty-seven and had recently married.[374] Abe was delivered unto God's Kingdom on April 5, 1919. His 265-acre farm, located four miles west of Corsicana, was left to the First Methodist Church of Corsicana to be used by the Waco Orphanage. Sister Louisa joined Abe on October 6, 1932.

The Mulkeys' greatest legacy was their support of the orphanage, currently called the Methodist Children's Home. Since its opening in 1890 it has served thousands of children. It currently offers several programs for youth in need and has an endowment of over $400 million.[375]

**Abe, Louisa, and Royal Mulkey**

Mulkey's popular "Ash Hopper" sermon, below, is not preachy. He pokes fun at himself more than anything. He advocates for tolerance among the different Christian churches and later extends his admonition to the "whole religious community."

"My wife was reared a Cumberland Presbyterian. I had known nothing else but Methodism. At her request I attended her church once. On my return she asked me, 'How did you like my people?' I petulantly answered, "Oh, not at all. I didn't like anything they did. Why, they read their sermons; sit down to sing and stand up to pray, and its all wrong—they ought to reverse everything and do like us Methodists.'"

*Louisa raised that long index finger*, and let it *fall* as *straight towards my pug nose as ever did the needle point*

*to the pole*, and said, 'I know what is the matter with you sir; you've got more of the *Methodist Church in you* than you *have of Christ.'*

"I tell you boys, it was a center shot and rang the bell on the inside of me. I backed away from her, feeling the rebuke and the next thing I knew I was in the back yard upon my knees behind an old ash-hopper. Thank God, if I didn't have the sackcloth I had a barrel or two of firstrate unbleached hickory ashes, and wept with deep contrition, as I said: 'Here Lord, is Abe Mulkey again; he is so full of conceit and sectarianism that he can't even speak a kind word of his wife's church.

" 'Lord forgive me of this meanness and littleness and make me liberal, broad and conservative,' and from that day to this I've had no trouble on that line.

"From what I see of the churches, they need an ash-hopper as big as the court-house or post-office building, and there needs to be a special day set aside by the city council and mayor to be known as "special dusting day," and the whole religious community needs to meet there and have one good wallow, at least once a week to give them brotherly love and unity.

## MULKEY AT WAXAHACHIE.

### He Is Bringing Sinners Nearer To The Throne Every Day.

*Dallas News.*

Abe Mulkey has got the devil on the run. That first sermon brought some of the luke-warm nearer the fold and at each meeting since the first some one has united with the church of their choice. Mulkey is a whole circus by himself; he can not cut the pigeon wing, but he can twist himself out of shape, turn his head round like an owl, and make more people feel bad in a minute than all the prosperity proclamations on earth.

Mulkey can not walk a tight rope, but he can walk down a plank balanced on a beer keg and preach the gospel with as much effect as if he had been practicing it all his life. Mulkey is a mimical contortionist; he can show an old sister just how she looks when she comes in and takes a seat before him for the first time; then, he can show her how she looks when she becomes insulted at what he has said and begins to pout; he can show a man how he looks when he is standing on the devil's territory and he can make him feel meaner than the man who stole a blind mule from an orphan's home.

Mulkey can not turn a back somersault, but he makes those on the front benches think he is going to do it;

Ω

There's no sure proof that Mulkey, Gulick, or Molloy's Hotel played any role in the Rope Walker saga except that they were made a part of the legend by Haslam, Rosenberg, and Campbell: no traction could be gained from Dr. Gulick's detailed biography; there isn't a ghost of a chance the secrets of Molloy's Hotel will ever check out; heaven only knows if Mulkey actually prayed with Rope Walker.

# Chapter 16

## MARY, MAX, AND A MR. SIMON

*it is not so easy to settle these plain things. I have ever found your plain things the knottiest of all. … Still, we can hypothesize, even if we cannot prove and establish.*

**Mary London**

Rachel Mae "Mary" London was born in Limestone County, Texas, in 1869[376]—the same year a man with a peg leg nearly killed himself trying to walk across a tightrope in Milwaukee—and came to Corsicana with her family when she was about eight. Her recollection of Rope Walker, more than a half century after his death, survives in John Sam Haslam's *Sun* story. Was her memory accurate and complete, or was it reshaped by what she heard from others—rumors, guess-work, and misinformation generated over the intervening fifty-three years?

It happened in the afternoon, "after children had been dismissed from Capt. J.A. Townsend's school," according to Haslam's "unsolved mystery." The school, on S. 18th Street, across from the western end of Collin Street, was a twenty-minute walk to Beaton Street, or fifteen minutes by skipping, and faster still if the destination was a visiting acrobat's tightrope perfor–mance.

James Andrew Townsend was one of the earliest educators in town, arriving in 1872 with his wife, the former Emma Davis. He was a teacher at Cedar Hall, one of Corsicana's early private schools,[377] and in 1882 became the first principal of the town's first public school, with a staff of eight teachers.[378]

According to *Love*, Capt. Townsend was

**faithful and conscientious and did much toward the education of the youth of Corsicana.**

The life of Mrs. Townsend, also a teacher, *Love* notes, was

**proof of the correctness of her theories and the virtue of her teaching.**[379]

On that fateful Saturday, Mary was thirteen and a half and was, presumably, at Townsend's school, probably with her brother, Meyer, who was ten. Mary's other brother, Jonathan Tobias "Tobie," was three years older than her and may have already graduated. The youngest, Julia, was five in 1883. A fifth sibling, Elkan, born in 1881, died on Feb. 20, 1883, only two weeks before the arrival of Professor De Houne.[380] Tobie also died young, at the age of twenty-two, on Jan. 20, 1890.[381] The four London children—Tobie, Mary, Meyer, and Julia—and their parents all might have been there to see the rope walker's performance.

Neither Mary nor Julia married. Julia had some sort of lingering illness as a young woman which might have made it difficult for her to find a mate.[382] She was not as outgoing as Mary, but neither of them, it seems, was the belle of the ball.[383] A review of over forty years of *Sun* articles reveals almost nothing about these women, none of the community involvement or social activity one might expect.[384] Julia and Mary died in Corsicana, one year apart, in 1951 and 1952, respectively.[385] Meyer married, settled in Austin, and brought up one child, Harold, whose descendants carry on the family line today in Texas and elsewhere.

Mamie Oppenheimer, Mary's cousin (their mothers were sisters), was adopted by the Londons in 1888 after her mother died young. Mamie and Mary, who grew up as sisters, were probably named after their maternal grandmother, Mina (Jacobowsky) Simon, who died in 1867.[386]

Julia London

Mary's father, Max London, the Civil War veteran remembered on the Hebrew Cemetery's historical plaque and cemetery record keeper when Rope Walker fell, was a stalwart, serious man.[387] Being raised under Max's rigid discipline may have been the primary reason why Mary and Julia be–came elderly spinsters—they never found a man, a Jewish man, who measured up to their father's high expectations.

Max London was born on July 20, 1838, in Grätz, Grand Duchy of Posen, Prussia, today's Grodzisk Wielkopolski, Poland.[388] He arrived in England at the age of thirteen, in May, 1852, joining his father Henry and brother Elkan, who preceded him.[389] The Londons was a family of London shoe and boot merchants.[390] Max was the only member of the family who came to America, arriving at New York on Oct. 22, 1853, at the age of seventeen. He then sailed to Galveston, arriving there in March of 1854.[391] Before the war he owned a "fancy store" in the Texas coastal town of Lavaca (now, Port Lavaca) and had an estimated worth at the time of $4,000.[392] After the war he lived in Houston, and then he set up a dry goods business in Halletsville. In October 1867 he married Bertha Simon (1846-1909), moved to Springfield, Texas, where her family lived, then to Bremond, in 1870, and, finally, the family came to Corsicana in 1877.[393] Professionally, he was a commercial insurance adjuster.[394] When he died in 1925, at the age of eighty-seven, he was the oldest past Grand Mason in the State of Texas.

On September 29, 1861, seven months after Texas became the fourth state to join the CSA, London traveled twenty-seven miles from his Lavaca home to Victoria to enlist in Capt. Alexander Hamilton "Ham" Phillips's Co. A of Colonel Garland's 6th Tex. Inf. under Major General Earl Van Dorn's Army of the West.[395] He was stationed at Victoria, serving as hospital steward[396] and acting druggist when, on Mar. 6, 1862, he was appointed a Hospital Steward-At-Large by Secretary of War Judah P. Benjamin[397] and sent with the 6th regiment to Tyler where it was made a part of the 1st brigade. He was next at Arkansas Post, Arkansas,[398] working at the hospital there under head surgeon Dr. Robert Archibald Burton, when Union forces attacked on Jan. 11, 1863.

**The Post's 5,000 troops were greatly outnumbered by the Union's 32,000 infantry and 1,000 cavalry. After heavy attack from Union gunboats, the Confederate troops surrendered.**[399]

Captured and sent to Gratiot Street Prison, in St. Louis, London worked in the prison hospital. After a month he petitioned his captors for release, averring he had never been in battle—except the attack on Arkansas Post[400]—and never owned slaves.

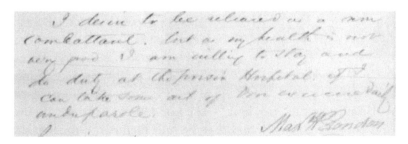

Statement of Max H. London at Gratiot Street Prison

*I desire to be released as a non-combatant, but as my health is not very good I am willing to stay and do duty at the prison Hospital, if I can take some out of Door exercise Daily under parole.*

**Max H London** [401]

London was part of a prisoner exchange at City Point, near Petersburg, Virginia, in April, 1863. He was then assigned to the chemical laboratories at Arkadelphia, Arkansas, and later to the general hospital at nearby Camden where he again worked under Dr. Burton, and remained there until the end of the war.[402]

Max H. London

Max London died on Christmas Eve day, 1925. Despite belligerent weather, a large crowd attended his funeral, including a large Masonic contingent which gave him full burial honors. Leading Corsicana citizens bore the casket to the grave: Attorney R.B. Molloy; W. P. (Perry) McCammon (lumber merchant and funeral home proprietor); Walter Beaton (grandson of Maj. Alexander and Jane (McKinney) Beaton); Dr. Homer Jester (son of C.W. Jester and brother of Judge Lee Jester); Trim Houston (dentist); Gus Wiedeman (baker and cofounder of Collin Street Bakery); P. Mayer (Corsicana postmaster); I.N. Cerf; Ivan Rosenberg; Henry Levi; K. Wolens; and Edmond Raphael.[403]

## Bernard Simon

Bernard Simon, owner of a grocery where the Jester Building/First State Bank now stands, was the Jew who recited Hebrew prayers with Rope Walker after the injured stranger learned he was dying—according to John Sam Haslam. Jay Silverberg said that Benjamin Marks and Ben Rosenberg were the local Jews who prayed with the rope walker. Marks and Rosenberg were closely associated with Corsicana's early Hebrew community, but who was Bernard Simon? There is no record that anyone with that name ever lived in Corsicana.

Bernard Simon was, however, the name of Mary London's maternal grandfather, but Haslam doesn't mention this. Maybe Haslam didn't know, or maybe there was some miscommunication between Mary and the re–porter, or maybe Haslam got his information mixed up.[404]

Bernard Simon, his wife Mina, and their two young daughters, Bertha (Mary's mother) and Ziror, emigrated from Prussia in the early 1850s. The next children, Henry and Theresa, were born in Louisiana, and the youngest children, Sarah Rosa, Julius, Hypatia "Beatrice," Isaac, and Dora, were born in Texas.[405] In 1860 the family lived together in Springfield, then the county seat of Limestone County.[406] In 1870, Bertha and her Simon family still lived in Limestone County, but by then she was "Bertha London" and the Simon family had expanded to include her husband Max and the first two London children, Jonathan T. (Tobie) and Mary.[407]

| 12 | 12 | 12 | B Simon | 38 | M |
| 13 | | | Mina " | 33 | F |
| 14 | | | A " | 22 | M |
| 15 | | | Bertha " | 13 | F |
| 16 | | | Aurora " | 12 | " |
| 17 | | | Henry " | 8 | M |
| 18 | | | Tinfa " | 6 | F |
| 19 | | | Sarah " | 4 | " |
| 20 | | | Julius " | 2 | M |
| 21 | | | Hy " | 1 | F |
| 22 | | | Louis Booth | 30 | M |
| 23 | 13 | 13 | G. F. Starley | 35 | " |

Simon family, Springfield, 1860

There is no evidence, other than the mention of the name in Haslam's article, that Mary's grandfather Bernard Simon or anyone else with that name owned or operated a grocery store in Corsicana. In 1880 Bernard Simon resided in Marlin, Falls County, seventy miles from Corsicana.[408] In 1900 he lived in Waco with the family of his daughter, Ziror Kiersky,[409] and he died and was buried in Waco in 1904.[410] If he wasn't the "Mr. Simon" who prayed with Rope Walker, but was simply the grandfather of Haslam's interviewee, was there a different Mr. Simon in Corsicana who *did* pray with Rope Walker, who had a grocery store at the end of his rope?

## Charlie Simon

Only one Simon family lived in Corsicana over the years, but no member of that family was named anything like "Bernard." Charlie Simon, however, was Jewish and was a Beaton Street grocer who, in 1883, might have had a store at or near the intersection of Beaton and 5th Avenue. Born in Russia in 1859,[411] Charlie was old enough to be a grocer in 1883 and he had already been in the U.S. since 1872 or 1873.[412] He probably lived in Houston before he came to Corsicana,[413] but exactly when he came to Corsicana is not known. He could not be located in the 1880 census. The earliest sign of him in Corsicana is in the 1895 Corsicana directory where he is listed as running a billiard hall, "over 217 N. Beaton,"[414] close to, but not quite the location mentioned by Haslam. In 1900, Charlie and his wife, Yetta (Finberg[415]), lived at 214 E. 3rd Ave. with Louis and Jane Blum and the Blum's daughter, Ethel. At the time, Charlie was reportedly a gambler.[416]

Charlie's sister was Sarah (Simon) Gottlieb Herman (she married twice), who came to Corsicana not long after Rope Walker's fall. Her residence in 1880 likewise could not be determined, but around 1883 she was just starting a family in Kosse, not far from Corsicana.[417] Charlie's nephew (Sarah's son), Sol Gottlieb, at one time ran the Blue Corner Drug Store, the store where, according to Haslam, the *other* end of Rope Walker's rope was tied—the end *not* tied to the building where "Bernard Simon's grocery store" was supposedly located. Sol did not have the store at the time of the accident but he did have it several years later. This confluence of facts might be getting close to the truth about a store owned by a Mr. Simon, but unfortunately, not close enough.

In later years, Charlie ran "Chas. Simon's," a combination candy store and deli, advertising in 1917 "all kinds of ready lunch goods." The shop was located at 105 N. Beaton and later at 100 S. Beaton, both at the intersection with Collin Street.[418] While this sounds something like a grocery store, it was long after 1883.[419] It's not known where Charlie's store was located on N. Beaton in 1883 or even if he had a store on the street at that time. To summarize, it's entirely possible Charlie Simon was the owner of the store at one end of the rope and he was the Jew who prayed with Rope Walker, and not Bernard Simon, but no certain evidence has been found.

Advertisement by Charlie Simon, 1922

# Chapter 17

## THE AMERICAN JEW AS PATRIOT, SOLDIER, AND ROPE WALKER

*Such, and so magnifying, is the virtue of a large and liberal theme! We expand to its bulk. To produce a mighty book, you must choose a mighty theme.*

The near-mythical Rope Walker narrative has now been examined from several perspectives, but back to the man himself, Professor De Houne, aka Professor Berg. What can be learned about, for example, his military service? Some newspapers said he served with the Kansas 7th Cavalry, a Union regiment, while others said he fought for the South, with Gen. Nathan Bedford Forrest's Texas 3rd Cavalry. Still others said he served with the Louisiana Tigers in the Louisiana 5th. When performing in the North he praised the noble cause of the Union. In the South he was a proud veteran of the Lost Cause. Did he fight on both sides? Some soldiers did.[420] One thing's for sure: the wounded soldier tailored his presentations based on the political sympathies of his audiences to maximize his income when the hat was passed around.

Until his true name is known, it's unlikely more about him can be dis—covered beyond the newspaper announcements about his performances, of which there are many. "De Houne" is the earliest and most common spelling used. A few reporters included his given name, Daniel. He per—formed as "Professor Berg" much less frequently.

One article reveals that De Houne was an alias and his real name was Joseph Berg:

Joseph Berg, *alias* Professor DeHoun, the one-legged rope walker, had a serious fall while performing at Vincennes, Ind., a few days since. He lost his left leg at the battle of Middleburg, Tenn., while serving in our army during the rebellion, and by this last fall he has had both arms broken in several places, and has had his face terribly lacerated. He was a daring gymnast, and wears two medals, one as champion of France, and another as victor over two hundred and forty-three tight-rope walkers in Great Britain. He is now in a critical condition at the Cincinnati Hospital.

The one-legged rope walker named, *Pittsburgh Daily Commercial*, 1869

According to the article, Joseph Berg was more than a so-so tightrope walker (the occasional mishap notwithstanding)—he was an award-winning champion! It also states that his <u>left</u> leg was amputated, lost at the Battle of Middleburg, Tenn. Other articles mention Middleburg, too.

Show business people often adopt their stage names. If that's the case here, historical records will be much easier to find under the distinctive "Daniel De Houne" than the prosaic "Joseph Berg." Any occurrence of "Daniel De Houne" would almost certainly be the correct person.

U.S. historical records from the 1850s through the 1880s show hardly anyone with the surname "De Houne," or similar. His name did appear in a list of passengers, in the *New York Times*. None of his shipmates appear to be connected to him, such as a family member or a fellow performer.

*In steam-ship General Barnes, for Savannah—Capt. Emmons, S. D. Clarke and wife, John Stetson. William Stetson, E. C. Bulkley, Mrs. Anna M. Starbuck. I. W. Hoyer, Prof. Daniel De Houne, C. W. Box, Charles S. Sprague, Charles S. Pearce, John T. Duke, William Frothingham and wife, Hugh McDonald.*

"Passengers Sailed," *New York Times*, January 24, 1873

On a June 1863 list of Cincinnati men exempt from military service (Class II—older or disabled men)[421] is one name which looks like "Daniel Dehune." If this forty-four-year-old German-born grocer is Joseph Berg, listed under his alias, it would mean the Corsicana rope walker was sixty-four when he died. That sounds unlikely, but worth noting, subject to finding corroborating evidence.

A "Dehun" family, of Omaha, indexed from the 1885 Nebraska State census, was probably not spelled that way in the census record itself because the indexer followed the entry with a question mark, indicating uncertainty of the spelling. No other record from Nebraska with that or a similar spelling was found.[422]

There was a family in Colorado and Los Angeles named "DeHoughne,"[423] with origins in Belgium. That's not too far from Alsace, where De Houne/Berg came from, according to one news article written after his fall in Corsicana.[424] There is nothing else about that family that suggests a connection to Daniel De Houne, so far. The family name "DeHoughne" is found on the Netherlands-Belgium border, but no discernable connection could be made there, either. And that is it—no federal census, city directory, or other records turned up under "De Houne," or any reasonable spelling variation, except as noted here.

In contrast, U.S. historical records include many men named "Joseph Berg." Most have a too-recent birth date to be Rope Walker. When narrowed down to Civil War veterans, only one Joseph Berg was found. Originally from Germany, he had once lived in Warsaw, Illinois, and had a family there. He served in the Civil War with a Missouri regiment—and died in 1925. Wrong Joseph Berg. Variations of the name (Joe, Jos., Burg, Berge, etc.) were also checked, all to no avail.

## AN ACROBAT'S FALL.

CORSICANA, Tex., March 3.—This afternoon, during a tight-rope exhibition given by a one-legged acrobat traveling under the name of Prof. Dehnon, the rope, owing to an insecure fastening, gave way, precipitating him to the ground, breaking his remaining leg just above the ankle and his right arm. The surgeons think there is a possibity of saving the leg, although it is badly shattered, both bones being broken. The sufferer is an Alsatian, and came from New York. He has a mother, sister, and wife dependent on him.

*Chicago Daily Tribune*, **March 6, 1883**

Biographical bits and pieces found in news articles about De Houne/Berg's performances could not be matched up to historical records for anyone named Joseph Berg. A *Chicago Daily Tribune* article, for example, said "Prof. Dehnon" was a New York Alsatian with "a mother, sister, and wife dependent on him." A few articles about his performances variously mention, briefly, a "son," a "brother," "Mrs. Berg," and "Miss Nellie Berg." At one performance, his "wife and child" were present.[425] "Miss Nellie Berg," presumably a young woman or girl when an 1879 article mentioned her, may have been his sister or daughter. The 1880 census lists several young Nellie Bergs, but none could be connected to a Joseph Berg. None of the clues about his family were enough to find an historical document about the amputee-veteran-acrobat Joseph Berg.

Articles mentioning Rope Walker's Civil War service provided con–tradictory information, as previously mentioned, depending on whether he was performing in the North or the South. Frequently, but only in northern states, newspapers said he served with the Kansas 7th Cavalry. Some reported he lost his leg at the Battle of Middleburg, Tenn. A few newspapers even gave a date when he was wounded: Dec. 24, 1862. For sympathy, is there anything sadder than losing one's leg on Christmas Eve? And was anyone more heroic to northerners (and detested by southerners) than a veteran of the famous Kansas 7th Cavalry, known as Jennison's Jay–hawkers?[426] A Jayhawker who lost his leg on Christmas Eve while fighting the rebels—what a compelling and lucrative narrative!

There is no Tennessee municipality called "Middleburg," but Civil War records do confirm fighting at a crossroads in an unincorporated area of Hardeman County, near Bolivar, where a "Middleburg Baptist Church" now stands. A Tennessee Historical Commission plaque mounted on a metal pole is planted in the middle of a grassy swell across the street from the church. It says the Battle of Middleburg occurred on August 30, 1862—not December 24.[427]

Simon Wolf's *The American Jew as Patriot, Soldier and Citizen*, mentioned in Chapter 2, was an attempt to list all Jewish American soldiers, especially those who fought in the Civil War. There isn't even one "Berg" (or "Burg"), and nothing at all close to "De Houne." Approached another way, a search was made of an online database created from the *Civil War Adjutant General's Report, 1861-1865 of Kansas*. There was a Moses Berg, two soldiers named Berger, one Bergman, but none of them named "Joseph" and nothing even remotely like "De Houne."[428] The entire military story appears fictitious, a clever sham used to elicit sympathy so audiences would open their purses for a wounded veteran. More likely, it seems, he lost his leg in a rope walking accident—he had a penchant for falling. To be sure, the Moses Berg listed in the database was checked. He was in Co. B of the 7th Cavalry, which would make him a Jayhawker, but no additional information was provided in the database.

**Middleburg, Tennessee**

The book from which the database was created was checked.[429] It shows Moses Berg was an "additional enlistment" in Co. B. He enlisted on Nov. 28, 1861 and was mustered the same day. He was discharged on April 7, '63, at Corinth, Miss., "on account of wounds received in action December 24, 1862, Middleburg, Tenn." Well, well. Looks like that *Pittsburgh Daily Commercial* article which called him "Joseph" was wrong, wrong, wrong.

# Chapter 18

## HEBREW POET REMARKS: "O LEGS!"

*I felt a sympathy and a sorrow for him, but for I don't know what, unless it was the cruel loss of his leg. And yet I also felt a strange awe of him; but that sort of awe, which I cannot at all describe, was not exactly awe; I do not know what it was. But I felt it; and it did not disincline me towards him; though I felt impatience at what seemed like mystery in him, so imperfectly as he was known to me then.*

Emma Lazarus, Jewish American poet, penned "The New Colossus" in 1883. The final lines are etched into immortality on the pedestal of the Statue of Liberty:

> **Give me your tired, your poor,**
> **Your huddled masses yearning to breathe free,**
> **The wretched refuse of your teeming shore.**
> **Send these, the homeless, tempest-tossed to me,**
> **I lift my lamp beside the golden door!** [430]

The start of the poem, not engraved, contrasts Lady Liberty—Lazarus's "New Colossus"—against the Colossus of Rhodes, the enormous statue which may or may not have stood over the harbor entrance of that Greek island, one of the Seven Wonders of the Ancient World. What became of the *old* Colossus? The brass was melted down and sold to a Jew—at least that's what some historians have said.

Lazarus's famous poem strikes a theme echoed in her other work. She frequently wrote about the desire and need of Jews to have a homeland. "The New Colossus" especially recalls a poem she wrote a year earlier, "In Exile," which begins with this epigraph:

> **"Since that day till now our life is one unbroken paradise.**
> **We live a true brotherly life. Every evening after supper we**
> **take a seat under the mighty oak and sing our songs."—**
> **Extract from a letter of a Russian refugee in Texas.**

The Texas epigraphnik and his comrades are free men, the poem explains, returned to the noble work of farming and they live in a "paradise." So why are they "in exile?" The poem only hints at the answer: they are working on a "glebe," which is land used to support a parish priest. The complete answer is found in the refugee's letter, printed in the *Jewish Messenger* in 1882.[431] The lengthy missive tells how the refugees are working on Saturdays and eating pork every day. Working on the Jewish Sabbath (Saturday) is breaking one of the Ten Commandants (Exodus 20:8), and eating pork is forbidden under kosher laws (Leviticus 11:7). The only thing these Jews are *exiled* from as they farm the glebe is their religion.

Two pages later, in the same issue of the *Jewish Messenger* where the refugee's letter was reproduced, is a brief item which may have provoked Ms. Lazarus to create the poem:

> SOME Russian emigrants, judging from their letter in our local columns, are making the best of the situation in Texas. Life is one unbroken paradise, they write, and after supper they sit under the mighty oak and sing their songs. Here is a theme for a poet.

*Jewish Messenger*, April 28, 1882

What does all this have to do with Rope Walker? Well, it touches on Texas Jews and Jewish identity, both tangled up in the Rope Walker story. He was nearly exiled from his Jewish identity for eternity, until, at the last minute—according to legend—he confessed, "I am a Jew." This discussion also concerns legs: Rope Walker lost his legs, while the Colossus "doth bestride the narrow world" (*Julius Caesar*, Act I, Scene 2).[432] No, the true purpose of this colossal distraction was to avoid titling this chapter: *The "Rope Walker": Moses Berg!* Even that sentence, the one prior to this, is buried in the middle of this paragraph, several paragraphs into this chapter. After all, what good is a mystery about an unidentified person if the big reveal is spelled out in huge, bold letters as a chapter title, runs along the top edges of certain pages, or is blatantly spelled out in the Table of Contents? Here, again, after well more than a century of bewilderment, as an anagram, is the long-sought answer to this mystery: *Hebrew Poet Remarks: "O Legs!"*

Ω

The Home for Disabled Veterans in Dayton, Ohio, kept a record of its residents, including a member of Co. B, 7th Kansas Cavalry who stayed there from May 14 to June 23, 1882. The entry says he was born in Prussia and was forty-seven; he enlisted on Nov. 28, 1861, at Kansas City, and was discharged Apr. 7, 1863, at Jackson, Tennessee; his disability was the "loss of left leg from cannon shot"; he last resided in Albany, New York and was married to "Mrs. Sarah Berg," also of Albany; he received a pension of eighteen dollars per month; he was a machinist.[433]

The North-Western Branch, National Home for Disabled Volunteer Soldiers, Milwaukee, recorded nearly identical information. His stay there began July 6, 1882, two weeks after his departure from Dayton. According to Milwaukee, he was "dropp[d] from rolls" on Aug. 9, 1883.[434] *Dropped* indeed!

Register, National Home for Disabled Volunteer Soldiers, Milwaukee

On Oct. 14, 1880, a veteran of the War of the Rebellion petitioned the Common Pleas Court of New York City to become a U.S. citizen, qualifying by virtue of his service in the Seventh Regiment of Kansas Cavalry. As a U.S. citizen he would be entitled to vote, and nineteen days later he could cast his ballot for president. Like nearly all northern states, New York went with Garfield, the Republican nominee, and this New Yorker, a Unionist who gave his leg in the war, likely voted Republican—Lincoln's party. Garfield won the popular vote by a narrow margin but carried the Electoral College handily to become the country's twentieth president.[435]

**Petition for Naturalization, Court of Common Pleas, New York City**

Not every immigrant became a naturalized citizen. Patriotic Max London, at an advanced age, was an enthusiastic supporter of WWI troops,[436] but unlike Berg he never became a citizen and therefore never voted in an election or served on a jury. An eighty-second-birthday tribute in 1920 in the *Corsicana Daily Sun* explained:

*Mr. London is a naturalized Englishman, his father having become an English citizen before he left that country, and although he has lived in Texas for sixty-five years, he has never taken out naturalization papers. He says that his great affection for Queen Victoria, who honored his family in many ways, prevented him from being naturalized during her lifetime, and after her death he was too old to do so.*[437]

Queen Victoria died in 1901, when London was sixty-three, so it's not clear why he was not naturalized after that—there is no age limit for citizenship. Isaac Adams, for example, a member of Waco's Jewish community, was naturalized in 1922 at the age of eighty-eight.[438] London was in England, as a youth, for only one and a half years[439] but lived in America for his entire adult life. If there is another, unstated explanation, it could be that he held a deep-seated, principled animosity toward the federal government, as shown by his sworn answers to the Federals in 1863 while a prisoner at the Gratiot Street Prison:

*Are you a southern sympathizer? Yes*

*Do you sincerely desire to have the southern people put down in this war, and the authority of the U.S. Government over them restored? No Sir.*[440]

Many years ago, on a delightfully sunny Saturday, a loosened iron rod brought together Max London and Moses Berg somewhere between Blue Corner, the Molloy Hotel, and the hallowed grounds where both are remembered today, well within eyeshot one of the other.

Ω

Citizen or not, every person in the country is supposed to be enumerated in the decennial federal censuses.[441] No 1880 census entry could be found for our hero, but frequently a person's name would be misspelled by a census taker, or, a century or so later, misread by an indexer while creating an online searchable database. In those rare cases when a person should be found in a census, but can't be found, even after checking spelling vari–ations,[442] it's sometimes possible to find the person by address, if their address is known.[443] Census takers went door to door, so everyone is listed in order by where they lived, more or less. In the case of Berg, his 1880 address *is* known, from his naturalization, and his entry in the census was indeed found using this back-door technique.

On June 10, 1880, on behalf of the U.S. Census Bureau, enumerator John Cosgrove visited 516 E. 12th St., in Manhattan's Little Germany neighborhood, Ward 17, next to the Lower East Side.[444] He recorded seven families there, none of them with the name "Berg." George and Elizabeth Hauck, however, had two boarders, Roos Louis and

*Burke Moses*

a white, male, thirty-eight years old,

*H M 38*

occupation "acrobat."

*Acrobat*

Column 15 asks, "Is the person [on the day of the enumerator's visit] sick or temporarily disabled, so as to be unable to attend to ordinary business or duties? If so, what is the sickness or disability?"

*Crippled*

For fifteen years, Berg and his cannonball-deprived left leg performed all around the country. He entertained thousands by walking across a tightrope and hanging from a trapeze. His audiences were of all colors, all religions, all nationalities, and all walks of life—anyone who could get to Main, Market, Broad, Fifth, or Elm at the appointed time. People tossed him a penny, a nickel, or a dime—or nothing at all. He used the gifts given him by God, Fate, and a rebel's cast-iron ball to earn a living. Strength, balance, fortitude, a sense of adventure, and a desire to amaze strangers were the tools he used to navigated murky seas to follow his destiny. *Crippled acrobat* hardly begins to do justice to this wounded warrior's accom-plishments; and yet, there it is—completely accurate.

# Chapter 19

## CERTIFICATIONS

*I care not to perform this part of my task methodically; but shall be content to produce the desired impression by separate citations of items ... and from these citations, I take it—the conclusion aimed at will naturally follow of itself.*

Application for accrued pension

The United States Pension Office was a sprawling bureaucracy in the decades following the Civil War. It sent monthly payments to many thousands of qualifying veterans, their widows, and their orphans. Larger amounts were paid to disabled soldiers, and those with missing limbs, in particular, received premium compensation. The office implemented constant vigilance to root out fraud. Every pensioner had to certify the legitimacy of his or her claim.

Pension Certificate 19378, issued to a disabled private from Co. B, 7th Kan. Cav., entitled him to eighteen dollars per month. After his death his widow requested a catch-up payment to cover an increase to the soldier's monthly money he was due while living but never received. The value of his missing leg had increased, according to federal law, but his monthly pension didn't, and so she applied for an additional payment.

Sarah Berg represented that she and her husband were married on April 10, 1881, in New York, and that he died on March 13, 1883. Her request for an additional six dollars per month, the difference between what he received and what he should have received, covering June 1872 until March 1883, totaling $840, at the time was equivalent to a modest annual salary. If the fees paid to William Morris, who represented her, were not too hefty, Widow Berg would receive a nice windfall.

She submitted supporting documents to meet the stringent requirements of the Pension Office, including a statement from her sister and brother-in-law, Hannah and Marques Ruben, who under oath averred that they were present when the couple got married.

Also personally appeared _Marques Ruben_, residing at _358 East 4th st, New York City_ and _Hannah Ruben_, residing at _same place_, who, being duly sworn, say that they were present and saw _Sarah Berg_ sign her name (make her mark) to the foregoing declaration; that they know her to be the lawful widow of _Moses Berg_, who died on the _13th_ day of _March_, 1883 ; and that their means of knowledge that said parties were husband and wife, and that the husband died on said date, are as follows: _that they were present when said parties were married; that their reason for believing that he is dead is from having read the letters hereto annexed_

(Signature of witnesses.) _Marcus Ruben_
_Hanne Ruben_

Sworn to and subscribed before me on this _8th_ day of _May_, 1883,

**Sworn Statement**

The Rubens' "reason for believing that he is dead is from having read the letter hereto annexed." Regrettably, no such correspondence is at–tached, it is not in the file, and its contents and whereabouts are unknown.

The Pension Office approved Sarah's application, issuing Form 3-562 on Oct. 24, 1883.

**Accrued Pension Approval**

Three other documents were submitted to the Pension Office in support of Sarah's application:

- Marriage Certificate

- Certification of death from the Clerk of the Navarro County Court

- Affidavit by a doctor who treated the soldier after his fall

**Marriage Certificate, April 10, 1881**

Reverend Abraham Wormser of Sheareth Israel, New York City, united in marriage Moses Berg and Sarah Höchster on April 10, 1881. Shearith Israel, known as the Spanish and Portuguese Synagogue, is an historic Manhattan synagogue dating to 1654, the oldest Jewish congregation in the U.S. It is also the name of synagogues in Nashville, San Francisco, and, once upon a time, in Wharton, Texas.[445] It was the name used by Abraham Wormser, with a minor spelling change, for a place of worship at No. 98 Avenue C, one and a half miles southeast from the famed Spanish and Portuguese Synagogue, which, in 1881, was located on 19th Street at 5th Avenue.[446] Wormser, identifying himself as "Reverend," was probably not an ordained rabbi, but if he was a rabbi, he was not a rabbi at New York City's iconic Shearith Israel Synagogue.

The certificate says Berg was *aus Weilar Preussen*, of Weilar, Prussia. *Lippincott's* 1880 edition was consulted. Like all highly respected author–ities—*Roget's*, *Bartlett's*, *Webster's*, and *Hoyle's*—the venerable gazetteer is monoymic.

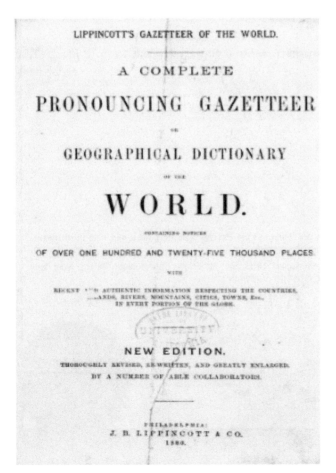

LIPPINCOTT'S GAZETTEER OF THE WORLD.

A COMPLETE

PRONOUNCING GAZETTEER

OR

GEOGRAPHICAL DICTIONARY

OF THE

WORLD.

CONTAINING NOTICES

OF OVER ONE HUNDRED AND TWENTY-FIVE THOUSAND PLACES

WITH

RECENT AND AUTHENTIC INFORMATION RESPECTING THE COUNTRIES,
ISLANDS, RIVERS, MOUNTAINS, CITIES, TOWNS, Etc.,
IN EVERY PORTION OF THE GLOBE.

NEW EDITION.

THOROUGHLY REVISED, RE-WRITTEN, AND GREATLY ENLARGED.
BY A NUMBER OF ABLE COLLABORATORS.

PHILADELPHIA:
J. B. LIPPINCOTT & CO.
1880.

*Lippincott's Gazetteer of the World* (1880)

Weilar, it says, is a village in Central Germany, in Saxe-Weimar, southeast of Lengsfeld, on the Fulda River. This is neither in, nor near, Prussia. Further down the page is a town with a similar spelling, "Weiler, or Weiller." That town is in Alsace—also not Prussia, but closer. Some newspaper articles said Prof. De Houne was an Alsatian, so the marriage certificate was possibly filled out incorrectly, maybe by someone other than the groom, someone who mistakenly thought Weilar, the groom's birthplace, was in Prussia. Or maybe Weilar, Prussia, was not one of the 125,000-plus places listed in the "thoroughly revised, rewritten, and greatly enlarged by a number of able collaborators" 1880 edition of *Lippincott's*. "Weiler" is the German word for "hamlet,"[447] so might it have been put on the certificate as some sort of generic place name placeholder? Weilar, according to *Lippincott's*, is something not in in the State of Prussia.

**WEI** 2371

**Weil,** a town of Switzerland. See WYL.
**Weilar,** wī'lar, a village of Central Germany, in Saxe-Weimar, S.E. of Lengsfeld, on the Fulda.
**Weilbach,** wīl'bäk, a watering-place of Nassau, E.S.E. of Wiesbaden, with a mineral spring, from which about 70,000 bottles of water are annually exported. Pop. 574.
**Weilburg,** wīl'böörg, a town of Prussia, province of Hesse-Nassau, on the Lahn, here crossed by an iron suspension-bridge, 28 miles N.N.E. of Wiesbaden. Pop. 2831. It has a castle, and manufactures of paper.
**Weil-die-Stadt,** wīl-dee-stätt, a town of Würtemberg, circle of Neckar, 13 miles W.S.W. of Stuttgart. Pop. 1765. It has manufactures of woollens and tobacco, and is the birthplace of Kepler.
**Weile, and Weilefiord.** See VEILE.
**Weiler, or Weiller,** a town of Alsace. See VILLÉ.
**Weilerbach,** wī'ler-bäk', a village of Bavaria, Palatinate, canton and near Kaiserslautern.
**Weilheim,** wīl'hīme, a walled town of Upper Bavaria,

Entry for Weilar in *Lippincott's Gazetteer of the World* (1880), p. 2371

Ω

Leaving the entry of his birthplace for another time, the next chapter presents solid evidence of Rope Walker's identity: a death certification and an affidavit by a doctor who tried to save him. A man of flesh and blood returns from oblivion.

# Chapter 20

## KERRSICANA

*So far as what there may be of a narrative in this book; and, indeed, as indirectly touching one or two very interesting and curious particulars … requires to be still further and more familiarly enlarged upon, in order to be adequately understood, and moreover to take away any incredulity which a profound ignorance of the entire subject may induce in some minds, as to the natural verity of the main points of this affair.*

Kerr families were all over early Texas. Those bearing the Scottish surname were some of the Old Three Hundred, the settlers of Stephen Austin's colony in the 1820s. One of them was the namesake for Kerr County and its county seat, Kerrville. Men named Kerr fell at the Alamo.[448]

Two Kerr families lived in Corsicana, both producing important citizens in the town's early years. It's easy to see how the two were confused: at the head of each was a James Kerr who was born in North Carolina and came to Texas via Tennessee. In 1883, two Corsicana Kerrs, one from each family, knew Rope Walker's true and correct name.

## Judge S.H. Kerr

At the head of the larger and better-known Corsicana Kerrs were James, a lawyer, and Nancy (Ross) Kerr. Both were born in North Carolina in 1788 and migrated to central Tennessee where they were some of the earliest settlers of Maury County. They moved to Corsicana in 1852 when it was just a toddler and the State of Texas not much older. "Corsicana was then a small place, being in fact only a straggling village"[449] with only primitive accommodations for new settlers. There was no stock of houses to purchase, and the family struggled in its first years.

Of their eight Kerr children, five, all sons, came to Corsicana with the parents. The oldest child, Andrew R., a teacher, met an untimely death in Mississippi, around 1848, and two married daughters remained in Ten– nessee. James and Nancy died in Corsicana in 1859 and 1865, respectively. One of the children, known as James Sr. (although his father was also James), born in North Carolina in 1817, was a highly respected and pro– ductive Corsicana citizen. Two others were physicians, David G. in Navarro County and William elsewhere in Texas. Calvin P. Kerr, the youngest in the family, was a popular Corsicanan.[450]

Samuel Harris Kerr is the son of interest here. He was a positive and influential presence in Corsicana from his first arrival, in November 1852, until his death, on Nov. 7, 1894, just shy of his seventy-first birthday. S.H. Kerr, as he was known, was born Dec. 24, 1823, in Maury County, Tenn., and raised there. He married Catherine Delia Smith on Oct. 20, 1846, at Lewisburg, Tenn.[451]

**Court House in Corsicana Burnt.**

On Tuesday night last the Court-House in this place was burned down. The burning is no doubt the work of an incendiary. The fire is said to have commenced in the District Clerk's office; the most of the papers of his office were burned. The thanks of our citizens are due to J P. Shipley, Thomas Johnson and John Bright who bravely rushed in the house and saved the greater portion of the papers belonging to the County Clerk's office, also to S.H. Kerr, T. J. Haines, and A. G. Birdsong, Esq., and others who aided

EXAMINATION OF MR. KERR'S SCHOOL.—
On last Friday Mr. Kerr had an examination of his students at this place. The day was pleasant and we noticed many friends and patrons of the school in attendance. Our duties were such, as not to allow our attendance throughout the exercises but we are informed the young men and ladies, acquitted themselves nobly—answering all questions put to them with a readiness, that clearly told that they had received the best of instructions. from able and learned teachers. At night there was an exhibition. Speeches were delivered and dialogues enacted, which would

Side-by-side articles about S.H. Kerr, 1855

For his first five years or so in Corsicana, S.H. Kerr taught primary school, a profession he had followed in Tennessee, and then he went into the wagon and buggy business. He was selected as foreman for the Corsicana District Court Grand Jury in 1859[452] and in 1861 was elected judge of Navarro County, an office he held for five years. In 1873 he became deputy clerk of the county and district courts and in 1876 he was elected county clerk, an office he held until 1886.[453]

*The records of the County Court are largely the work of his hands, and they give abundant evidence of the care and efficiency with which he served the people of Navarro county in one of the most responsible positions within their gift.*[454]

The large, hefty ledger books recording Navarro County official business from those years are testament to his industriousness as county clerk. Innumerable transactions are listed, all in his hand, all with his signature.

Judge Kerr had eight children, nearly all of them Corsicana residents.[455] His daughter, Louisa Pratt Mulkey, wife of Abe Mulkey, was introduced back in Chapter 15. The Mulkey home, in fact, was built at the public square, where S.H. Kerr once had his buggy shop.[456] Frank S., another child, married Ada Taylor, daughter of Corsicana's first mayor.[457]

Judge Kerr's certification of Moses Berg's death, dated Sept. 13, 1883, was filed in the U.S. Pension Office as part of Sarah Berg's application:

Certification of death

Sept. 13, 1883

I, S.H. Kerr

Clerk of the County Court within and for Navarro County and Ex Officio Recorder.

Do hereby certify that Moses Berg Died in the City of Corsicana Texas On the 13th day of March A.D. 1883.

To Certify which I hereunto Set my hand and Seal of Office at Corsicana Texas this Sept. 13th 1883

S.H. Kerr Clerk

County Court

Navarro County,

Texas.

No Regular Record of Deaths Required by law in my office, but certify the above from my Personal Knowledge as county clerk.

you can forward $4.00 for certificate and affidavit of Dr. W.J.W. Kerr.

S.H. Kerr

The closing request for payment for an "affidavit of Dr. W.J.W. Kerr" segues nicely into Corsicana's other Kerr family.

## Dr. W.J.W. Kerr

William Jacob Warren Kerr was a longtime Corsicana doctor and the official county physician for Navarro County in the 1880s and early 1890s. He was also a surgeon for the H&TC Railroad and an examining surgeon for insurance companies.

William Jacob Warren Kerr

His father, a Cumberland Presbyterian min–ister from the age of twenty-one, was James Milas Kerr, born in 1811 near Charlotte, N.C. Rev–erend Kerr was brought to Giles County, Tenn., in 1823, and ten years later married Delia Newton Lowrance, Dr. Kerr's mother. She was the daughter of Lt. Jacob Lowrance, a Revo–lutionary War veteran. Rev. James and Delia (Lowrance) Kerr had two other children, also sons: Donnell Hugh Modell "D.H.M." Kerr and James Carson Reid "J.C.R." Kerr, both Navarro County farmers. Delia Kerr died in 1880 and Rev. Kerr died at his son Donnell's farm, near Chatfield, on Aug. 8, 1896.[458] All three boys served for the entirety of the Civil War and all lived into their eighties, an unusual feat for three brothers.[459]

Dr. W.J.W. Kerr, as he was known, was born in Giles County on Dec. 1, 1834. He married at the age of nineteen to Martha J. Nelson[460] and they had one child, Albert, born in Tennessee, in 1854. Martha died in 1870, and that year the doctor remarried to Martha Caroline "Mattie" Cowan, age twenty-four, a South Carolina native. At the age of thirty-seven, in 1872, he moved to Corinth, Miss., where he practiced medicine. He also was a doctor for a few years at nearby Kossuth. His extended Kerr family moved to Texas, arriving in Corsicana in January, 1873.[461] Reverend and Mrs. Kerr stayed for about a year, and then moved to Chatfield with other family members while Dr. Kerr remained in Corsicana.[462] Mattie, Dr. Kerr's second wife, gave birth to four children, of whom two survived to adult–hood: James Wade Kerr and Maggie Sanders, wife of Samuel Sanders of Fort Worth. Mattie succumbed to "floating spleen exhaustion" in 1897 at the age of fifty-one.[463] The doctor married for a third time, to Mary Ellen (Smith) Burge, a widow. She survived him and died in 1936.[464]

Dr. Kerr was self-educated from an early age with a keen interest in mathematics and at one point was a teacher. In 1859 he studied medicine at Nashville, and by 1860, apparently not yet a graduate, he nevertheless identified himself as a physician.[465] Following the war, in June, 1865, he returned to West Tennessee,[466] resumed his studies, and graduated at Nash–ville in 1869.[467]

W.J.W. Kerr proposed the creation of the Odd Fellows Orphans Home at the Grand Encampment and Grand Lodge of Paris, Texas.[468] He was an IOOF Grand Patriarch, a Mason, and a member of the Knights of Honor. He was medical director of the Texas Division of the United Confederate Veterans, holding the rank of colonel; surgeon at Camp Winkler, the UCV home in Corsicana; and a member of the Cumberland Presbyterian Church. Dr. Kerr died at home in Corsicana on Nov. 12, 1916, following a lengthy illness. He was eighty-one.

Dr. Kerr's affidavit bears the date of Sept. 13, 1883, the same as Judge Kerr's death certification. It was the third document Sarah Berg submitted to the Pension Bureau with her application.

Physician's
Affidavit

*Matter of the claim of Sarah Berg as widow of Moses Berg late a pensioner under Certificate No. 19378 for accrued pension to date of soldiers death*

*State of Texas County of Navarro ss:*

*W.J.W. Kerr being duly sworn says he is a practicing physician & surgeon, that he resides at Corsicana, Texas; that on the 6th day of March 1883 deponent and Drs. S.F. Starley, J.M. Blair, H.F. Witherspoon and A.C. Sloan found it necessary owing to fractures sustained by falling from a tight-rope to amputate the right leg of Moses Berg late a soldier whose left leg had been amputated prior thereto and to deponents personal knowledge said Moses Berg died at Corsicana, Texas on the 13th day of March 1883 in consequence of said injuries & Surgical operation above described.*

*That he has no interest in this claim and that his post office address is Corsicana Texas.*     *W.J.W. Kerr, M.D.*

*Sworn to & subscribed before me this 13th day of Sept. 1883 and I hereby certify that affiant is well known to me to be a practicing physician in good professional standing and that I have no interest in the matter.*

*To certify which I hereunto Set my hand and Seal of office at Corsicana Texas this Sept. 13th A.D. 1883*

*S.H. Kerr clerk*

*County Court*

*Navarro County Texas*

The five surgeons who operated on Berg were seasoned medical men with impressive credentials, decades of experience, and sterling reputa—tions—no simple country doctors they. These were authors of journal articles and leaders of medical societies. Nearly all of them served in the Civil War.

Doctors S.F. (Silas Fletcher) Starley, J.M. (James Monroe) Blair, H.F. (Hezekiah Ford) Witherspoon, and A.C. (Alexander Colvin) Sloan, with Dr. W.J.W. Kerr, amputated the right leg

♎

John W. Gulick was not one of them. He certainly had as much experience as the other five, having once been a regimental surgeon. The popular town doctor in 1886 had his office right at the intersection where the accident happened.[469] In fact, Gulick and Kerr had their practices in the same building, as shown in Chapter 14, and therefore might very well have had a joint practice.

Gulick garnered the utmost respect from his fellow doctors. The bio—graphical note reproduced in Chapter 15 describes him as

> *a man who has always enjoyed the unbounded confidence of those among whom he has practiced and is highly esteemed also by his medical brethren. He has always made it a point to be honest with himself and with his patients, not pre—tending to do more than he could do nor assuming to know more than he really knew. He is a great stickler for the ethics of his profession, being always courteous to his medical brethren.*[470]

Although Gulick was not listed as one of the surgeons who operated on the injured rope walker, he may have helped to care for him just the same, either immediately after the fall or during the ten days between the stranger's fall and death. For some unknown reason, Gulick did not join his medical brethren in the O.R. The one doctor named in the legend, oddly enough, was not one of five doctors named in the historic record.

# Chapter 21

## CONFEDERATE DOCTORS

*I would fain advance naught but substantiated facts. But after embattling his facts, an advocate who should wholly suppress a not unreasonable surmise, which might tell eloquently upon his cause—such an advocate, would he not be blameworthy?*

If anyone in Corsicana, besides the Kerrs, knew anything about Rope Walker—his name, for starters—it would have been the four other surgeons named in Dr. Kerr's affidavit. Wouldn't their care for their patient bridge the cool currents that usually flow between strangers, as they tried to nurse him back to life, as they took off part of his leg? Wouldn't they have told Max London and others in the Jewish community what they knew about the identity of the man, when they turned over the corpse for burial?

Newspaper accounts disagreed on whether doctors could "save the leg." A broken leg, in those days, was dangerously at risk of infection, gangrene, and other complications, one of the reasons why medical tents during the Civil War raised mounds of sawed-off arms and legs. Many thousands of veterans had missing limbs. Eighteen years after the end of the war, in a guestroom at Molloy's hotel, a highly experienced medical team exercised its professional duty and removed one more soldier's leg. How many amputations did those five surgeons perform during the war, and later due to train accidents and such, before they removed Berg's right leg? Hundreds? Probably more. How many agonizing deaths did they witness? Thousands. Dr. Kerr alone, based on his wartime experience, witnessed the deaths of several thousand men.

Doctors Starley, Kerr, and Blair, in 1883, were well-established Corsi-cana residents. Witherspoon and Sloan were longtime residents of nearby towns, Chatfield and Dresden. All were married with families. Some had lost a wife or children to early deaths. Dr. Starley had thirteen children, but only eight outlived him. Dr. Blair had ten, and only six survived him. All except Dr. Blair had lost their first wife by 1883. These men knew death and suffering—on the battlefield, in their own homes, in the homes of their neighbors, and in the streets in and around Corsicana. These were the times they lived in—a bloody war, a lost cause, and life-and-death struggles in a frontier Texas town.

## Dr. Kerr, Redux

Dr. W.J.W. Kerr's biography, in the previous chapter, left out his military experience and the role he played in Civil War history, a dramatic scene which began to play out around three quarters of the way through the course of the war.

**When the conflict between the North and South burst upon the country, the Doctor enlisted in Ford's Battalion of Graybeards, being a company of 118 large men, 116 of whom were married, and represented 516 children.**[471]

During a period of illness he was taken prisoner near Jackson, Tennessee, and held for several months at Camp Douglas, on the south side of Chicago, and later, in the winter of 1862, at Point Lookout Prison. Camp Douglas has been judged the worst of Union prison camps, and Point Lookout, in Maryland, while not as bad, was also subject to overcrowding and other deprivations.[472] Dr. Kerr was part of a prisoner exchange, in 1863, and then became a hospital steward and assistant surgeon, working in the field and in hospitals. In the summer of 1863 he had charge of the smallpox hospital at Chattanooga, and after that, was a surgeon on a train.[473]

He was then assigned to Camp Sumter, in Georgia, which was outfitted to hold Union prisoners. Located near a railroad depot named Anderson, the prison quickly became known as "Andersonville."[474] He was hospital steward[475] under the command of Captain Henry Wirz and served out the remainder of the war there. Prison conditions at Andersonville represented one of the most infamous chapters in Civil War history. Internment there was tantamount to a death sentence. After the war, Captain Wirz, Dr. Kerr, and several others were indicted by the U.S. government for inhumane treatment of Union prisoners. Wirz was singled out for committing specific acts of cruelty and murder. Evidence against him was that he not only ordered others to commit atrocities, but he committed murder by his own hand as well. While much of the court testimony was hearsay, nonetheless, he was convicted. Wirz was hung in Washington on November 10, 1865.

A number of historians say Wirz was a scapegoat, blamed for deplorable conditions over which he had no control. He tried to get more food, better water, and to improve conditions. Overcrowding in the camp was due in part to the inability of the two sides to exchange prisoners. Critics cite the equally horrible conditions in Union prison camps, like Douglas and Point Lookout, and observe that a larger percentage of prisoners died in Union camps than Confederate camps. The South was severely in need of supplies for its own troops, so prisoners, predictably, were a lesser priority. It was observed that many guards at Andersonville also suffered and died from hunger and disease, albeit nowhere near the same rate as the prisoners.

Andersonville opened in February 1864, and by the end of April there were close to ten thousand prisoners, its full capacity. In another six weeks its population doubled, and by mid-summer, 1864, it had tripled, to over thirty thousand prisoners. It was horrifically unhealthy, with open sewage, no clean water for drinking or bathing, food shortages, and no shelter from the sweltering heat. Disease was so rampant that nearly one third of those imprisoned died. At its peak, more than a hundred prisoners dropped dead each day.[476]

Dr. Kerr was a man of many accomplishments and accolades,[477] "a man of good mind and strong and resolute character, and always took an active and zealous position in any course he espoused."[478] Additionally, the *Sun* wrote,

> *[Kerr] knows doubtless as much Confederate history as any man living, for the reason that he spent four full years of the war in positions which gave him an opportunity to not only see history made but to be a part of its making ...*[479]

One thing more than anything defined Kerr's legacy—his time at Andersonville. Indicted with Kerr and Wirz were C.S.A. President Jefferson Davis; General R.B. Winder, who was nominally in charge of the camp; the surgeons who ran the hospital; and others. Curiously, in no instance in the trial record was Kerr's first name or initials used, unlike every other defendant, even to the point that hundreds (maybe thousands) of newspaper articles, quoting the court order condemning Wirz to die, referred to him as "——— Kerr, late Hospital Steward at Andersonville."

Following Kerr's death, the *Sun* published a letter written by his friend, Menzies Cumming, who warmly remembered Kerr and praised his con–tribution to the founding of the IOOF Orphans Home. No mention was made of Kerr's time at Andersonville, but Cumming said Kerr left a

> *monument ... that would prove "this world was made better, that he lived in it" ... his published vindication of "The True Character of Capt. Henry Wirz" ...*[480]

No record of criminal proceedings against Kerr has been found. One obituary said he served time in a "federal prison," but the ambiguous state–ment might have been referring to his time as a prisoner of war.[481]

Ulysses S. Grant, secretary of war *ad interim*, on Dec. 5, 1867, submitted to Congress the court record of the trial of Henry Wirz.[482] Dr. Amos Thornburg testified he had a concern that requisitioned hospital supplies were not being received, that they were diverted elsewhere:

> **Mr. Kerr, to convince me that these things were sent in, showed me the weekly statement for that week. In looking at it I remarked that those things never came into the hospital—at least, that no considerable part of them had come in ... and we began to talk about having an investigation. ...and on examination we found that large quantities of things which appeared by the book to have been bought had never come into the hospital.**[483]

Nothing further about missing hospital supplies is mentioned in the transcript.

The testimony of Benjamin F. Dilley was particularly damning. Dilley stated that robbing of care packages for prisoners was done by "Wirz's sergeants," of whom Kerr was one.[484] Referring to Kerr, Dilley testified:

> **I have seen him come into the hospital enclosure and strike a man across the face with his pistol for merely standing and talking to a guard. He carried a heavy pistol. He would strike a man right across the forehead. This he did frequently, although I never saw him do it but once, but I saw men whom he had struck. Once he robbed a man. He went and took some staff buttons [used as money in the camp].**[485]

Witnesses' testimony can be believed or not believed, but Dilley's was highly credible because he had been an Andersonville prisoner and was actually testifying in *favor* of Captain Wirz.[486]

Dr. Kerr's role in Andersonville was discussed in *A True History of Andersonville Prison: A Defense of Major Henry Wirz* (1908). Second Lieutenant James Madison Page, Co. A, 6th Mich. Cav., another Andersonville prisoner, in collaboration with author Michael Joachim Haley wrote, at page 87:

> **Chief among the surgeons were Drs. White, Stevenson and Kerr and no medical men, North or South performed their duty more laboriously or conscientiously than the above named gentlemen.**

## Dr. Silas Fletcher Starley

S.F. Starley was one of the top surgeons in Texas when, at the age of fifty-eight, he assisted in the amputation of a trapezist's right leg.

Born in Autaga County, Alabama, Sept. 5, 1824, Silas Fletcher Starley was the son of Daniel and Rebecca (Thomas) Starley. His father died before he was six and his mother remarried to Reason Franklin. He was educated at Hayneville Academy in Alabama and received his medical degree from the University of Louisville in March, 1854.

In 1842, living in Nacogdoches, Republic of Texas, Starley's stepfather Reason Franklin made a contract with one John Mooney wherein Franklin would pay Mooney $150 if Mooney would be a military "substitute" for young Silas. Mooney signed up to fight against Mexico, as agreed, and Silas was spared military service. The contract was the subject of an 1847 court decision, one of the earliest in Texas state history. Franklin had refused to pay Mooney because Mooney didn't actually go to Mexico and didn't have to do any fighting. Franklin lost the suit and had to pay Mooney the money, plus interest.[487]

Dr. Starley married Nancy Skinner at Nacogdoches on Oct. 19, 1842.[488] Their first child, William F. Starley, was born a year later and after another year the doctor perfected his headright certificate to get title to 320 acres in the county.[489] In 1859 he inherited his stepfather's 440-acre estate in Cher–okee County, including cattle.[490]

In 1860, Starley and his second wife, Margaret, lived in Springfield, Limestone County, adjacent to Bertha London's Simon family, as shown in Chapter 16. At the time, Starley had six children living at home: William F.; Martha A.; Jonathan F.; Amaretta; Emma R.; and Lockland A. Other children, born later, were Emma I.; Lemuel; Mary L.; Maggie B.; Sallie O.; and a second Lockland.

Starley lived in Fairfield, in nearby Freestone County, prior to his 1874 arrival in Corsicana.[491] He registered to practice in Navarro County on Apr. 11, 1874. Two of his sons, William and Jonathan, were also licensed physicians in the county, also starting their practices in the 1870s.[492]

**Silas Fletcher Starley**

During the war, Starley was a surgeon with the CSA, but he was dismissed, in January 1863, "having been rejected by the Army Medical Board," probably due to age.[493] His son-in-law, L.J. Farrar, on the other hand, served in Parson's Brigade at Little Rock and rose to the rank of Battalion Major. Farrar became a state senator in 1882, representing the citizens of Navarro, Freestone, and Limestone Counties.[494]

Starley received an honorary degree from the Medical Department of Soule University, Chappell Hill, Texas, in 1867. His specialty was obstetrics and gynecology and several articles he wrote were published in distinguished medical journals, especially in the 1880s.[495] He was surgeon for the H&TC Railroad for the nine years he lived in Corsicana and was elected president of Navarro County's Board of Medical Examiners for three terms. He ascended the leadership ranks of the prestigious Texas Medical Association and became its president in 1882.

In Sept. 1879 he joined other leading citizens, including Jewish merchants Fox, Cerf, and Raphael, to create a large lake and standpipe outside of Corsicana to supply the town with water, primarily for firefighting. This was completed in 1883, at which time the first fire department in town was organized.[496]

In 1883 he moved to Tyler. On April 24, 1883, at the Tyler Opera House, he led the annual meeting of the Texas Medical Association,[497] only a little more than a month after he operated on Moses Berg. Then, only weeks after the conference, his unmarried daughter, Mary, about nineteen years old, died of pneumonia.[498]

Dr. Starley died in Tyler on Dec. 19, 1887.[499]

*In the death of this estimable gentleman and able physician, the whole State of Texas has suffered a severe loss, and the State Medical Association has lost one of its oldest, ablest and most zealous co-laborers. But three short years ago, Dr. Starley, then, though past 60 years, in the prime and vigor of manhood, presided with dignity over the deliberations of that body at Belton, and contributed much to the eclat which has caused that meeting to occupy a brilliant page in the medical history of Texas.*[500]

Tributes included a resolution from a committee of Tyler physicians:

### IN MEMORIAM.

*... as a physician and surgeon Dr. Starley stood in the front rank of the profession in Texas, and has contributed largely to the development of medical science in this State. ... In his relations, personal and professional, to his medical brethren he was ever affable, generous, courteous and kind, always ready, and with apparent disregard of self, to assist a brother physician in any way that he could; as a citizen and member of society, he at all times, met in full measure the demands of his station.*[501]

## Dr. Hezekiah Ford Witherspoon

Ford Witherspoon—he went by his middle name—was forty-eight when he and four other surgeons operated on an injured tightrope artist. He was born in Mississippi, probably Franklin County,[502] and by 1850 he was living in Texas, in Marshall.

In September 1861 President Davis appointed him Assistant Surgeon to the 9th La. Inf., a regiment that suffered high casualties. In the summer and fall of 1862 those troops served as part of Stonewall's Brigade in Maryland and fought at Antietam where a mutual slaughter in September left tens of

thousands dead. Witherspoon was captured, but re-leased in a prisoner exchange a few months later. He took ill after that and was hospitalized for several months in Petersburg and Richmond, Virginia, and then resigned on Feb. 29, 1864.[503] Following the war he joined his brother, Norris, who was then a doctor in Chatfield, a dozen miles north of Corsicana.

Witherspoon was the son of John Ford and Maria (Cheney) Witherspoon, the paternal line from South Carolina and the maternal line Louisiana. His first marriage was to Martha Ellin "Mattie" Hodge, in 1868, but four short years later she was dead, at the age of twenty-two.[504] They had a son, Robert Hodge

**Hezekiah Ford Witherspoon**

Witherspoon, and a daughter, Nettie. The doctor remarried to Lena Clara Newman, twenty-seven years his junior, and two more children were born: Tenie, who married Walter Holsey and lived in Corsicana, and H. Ford Witherspoon, who became an oil company executive in San Antonio. The Witherspoons' Corsicana household in 1880 consisted of the doctor, forty-five; his wife Lena, nineteen; his son Robert, nine; and his mother-in-law, Meg Newman, forty-three. Robert was enumerated that year a second time, with his grandparents, the Hodges, who ran a store and operated a cotton gin in Chatfield for fifty years.[505]

Ford's brother, Dr. Abel Norris Nelson Witherspoon, married Lena's sister, Dora Newman, in 1872. There was a twenty-six-year age difference between those two. A.N. Witherspoon lived in Corsicana before the Civil War, one of the town's many residents who owned slaves.[506]

Dr. H.F. Witherspoon died in 1894, at the age of sixty. Mrs. Lena (New-man) Witherspoon died in 1928, aged sixty-seven.

## Dr. James Monroe Blair

J.M. Blair was a native of Tennessee and sixty years old when a German Jew from New York lost his second leg to him in Texas. An 1849 graduate of Transylvania University, at Lexington, Kentucky,[507] in the 1860s James M. Blair and his family lived in Henderson, Rusk County, Texas,[508] and then came to Corsicana sometime in the 1870s. He was married to Elizabeth Upton (1825-1904) for more than fifty years[509] and they had ten children, six of them outliving their parents.[510]

Their oldest child was Annie, born in 1848, who married Dixon Bolling Hall, from a prominent Alabama family, and settled in Henderson. Second oldest was William S., who also became a Corsicana doctor. Mary and Bettie, who may have been twins, were next. The remaining children were Nannie, James, Upton, Inez M., and Helen Martha "Mattie." Mattie, born in 1869,[511] and her husband, Joseph P. Goodman, were longtime Corsicanans.[512] James Jr. was stabbed to death in 1885. Daughter Mary married James Kerr, a nephew of Judge Kerr.

Son Upton Blair (1864-1923)[513] was a locomotive engineer and president of Corsicana's Texas League baseball club. His team is famous for its 1902 record of twenty-seven consecutive wins. The team set another record that year, on Sunday, June 15, when they killed the Texarkana Casketmakers, 51-3.[514]

On the day Rope Walker fell, Dr. Blair's nephew, James B. Upton, of Stillwater, Tenn., was visiting his Corsicana relatives. The young man was there to improve his health and left to return home on March 13. He dropped dead on a train station platform in Houston while waiting for the Knoxville train. It was the same day another patient of Dr. Blair, an itinerant acrobat, surrendered to his injuries. Dr. Blair retrieved his nephew's body the next day. Said the *Fort Worth Daily Gazette*, "deceased was consumptive and had no hope of living long when he was [in Corsicana]."[515] In that same report of Corsicana news, Upton's death was the topmost of five items and a rope walker's death the fourth item, more newsworthy than the last item, about a runaway mule (Chapter 12).

Dr. Blair was almost forty when the Civil War started, too old for the draft. There is no record of his participation in the war, the only one of the five doctors (six, if Dr. Gulick is included) who did not serve. His sons were too young to fight. Another reason Blair may have avoided service was the Confederate States' slave exemption. Initiated in 1862, it allowed one (white) man to forgo service for every twenty slaves owned, later lowered to fifteen.[516] In the slave schedule to the 1860 U.S. census Blair is listed as the owner sixteen slaves, ranging in age from three months to fifty-eight, half males and half females, in the town of Henderson.[517] In 1850, ten years earlier and recently married, Dr. and Mrs. Blair only had nine slaves, although her father, Thomas L. Upton, living nearby, owned thirty-five.[518]

A household of African Americans was enumerated directly following Dr. Blair's family in the 1870 census. Polly Blair, Lorenzo Blair, Charles Blair, and Jack Upton undoubtedly received their surnames from their former "owners."

Blairs, black and white, Henderson, Texas, 1870. Columns: Name, Age, Sex, and Color.

Ten-year-old Betsey Camsan (?) was a "Domestic Servant" (not shown) to the white Blairs.

Inez Blair (last entry) was enumerated with the black Blairs, but with the help of an arrow (not shown) her entry is moved up seven rows, reuniting her with her white family.

Dr. Blair, a longtime Corsicana resident, did not possess the professional acclaim of the other doctors—no biography of him or publication authored by him could be found.[519] He died in 1903 and was buried in Corsicana's Oakwood Cemetery.

## Dr. Alexander Colvin Sloan

Dr. Sloan was just about forty when he participated in removing the last leg of a crippled acrobat. A native of Montgomery, Alabama, he received his medical degree from Louisville University on March 12, 1869.[520] Dr. Sloan registered as a Navarro County physician in 1873.[521]

His parents, Hugh Sr. and Eliza (Colvin) Sloan, emigrated from North Carolina to Alabama in 1842, where they farmed and brought up a family of nine children. In 1850, Hugh Sr. had a plantation with ten slaves in Lowndes, Alabama, while the nearby Colvin family, presumably relatives of Mrs. Sloan, also used a sizeable number of enslaved workers. Moving to Texas, Dr. Sloan's parents first lived at Hill County and later at Ellis County. Several of their offspring also lived in Texas, including Alexander's much younger brother, Hugh Jr., who was also a Navarro County doctor.[522]

**Alexander Colvin Sloan**

A.C. Sloan's early education was at the Magnolia Academy in Montgomery. At the age of seventeen, in 1861, he enlisted with the 1st Ala. Cav. and served with that regiment until the surrender. He was wounded three times and two of his horses were killed.[523] After the war he completed his education and came to Dresden, fifteen miles west of Corsicana, where he practiced medicine for twelve years. He spent a year in Europe attending Guy's Medical College, in London, and upon his return, in 1882, he studied at Bellevue Hospital Medical College in New York. In 1882 or early 1883 he came to Corsicana and again took up the practice of medicine. A physician and surgeon with a broad range of interests in medicine, Dr. Sloan established a highly successful practice which allowed him to acquire extensive real estate holdings in Corsicana and elsewhere in Navarro County.[524]

His first marriage was to Lucy N. Shackelford. They had two children, Alex Y. and Benjamin L., and another child, Lucy Ruth, died in infancy. The doctor's wife died at Dresden, in 1879, and five years later he married again to Henrietta "Etta" Ornsby Blanding of Sumter, S.C. They had one child, James Blanding Sloan. Three years after Etta's 1888 death he married Leila F. Smith, of Oxford, Miss.[525] A.C. Sloan died in Corsicana on Nov. 30, 1906. His widow lived to eighty-six, dying in Corsicana in 1945.[526] Their final resting place is Oakwood Cemetery.

Gravestone of A.C. Sloan,
Oakwood Cemetery,
Corsicana

*NOT ON THIS PERISHING STONE, BUT IN THE BOOK OF LIFE, AND IN THE HEARTS OF HIS AFFLICTED FRIENDS, IS HIS WORTH RECORDED*

Sloan's epitaph is a sentiment commonly found on children's gravestones, throughout the U.S., usually beginning with: "Farewell/Thy years were few but thy virtues many."

Sloan's ultimate legacy is rendered in large, block letters:

**A CHRISTIAN AND SOLDIER**

♎

Before Professor De Houne fell, he likely told the crowd gathered on Beaton Street he was a confederate veteran, the same thing he told his audiences in other southern towns. In the North he told crowds the truth, but not in Dixie. At what point did those five confederate doctors and his temporary hospital host, hotel owner Henry Molloy, realize he was lying about his wartime affiliation? How did they feel about him collecting money while masquerading as a Johnny Reb, when in reality he may have killed their family, their neighbors, their friends, and for that matter, their economic livelihood and their way of life?

They found him out at some point. The pension certificate Berg would have carried with him (so he could collect his payments) gave his full legal name and identified the regiment with which he served. The certificate would have revealed to the doctors, Henry Molloy, Max London, to the whole town that this injured rope walker was a lying, carpetbagging Yankee, and the very worst of that kind: a Jayhawker, a soldier of the Kansas 7th Cavalry, the most despised regiment in the entire Union army, one of those lawless brigands who tried to justify their crimes as high-minded fighters against slavery.[527] And not only that: the Rope Walker legend says Berg pretended to be a Christian, only to reveal later he was a Jew. Lies upon lies, an affront to Christian and Jew alike. At least one of the doctors, Dr. Sloan, was deadly serious about his faith.

How did these men feel about spending their valuable time and energy dealing with the predictable outcome of this deceitful man's foolish,

ridiculously dangerous circus stunt, carrying a stove across a rope with a peg
leg? These men of consequence, with critically important responsibilities,
must have been angry beyond limit. Dr. Blair was trying to care for his
deathly ill nephew. Dr. Starley was preparing to lead a medical meeting that
would cap his illustrious career, and probably attending to his sick daughter.
Instead of their patients and family, who deserved their valuable attention,
they were laboring to save the limb and life of this pathetic imposter.

Only one thing is known about what happened during Moses Berg's
final ten days, after his agonizing descent but before that final blissful ascent
awaiting all mortals—he was cut down by a foot. One can speculate as to
what else transpired during those days and nights, what Berg said to the
people with whom he interacted and what they said to him.

The presumption must be that all the doctors were men of integrity with
extraordinary dedication to their profession and that they did their utmost.
They had all taken an oath and subscribed to the American Medical
Association Code of Ethics, which was established long before the Civil
War. Without proof to the contrary, it is only fair to assume their efforts to
save the soldier were sincere and thorough.

Ill feelings against a manipulator like Professor De Houne might not
have affected the doctors, to keep them from carrying out their medical
duties, but other Corsicanans may have felt an artillery of resentment against
him. The town was filled with people who had lost sons, husbands, and
brothers in the war. Henry Molloy lost one brother (R.B. Molloy's father)
to bushwhackers, who were probably considered Jayhawkers, even if tech–
nically they were not from the Kansas 7th Cavalry,[528] and another brother, a
beloved town educator and captain, was killed in battle. Corsicanans like
Max London suffered deplorable conditions in Union prison camps. All
Southerners suffered a demoralizing defeat, years of economic hardship,
and humiliating, forced attempts at social rehabilitation under their victors'
ideas of racial justice: Reconstruction. If De Houne had successfully
performed in Corsicana, pleading for donations as a poor, crippled, Con–
federate veteran, and was then exposed as a fake—and one of Jennison's
Jayhawkers to boot—he would have been run out of town, if he were lucky,
and likely would have suffered a lot worse. The Jayhawkers' reputation was
no less than thieves and murderers. So reviled was the Jayhawker that it was
used as an epithet and applied to anyone who fought for the end of slavery.
This lying, dirty-dealing, thieving, negro-loving Yankee would have had
good reason to be concerned for his life as he lay helpless on that hotel
room bed. They won't forget and they'll continue to stage Confederate
Memorial Day parades.

It's not too far-fetched to surmise that some dastardly deed occurred in the makeshift operating room. Surrounding the fallen acrobat were these ex-Confederates, one an accused war criminal—a real tough character. One doctor once owned sixteen slaves. As Christians, maybe they subscribed to the biblical mandate for retribution: an eye for an eye. Here they had their sacrificial lamb, their scapegoat, a non-believer, a fraud, a killer of Southern boys—a killer of Christ. How many different ways to make him suffer? No one would ever know.

Nevertheless, this hazy, imprecise record declines to draw any such inference. There is no substantive evidence that it went down that way. The only evidence at all of what happened is the affidavit of Dr. Kerr. These doctors, after all, had an ethical duty to treat the sick and injured. These were Christian men, taught to turn the other cheek, men who were taught that all (white) people are God's children.

# Chapter 22

## BLACK DIAMOND

*Nor, credulous as such minds must have been, was this conceit altogether without some faint show of superstitious probability.*

Circuses have performed in the United States almost as long as there has been a United States.[529] At first, circuses were simple equestrian exhibitions, expert riders going around a circular path inside a building; thus, the name. The variety of entertainments expanded and they started to travel, merging with the centuries-old traditions of itinerant acrobats, rope dancers, mena—geries, and human oddities to create the carnival mood of the modern circus. In the early days there were "mud shows," named for the roads that would literally mire down a troupe. With the advent of railroads, circuses travelled further and faster, grew larger, and became more profitable. Competitors vied to be "The Most Stupendous, Spectacular Show Ever!", piling on the superlatives.

### Circusicana

The circus came to Corsicana every year, and it was a big event. Not only was it an unparalleled form of entertainment, especially before the advent of movies, but it was also an opportunity for local merchants to draw extra business from circus workers and the large influx of spectators who came into town from surrounding areas.

When the H&TC railway reached Corsicana, in 1871, the town became a place where circuses could stop and put on a big show. *C.W. Noyes' Great Crescent City Circus's* nineteen-stop train tour in Eastern Texas in the fall of 1871 included Corsicana,[530] and *The Great New York and New Orleans Zoo—logical & Equestrian Exposition* performed at each stop along the line a few years later, stopping at Corsicana on May 7, 1873.[531]

Mary Miller, one of Diadema Jester's sisters and one of the town's earliest residents (Chapter 11), recalled, "the first circus I remember seeing was Robinson's circus that was traveling through the country. Of course it had to travel by wagons as there were no railroads here then."[532] It set up "where the 3rd ward school is now," at West 1st Ave. and 13th Street,[533] but Mrs. Miller didn't say when. Robinson's circus did tour through Eastern Texas, in the spring of 1857, with a stop scheduled for Corsicana on June 8 and 9.[534]

H. Buckley & Co.'s Great National Circus performed in Corsicana on Oct. 2, 1858, bringing with it the earliest rope walker known to perform there, Mademoiselle Durand.[535] Mabie's Circus and Menagerie played in Corsicana on May 4, 1860.[536]

```
Admission, (Reserved Seats-only,) 50 Cents.
Children and Servants,  -  -  25  "
        A VISIT TO THE CLOUDS!
MDLLE DURAND, will walk a single wire
from the ground to the top of the Pavillion
centre pole, a distance of 300 feet, outside the
Pavillion, immediately before each perform-
ance.
    This unrivaled company will also exhibit at
Dresden,           on  Friday, October 1st
Corsicana,          "   Saturday,   "   2nd
Porter's Bluff,  .  "   Monday,     "   4th
Kaufman,            "   Tuesday,    "   5th
Prairieville,       "   Wednesday,  "   6th
Canton,             "   Thursday,   "   7th
Athens,  on Friday & Saturday,  8th & 9th
Kickapoo,        on   Monday, October 11th
```

Advertisement for H. Buckley's Circus, 1858 (detail)

Demonstrably, Rope Walker was not the first circus performer to show up in Corsicana, and surprisingly, he was not the most memorable, either. That distinction belongs to Black Diamond, a towering nine-ton Asian bull elephant, a runaway and a killer. His tusks were blunted and a flat metal bar bolted across them prevented him from lifting his trunk, an effort to curb his violent urges. He was restrained when necessary by chains attached to tusks, ankles, and body, and yoked by chains to the more docile cows to keep him from bolting.

The Al G. Barnes Circus brought Black Diamond to Corsicana on Oct. 12, 1929. Early in the afternoon, during the parade from the train yard to the fairgrounds, without provocation, he savagely attacked and killed Eva Speed Donohoo, a farmer from the Kerens area, twelve miles east of Cor-sicana. The once-widowed, twice-divorced grandmother was specifically targeted for the hulking fiend's wrath. The story of Black Diamond, Al G. Barnes Circus elephant, like Rope Walker, is etched deep into Corsicana's memory.

## Diamond

"Diamond," his original name, was captured in the wild when just a calf and brought to the U.S. by the Hagenbeck Circus in 1900.[537] He and three other untrained elephants were subsequently purchased by the Gentry Bros.[538] He was part of the Gentry dog and pony shows until 1914 when he and another male, Trilby, were sold to Wm. P. Hall. In 1915, Diamond and four other bulls were being leased by Hall to the Barton & Bailey Shows.[539] The following year the herd was sold to the Wheeler Bros Enormous Shows, who in turn sold the five to the R.T. Richards Circus in 1917.[540] Following that season, Diamond and three others were sold back to Hall while the fifth went to a Milwaukee zoo. Diamond was sold to the Atterbury Wagon Show, in the winter of 1919/1920, and for the first time he worked without a herd. R.L. Atterbury owned him until the show was sold, with Diamond, to A.M. (Albert) Cauble, in August, 1924. Cauble had previously owned that show but had sold it to Atterbury years earlier. Atterbury had purchased Diamond in the interim and then sold the same show, now with Diamond, back to Cauble.

With the repurchase, Cauble had to replace some of the old animals and fix up the show. It was in poor shape—Diamond was the only attraction worth seeing; he was, in fact, the main draw. All personnel stayed with the show because it was up north, heading south for the winter. It travelled quickly toward the Gulf of Mexico, breaking records as the fastest moving wagon show. Diamond travelled on foot, as far as fifty-five miles in a day, and then he would do a show in the evening. Boots were made to alleviate his sore feet. The show arrived in Texas before winter.

## Black Diamond

**Diamond with Trainer Bill Woodcock, ca. November, 1925**

Elephant trainer Bill Woodcock joined the Atterbury Show in 1924, shortly before Cauble repurchased the outfit and took on Woodcock and Atterbury's other staff. He replaced Curly Prickett, the bull man working with Diamond up to that point.

Cauble didn't change the lettering on the wagons for the balance of the season, so in 1925 the show was presented as "Monroe Bros." In addition to Diamond, the show had two cages of animals, one with lions and one with a bear and monkeys. Claude and Pauline Webb's side show included snakes, baboons, and monkeys. Diamond was billed as "Congo" while traveling with the Monroe Bros.[541]

Woodcock, the new bull man, found that Diamond was not good at following commands, but he taught him to do the three-leg hop, to shimmy, and to dance on front and rear legs. Sleigh bell bracelets were put on his legs for some dancing. Diamond could also ring a cowbell, do a headstand, and stand on his rear legs.

*As a finale, Woodcock called for volunteers out of the audience to ride him. Put about four guys on his back. Had collar chain on his neck for front guy to hold; and made others hold onto man in front. Then around the ring doing the three leg hop. This shook the riders up good and caused much amusement and was a good finish for this type show.*[542]

Around 1925, Woodcock renamed him "Black Diamond," because of his dark mood. He found the name in a dime-store novel, and it fit. The name "Diamond," alone, was "just plain, dumb."[543]

When younger, he was not so vicious, but he would run away. That was why the Gentry Show sold him to Hall, in 1914.[544] On Dec. 10, 1926, he went AWOL over a long weekend. Departing from Quenemo, Kansas, he made it across five counties and drew a lot of attention until a posse was dispatched and the fugitive tracked down.[545] Exactly a year earlier, in 1925, a wire story about an elephant escape, south of San Antonio, near Sabinal, appeared in many newspapers, including the *Corsicana Daily Sun*. The meandering mastodon's name wasn't given, but one paper identified the show as the "Morris Brothers," which sounds a lot like "Monroe Brothers."[546] According to Curly Prickett, who probably knew Diamond better than anyone, the humongous Houdini took off while Atterbury's circus was in Earth and another time near Hebbronville, both in Texas. Earth is located near the Texas Panhandle. Hebbronville is close to Sabinal, confirming that Diamond was the 1925 escapee. Woodcock confirmed that the Sabinal runaway was Diamond.

**Corsicana Daily Sun**

# CIRCUS ELEPHANT RUNNING AMUCK

Four years before Black Diamond came to Corsicana

## Ben Sweet

Prior to Corsicana, Black Diamond had already killed three times, according to some,[547] although the only victim ever identified was Ben Sweet, known by many as Captain Benjamin Reed. When Atterbury sold his show to Cauble, in 1924, "Old Ben," as some called him, was included. He was the only one except Bill Woodcock who could go near Diamond. Ben had been with the Atterbury Shows for years where he had handled an old bull named "Tommy," walking him over the roads and working him in the ring. He first handled Diamond in 1920, after Tommy died, when Atterbury purchased Diamond.[548] Ben was in his late sixties in 1924 and not the handler he once was. It wasn't safe for him to be around a dangerous bull, like Diamond, according to Woodcock, who was working Cauble's "Monroe Bros." show at the time. Diamond killed Sweet "for no apparent reason only that he was trying to replace a leg chain," said Woodcock, who was eating supper elsewhere when the attack occurred. Ben didn't show authority over Diamond, said Woodcock, and Diamond crushed him.

No death certificate, newspaper account, or other documentary evidence substantiates the story about Ben Sweet/Benjamin Reed. According to Woodcock it occurred on New Year's Day, 1926, in Oilton, Texas, a town close to the Mexican border.[549] A few weeks earlier Black Diamond was "running amuck" near Sabinal, not far from Oilton.[550]

Of the four deaths attributed to Black Diamond, two are completely unknown, and only Eva Donohoo's is documented. Nevertheless, clearly, he had at least a *reputation* as a killer.[551]

## Al G. Barnes Circus

In 1927 Cauble sold Black Diamond to his nephew, Wilson Fulbright, who briefly ran "Wilson's Greater Shows."[552] Fulbright in turn sold him the following year to the Al G. Barnes Circus, which was known to have mis-behaving bulls. One of them, Tusko, was sometimes too agitated to go on the road so Black Diamond would take his place. When Tusko and Diamond were on the road together, Diamond was billed as "Tusko," and Tusko was "Mighty Tusko."[553] Tusko was presented as "the World's

Meanest Elephant," celebrated for his rampages;[554] but those who worked
with Diamond knew he was not just mean, he was a killer.[555]

## Corsicana, Oct. 12, 1929

The Al G. Barnes Circus was near the end of its twenty-eight-week
season having covered several states and a good bit of Canada when it
arrived in Corsicana. [556] Black Diamond was being billed as "Tusko."[557] No
one noticed the great, gray omen. No one knew it was twelve days before
Black Thursday and seventeen days before Black Tuesday, that the world
would shortly be bullhooked[558] into the Great Depression. When Black
Diamond arrived, Saturday, Oct. 12, 1929, no one knew it would be a black
day in Corsicana history.

Animals disembarked from train cars to march to the fairground, where
the big top was being set up. Elephant cows were chained to each side of
Black Diamond to keep him from running. Curley Prickett, who had left
circus life and was then working on Eva Donohoo's farm, was given
permission from Jack O'Grady, then trainer of the massive beast, to walk
his former charge in the parade to the fairgrounds.

The procession paused at the Third Ward School on 1st Ave. to water
the animals from an open hydrant. Prickett pulled Diamond between two
parked cars to wait for a turn. [559] Slim Lewis and Blumer English, two bull
handlers with the show, were right behind them and saw everything.[560]
Donohoo approached Diamond while he was waiting to take water. "She
wanted to pet him."[561] Donohoo raised her hand to the side of Diamond's
head and he whirled in a flash. He caught Prickett with the side of his

shortened tusks and hurled him completely over
the top of a nearby car. Said Lewis, "before
Bloomer [sic] or I could catch our breath,
Diamond had turned on Mrs. Donehoe [sic]."
Diamond knocked her to the sidewalk and ran his
tusks through her body. She gave one short
scream.[562] She was rushed to a hospital but died
soon after. Prickett suffered a broken wrist.

### Curley Prickett

Homer Douglas Prickett, "Curley," was born
Sept. 5, 1888, in Fort Worth.[563] One of his earliest
circus jobs was cooking for the Foley and Burke
show. Before that he was in the army for three
years, in California and Idaho.[564]

Curley Prickett, "after
Diamond broke his arm"

He was Diamond's trainer from 1920 to 1928,[565] but not throughout that time because in 1924 he was replaced on the Atterbury show when Woodcock became the bull man. Prickett probably worked with Diamond on the Wilson and Barnes shows,[566] and left when he was hired to work as Donohoo's "animal man" on her farm.[567]

Curley believed Diamond's attack was a rage of jealousy.

*Prickett said the elephant saw Mrs. Donohoo with him when he said good bye to it and to the circus. Prickett believed the elephant remembered and charged the woman because it had seen him leave with her.*[568]

When he was Diamond's trainer, Prickett recalled,

*[When] talking with my wife, he often reached out and gotten me and pulled me away from her. I would pet him a minute and slip around behind him and rejoin my wife and the same thing would happen. He was awfully jealous of me.*[569]

Curley Prickett died in Pensacola on Dec. 3, 1938 and was buried in Fort Worth.[570]

## Eva Donohoo

Eva Donohoo was "well known and well-liked by the people of Kerens, and had a host of friends who were shocked over her death" read the brief report of her funeral. She held memberships, the paper added, in Daugh–ters of the American Revolution, United Daughters of the Confederacy, and the East–ern Star.[571]

Mary Evelyn "Eva" Speed was born in 1878, in Hale County, Texas, into the extensive Speed family, a clan with American roots reaching back several generations. One of her several siblings was Carlton D. "C.D." Speed, a Corsicana oil man. A nephew, Carl Miller, was an actor who appeared in several movies, including two Charlie Chaplin features.

Eva Speed Donohoo

Her father, L.E. (Lafayette Ebenezer) Speed (1848-1914), owned sizeable Texas properties. In 1911 he bought a large spread, eight and a half miles southeast of Kerens, for $75,960. The Speed family's presence in the area predated the purchase, however, because G.W. (George Washington) Speed (1846-1942), a cousin once removed of Eva's father, worked land in that vicinity of Navarro County much earlier.[572] Both men came from Mississippi.

Eva's maternal grandfather was Dr. John L. "Leonard" Randal, a citizen of the Texas Republic who arrived in the future state around 1838, shortly after Eva's mother was born. In San Augustine, where Dr. Randal first settled, he built a house which also served as a hospital for his patients. He was elected to both legislative houses of the Republic and in 1859 received a grant for 640 acres in Starrville, Texas, a few miles northeast of Tyler. Dr. Randal was regimental surgeon for the 28th Texas Cavalry, brought into service at the age of sixty-two by his son, Horace, who was then a colonel. The elder Randal served for only one year, due to failing health, but Eva's uncle, Horace Randal, went on to become a general and the man for whom Randall County was named, or more accurately, misnamed—Eva fre–quently lamented the injustice of the extra "L," mistakenly added by the Texas legislature when the county was established and never remedied.[573]

When Eva inherited a part of her father's Kerens property after he died in 1914 [574] she was living in Houston, and then in 1921 she permanently relocated to the farm.[575] She was considered a wealthy land owner, "owning one of the richest black land farms in east Navarro,"[576] a property she referred to as "Shoe String Plantation."[577] Calling her farm a "plantation" recalls the antebellum southern slave economy, with scores of enslaved black people laboring in the fields, which she obviously did not have in the 1920s. Running the plantation did, however, for Eva, conjure romantic images of a bygone era gilded with patrician nostalgia, and in all likelihood her plantation's laborers were the children and grandchildren of slaves.

*A very delightful program was enjoyed Friday morning by the Sorosis club.[578] ... In a very entertaining paper, personal experiences and reminiscences were given by Mrs. Donohoo of plantation life, with all its solitude and weird witchery, its tragedies and comedies in the negro quarters, failures and successes with craps, all were given with a touch of the master hand. Interwoven were life stories of beloved and honored ancestors whose names are held dear as pioneers of Texas. A humorous thread in the paper might aptly be called "A Quest for a Coat of Arms," and caused much amusement. Mrs. Donohoo had many pictures of the old homes and scenes on the plantation and of an old darky, of "befo' de war" type.[579]*

Antebellum plantation culture was something Eva learned about from her parents, who were seventeen and twenty-eight years old in 1865[580] when the end of slavery came to Texas—a few years after the Emancipation Proclamation was issued.[581] Both were reared on slave plantations. Eva's Randal grandparents held seventeen people in bondage in the Starrville area of Smith County, Texas, in 1860.[582] Her Speed grandparents only had two slaves, in 1860, in Smith County, Mississippi, but in the neighboring county of Covington the well-established, extended Speed family had dozens.[583]

Eva Speed married William J. Donohoo, son of a Texas banker, in 1897. They had a daughter, Louisa, the next year. Six years after that he died, in 1904, at the age of thirty-three.[584] Eva remarried in 1905 to Dwight H. Skinner, a recently widowed Houstonian with five small children, the youngest an infant, but they divorced three years later.[585] In Houston, following her divorce, she was said to be society editor for the *Houston Post*[586] and later a public stenographer at the Rice Hotel.[587] Eva married a third time, to W.T. "Buck" Griffin, in 1925, but that marriage also ended in divorce, in 1927.[588] Griffin was there when Donohoo was attacked. He was hailed as a hero by removing her before Black Diamond could do more harm.

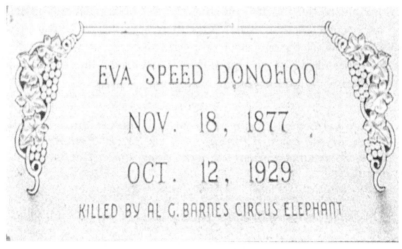

EVA SPEED DONOHOO

NOV. 18, 1877

OCT. 12, 1929

KILLED BY AL G. BARNES CIRCUS ELEPHANT

**Grave marker for Eva Speed Donohoo**

Ω

Following the tragedy, the circus moved on to its next scheduled stops. Black Diamond was kept locked-up in a train car and his days were numbered. One circus manager remained in Corsicana to pay claims for five damaged automobiles. Louisa (Donohoo) Mahan, Eva's daughter, sued the Barnes Circus and won $2,500.

## Dead Tusker Walking

Two days after Donohoo's death, the circus was in Bay City for a show.

*"Black Diamond," the killer elephant, lay trussed in his death cell today, his little eyes aglow with a jungle lust to kill and his heavy chains a clanking badge of shame, while his owners, the operators of a circus, already ordered to take his life, deliberated on the method they would use to carry out the death mandate.*[589]

John Ringling, who had recently bought the Barnes circus, authorized the execution. The original plan was strangulation:

*Three of the killers companions will be hitched to the end of a huge chain and three to the other and the elephant's neck will be caught in a slip knot in the center.*[590]

Attempts had been made to poison him with cyanide-laced peanuts, but Diamond picked out and ate only the untainted ones. They tried the same thing with oranges, but he wouldn't eat them.[591] In the end it was decided to shoot him. While the circus was stopped at Kenedy, on October 16, five men with rifles filled him with more than 150 bullets. A final shot was fired into his brain, for good measure.[592]

*Circus performers, tight wire artists, aerial queens and others of the big top family wept as Black Diamond, the majestic trouper of them all, went down under the fusillade of bullets.*[593]

Curley Prickett was still in the hospital when told of the elephant's end.

*"Feller, if I ever loved an elephant, I loved that Diamond. Wish John Ringling would have given him to me." ... Prickett moistened his lips nervously and his voice was thickened by emotion as he talked after receiving the news.*[594]

## Elephant in the Room

The director of the Houston Zoo and a taxidermist attended the execution and took Black Diamond's head for display at the Houston Museum of Natural Science. Actually, they only took the hide from his head and his tusks, and for forty years his head was mounted on a wall at the museum. The exhibit then went into storage in the museum's basement.[595]

In the early 1990s, Carmack Watkins, a Corsicana-area businessman, with the help of Navarro College personnel, acquired the head from the museum and restored it. Watkins's interest in Diamond began on the day of Eva Donohoo's murder—he witnessed the beginning of Black Diamond's rampage while sitting atop his father's shoulders. He learned where the carcass was buried and had the skull dug up. Both are displayed along with other animal specimens at his Corsicana construction firm.[596]

## Gray Matter

Several reasons, other than Prickett's jealousy theory, were given for Black Diamond's assault. Slim Lewis, one of the handlers there when the attack occurred, believed that a dangerous elephant like Diamond could only be commanded by one handler at a time, and at the time, it was Jack O'Grady.[597] It was well-known, said Lewis, that Black Diamond had killed and was dangerous enough to kill again.[598] Some attributed Diamond's violent outburst to years of forced submission, the restraint of massive chains, and the frustration of not being allowed to lift his trunk. It was said he had an abscessed tooth. Others believed he was in musth, a state of hormonal elevation, when bull elephants are said to be most dangerous.[599] Certain academics attribute human-like emotions to bull elephants and believe their aggression is a byproduct of past traumatization or a breakdown of social boundaries within the herd.[600] No one knows for sure.

## End of a Peculiarly Spectacular Institution

The Black Diamond tragedy was a turning point for attitudes about circus elephants, especially male elephants. Eva Speed Donohoo's death "effectively signed the death warrant for every living bull elephant in America."[601] In more recent years animal rights activists have changed popular opinion about all circus animals—but especially elephants—leading to an unimaginable consequence: The Greatest Show on Earth, the 146-years-old Ringling Bros. and Barnum & Bailey Circus, ceased operations on May 21, 2017.[602] The end was precipitated by the decision, a year earlier, to remove elephants from performances, a change traceable in part to one

singularly savage attack by one particular pachyderm martyr who had finally
had enough.

Black Diamond's body, what's left of it, lies moldering in a Kenedy
grave, but his soul is marching on.

"Diamond's last day, October 16, 1929, Kennedy [sic], Texas"

# Chapter 23

## THE REAL MYSTERY

*Wonderfullest things are ever the unmentionable; deep memories yield no epitaphs*

It took 135 years—one and a third centuries—to find out the name of Corsicana's Rope Walker. The Rope Walker legend was repeated inside and outside of Corsicana homes, in newspapers, in books, and online. Out-of-towners visiting the Hebrew Cemetery would see the peculiar epitaph and hear an incredible story about a one-legged performer. Despite all of that curiosity and publicity, however, there is no evidence, during all those years, except for a few, minor, recent exceptions, of any attempt to determine the man's identity. There wasn't a "search for his identity which gripped the community," as the historical plaque at the cemetery claims. Haslam's 1936 article, Campbell's article thirteen years later, and Tolbert's columns several years after that are all efforts to describe the mystery, but not to solve it. Even Tolbert's "Theory" article (Chapter 7) did nothing to solve the mystery, although Samuel F. Tulhill, of Dallas, who made the initial deducement suggesting his identity, does get credit for contacting Tolbert. Babbette recalls a fraternity—from which college she doesn't remember—at one time required new pledges to seek out the identity of Rope Walker as an initiation rite—snipe hunting in Corsicana's Hebrew Cemetery. What about efforts before 1936? Fifty-three years after he died, according to Haslam, his identity was already an "unsolved mystery." Haslam reported nothing about efforts, before then, to discover Rope Walker's identity.

No query or notice asking for help to identify the stranger was placed in the *New York Clipper* or its successor, *Variety*, the nation's widely read enter-tainment industry newspapers which were published going back well into the nineteenth century. There was one inquiry, by a genealogist, in 2008 (Chapter 10), but that effort, based as it was on an out-and-out fabrication, was doomed from the start. There is no record of any inquiry to circus historical societies, except those discussed in Chapter 12 (which don't count because the inquirer, your author, had already solved the mystery and was only checking for additional information, a detail Chapter 12 failed to mention). It seems nearly certain that when circuses came through Cor-sicana someone would ask the circus people if they had ever heard of a one-legged tightrope performer. Whatever might have been learned from those inquiries, unlikely anything, nothing ever came of it.

There is one reason why finding an answer was difficult, to the extent any effort was ever made, and it might explain why the mystery persisted for so long. So certain was everyone of this one fact—he fell and died in 1884—that it was put on the cemetery's historical marker and the granite marker placed next to the original gravestone. And it is totally under–standable why everyone thought so: the original cemetery book, which was already "ancient" in 1936, according to Haslam, gave that year as his date of death. This one, key piece of data was copied into the current record book, into the walking tour guide, and everywhere else. Anyone who wrote any–thing about Rope Walker unwittingly repeated the error.[603]

Did anyone ever try to search for his identity in 1884 records? In 1936, when the mystery was well-known, maybe there still existed a full run of some 1884 Corsicana newspaper.[604] At any time someone could have re–viewed issues of the *Dallas Daily Herald* or any of the other nearby city newspapers with available 1884 issues for a Corsicana news item about the accident. Many of those newspapers still exist even today—see Chapters 12 and 13. Back then, without computer searching, it would have been quite a chore to read a year's worth of newspapers, and what a devastating letdown when nothing about Rope Walker was found, even after checking a few months back into 1883 and a few months forward into 1885.[605] Had the correct year been known, however, the labor of a manual search would have been worth the effort and the mystery would have been solved long ago.

**Navarro County records**

Someone could have searched 1884 municipal records in the Navarro County courthouse—probate and sundry other government and legal documents—and likewise come up empty. It wouldn't take more than an afternoon, even if the scope of the search were extended into 1883 and 1885, as any prudent researcher by habit would naturally extend the review beyond just the one calendar year.

A search of Navarro County's Probate records for 1883 and a few years after found nothing for "Moses Berg" or "Daniel De Houne." Indexes were checked using various spelling variations, even "Rope Walker" and "Walker, Rope." A series of index entries dated in mid-March, 1883, under the heading of "Walker," looked promising. Lucinda Walker died on February 4, 1883, leaving an estate worth at least $6,000, mostly real estate. Her widowed husband petitioned to become guardian of the two minor children, Rice and Roxy Walker, who would receive a share of the estate with the rest of the family. And that's it for probate. Rice and Rox, yup; Rope, nope.

Other Navarro records from 1883 which might have a reference to Rope Walker were also checked. Land records were not looked at; it seems unlikely that an itinerant acrobat who stopped in Corsicana for a few days to walk a high wire would also buy a house or land. The book of registered brands, in a similar vein, was not checked.

The "Minutes of Commissioners Court" was checked. One volume consists of indexes to the other volumes, over a hundred indexes arranged alphabetically with a table of contents for the indexes at the front. Sixteen indexes, for example, are listed under "P":

Commissioner's Court, Navarro County, Indexes book, "P" indexes

The index to "Paupers" entries was checked to see if Rope Walker was listed there. In the days before Social Security and Welfare, if there was no help from family, church, friend, neighbor, or charity, in a time of need, the County would step in to help. The pauper entries, indexed chronologically, show payments made by Navarro County for the support, care, and burial of the poor.

Index entries under Pauper, Minutes of Commissioner's Court, Navarro County

The index gives the page and entry numbers of the actual proceedings (minutes), which are found in other volumes. Over five hundred entries record reimbursements paid for the support of paupers, 1856-1942. In the spring of 1883 there is only one reimbursement, ten dollars paid for the burial of E. Moody, not a known alias of Moses Berg. For all eighty-seven years there is not one Jewish-sounding name; the Jewish community, like other religious communities, took care of its own, including Rope Walker.

Rope Walker's death might have been the subject of an inquest. Medical examiners and other officials were responsible for determining whether a death was caused by a criminal act, and if not, whether a judge or jury should investigate it for some other reason in the interest of public safety. There are fifty-three entries in the commissioner's index for inquest expense reim–bursements, covering 1852-1914. Some entries don't name the deceased, requiring a look at the minutes themselves. There were four entries for 1883. A review of the actual minutes found nothing about a rope walker's accident.

Index entries under Inquests, Minutes of Commissioner's Court, Navarro County

Having found nothing by checking a few select indexes, resort was made to simply read through the court's minutes for the applicable timeframe. Here are found entries in chronologically order related to paupers, inquests, and all the other day-to-day business of the commissioner. Three con–secutive entries from the May 1883 term illustrate how many of Corsicana's early citizens are now familiar names:

*596. It is ordered by the Court that S.H. Kerr County Clerk be allowed the Sum of $63.68 Dollars for Transcribing 919 Brands, Receiving County Deed from Mrs. Haynes & Postage and that a warrant be drawn on County Treasurer for the Same.*

*597. It is ordered by the Court that A.H. Mulkey & Co. be allowed the Sum of $3.09 Dollars for Nails, Brooms & Oil for County and that a warrant be drawn on County Treasurer for the Same.*

*598. It is ordered by the Court that A. Fox & Bro. be allowed the Sum of $13.50 Dollars for Blankets for Jail and that a warrant be drawn on County Treasurer for the Same.*

Further on is entry 626:

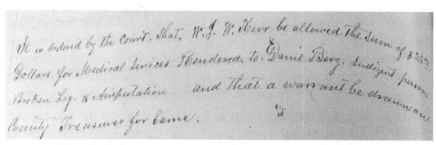

Navarro County Commissioner's Minutes, May 1883, entry 626

**626. It is ordered by the Court, that, W.J.W. Kerr be allowed the sum of $25.00 Dollars for Medical Services Rendered, to Danil Berg, Indigent person Broken Leg & Amputation and that a warrant be drawn on County Treasurer for Same.**

If a researcher trying to find Rope Walker's identity looked into county records and came across entry 626, she would have recognized "Berg" as a German surname and possibly Jewish. The mention of an "amputation" would have made the entry stand out, even though the legend states that Rope Walker had an amputated leg before he got to Corsicana. Still, that one word would have piqued a researcher's interest and triggered a deeper investigation into 1883 records, inevitably leading to one of the many news stories in March 1883 which described the accident. Unquestionably, a researcher who had read Tolbert's 1968 "Theory" article about "Professor Berg" would have recognized in this municipal record a connection which would have led to the realization that 1884 was not the year when he was killed. But no one ever searched county records. If they did, they would have found that record and the mystery would have been solved already.

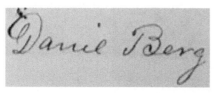

**Detail from entry 626**

Any confusion about Rope Walker's name ("Danil Berg") in May of 1883 was cleared up by September when the death certification and doctor's affidavit were written. S.H. Kerr and W.J.W. Kerr definitely knew the man's full, legal name at that point.

Anyone with an interest in finding out the man's name back then, like the cemetery administrator, would have known to ask Judge Kerr or Dr. Kerr for it. The judge knew about everything that happened in the county. Every entry in the Commissioner's Minutes in those years bear his signature and his authority extended to probate, real estate, and all other sorts of legal matters. Doctor Kerr was the county's public physician.

Others probably knew his name, too, or knew that the judge or doctor knew it: the other four surgeons; Dr. Gulick, maybe; people at the Molloy Hotel; possibly Abe and Louisa Mulkey; Bernard or Charlie Simon, Ben Marks, and other local Hebrews who spent time with Berg during his final earthly days; and presumably the Jews who buried him—Max London for sure, and potentially many others. Hundreds, even thousands of locals read the newspaper accounts, which mentioned his name, albeit his stage name.

Why is it, then, that there is <u>no</u> name whatsoever on the gravestone? When the body was transported to the Hebrew Cemetery and placed in the care of Max London, or some other member of the Jewish community, why was his name left behind, and never retrieved? Why did this mystery exist in the first place? Anyone who visited the Hebrew Cemetery and saw the unfinished gravestone in the decades immediately following Berg's death could have investigated and easily connected with one of those two Kerrs to find out the dead man's name, or some version of his name. S.H. Kerr lived until 1894 and W.J.W. Kerr until 1916. Max London, who lived until 1925, certainly must have known that one of the two Kerrs knew the man's name. Any one of them could have cleared up the mystery with ease. His stage name—Prof. Berg, Prof. De Houne, or some variation—would have been better than "Rope Walker." Even "Danil Berg" would have sufficed. The real mystery is why a name, any name, was not put on the gravestone.[606]

Formulate two groups of people in Corsicana during the months, years, and even some decades after Rope Walker's death: one, those who knew something about his name and identity, or knew of someone who knew something about his name and identity; and two, those who knew of the gravestone with the missing name. Why was there never any connection made between those two groups so the gravestone could be corrected?

# Chapter 24

## HEBREWS AND SHEBREWS

*It's a mutual, joint-stock world, in all meridians*

The tightrope walker's fatal fall was a shocking event which took place in front of hundreds of people, was reported in newspapers across Texas and the country, and certainly must have been the talk of Corsicana for quite some time. Within months the county court clerk and county physician, two leading Corsicana citizens, created official documents which bore the dead man's actual name. The mangled acrobat's survival had been entrusted to five skilled surgeons from Corsicana and nearby towns. The Navarro County commissioner compensated one of the doctors for his troubles. After he fell, he was brought to the popular Molloy Hotel, it seems, where he lived for another ten days. Downtown businessman and emerging religious leader, Abe Mulkey, and one or more local Jewish merchants offered him spiritual succor, or something like that.

So how is it, with all those Corsicanans so closely connected to Rope Walker, no one in the Jewish community, including those who buried him and those in charge of the cemetery, was able to get his name—all of nine letters—etched into his gravestone?

One might conclude there were social barriers and limited social inter–course between those who certainly knew his name—certain prominent, gentile citizens of Corsicana, the two Kerrs in particular and a passel of confederate surgeons—and those who needed to learn his name, that is, generally speaking, Corsicana's Jews, and specifically Max London and others in charge of the Hebrew Cemetery. In stark terms, it must be the case that Corsicana Jews and Gentiles didn't communicate with one another. How else to explain why the men who knew the itinerant performer's name didn't give it to the Jews when they turned over his body for burial? In the same vein, and more importantly, why did the Jews not ask those Christian townsmen, "Do you know the name of the dead rope walker?"

There were obvious cultural and religious differences between Jew and Christian, but nothing divisive. To the contrary, early Corsicana history shows that the town's Jews were fully integrated citizens. They were popular merchants and fellow Civil War veterans. They held positions of respons–ibility, belonged to the nonsectarian civic groups and fraternal organizations, and even helped run the town.[607] They were Jews, yes, but they were Texans, too. Almost everyone in Corsicana came from somewhere else, and the

Hebrews were no different. Not only that, but the Jews themselves were diverse—from religious to agnostic, from government officials to gamblers, from leading businessmen and bankers to ex-cons—it's hard to lump them together as one people, let alone a people set apart. They were just people. The Jews' only distinction was their ancestry and the theology they inherited from their forebears. The Christians knew something about their Jewish neighbors' background because the history of the Israelites was in the Holy Bible. And the Jews knew about the Christians because Jews had been living in Christian society for millennia. And of course, as everyone knows, Jesus was a Jew.

Reverend Mulkey defended the presence of Jews amongst the Gentiles, even at one of his revival meetings, according to this anecdote from his 1897 *Budget*:

> One worker rose and said: "The Hebrews are attend-
> ing the meeting." "Thank God, I have seen some She-
> brews also, and have shaken hands with them and invited
> them back again."

**Hebrews and Shebrews**

Mulkey's message? Fear not, these men and women are just like everybody else.

Before and after a rope walker's body made its way to Corsicana's Hebrew Cemetery the town's Christians and Jews jointly participated in many enterprises, commercial and social, and held each other in high esteem. There was no discernable division. In some cases, as the following examples make clear, these labels—*Jew* and *Christian*—don't even apply, and it seems certain that lines of communication were unimpeded by nationality, race, religion, or creed.

## The Merchant of Ennis and a New Daughter of Israel

Phillip "Pete" Freeman of Ennis, a Jewish immigrant from Russian Poland, was a dry goods merchant and director of the Ennis National Bank.[608] He and his wife, Theodosio "Docie," lost two of their infant children in 1878, but because there was no Jewish cemetery in Ennis the babies were buried in nearby Corsicana's Hebrew Cemetery. Although the Freemans lived in Ennis, their unusual story is exemplary of the close bond between followers of the Jewish and Christian faiths, and they could just as likely have been Corsicana residents.

In 1874, Pete and Docie got married in Galveston:[609]

### Conversion and Marriage.

*On Sunday the Synagogue was crowded to its utmost capacity by an audience eager to witness the dual ceremonies of the reception of a convert to Judaism, and her subsequent marriage to a gentleman of that religion. The Holy Ark – the reader's desk, and the small stand in front of the ark, were covered with white drapery embroidered in silver.*

*The convert was Miss Theodosia Rushing, daughter of Col. Rushing, editor of the Ennis Argus. As the bridal party – consisting of the bridegroom, Mr. Phillip Freeman, and the bride, Miss Rushing, Col. Rushing and Mrs. Rabbi Blum – advanced up the broad aisle of the Synagogue, the choir sang a selection of Hebrew songs. Rabbi Blum, then standing at the reader's desk, addressed the congregation upon the solemnity and the rarity of the ceremony he was about to perform, saying that there were but few converts to Judaism, because Jews seek to make no converts; on the contrary, they rather discourage those who propose to enter the ancient faith of Israel, bidding them to remember the rigors of the ceremonial law and the opprobrium that a cruel world still bestows on the children of Abraham.*

*If the convert still remains firm in his desire to be incorporated into the household of Jacob, he is then instructed in the faith of Moses, and received into the synagogue. The bride having been placed on the platform by the side of the reader's desk, she was asked if the act she was about to perform was of her own free will. She replied that it was. The rabbi then demanded to know if she had been persuaded to it by any Jewish minister. She responded, "no."*

*Rabbi Blum then asked her father if it was with his consent, and with that of her mother, that Miss Rushing was about to enter the Jewish religion. He arose and declared that it was. The Rabbi then proceeded to examine the candidate catechetically on the principles of the Jewish religion and its observances. She answered his interrogatories clearly and properly. The bride was led to the higher platform, the curtains of the Holy Ark were drawn aside, and, in the presence of the whole congregation, with firm and audible voice, she made the declaration of her religion, both in Hebrew and in English.*

*Hear, O Israel. God is our Lord. God is one. She then descended to the reader's desk. The bridegroom, Mr.*

*Freeman, advanced, and the nuptial ceremony was performed, after which the bridal party retired, Prof. Lieberman performing Mendelsson's Wedding March, from the Midsummer Night's Dream. The whole ceremony was impressive, and conducted with great propriety. A large proportion of those present were Christians.*[610]

Freeman family plot, Jewish section of Myrtle Cemetery, Ennis, Texas

Theodosio gave birth to seven children, but only four, all daughters, survived to adulthood.[611] Phillip and Theodosio's final resting place is the Jewish section, established by 1893, of Myrtle Cemetery, in Ennis.[612] All four daughters, an infant child, and several of their grandchildren are buried in the family plot.[613]

It is not known if anyone from the Freeman family visited the graves of the two little babies buried in Corsicana, but if they did, and if it was after Rope Walker's stone was put up, any inquiries they made about the incomplete tombstone did not reach the right ears. Rope Walker's epitaph remained deficient.

## Fire Chief, Colonel, Carrie, and Kin

Further evidence of the close relationship between Jew and Christian can be gleaned from a look at the four Freedman siblings of Corsicana (*Freedman*, with a "d"; no known connection to Phillip Freeman). Two of them, possibly three, were already living in Corsicana when the rope walker died. These Jewish immigrants from Mariampole, Lithuania, children of Hirsh and Bashe Freedman, boldly penetrated Corsicana's cultural fabric, holding their own nose-to-nose with their native-born Christian friends and colleagues. Day in and day out they interacted with Corsicana's Christian establishment, including men who could have easily given one of the Freedmans the correct name of the rope walker.

Brothers Ruben and Solomon arrived in Corsicana first, sometime in the 1870s, followed by their sister Esther Blumrosen and her husband Jacob several years later, in the early 1880s. Brother Alex was the last to come, arriving from Flint, Michigan, sometime after 1885.[614]

**Reuben "Rube" Freedman** was Corsicana's fire chief and a leader in the Texas Republican Party.[615] He was responsible for creating the

MAN TO WHOM FIRMEN'S MONUMENT WAS DEDICATED

Rube Freedman

memorial honoring deceased Corsicana firemen, erected at the southeast corner of the courthouse grounds shortly after his death. Standing on a pedestal of Barre granite, the Italian-made figure cost $4,000. An inscription near the top of the base says, "Dedicated to our Chief, Rube Freedman – 1859-1917."[616]

The unveiling of the statue on June 15, 1919 was an opportunity to reflect on the history of the department, one of the best in Texas, founded in Dec. 1883 by E.H. Church, Abe Mulkey, Capt. James Garitty, Edmond Raphael, and others. Freedman, first elected chief in the nineties, was celebrated for creating a firemen's fund which included funeral benefits.[617]

Praise for Freedman was gushing, with words of gratitude from two judges, one observing that

> *He labored for the welfare of the department, his ideal always being to care for the members of the department, render service to the city and to build up and equip a fire department which would be suitable to Corsicana. ... devoted to the citizens and loyal to his friends. His love to the city was second only to his love for his family.*[618]

The other judge noted that

> *Men whose parents came to this country from different nations are joined together to protect the city, all being immensely American and interested in the city's welfare. I know of no man who was as American as Rube Freedman. His idea of true Americanism was the same as Roosevelt's.*[619]

The Jan. 16, 1918 CFD annual election of officers was a festive affair with over 125 attendees, speeches from prominent Corsicanans, and a delicious culinary spread. P. Mayer, acting chief since Freedman's passing four months earlier, was easily elected as the new chief. Isaac Levy was voted in for his twelfth year as treasurer.[620]


**Solomon Sampson Freedman** was an intimate of powerful men at the local and state levels—and was one himself. Governor Jim Hogg appointed him a state advisor, making Freedman a "Texas Colonel."[621] In 1885 he served on the committee for sending a local contingent to the St. Louis Exposition and[622] three years later he was one of the incorporators of the Navarro Land Investment Company, created to set aside property for schools, a university, and other public institutions.[623]

Like his brother Rube, Col. Freedman was a fighter for justice.[624] He was a litigant in numerous lawsuits, two of which caught more than a little attention from the press. One was against the Cotton Belt Railroad, which negligently caused a horse to throw his daughter, Ida, injuring her leg. He won, though much less than the $12,000 he sought.[625] In another, in 1891, he fought a fifty dollar fine imposed on him for repairing the sidewalk in front of his house, an unjust penalty considering that the town had damaged it while installing curbing. He was so incensed at having lost in city court that he hired two of the town's best lawyers, Neblett and Simkins, and, following an appeal to the district court, won.[626]

He was tough, as shown by a very public tiff he had with the aforementioned Neblett with whom he was temporarily on the outs. The feud was prosecuted in an 1888 Corsicana newspaper:

> **To the ex-Mayor and Circus Rider:**
>
> **The circular in yesterday's COURIER signed by Robbins Stuffins Neblett is very dull for so great a man as Robbin Stuffins Neblett professes to be, to write with the aid of his overseer, L.B. Haynie, and other aid de camps. I am not a lawyer, but will hit Stuffin Nible so hard in a circular reply to his offensive burlesque on me and other nationalities that he will not seek another office for a score of years. I am not an office seeker or do I belong to any clique or organ grinder as our friend Robbins Stuffins Neblett.**
>
> **S.S. FREEDMAN** [627]


**Carrie (Frank) Freedman**, Col. Freedman's wife, was the most Jewish-minded member of Corsicana's early Jewish community. Through her ef-forts Corsicana got its first synagogue built, Beth El, which is still standing.

She and three of her sisters, all Corsicanans and all native-born Americans, are profiled in Supplement I.

**Esther (Freedman) Blumrosen**'s husband, Jacob, died in 1893, leaving her to bring up two young children on her own.[628] She ran a grocery and saloon and owned various properties, including rights to wells in the nearby Powell Oil Field. In 1897, Esther was charged with a misdemeanor offense for keeping her business open on a Sunday, the (Christian) sabbath. City court set the hearing for Tuesday, Sept. 28, but when informed it was the second day of Rosh Hashanah—the Jewish New Year is celebrated for two days—the court willingly postponed the hearing.[629] Esther died in 1945 at the advanced age of eighty-five.

**Alexander "Alex" Freedman** owned properties in Corsicana and Navarro County,[630] including downtown lots in Blocks 33 and 60, straddling both sides of $7^{th}$ Street (aka Commerce Street, aka Hardin Street) between $5^{th}$ Ave. and Collin Street, walking distance from Beaton. Early Corsicana city directories list him as a saloon operator, and later, a soft drink purveyor. Alexander's niece, Frankie, received the properties just before her bachelor uncle passed away, in 1928.[631] The transfer on the eve of his death is probably why Esther Blumrosen, Alex's sister and Frankie's aunt, contested his will. Uncle Alex left everything to his unmarried nieces, S.S.'s daughters Frankie and Ida.

Ω

All four Freedman siblings and their families were buried in the Hebrew Cemetery. In the burial ground's old section, where Rope Walker's gravestones (the original one and the recently added one) are located, are the small graves of Mabel and Daisy Freedman, Col. S.S. and Carrie Solomon's infant children, who died six months before and nine months after Daniel De Houne's death. The grave of two-year-old Lillie Polasky, who died five months after De Houne, is embraced by her two Freedman cousins, their mothers being sisters. Rebecca Blumrosen, who died in 1885, the infant daughter of Esther and Jacob, lies alongside her little cousins as well. See Supplement III.

Freedman family members visiting the cemetery would have cast their eyes upon Rope Walker's peculiar epitaph numerous times. Still, even with their lofty positions of respect and access to the town's most powerful citizens, they never found out the unknown man's name to have it etched into his gravestone.

## Rich Relations

The Rich family lived in Corsicana and later in a farming community outside of town. Unlike the Freedmans, who interacted with the town's Christians through commerce and civil service, many members of the Rich family connected with their Christian neighbors by marrying them and adopting their spouses' religion.

**Harriett (Hart) Rich**, the family matriarch, died at the age of fifty-five (or so) on March 9, 1883, four days before De Houne's death.[632] She and her husband, Isaac (ca. 1825-Sept. 1908),[633] and her stepson, Charles (June 3, 1852-1885),[634] were buried in the Hebrew Cemetery. All other members of the large Rich family were buried elsewhere.

Harriett and Isaac raised nine children, all born in Louisiana except Abe, the youngest, who in 1871 was born in Texas.[635] The two oldest, Charles (whose birthname was "Salomon") and Regina, were the children of Isaac's first wife, Rebecca.[636] The other seven, born to Harriett, were Morris, Sally, Carrie, Benjamin, Barbara, Nathan, and Abraham.[637] The children who married all did so outside of their parents' faith,[638] and all of Harriett's seven children were buried in non-Jewish cemeteries.[639] In 1880 the Riches were living in rural Navarro County on land abutting the farm of Donnell Hugh Kerr, home also of the farmer's aged parents, Rev. James and Mrs. Delia Kerr—Dr. W.J.W. Kerr's kin.[640]

**Charles Rich** served nearly two years of a five-year sentence for a theft conviction at the Texas State Penitentiary at Huntsville.[641] His cause of death, at thirty-one, is not known, but many an ex-convict who died young did not die of natural causes.

**Isaac Rich**'s obituary shows he was popular Corsicanan:

> *Mr. Isaac Rich, an old citizen of this place until recently, died in Houston Tuesday night. The remains were brought here for interment in the Hebrew cemetery. Deceased is survived by three sons, N.R. Rich and A.C. Rich, Houston and Ben Rich of this city; also a daughter, Mrs. Barbara Barnaby. He was 79 years of age and had many friends here.*[642]

Four of the Rich children established families in Corsicana and produced sixteen progeny amongst them in the next generation, all brought up in town. Over the years, some of those descendants, many with the surname

"Barnaby," might have visited their Rich grandparents in the Hebrew Cemetery. They would have seen Rope Walker's gravestone—right in front of Harriett's (see Chapter 5)—but no one from that family was able to get the faulty gravestone corrected.

## Isaac Baum

The Freeman, Freedman, and Rich families were pioneer Jews living in (or near) Corsicana who did not adhere to the stereotypical notion of Jews as an insular minority. They blurred and even erased cultural and religious distinctions by connecting with their non-Jewish fellow Texans in politics, family, and religion. Isaac Baum's story presents a unique variation on the same theme.

Baum, a native of Alzey, Germany, was twenty when he arrived in the U.S.,

**Isaac Baum**

at Galveston, where he started out as a janitor at the Tremont Hotel. He eventually became a millionaire.[643] His good turn of fortune is on full display by the classically elegant and unquestion-ably expensive Baum-family monument in the Hebrew Cemetery. His name was also chiseled into two buildings on Beaton Street, both still standing, one of them Hashop's, where one end of Rope Walker's line was attached.[644] At the time of the 1880 census, Baum, a bachelor, was in Corsicana boarding with the Jewish family of Adolph and Mary Cahn. A year later he was married to Mary's sister, Sophia Mindek.

Baum was not Jewish, at least not by birth, as his son, George Frederick Baum, Sr., explained to a newspaper reporter:

> *Baum is not really a Baum. He has spent many dollars verifying and documenting his heritage. ...*
>
> *Baum's natural grandfather, according to documentation, was Barron Eric von Amster, a Bulgarian revolutionist who lived in Budapest. Fleeing his country with his wife, the barron found refuge in the home of a sympathetic Jewish family in Alcey, Germany, about 20 miles from Worms. The name of the family was Baum. Two days after the barron's family arrived, the wife gave birth to a son. Soon afterward, the barron was found and imprisoned, and the wife died. The kind Jew, looked at the unnamed orphan and called him "Little Isaac." The name stuck. When little Isaac entered school, he had to have a last name; he took the name Baum.[645]*

Three of Isaac and Sophia's children, George, John, and Carrie, married non-Jewish spouses and were buried in non-Jewish cemeteries. Ed, another child, never married and was buried with his parents in the Hebrew Cemetery. Isaac's impressive monument, his Jewish-sounding name, his adoptive parents' and his wife's religion—taken altogether, it seems Isaac Baum considered himself Jewish. George Baum didn't consider himself Jewish, but if requested to finance a corrected gravestone for Rope Walker, one which included at a minimum an accurate name, he probably would have done it. But no one ever made the request, it seems, and neither George F. Baum, Sr. nor anyone else for that matter, over so many years, ever spent a single dollar attempting to verify or document Rope Walker's real name.

## Adolph Zadek—One for the Books

George F. Baum's family origins were explained in a 1976 *Sun* article about Corsicana's First National Bank, which was honoring its two oldest customers, one of them Baum. The other was Bertha (Zadek) Ellis, whose thoroughly assimilated family also had an unusual relationship with its Israelitish roots. Her great uncle, Adolph Zadek, was a pioneer Corsicana Jew who arrived in the town in 1872. He was one of three trustees who purchased land to create the Hebrew Cemetery and one of the seven founders of the Corsicana Hebrew Cemetery Association.[646]

Adolph Zadek was a highly respected citizen of Corsicana and known throughout Texas as a Republican Party leader, not unlike Rube Freedman. His biography in the 1893 *Memorial History of Navarro, Henderson, Anderson, Limestone, Freestone and Leon Counties* lies alongside Corsicana luminaries like businessmen Alex Beaton and Charles Allyn, Judge Kerr, Texas legislator George T. Jester, and celebrated doctors J.W. Gulick, W.J.W. Kerr, A.C. Sloan, and A.N. Witherspoon. There are over four hundred biographical sketches (all men), but only two with Hebraic origins. One is the early Texas patriot, Adolphus Sterne, whose fascinating biography (posthumous in 1893) is well-known to Texas historians. The other is Zadek.

He was born in what is now Gliwice, Poland, in 1832. He noted[647] that his ancestry could be traced back to "the high priests of Judea," a claim he could make because the Hebrew word "*tzadik*," meaning "righteous," was used to describe the biblical Hebrew priests.[648] He initially came to the U.S. in 1855, landing at New Orleans, where he then worked in the saddlery and hardware business until April 1862, when Union General Benjamin Butler took the city. Although Zadek voted against secession and was a Union sympathizer, he left the city,[649] travelling to Europe to visit his mother. Ten months later, back in New Orleans, he decided to go to Mexico, where he was in business in Matamoros, just over the Texas border, until the end of the war. He returned to New Orleans and worked in the cotton business there and in Alabama. In 1866 he again went to Europe. When he came back this time he lived in Navasota, Texas, where he again engaged in the cotton business. He followed each new extension of the H&TC railroad as it progressed northward, living in Millican, Bryan, Calvert, Kosse, and Groesbeck. Finally, in the summer of 1872, he reached Corsicana where he established a grocery and cotton business and settled permanently.

He was a close friend of Governor Edmund J. Davis, the federal government's Reconstruction appointee for Texas. During the election of 1872 Zadek was authorized by Gov. Davis to establish policing of the polls to ensure a fair election. The years of Reconstruction were difficult times for Corsicana, as it was throughout the South, but Zadek's "fairness and non-partisanship was strongly brought out in his exercise of the trusts committed to him."[650] He was appointed U.S. Commissioner in 1873 and held that office until 1882.

Davis made Zadek an alderman of Corsicana, which Zadek accepted

> *with the condition that all the officers, from mayor down, be removed and others appointed, which was done. He served as Alderman until an election took place. During this year he, under the authority of the late Governor Davis, established the first free public schools in Navarro and Hill counties. He was president of the school board.*[651]

Zadek published the *Progressive Age* in 1872, the first Republican newspaper in Central Texas, which existed for one year. He became chairman of the State Republican Executive Committee in 1873 and was a delegate at large at the 1876 National Convention, voting to nominate Oliver P. Morton for president.

> *In 1884 he was appointed Postmaster of Corsicana by President Arthur, and held the office until he was indicted upon false charges preferred by political enemies.*[652]

He proved his innocence in a Dallas Federal Court in 1885 and returned as Corsicana's postmaster in 1889, reappointed by President Harrison.[653]

He never married. He lived with his mother prior to her death, his widowed sister Bertha Casper, and Bertha's son Bismarck. Zadek adopted his nephew, Bismarck, who adopted his uncle's surname, Zadek. This is why Bismarck's daughter, Bertha Ellis, one of the two bank customers written about in the 1976 *Sun* article, had the maiden name "Zadek." Shortly after the end of World War I, on Dec. 10, 1918, Bismarck legally changed his name to Bertrand Caspar Zadek. He told the court that he was born in Bryan, Texas, in 1870, the year of the Franco-Prussian War, and that was why his mother gave him the unusual name.

> [He] *never liked the name, and has never had any use for the Prussians or their treatment of France in 1870, and that now since they have tried to subjugate the rest of civilization he desires to be rid of the name.*[654]

Postmaster Zadek was a follower of Robert G. Ingersoll, a well-known orator and statesman of the era, famous too for his promotion of agnosticism. The descendent of the high priests of did not ascribe to the tenants of Judaism. Despite being a founder of the Hebrew Cemetery, when his time came, in 1895, at the age of sixty-three, he would be buried in Corsicana's Oakwood Cemetery.[655] His mother, Rosalie Zadek, died in 1880 and was buried in the Hebrew Cemetery, her ornate gravestone listing her three children: Adolph, Oscar, and Bertha (see Supplement III).[656]

Zadek was closely connected to the Jewish community, even if theologically he was not one of them. He was closely connected to the town's leading citizens, even if his politics placed him in a small minority, Corsicana then being overwhelmingly Democratic. Zadek *was* a leading citizen, despite his unconventional political and religious predilections. He had a major role in establishing the Hebrew Cemetery and his mother's grave is located next to Rope Walker's grave, together strongly suggesting that he was well aware of Rope Walker's defective memorial. If asked, Zadek probably could have easily looked into the matter and had "Danil Berg," or some variation thereof, engraved into that piece of marble.

♎

Those who knew the tightrope performer's name and those who could have put a name on his gravestone were on an equal footing, working and living close together while jointly building Corsicana into the city it is today. Back then it didn't matter if one called himself a Jew or a Christian. There was no lack of communication or cooperation that explains why Rope Walker's true name, which was known, was never put on his gravestone. There must have been some other reason to explain why his epitaph was missing.

Corsicana Fire Department statue on the grounds of the courthouse

# Chapter 25

# THE JEWISH CHURCH

*Faith, like a jackal, feeds among the tombs, and even from these dead doubts she gathers her most vital hope*

After Rope Walker's brief appearance, other Jewish performers came to Corsicana. These men walked a figurative tightrope: not a line stretched between two buildings but a chain linking the strictures of ancient traditions to the modern exigencies of Main Street merchants. These were the rabbis of Corsicana, envoys representing a minority amidst an overwhelmingly dominant Christian culture and ethos, presiding over what local histories and town directories frequently referred to as the "Jewish Church." The histories of Corsicana's two Jewish churches, Beth El and Agudas Achim, are found in Supplement I. Biographies of Corsicana's rabbis are presented in Supplement II.[657]

Those who ministered to Corsicana's Jewish community visited the cemetery frequently and therefore must have seen the peculiar grave marker there, or at the very least heard about it.[658] They had a moral, perhaps even a divine duty under Jewish law to find out the identity of the unknown Jew buried there. Was he not some mother's son, a widow's husband, an orphan's father? Would not his widow be prevented from remarrying, not knowing if her husband was dead? What of his mother's inexorable grief for her missing son? Would his children grow up thinking their father had abandoned them? How is it that these highly educated, intelligent com‑munity leaders never tracked down the identity of this forgotten soul? Did they simply concede that the mystery was unsolvable, his identity unknow‑able, like God Himself?

Two rabbis lived in Corsicana before 1900, the year when Beth El was built—Abraham Israel and Solomon Solomon—but no rabbi was in town as early as when Rope Walker died, as correctly stated in the legend. Altogether, twenty-one rabbis led the Beth El congregation, beginning with Rabbi Magil in 1900. Congregation Agudas Achim had ten rabbis, starting with Rabbi Ratner in 1901. Another four rabbis from neighboring communities frequently officiated at funerals and weddings and led holiday services during pulpit vacancies. There is no evidence that any of those thirty-five rabbis made any effort to figure out the identity of Rope Walker. Rabbi Joseph, Corsicana's last full-time rabbi, in 1989 wrote up a straightforward summary of the Rope Walker legend for the Texas Jewish

Historical Society, but there is no evidence that he undertook an inves–
tigation to learn the man's identity.[659]

Corsicana's Jewish clergy certainly had the smarts to figure it out—their
collective resume of advanced degrees rivaled that of a small college's fac-
ulty.[660] They had connections to hundreds of Jewish communities throughout the country,[661] useful when asking if anyone had ever heard of a Jewish
one-legged entertainer/acrobat. Beyond that, it's not altogether clear what
they *could* have done without newspaper databases available at their fin-
gertips. In any case, if they did try, they didn't succeed.

Beth El Temple's second leader, Rabbi Stollnitz, delivered a Confederate
Memorial Day sermon at the Hebrew Cemetery on May 30, 1904. There
were sixty-five graves at the time—forty of them children. He spoke broadly
on the topic of honoring the dead:

> *We derive a very important lesson by visiting these grounds
> that God intended no man to be better than his fellows, for
> just as there is no distinction here so should we be mindful
> that the advantages of this life were by Divine intention
> designated to be for the common benefit of all. With the same
> readiness as we to-day pay tribute and honor to the dead, so
> should we ever willingly, and wherever we can, help to
> smoothen the paths of our brethren in this life ...* [662]

Surely there is some third measure of life between the oblivion of death
shared by all equally and the inequities all experience above ground. It is the
acknowledgement that a person came into this world, bravely lived, loved,
felt pain, succeeded, failed, and left. It is the recognition and appreciation
everyone deserves. It is not too much to ask for some sign, some memorial,
some record to remain to say, "I was here, and now I'm gone."

The vague statement on the historic plaque about "a search for his
identity which gripped the community," a reasonable assumption, is ultimately proven wrong. Rope Walker's simple stone and its puzzling epitaph
remained, year to year, decade to decade, century to century, rabbi to rabbi,
*dor v'dor* (generation to generation).

# Chapter 26

## TILL LIFE BECAME A LEGEND
## OF THE DEAD[663]

*in some spiritual sense the coffin is, after all, but an immortality-preserver*

Most of the uncertainty and mystery connected to the Rope Walker legend is gone. *Who*, *where*, and *when* are known. *What* happened on Beaton Street that Saturday has always been known, in some sense, even if proof is sorely lacking that events happened as detailed in the legend. The basic story of a one-legged Jewish tightrope walker who fell and died in Corsicana is fact.

But there is still the question of *why*. Why did no one in Corsicana's sizeable Jewish community put this man's name on his gravestone, and perhaps, if it's not asking too much, his date of death and the other information typically found on a nineteenth-century Jewish American's gravestone? The answer lies in that burial ground, or more accurately, it lies with the early administrators of the cemetery. They failed to carry out what surely was one of their basic responsibilities. They didn't deem it important enough to make sure that the deceased received a proper gravestone when he died, and, through mismanagement, allowed the defective memorial to remain uncorrected in perpetuity. A close look at the early history of the Corsicana Hebrew Cemetery Association (CHCA) leads to this conclusion.

But the CHCA was not the only nineteenth century Corsicana Jewish institution to suffer setbacks and administrative failures. Although the Hebrew Cemetery and two synagogues seemed to define Corsicana's Jewish community, its B'nai B'rith lodge was also an important factor in the community. The *Jewish Monitor*'s 1920 history of Corsicana's Jews, from Chapter 4, describes Jewish institutions current at that time, including a children's religious school, a Council of Jewish Women, and B'nai B'rith (IOBB) Lodge No. 275.[664] The article misreported that the lodge was founded in 1919. In truth, the lodge's charter was granted on April 18, 1877,[665] and its constitution was one of the documents placed in a time capsule in the cornerstone of Corsicana's newest courthouse in 1881.[666] In May of 1879, twenty-one years before the town's first synagogue was built, the lodge was said to be "in very good condition and full of life and debate". Evidence suggests this means it was full of rancor and discord, but these characteristics are not necessarily incompatible.[667]

## Some Brass—Aluminum Gaps and Discrepancies

A burial ground is almost always the first Jewish institution established in a nascent Jewish community, but the Hebrew Cemetery's Historic Texas Cemetery marker (Chapter 2) says the land was purchased in 1881, years after the town's B'nai B'rith group began.

JEWISH POPULATION WAS WELL ESTABLISHED IN CORSICANA AND NEEDED A CEMETERY. IN 1881, THE HEBREW CEMETERY ASSOCIATION PURCHASED THIS PROPERTY FOR USE AS A BURIAL GROUND. HOWEVER, THE LAND HAD BEEN USED FOR JEWISH INTERMENTS PRIOR TO THIS TIME; THE EARLIEST KNOWN BURIAL DATES TO 1877. IN 1887, THE LADIES HEBREW CEMETERY ASSOCIATION FORMED TO RAISE FUNDS FOR CEMETERY UPKEEP. IN 1951, ADDITIONAL PROPERTY WAS PURCHASED.

Historical plaque at Hebrew Cemetery (detail)

It also says, "the earliest known burial dates to 1877," which means someone permitted four years of Jewish burials on their land before it became a cemetery. Another plaque, attached to an entry gate post only a few yards away, donated by James Cerf, son of I.N. Cerf and grandson of Louis Cerf, says the cemetery was established in December 1875. Which is it, 1875 or 1881?

A short history, written up in the CHCA's 1951 *Revised Constitution and By-laws*,[668] names the CHCA founders, the same seven on James Cerf's plaque, and says the land was purchased in December 1875.[669] It turns out that the original deed, from 1875, was lost and therefore never filed with the county, a glaring example of mismanagement. Another sign of early mismanagement is that the CHCA improperly used a portion of the Catholic

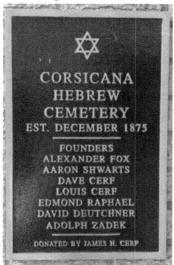

Founders plaque

cemetery, its neighbor to the east. The additional property purchased by the CHCA in 1951, mentioned on the State Historic Cemetery plaque, was not for more space— the CHCA had then and still has plenty of space. Instead, the CHCA needed to purchase a sliver of land it had taken by mistake.[670]

On June 6, 1881, William F. Henderson created a Deed in Substitution, legally conveying (reconveying) the Hebrew Cemetery property to Alexander Fox, Adolph Zadek, and David Deutschner.[671] This time, the deed was duly recorded.

*The State of Texas*

*County of Navarro*

*Whereas heretofore to wit, in or about the month of December A.D. 1875, I William F. Henderson of the County of*

*Navarro and State of Texas, made, executed and delivered unto the trustees of the Corsicana, Hebrew, Benevolent Association, a good valid and sufficient deed of con- veyance to four and 96/100 acres of land hereinafter described the consideration of said deed being the sum of twelve and 50/100 dollars per acre of good and lawful money of the United States to me then in hand paid by the said Trustees of said association and whereas the above described deed was lost or destroyed*

*... therefore I make the following deed in substitution.*

*... by these presents grant, bargain and convey unto A. Fox, A. Zadek and D. Deutschner Trustees ...*[672]

The nearly five acres came out of a spread of 1,475 acres granted by the Republic of Texas to Henderson, land which he patented—legally estab- lished with full, private ownership rights—in 1841.[673] Thanks to Henderson, the Jews of Corsicana were able to take the first and most important step needed to emboss their presence in the twenty-seven-years- young town.

A few years after Texas Independence, William Fenner Henderson was a twenty-one-year-old land surveyor and one of twenty-four (twenty-five, by some accounts) men who surveyed land in what would later be, for the most part, the southwestern part of Navarro County. The surveying party started in the town of Franklin and spent the first night in the home of Dr. George W. Hill, said to be the first permanent white settler in what became Navarro County. The next day, setting out, they were attacked by a large number of native inhabitants who understood, correctly, that the white men's purpose was to take away their valuable hunting grounds. A pro- longed battle ensued, the Indians killing fifteen of the remaining twenty-two Whites (prior to the attack, two from the party were dismissed to retrieve a better compass). Six, including Henderson, made an escape. A wounded man, left behind in hopes of being rescued once the others returned, survived. The Indians also sustained numerous casualties. The scene of the bloodshed became known as Battle Creek.[674]

Henderson went on to become a lawyer and district attorney and died in Corsicana on Oct. 12, 1890.[675] Mary Miller candidly recalled:

> **W. M. Love built the first house in this County down near Patterson Lake.**[676] **Among the early settlers was R. H. White,**[677] **who came here very soon after we did. Col. Henderson who came about the same time and built a house where the Third Ward School is now. He was a lawyer but he didn't practice much. He had a rich brother in New Orleans who sent him money all the time, and he didn't do much of anything but chess.**[678]

W.F. Henderson was no stranger to Corsicana's Jews—in 1860 he and his family resided with Alex Michael in the public square, then the heart of Corsicana.[679]

## Mortality Disorder

The 1951 CHCA history says that "The first recorded burial was a child of Mr. and Mrs. Alex Fox on March 18, 1877." Were there *unrecorded* burials before then, during the cemetery's first fifteen months, before the death of little Leo Fox? Is that what the historical plaque means by "the earliest *known* burial dates to 1877"? In those early days there were several Jewish families in town and infant mortality was high. If there *were* any burials in 1876 or in the first few months of 1877 they were not recorded, and no evidence of them, including markers, currently exists.

Shoddy record keeping was evident right from the start, when the original deed was lost, and persisted for years. To its credit, the CHCA acknowledged these problems in its 1951 historical summary:[680]

> No records are available during the years from 1908 to 1918. The above information was gathered from many sources since some of the records are lost, and those available are scattered.

Constitution and By-Laws, Hebrew Cemetery Association, 1951 (excerpt)

Currently, the only early records to have survived are the CHCA's compiled meeting minutes, covering meetings from Oct. 11, 1918 through Feb. 20, 1956,[681] a 1958 cemetery plot map, and the information recorded in the (current) record book. The location of all records prior to the 1950s, other than meeting minutes, is not known. Pre-1908 records and the original record book, the "ancient volume" mentioned in Haslam's 1936 article, may have been destroyed after information was transferred to the newer record book, in 1952, but no one knows.

The notation about Rope Walker in the original record book must have been made long after he died because his date of death was off by an entire year and tellingly omitted a specific date. In all likelihood the entry was recorded many years later, retrieved from either a scrap of paper or a scrap of memory. "It was some time later before the little marble tombstone was put at the head of the grave," according to Haslam's information, presumably supplied by Mary London. The old record book also said he "Fell from Trapeze," as discussed in Chapter 13, but it is doubtful that notation is accurate because an important detail like that would have been mentioned in the news articles written at the time of the accident. The early CHCA administrators, it must be concluded, did not carry out their re-sponsibilities. If they did, a proper record of Moses Berg's death would have been made and his gravestone would have a proper epitaph.

Regardless of the mismanagement and record keeping irregularities in the early years of the CHCA, those members of Corsicana's Jewish com-munity who contributed time, labor, and money to create and care for the Hebrew Cemetery, a sacred duty, deserve respect and gratitude. A brief chronology, assembled from the limited sources available, is a small but worthy offering of tribute and appreciation for their sacrifices.[682]

# Chapter 27

## GONE AND FORGOTTEN

*these mysteries were therefore destined in the end to moulder away with the living parchment whereon they were inscribed, and so be unsolved to the last*

The rope walker's widow learned of her husband's death by May 8, at the latest, less than two months after he died, and yet she never arranged to have a proper gravestone put on his grave. Newly widowed, a gravestone may not have been an expense she could afford. Even though she received a bundle of money from the Pension Office before the year was out (Chapter 19), just how much did she owe this man, pension money notwithstanding, who married her, took off across the country without her, and promptly got himself killed? No spouse or relative of Moses Berg, no friend of Daniel De Houne, no benevolent co-religionist or kindly Christian neighbor provided a proper memorial for the itinerant, indigent rope walker. Instead of the oft-used funereal sentiment, "gone, but not forgotten," inscribe this one "gone and forgotten."

Close family and friends put up gravestones honoring the memory of their dearly departed. In a few generations those caring survivors also perish and nobody is left who remembers the earlier, deceased generation. People seldom visit the graves of their grandparents, let alone their great-grandparents. Within a hundred years of death remembrance becomes the provenance of the devout, family historians, and cemetery administrators. Life's day-to-day struggles allow little time, money, or emotional energy to attend to the dead; less so for the dead who are distantly or tangentially related; and nothing for the stranger. What becomes of the friendless departed, all alone like Berg? Eleanor Rigby was buried along with her name; Rope Walker didn't even get that.

Sarah cannot be accused of entering into a meretricious marriage, just for his pension money. The man she married was intent on getting himself killed. She and others within the personal sphere of the death-defying daredevil are indemnified against mourning his death or caring whether or not he received a worthy memorial stone. He was mourned enough in life and his epitaph appeared on every handbill announcing the incredible feat of walking a tightrope with but one leg. Alone he greeted crowds of strangers eager to pay for a chance to see him die. He kept up his routine until one day he finally urged fate one-too-many times. Parent, brother, sisters, children, wives, lover, friends—why should anyone care for a man who cared so little for himself? No wonder none of them erected a proper stone in his memory. No one ever visited his grave to discover his odd gravestone, to discover it needed to be corrected.

An unfair presumption? Too harsh? Was he expected instead to grind a hand organ on a street corner for handouts, like thousands of other veterans with sawed-off legs, or sit at home with his modest pension, poor and bored? His spirit of adventure, his courage, his jousting with the fates was a lifestyle worthy of respect and deference from those who cared for him. They should have let him live the life he wanted to live. Whatever pursuits his loved ones chose for themselves, they could hardly assume the power to choose for him his life to live. They should have viewed his chosen profession with awe, not just fear. When his life story is written—this memorandum being only the story of his death—then his full life will be celebrated, and not just lamented, in chiseled verse.[683]

The failure to act by those with personal connections to Berg were not remedied by the local Jewish community, which at the time showed a similarly blunted absence of care and empathy for the performer. Inad–equate attention to cemetery responsibilities was just one symptom of a general neglect of religious commitment among Corsicana's early Jewish community. As shown in Supplement I, it took many years, until the late 1890s, and a set of newcomers, to get the town's first synagogue built.[684] Then, despite having a synagogue, there was a persistent inability to keep a rabbi for more than a few years and for many years there was no rabbi at all.[685] In 1913, an entire reorganization of Beth El's leadership was necessary because it had fallen into such a stupor.[686] Corsicana's pioneer Jews

**for the most part hailed from cities and communities where no effort was made in the direction of [institutional] org–anization.**[687]

The failures of those men and women to act as a responsible Jewish community were painfully manifest to Charles Wessolowsky (1839-1904), associate editor of the *Jewish South*, who stopped in Corsicana on May 27, 1879, during his travels through the South. The purpose of his tour was to encourage greater involvement in religious practices and procure more subscribers for his newspaper. The *Jewish South* published his peripatetic missives, addressed ostensibly to the paper's editor, Rabbi Edward B.M. "Alphabet" Browne. A frequent subject was children's education. Wesso–lowsky reported that

*Among the 4,000 inhabitants of this city, there are about twelve Jewish families. Here again, we found that the young are neglected and that the command, "Thou shall teach it diligently to thy children," is entirely forgotten. ... We hope that ere long, parents in Corsicana will awaken to their duty and let their children at least receive the necessary instruct-tion in the Jewish religion. Otherwise our Israelitish breth-ren here seem to be prosperous, and are carrying on exten-sive business.*[688]

He added that

*The Sunday School established some time ago by Rev. Mr. Blum,*[689] *of Galveston is out of date, no pupils and no teacher to be found, no one cares and thus it rocks along to the injury and neglect of the Jewish children. We took occasion to speak to some of the ladies in its behalf and in our lecture in the B. B. Lodge made mention that it is one of the teach-ings and purposes of the order.*[690]

Wessolowsky spared Corsicana's Jews the harsher criticism he unleashed against the Jews of some other towns he visited, like Brenham, Texas.[691] He was more accepting of Corsicana, perhaps, because he received a nice reception there. Following an unexpected delay in Waco, in Corsicana Wes–solowsky

*spent our Shevuos, the Feast of Weeks, but not in such a manner and place as we would desire, as there is no temple... We made ourselves satisfied spending the day in getting acquainted with our brothers, whom we found to be pleasant and agreeable.*[692]

No mention was made of the cemetery, which, at the time of his visit, had a population of seven—six infants and one newborn.

Ω

Chapter 26 concluded there was poor management of the Cemetery Association in its early years. At one point the wives formed their own association to raise money for cemetery upkeep. It's not known what care the cemetery needed, but it may have included the procurement of headstones for stoneless graves. The Shwarts family, strong supporters of the cemetery, at that same time became part owners of a Vermont marble quarry.[693] What purpose could there be for a Jewish family of cotton dealers in 1880s Texas—Aaron, the family head, a founding member of the CHCA, Caroline, his wife, on the Cemetery Affairs Committee of the Ladies Hebrew Cemetery Association, and their boys, Abe and Kal, cotton brokers—to own a quarry amongst the snowy mountaintops of Vermont, other than to ship some of that fine marble two thousand miles back to Corsicana so gravestones could be put up in their beloved Hebrew Cemetery? If they did is a black and white question to which the simple answer, yes or no, could fit on a postage stamp, but that's a mystery for another day.

**Fountain plaque at Hebrew Cemetery**

According to the Historic Texas Cemetery plaque, the Ladies' Hebrew Cemetery Association was formed in 1887 "to raise funds for cemetery upkeep." According to an *American Israelite* story, though, it was formed not in 1887, but in July 1891:

> **CORSICANA, TEXAS.**
>
> **JULY 27:-- There are about three hundred souls in this community that profess the Jewish faith. They have not done much as yet, however, toward promoting Judaism or instructing their offspring in the tenets of our religion.**
>
> **The Ladies' Hebrew Cemetery Association was formed about two weeks ago...**
>
> **The membership numbers forty-two, all married ladies, as no unmarried ladies are admitted. Their object is to give festivals, etc., in order to raise the necessary funds to improve the cemetery grounds.**[694]

The article describes a fund-raising event on July 22 at the home of Mrs. Freedman. She and other officers ran the fair with help from more than a dozen young Jewish women, including "Mamie" (Mary) and Julia London.

> **Miss Sophie Raphael [was voted]** *most popular young lady;* **Mrs. L. Cerf** *as the most popular married lady, and Mr. M.A. Goldsmith "took the cake" as the ugliest man.*
>
> *The cake voted to Ms. Raphael netted the handsome sum of $155.60. The one to Mrs. Cerf realized $10. There were quite a number of Christians present, who helped to swell the fund. The festival netted $260, quite a handsome sum for their first entertainment. Another festival is contemplated in the near future.*
>
> *As the holidays are approaching our Jewish brethren are getting very pious, and are building synagogues and temples (in their minds), but after the holidays all enthusiasm vanishes, not to be heard of again until the next year.*
>
> **Promoter.**[695]

In the summer of 1891, there were thirty-four burials in the cemetery. Improvements might have included putting up tombstones on the graves of those who had long gone without, perhaps Rope Walker's, enhancing the landscaping, installation of fencing, curbing of family lots, and maybe some effort to improve record keeping. Eight years after Rope Walker's death would be a sufficient passage of time such that his year of his death, finally moved from recollection to written record, would be misremembered by one year, and long enough that any readily accessible way to learn his name would have long-since disappeared. If the original (now lost) burial record book was started around 1891, by 1936 it would be "somewhat ancient," with "yellowed pages," as described by Haslam.

Twenty-seven deaths were recorded before 1890 (Supplement III):

- thirteen were under the age of three
- three were aged three to six
- Louis Shwarts was fifteen
- three were adults who died young
- four were adults who lived out full lives
- the ages for three could not be learned

In other words, early death accounted for roughly five out of six pre-1890 Jewish deaths in Corsicana.

With so much death so close at hand, sustained grieving for the dead would have been an emotionally dangerous luxury few could afford. Death and dying was a far-too-common business and clinging to memories of lost loved ones a heavy burden, a distraction from life's daily struggles. "Bury them and move on" would have been preferable to "remember the dead." Max London might have adopted the former philosophy in early 1883, a month before Moses Berg's death, when he lost his infant son, Elkan. Unlike the elaborate and informative 1877 gravestone for Leo Fox, who died just short of his first birthday, the plain slab for Elkan London, about two years old, bears his name, and nothing more.[696]

♌

A review of the pre-1890 Hebrew Cemetery burials in Supplement III reveals which of those individuals were quickly forgotten once they were gone. They were the ones without local ties and without Corsicana friends and family, like Rope Walker, and their gravestones, just like Rope Walker's, are missing essential, basic information. The stones for *Morris* (1878), *Brin* (1887), and *Abraham* (1887) have nothing but one word on them, a name. The cemetery record book's entries for those three show a year of death but not a particular date—just like the entry for Rope Walker. Who's to say any of *those* years are accurate? The tablets for *Elkan London, Charles Rich*, and *Joe Goldberg* have a first and last name, and nothing else—no date of death. The death dates for those three are likewise only found in the CHCA record book, and Charles Rich's notation there likewise only records a year. There's a good possibility Goldberg's recorded date of death is grossly incorrect and not only that, but "Joe Goldberg" may not even be his correct name, as discussed in Supplement III.

These are not unreadable stones, as the table below and the photos in Supplement III make plain. Gravestone engravings do become illegible over time, as some other gravestones amply demonstrate, but that's not the case here. These gravestones <u>never</u> had key pieces of information: no first name, no last name, no date of death.[697]

A delay in erecting these markers and the stingy information etched into them were probably the consequences of dying without family or friends (or an estate) to pay for and oversee the creation of a proper memorial. Instead of being buried in unmarked graves in a potters' field, these friend–less, penniless Jews at some point after burial received a very basic marker, about ten letters carved into it, and nothing more, probably financed by a bake sale.

Ten gravestones have so little information on them, like Rope Walker's stone, it seems they were created much later than when those people died, as was the case with Rope Walker's. Eight of these ten were for deaths before 1890, and of these, only Joe Goldberg's record book entry has a date more specific than just a year. Again, like Goldberg's recorded name, there is doubt about the accuracy of his date of death, which may be off by more than two years.

Not only do these ten markers have similarly sparse information, but eight of them have an identical shape and inscription style. The other two, for Elkan London and "Abraham," have squared-off tops, not rounded, and different lettering styles: "Elkan London" is engraved in a curve, while all others have the letters going straight across; and the letters comprising "Abraham" are spaced far apart, unlike the others. Elkan London's stone is quite exceptional because his father was secretary of the cemetery association and young Elkan should have had a nicer stone. Wholly inex–plicable.[698] Because of these distinctions, the Elkan London and Abraham gravestones are excluded from further analysis. The remaining eight tablets are listed below. All have a rounded top that smoothly curves into vertical sides. All have the same style of lettering.

Plausibly, these eight similar stones were bought for the graves of the poor and friendless, maybe created from stone shipped from the Shwarts's Vermont quarry. They are the simplest and therefore the least expensive. All of the people buried beneath them, except Charles Rich (see Chapter 28), were without known ties to Corsicana. No request for reimbursement was made to the county commissioner for the burial of these poor Jews.[699] If you were Jewish and died in Corsicana, you got a proper burial, and, in time, a gravestone.[700]

Most of the other early gravestones in the cemetery as old or older than any of these eight have ornate carvings and detailed inscriptions. It's obvious, after a review of Supplement III, that the more elegant markers were put up by local families. The earliest, for example, for Leo Fox, has complete information about the boy and an intricate, artistic design. This is also true, in various degrees, of many other early memorials, i.e. those erected by Corsicana families before 1920. Later monuments, i.e. those after 1920, don't have fancy carvings, but they do contain at least the minimum information expected: full names and birth and death dates.

# GRAVESTONES LIKE ROPE WALKER'S GRAVESTONE

| Stone | Died | Writing on Stone | Record Book |
|---|---|---|---|

## Burials to 1890—See also Supplement III

| Stone | Died | Writing on Stone | Record Book |
|---|---|---|---|
|  | 1878 | MORRIS | Twins infants of C. Morris 1878 |
|  | Mar. 13, 1883 | ROPE WALKER | Fell from Trapeze 1884 [from the original record book] |
|  | 1885 | CHARLES . RICH | Rich Chas Son of Isaac & Harriet Rich 1885 |
|  | Aug. 11, 1884 or Oct. 31, 1886 | JOE . GOLDBERG | Goldberg Joe 8/11/1884 Nephew of Joe Reisman, Ennis Texas |
|  | 1887 | BRIN | Brin 1887[701] |
|  | Unknown | MORRIS ROSENBAUM | Rosenbaum, Morris No information[702] |

## Burials 1890 and Later

| Stone | Died | Writing on Stone | Record Book |
|---|---|---|---|
|  | July 14, 1904 | OSHUA N. CAHN | Cahn Joshua, Infant of Mr & Mrs Nathan Cahn 7-14-1904 |
|  | Feb. 11, 1905[703] | LEUIS NIVETH | Niveth Louis 2-12-1905 |

An odd part of the Rope Walker legend was the test given to the dying acrobat to verify that he was, in fact, Jewish. It was not enough for him to say he was Jewish; he also had to recite a prayer in Hebrew. And woe to him if he made a mistake or his Hebrew wasn't so good! Haslam's version has Rope Walker telling Mr. Simon "He had been 'joking' when he said he was a Methodist, but really was an Orthodox Jew, which was proven to Mr. Simon's satisfaction ..."

Ivan Rosenberg's version in the cemetery record book says: "A Jewish merchant ... requested the dying man to repeat a Certain prayer, which he did in excellent Hebrew and there was no doubt that he was a Jew."

Campbell's "Walk into Oblivion" pushes the idea to parody:

> *The dying man told the merchant he was an Orthodox Jew.*
> *It is not easy to fool a Jew about his religion. He asked the dying man to repeat certain prayers. He did, readily, in excellent Hebrew.*
> *He was a Jew all right, the merchant said.*

Certified Kosher! He was not one of those numerous Gentiles who presumably came to Corsicana in early pioneer days who, on the edge of death, falsely claimed to be Jewish just so they could get a free burial and gravestone.

# Chapter 28

## CRUSHED

*chance, free will, and necessity—no wise incompatible—all interweavingly working together*

Haslam and Campbell both said Rope Walker was "crushed" by the stove he attempted to carry across the rope. This stove then became the focus of speculation, and later repeated as fact, that he was a stove salesman, notably by Jay Silverberg and Frank X. Tolbert. Contemporaneous accounts of the accident in several newspapers confirmed he was carrying a stove when he fell,[704] but none said he was crushed by it or reported injuries consistent with him being "crushed." The stove, it turns out, was part of his act—he cooked pancakes up on the wire.[705] He couldn't possibly have carried, unpacked, and cooked on a full-sized, four-hundred-plus-pound iron stove, all the time balancing on a rope. It must have been a fairly small stove. Rope Walker was not crushed by a stove.

A Serious Accident--A Fair Journalist.

Special Telegram to the Examiner.

CORSICANA, March 9. Mr. Richard Maynard, a much respected citizen, was to-day very badly crushed by a safe which he was moving to the second story of the Mallory & Allen building, falling on him. The pelvis bone is broken, and there is hardly a chance of his recovery.

Miss Eva Britton, the editress of the Hurricane, of Charleston, South Carolina, is in the city in the interest of her paper.

More news from Corsicana, March 9, 1883

## Richard Maynard—Crushed

Six days after Rope Walker fell and four days before he died, Richard Maynard, a Corsicana bricklayer originally from England who had recently arrived from Toronto with his wife and three small children, <u>was</u> crushed—by a safe. He was trying to move it up a stairway at the Mallory & Allen store, in the Wilson Building—pretty much the same location where Rope Walker fell.[706] Maynard's fatal accident was in such close proximity in both time and place to Rope Walker's fall, surely the two events became conflated and people began to say that Rope Walker was "crushed."

## August Blum—Crushed

Four months after Maynard's safe accident, his widow married another Corsicanan, August Blum.[707] Blum was also widowed, and he had a daughter, Matilda, from his first marriage,[708] while Mrs. Maynard had three of her own.[709] Before long, alas, the new Mrs. Blum, formerly Mrs. Maynard, was also dead.[710] Three weeks after that, August Blum wed another widow, Mrs. Carrie (Rich) O'Daniel.[711] The newest Mrs. Blum had a daughter from *her* earlier marriage, and Blum still had Matilda. The three Maynard orphans, ages eleven to sixteen, went to live elsewhere.[712] Ida, the product of August and Carrie's union, joined the new family.

People still marry and give themselves away in marriage in Corsicana frequently. The Observer says:

If August Blum, the baker, keeps on at the same rate he has been marrying the last few months, by the time he is an old man Bluebeard will not be a circumstance. He lost a wife some time in the spring. Three moons had hardly waxed and waned before he, through an agent, had contracted for and married a widow, who had very recently lost her husband, and who had a house full of children. She scarcely lived through the honeymoon, though from reports there was not much honey in the moon for them, before she too was laid beside his first wife. In about three weeks he contracted for another, a buxum young widow. He met her at 1 o'clock last Sunday evening, and at 3 o'clock the ceremony of marriage was performed.

The many marriages of August Blum

Carrie did not leave August a widower, but left him just the same, divorced, sometime in the latter part of the 1880s.[713] She remarried, again, on August 11, 1890, to Dave King,[714] who was also previously married, and he too had children from his former wife. Together, over the next several years, the Kings added to their brood. In 1900 their farmhouse boasted: three of their own, jointly produced offspring; four from King's previous marriage; one from her first marriage; Matilda, from August Blum's first marriage; and Ida, the daughter of Carrie and August. In 1903 the Kings welcomed Hallye, making a total of eleven. On the ninth day of 1906, Carrie succumbed to pneumonia on the family farm near Blooming Grove, just outside of Corsicana.[715]

August Blum had lots of legal troubles to go with his marriage troubles. In one case, he and Carrie's father, Isaac Rich (the same Rich family from Chapters 5 and 24), were arrested for fraud. They were eventually found not guilty, on appeal.[716]

Charles Blum, August's brother,[717] lived in Corsicana as early as 1873.[718] His wife, Ella (Louella), "Lou," died Sept. 7, 1889,[719] Charles died Oct. 29, 1890,[720] and their son, Grathe, reunited with his parents on Dec. 1, 1893, at the age of four.[721] Charles, Lou, and Grathe were interred in Corsicana's Oakwood Cemetery. Louis Blum, another brother, was a successful Corsicana baker and confectioner.[722] In 1902 his wife Jane left him. She stopped at the house a few days later to discover a terrifying scene: Louis had stretched a string between a shotgun's trigger and his foot.[723]

People were not fond of the hard-luck Blums. In June, 1886, for example, August Blum filed a lawsuit against Anderson Teague, "charging him with disturbing the peace of Blum's family." Teague was acquitted, and then sued Blum for libel.[724] Then there was the time a Roman candle was tossed through a window of Louis Blum's store on Beaton Street, Christmas morning, igniting a fire but causing little damage.[725] It was ten years after a fire burned down Charles's business on Beaton Street.[726]

Twice widowed, divorced, with failed businesses, criminal charges, civil suits, and sundry other indignities and travails, August Blum lost his mind. On Jan. 4, 1890, he was committed to the Austin Lunatics Asylum where he lived out his life until, finally at rest, he passed away on Aug. 7, 1914.[727]

Navarro courts were kept busy dealing with the estates of the three Blum brothers and Wilhelmina Blum (she was adjudged a lunatic, like August, and was somehow related), who all owned real estate in Corsicana. While no proof of the Blum family's Jewish ancestry has been found, those involved in the disposition of their properties included Rube and S.S. Freedman, I.P. Levy, and Max London, all Corsicana Jews.[728]

## Eva Britton—Crushes

The clipping reproduced at the start of this chapter had two items, the second about a "Fair Journalist," Eva Britton of Charleston. During the short time Rope Walker lived (and was dying) in Corsicana, the teenage editress of the *Hurricane* was visiting, one of her many stops, taking subscriptions.

Little Eva Britton, a child, and yet the most hoyden, coquettish, a perfect little sparkler, aged about 11, and was in town to-day drumming for her paper called the *Hurricane* and published in Charleston, S. C., it was 50 cents a year, and she received a number of subscribers. What a fascinating little witch she was, I believe all the young men fell in love with her, and oh! she had travelled, Canada, New York, Boston, was then on her way to New York and would stop in Danville, she has evidently had stage training, and probably made one of the "Pinafore" troupe, a number of young men attended her to the train, and she flirted with them all, as one concluded a neat little goodby speech she exclaimed, "I'll see you later!" to another she said, "If I don't see you again——hello!" Another was evidently mashed, and as he shook her hand a long while and finally darted from the car she turned to a passenger and said, "Quite confectionary, wasn't he?" And this lone child travelling in this big world and perfectly at home, holding herself with all the airs of a little lady, fascinating and at the same time repelling familiarity, quick at repartee and bewitching in manners—and only 11 years old, at that—certainly there is no school like travel and no polish like that caught from the world's great mirror

Eva Britton visits Reidsville, N.C., 1880

Half a year after her visit to Corsicana, Eva found herself in the New Orleans calaboose. She had sold a number of subscriptions in the Big Easy, in July 1883, and when she returned that September, with nary a wisp of her publication, a news-forlorn Leeds Foundry worker, young George B. Mitchell, had her arrested.[729] Other towns also felt they were cheated by her and she got a reputation across the country as a swindler.

Eva did charm half a dollar out of thousands of men in towns across the country, and she did fail to timely fulfill their subscriptions, but contrary to accusations, the *Hurricane* did exist. Scattered issues survive from 1882 and 1883. The numbering in the mast head demonstrate that the paper was a monthly begun in late 1879.[730] In truth, the "perfect little sparkler" had printer's ink coursing through her veins. Her mother was a newspaper publisher, her father a printer, and her grandfather, Edward H. Britton, was a highly esteemed Charlottean news publisher.

Did Ms. Britton print anything in the *Hurricane* about the fall and subsequent death of Prof. De Houne? Probably not[731]—little Eva's newspaper had no discernable *news*. Instead, it was filled with chit-chat, advice, musings, and poetry—the precocious sunbeams and petulant bluster of a bright and perky fourteen-year-old girl.

♎

In 1884, Eva became Miss Lillian Markham, singer and actress. She received glowing reviews for her angelic contralto voice. Her career lasted well into the 1890s, after which time her name, original and assumed, no longer made the notices.

### A GIDDY GIRL.

#### The Career of Eva Britton alias Lillian Markham.

*The people of Cleveland will remember a little girl named Eva Britton who first came here two or three years ago soliciting subscription for her paper, called the Hurricane, printed in Charleston, South Carolina. After reaping quite a harvest, she left and was next seen here on the stage of the White Elephant in a song-and-dance act under the euphonyious name of Lillian Markham. Still more recently she appeared on the stage of Drew's Dime Museum in the same capacity, having a remarkable voice. From a Columbus paper it is learned that "Mrs. Mary Britton, of Charleston, South Carolina, was the other day in search of her daughter, Miss Eva Britton, now singing on the variety stage under the name of Lillian Markham. The young lady was in that city last week, but has gone to Indianapolis. Some years ago Miss*

*Britton visited Columbus when the Legislature was in session, and roped in the members to the extent of fifty cents apiece in the way of subscriptions to a paper called the Whirlwind, which she claimed to be printing in Charleston. The members never saw the paper further than the number which the little solicitor carried with her. She was then but a child, and was interviewed by newspaper men and petted by every one."*

*"Little" Eva Britton—she is eighteen years old—is quite well known in Charleston. Some seven years ago her mother, Mrs. Mary Britton, started a "literary" paper ... and when its failure was patent to everyone, Mrs. Britton sent little Eva out to solicit subscriptions. The warmhearted Charlestonians would not refuse the little girl as they did her mother and the paper was helped to its feet once more. Those who subscribed did so out of sympathy for the little solicitor, who at that early age already displayed an extensive knowledge of the world and its wicked ways. If Eva Britton has turned out what she was taught to be by the course she was obliged to take her mother who now is "in search of her daughter," has no one to blame but herself.*[732]

In her later years, Eva worked as a government clerk in Washington, D.C., and lived with her mother. Her brother Edward, secretary to the secretary of the navy, also lived in D.C. According to a great-niece, Eva was once engaged, but her fiancé died in an airplane crash. She kept her stage name for the remainder of her life, dying as Lillian Markham in Washington in 1941 at the age of seventy-three.

Eva Britton, alias Lillian Markham

Chapter 29

## THE REDEMPTION OF BILLY POWERS

*I may as well say—en passant, as the French remark—that I myself ... am a strict total abstinence man*

### Private Hospital

In the year of '82 Dr. John Starley came into Mr. Mulkey's grocery store and said, "Mulkey, Billy Powers, a citizen of thirty years in this town, is in the upper back room of Col. Croft's store house dying for want of human aid. I have attended to him as long as I can. I turn him over to you." He then walked out of the store. Mr. Mulkey leaned over the counter and prayed to God to know what to do with this man. After praying, he went and arranged for two rooms and secured the service of Harry Hanson, a Norwegian who loved God and loved humanity, and established a temporary private hospital, where he brought in four other sick men. He was delirious for several days after getting into his room. Judge Kerr, A.M. Wilson, Capt. Allen, Judge Bright and others, hearing of this act, contributed freely toward sustaining this enterprise. One day, while Mr. Mulkey was nursing him to let the attendant eat his dinner, the patient opened his eyes and said, "Where am I?" He said, "you are in my house." He answered, "Is it possible? After you have fought whiskey and saloon men as you have to then take me in this condition into your own home?" He replied to this, saying, "Billy, you are mistaken. I have never fought the saloon man, but the traffic only." He says, "Where does this spirit come from?" He then pointed him to Christ the Savior of men. He began to weep and said, "I want to know such a Savior." "Billy, you may know him; let us pray." He tried to get out of bed on to his knees. He said, "Billy you can't do that." "But, I want to get out on my knees; I have not prayed in thirty years." He called in four men. They lifted him out. His flesh was so swollen it was bursting, and, all wrapped in cotton and oil, they let him down on a pillow. He clasped his hands, looked Heavenward and said, "O God, can you forgive a sinner like me, who has been selling whiskey and has thirty years of woe to his account?" In a few days he died, and was buried from Mr. Mulkey's parlor. Twelve or fifteen saloonists came up to attend the funeral. The services consisted of a few remarks from Harry Henson, the attendant; a song by Mrs. L.L. Jester and myself—"Think of *the Home Over There." He was carried to the city of the dead and while letting his remains down in the grave, Arthur Sutherland, the undertaker, an Odd Fellow, said: "Abe, aint this man being buried in your grave lot?" To which he answered, "Yes." "Why this?" "Because, to put him in the potters' field I could not stand." Arthur says, "Abe, in the days of resurrection this will be a beautiful scene for your own family—these little orphan children and the redeemed saloon-keeper, Billy Powers, all to be raised from the dead to newness of life. God will bless you for this." [733]*

This anecdote, printed in *Abe Mulkey's Budget* (No. 1), bears comfortable similarities to the part of the Rope Walker legend about Mulkey. The Billy Powers story is genuine; Mulkey's two *Budget* books are nonfiction and Billy Powers's gravestone, just as the story says, is found in Mulkey's plot in Oakwood Cemetery. This is not a Mulkey parable about the evils of alcohol and the death of will power(s).

Rope Walker was injured at virtually the same location, at roughly the same time, and had the same one-foot-in-the-grave condition as Billy Powers. Abe Mulkey, as this story confirms, was the religious Beaton Street merchant go-to guy in the early 1880s for those of broken body seeking spiritual succor in downtown Corsicana. It seems quite possible the fallen aerialist was indeed one of Mulkey's patients at his makeshift hospital.

Two key points differ between the "Private Hospital" story and the Rope Walker legend. Billy Powers was wide-open and receives salvation—touchdown! Mulkey and God win! Not so with Rope Walker. In the end, the tightropist's zone of comfort is his Jewish faith and the Methodist preacher fails to make the deathbed conversion.[734] The other difference: it was not Dr. Gulick who summoned Mulkey to help Billy Powers; instead, it was Dr. John Starley (son of "Confederate Doctor" Silas F. Starley[735]).

It's not clear in "Private Hospital" where the hospital was located. Initially, Powers is found in Col. Croft's store, and later, Powers is surprised to find himself in Mulkey's house. Before leaving Croft's store, Mulkey "arranged for two rooms," phrasing which implies the rooms were someplace other than in Mulkey's own home. If those arranged rooms—the hospital—were in the Molloy Hotel, as an intermediate location before Powers was moved to Mulkey's home, that would conform to the narrative in the Rope Walker legend.

Mulkey's "Private Hospital," whether in his house, at Molloy's hotel, or elsewhere, was a place where ten men—Mulkey, Powers, "four other sick men," and the four men who lifted Powers out of bed—came together and prayed. It certainly seems possible Rope Walker was also treated at Mulkey's hospital, and it's also possible that Rope Walker prayed with nine or more men, all Jews, the *minyan* (prayer group of at least ten men) required under Jewish law: Louis Cerf, Ed Raphael, S.S. Freedman, Rube Freedman, Aaron Shwarts, Dave Deutschner, Alex Fox, Ben Marks, Max London, Abe Solomon, Adolph Cahn, Louis Cohen, Isaac and August Levy, some Mr. Simon, maybe others.

Ω

If Mulkey and Rope Walker did meet, as legend has it, why was their interaction not recounted in either of Mulkey's books, in his *Budget*s? Was it because Mulkey could not intercept the dying man's faith or recover Rope Walker's soul, as he did with Billy Powers? Or was it too sensitive a subject for his books, one that might create hard feelings between Mulkey and his Jewish friends and neighbors, not to mention Jewish donors to his orphanage? If anyone could have taken the story of a fallen one-legged rope walker on the verge of death and shape it into a meaningful parable on piety, faith, tolerance, and justice—it would be Mulkey. Even if presented solely as an interesting story, it should have found its way into one or both *Budget*s. As the title "Budget" makes clear, the books are grab bags of miscellany, including all manner of newsy and self-effacing stories having nothing to do with faith and salvation.[736] For this reason alone it seems Mulkey had nothing to do with Rope Walker. Very likely the widely read story about Mulkey and Billy Powers[737] became conflated with the Rope Walker legend in the same way Richard Maynard being crushed by a safe became confused with Rope Walker's injuries.

Ω

There was an inherent conflict between an evangelical Christian like Mulkey, whose goal was to bring people into the fold by convincing them of the redemptive power of faith in Jesus Christ, and Jews, who believe that Jesus was not the Messiah. And yet, Mulkey was tolerant and respectful of the Hebrews and Shebrews of the Jewish Church. His "Ash Hopper" sermon (Chapter 15) is all about religious tolerance.

Jews, other than biblical Hebrews, do come up a few times in Mulkey's books. In one case he republished an 1897 newspaper article which quotes David Brin, a merchant from Waxahachie who endorses Mulkey's resti–tution sermon. Brin praised the preaching of repaying debts as "practical religion." Mulkey doesn't say Brin is Jewish, but he was (see Supplement III). Mulkey was closely associated with Corsicana's Jews, most of whom, like himself, were merchants. At one time he worked for Alexander Fox.[738]

In Dec. 1883, Mulkey and Edmond Raphael, a Jewish Corsicana merchant, were some of the men who organized the town's first fire department—Mulkey was assistant chief.[739] It was no slur for Mulkey to speak of a "Jew Store," as he did in the *Houston Post* in 1906, so ubiquitous was the Israelite dry goods merchant in the frontier towns of a growing America.

> "I went down to Bryan and stepped into a Jew store. 'I want a pair of pants for courting in,' I said. Couldn't afford anything but the pants then. He got out a pair, tried 'em on me, fit just fine, and I went back and met the girl.

A Jew store in Bryan, 1869, when Abe met Louisa

Mulkey's father instilled in him an unbiased tolerance and love of others. When a boy, Abe was sent on an errand many miles from his home. Reaching his destination, the lady asks him if he knows of an old man in Waxahachie, Mulkey's town, who preaches to the "negroes." She tells him her husband and nine other men intend to "tar and feather that preacher, ride him on a rail, and hang him." Abe would have run out of her house then and there except he was more afraid of the hungry wolves he imagined right outside the door than he was of the mean woman. Also, by completing the errand he would earn five dollars to buy his mother a set of cups and saucers. He listens in terror and doesn't deny knowing the preacher until, finally, he bursts: "Yes, I do know him, he is my father, and he is the best man that ever lived."[740]

Mulkey recounted his first teaching of scripture:

> *My first audience was an old negro man who sat on the curb stone of Col. Huey's residence. We both were blessed. He went down 6th Avenue shouting, and I went up 12th street praising God.*[741]

Mulkey wrote many articles for the *Sun*. Even those not signed by him have his signature voice. One "Mulkey's Epistle," written about a year before he claimed his final reward, illustrates his homey writing style and jocular, devil-may-care attitude. It also shows his dedication to charity work and his fearless fundraising skills, which in this case was to raise money to buy beds for his orphanage. The article's ecumenical outlook reflects a liberal attitude toward his Jewish fellow citizens.

There are just fourteen beds left
for the orphanage. I'm going to ask
Mrs. Bill Dunn, Mrs. Albert Wortham
Mrs. George T. Jester, Mrs. George
E. Jester, Mrs. Perry McCammon,
Mrs. Fannie Halbert, Mrs. Sue Cas-
tles, Mrs. Byron Cheney, Mrs. Bank
Sutherland, Mrs. Tom Walton, Mrs.
G. J. Heflin, Mrs. Ralph Beaton, Mrs
John Thompson and Mrs. Harry
Kaufman to please mail me a letter
telling me that they each will furnish
one of the beds, and if you can't
please write me the reason why so
that I can select another prospect.
The first time your little one gets sick
or your neighbor's little one, you'll
think that you've laid down a bed for
one of God's little ones and if you
don't feel kind of pious I'll lick your
husband the first time I see him. I
know it because I have tested it.
One says: "Bro. Mulkey, why is it
you go out of your own pail to select
these women?" Because the orphanage is undenominational in the reception of children. A Jew is one of the
most liberal supporters the institution has. I'd give his name but I'm
afraid some Baptist would take him
over. Have you got any sense?
There are more children in the or-
phanages of other denominations than
our own. Now don't delay because
the option will soon be closed as others will take it.

Mulkey protects a Jew from the Baptists

Ω

Unlike the inferential evidence showing Rope Walker was not crushed, there is little evidence set down, one way or the other, to prove that he initially claimed to be a Methodist and prayed with Mulkey. It's hard to imagine that if Corsicana's unrestrained and audacious evangelist did play some part in the Rope Walker tragedy that he would not have tackled the story in one of his books, or touch on it in one of his newspaper pieces. The Mulkey piece of the legend remains just that—legend.

# Chapter 30

## THE GOOD, THE BAD, AND THE UGLY TRUTH

*be it recorded, that, in this matter, I am not free to utter any fancied measurement I please*

Histories are based on a string of connected events, things that *actually happened*—which sounds obvious—except that what passes for "history" is often built on a foundation of unverified events and facts only assumed to be true and accurate. Events should only be asserted when evidence proves they actually occurred. When events are not well-proven there is less certainty that they occurred, or occurred as described, and that uncertainty casts doubt on historical accounts. In some cases, a presumed historical fact, following a strict, disciplined inquiry, is shown to be untrue. Historical inquiry and analysis require much more than uncritical acceptance of events as true. In this sense, the verification of the events themselves, and the facts that comprise those events, all collated, analyzed, and packaged into some—thing called "history," are not so much true or false as they are "good" or "bad," a measure of the effort used to confirm their accuracy.

Good historical exposition is supported by clear, unambiguous facts, facts which do not lead to obvious questions challenging their accuracy. Related information supports the truth of the facts. It all makes sense and everything fits together.

Bad historical exposition hardly deserves to be called history. References are lacking, untrustworthy, or cannot be traced back to a reliable origin to verify their accuracy. An historical "fact" repeated over and over again doesn't make it any better. Bad facts are derived from unspecified suppose—itions and likelihoods which can't be verified. They are justifiably subject to doubt and refutation if they are accepted without question. They are not concrete evidence.

The ugly truth is that histories contain both good and bad factual exposition. The better histories identify which is which, where failed attempts to prove the truth of facts are acknowledged instead of ignored and glossed over. Argument and persuasion are used to explore the like—lihood that events actually happened, fully acknowledging the uncertainty inherent in that advocacy. Facts presented without identifying their sources are fine for storytelling, but if presented as *history* they need to be supported by citations, explanations, qualifications, disclaimers, and analyses of evi—dence. If supported by some previous historical account, the previous account bears the same burden, *ad infinitum*, back to some source which is either trusted for its accuracy or acknowledged as less than fully reliable for proving the truth of the asserted facts.

The truth about the history of Rope Walker is that there simply isn't a lot known about those dramatic days in March 1883, even after extensive inquiry and the occasional immersion into peripheral matters. What *is* now known, with guarded certainty, are several biographical details about Moses Berg and a few snapshots, several of them quite fuzzy, of what happened at his life's conclusion. The true roles of Mulkey and Gulick remain unknown. No detailed, first-person, contemporaneous written account is known to exist. There was no Zapruder film.

## *Golden City* Disaster, Golden Opportunity

Someone notified Recorder Davies of the New Orleans Court that Professor De Houne, the accused, was on the *Golden City* when the steamer, with a good part of Stowe's circus on board, erupted into flames and sank near Memphis in the early morning hours of March 30, 1882. The defendant failed to show up for his April court date because he may have been killed, the judge was told, and so a continuance was granted. De Houne, who had been out on bail, was to go on trial for the assault and battery of one C.M. Gilley.[742] The sinking of a circus was just what he needed to avoid a court appearance and possibly a prison sentence.

Most of the Stowe Show performers aboard the ill-fated ship survived, but the owner, young William H. Stowe, and his family, perished. Sideshow man Lucius Cronk was killed, as were another thirty or so non-circus passengers. Many highly valued animals were lost along with valuable circus equipment.[743] Reports of the disaster listed numerous victims and survivors, but none mentioned De Houne or Berg,[744] and there is no evidence that he was ever associated with Stowe's circus.

A month earlier, De Houne and his assistant at the time, R. Dietel,[745] were arrested in New Orleans for grand larceny, accused of taking clothing and fifty dollars cash from the sleeping quarters of Michael Hackett's clerks, above Hackett's Market on Dryades Street. They entered the bedroom on February 4, with permission, to secure one end of the rope they would use for the next morning's performance. Instead of putting on a show, though, they were arrested and locked up in the parish prison. Neither could come up with the $1,000 bail at the time,[746] but they managed to get out by the 12th.[747] The news story of their arrest makes no mention of C.M. Gilley or an assault and battery, so it's unclear how, or if, the two criminal matters were related. There is no independent news story about the assault, only its mention as related to De Houne's non-appearance in court.[748]

De Houne's whereabouts between his release from jail, on Feb. 12, and May 14, when he showed up at the Dayton Soldiers home,[749] is unknown, except for a performance at Vicksburg on March 28, two days before the *Golden City* went down.[750] The steamer did travel past Vicksburg on its way up the Mississippi toward Memphis toward its final destination, Cincinnati. Professor De Houne was in the right place, at the right time, and may or may not have boarded.

He would be in the clear so long as the court believed he died on the *Golden City*, but if he was on the lam, the fall in Corsicana less than a year later would have put his freedom in jeopardy. The New Orleans authorities would hear he was still alive and he would have to answer not only for the theft and/or assault, but also for jumping bail, and perhaps for orchestrating a charade about his death on the *Golden City*. Keeping his name out of the papers would be paramount to keeping his freedom, and here then is a new, alternative explanation for the deficient epitaph. The part of the story told by Haslam and Campbell/Rosenberg, where Rope Walker refused to give his name, might be true—he was a wanted man in New Orleans. Further proof he was afraid of being caught is that up to and including his arrest in New Orleans he was "Professor Daniel De Houne." That was the name of the man accused of assaulting Gilley and stealing from Mr. Hackett's clerks. Following his arrest, however, he performed as "Professor Berg."[751] Despite his efforts to stay anonymous and keep things hushed—so goes the reasoning under this theory—newspapers did pick up on the story, and instead of using the name he was using at that time, Berg, they used his usual name, De Houne.

Eva Britton changed her name, too, to "Lillian Markham," shortly after her New Orleans arrest, but she had the good sense to cease shilling her windy sheet and take up a new line of work.[752] Not so the one-legged rope walker.

New Orleans papers carried the story of De Houne's accident at Corsicana and his amputation, but not his death.[753] Would Recorder Davies, of the New Orleans Court, check with Judge Kerr, in Corsicana, and learn of the fugitive's death? This time, for certain?

Or maybe, just maybe, the legless man made an escape: he didn't actually die in Corsicana; the Kerrs were duped into believing the injured man had expired and the gravestone was part of a ruse to help him escape a prison term in New Orleans (and heavens knows, other warrants, obligations, and burdens). Under this scenario, those who put up the gravestone didn't misrepresent his death because it didn't actually have his name on it. Maybe it <u>was</u> only his leg which was buried in the grave, as suggested in Chapter

12, and he lived out his days under an alias as a legless New York City taxidermist.[754]

And those are the not-so-pretty facts providing another possible explan–ation for the marquee marker in the Jewish cemetery in Corsicana, Texas.

## Fruitcake Imbroglio

Discovering historical facts is both an art and a science. What occurred in the distant past is difficult to determine through the haziness of memories, intervening events, and the constant revisions of oft-told tales. Adding to the challenge is the intentional misstatement of facts, either at the time of an event or in recounting the event at a later time. Misinformation peddled by presumed-trustworthy sources is not easily unmasked. Of mistake, misperception, and deception, the last makes accurate historical discovery the most difficult.

And when it comes to deception, Sandy Jenkins takes the cake, and more. He was comptroller of Corsicana's Collin Street Bakery in 2006 when profits began a precipitous decline. Make no mistake, this is no little corner bakery; it is the fount of Corsicana's greatest claim to fame. The Rope Walker legend, while quaint and curious, has never been a famous story outside of Corsicana, Corsicanans, and some Jewish and Texan taphophiles. The same holds true of Black Diamond; known by many Corsicanans and some circus enthusiasts—but not famous. Corsicana is truly famous for one thing only: fruitcake![755] Not the fossilized, five-pound doorstop disparaged by late-night comedians but the deliciously rich and gooey confection which is a Christmastime favorite. Collin Street Bakery's DeLuxe brand fruitcake is legendary. Each year the bakery ships over a million of them around the world and claims scores of celebrity devotees.[756]

**DeLuxe brand fruitcake**

The bakery has a strong connection to the circus, of course. In 1914 the entire Ringling Bros. Circus, including John Ringling, was in town during Christmas and visited the shop. They loved the fruitcake so much that they wanted to send them to friends and relatives, and that's how the bakery's mail order business got started. The circus was an important, regular customer.[757]

In 2014, the bakery's quiet and unassuming financial manager pled guilty to "conspiracy to commit money laundering, mail fraud and making a false statement to a financial institution." Why did these minor improprieties by Controller Jenkins result in a ten-year prison sentence? Because he stole—embezzled—over the course of eight years, an astounding $16.7 million.[758] At the time of his guilty plea, $4 million worth of property and cash had been returned to the bakery, as partial restitution, and he still owed $12,697,921.79.[759] On March 28, 2014, an estate sale was held at the Jenkins's home in Corsicana where luxury items bought with the stolen funds were available for purchase. A queue of curious locals extended around the block as bakery president Bob McNutt served goodies to the multitudes, buttering them up for generous bids to help replace some of his company's lost dough.[760]

Mulkey:

> *You let a poor fellow run his fist into a show case and take out a piece of bread, and you will hear the people all cry out, 'Catch the thief.' But you let one of those dandies* [respected men, usually bearing a military title such as "major"] *embezzle, escheat, hypothecate or imbroglio, and get loose, and the officers would not know which way to run and what to run after. They would think a rhinoceros had gotten loose. Those names I have called out are to cover the title of thief and give it to him easy. You let Jim Garitty, Geo. T. Jester, or Fred Fleming, or any of those banking concerns at Corsicana* [force them into bankruptcy] *and take off the substance of those people. Why, bless you, here is a fellow that won't say escheat, imbroglio, or any of that kind, but I will say, 'you dirty old thief, you stole that money.' He is a thief, I care not whether he steals a million dollars or thirty cents, he is a dirty thief on all parts of the ground.*[761]

## Inconsequential Untruths

Some deceptions are expected, lawful, and even encouraged. The greatest aerialist to ever come out of Texas was a master (mistress) of deception. Barbette was born in 1899 in Round Rock, a community slightly north of Austin. She captured the imagination of audiences in the U.S., Paris, and elsewhere in Europe with her death-defying tightrope and trapeze performances. Writer and filmmaker Jean Cocteau described her as:

> *a graceful daredevil* [and] *one of the most beautiful things in the theatre ...* [with] *female glamour and elegance* [like] *a cloud of dust thrown into the eyes of the audience ...*[762]

In Barbette's signature closing he removes his wig and flexes his muscles. Audiences ate it up. Vander Clyde Broadway, aka Barbette, the greatest tightrope walker and trapeze artist in Texas history.

Another performer whose stock in trade is deception originated closer to home: Terry Fator, born in 1965, grew up in Corsicana. He was the winner of television's "America's Got Talent" competition in 2007. His act combines two very entertaining deceptions. The ventriloquist's puppets perform a full selection of celebrity impersonations. The star and his diminutive entourage currently headline *The Mirage.*

## Historical Fictions

Sad Hill Cemetery in New Mexico, between El Paso and Santa Fe, like Corsicana's Hebrew Cemetery, has a circular center. Thousands of grave markers radiate from the stone-paved middle, mostly planks of wood and misshapen wooden crosses presumably erected hastily to mark the graves of soldiers killed at a nearby Civil War battleground. Other markers are made of marble, limestone, and granite, installed no doubt when time seemed less precious, monuments presumed to last for centuries. In the whole cemetery, only two epitaphs have ever been catalogued. One is the grave of Arch Stanton, who died Feb. 3, 1862. The other is marked, simply, "Unknown."

Sad Hill Cemetery was built in what looks like a valley, not on a hill, and it is not real. It is the cemetery in the exciting finale of Sergio Leone's iconic movie, the basis for this chapter's title. The entirely fictional historical fiction story is set in the U.S. Southwest, but the fake cemetery was fabricated where the movie was filmed, in Spain.

**A Jew looking for a gravestone. The Man with No Name knows it's Unknown.**

Eli Wallach, a second-generation American Jew, played the film's "ugly" character, Tuco. His search through the cemetery for Arch Stanton's grave is a celebrated piece of cinema and the most famous instance of a Jew searching for a gravestone. Tuco, however, was searching for the wrong grave. To find the buried loot he should have been looking for "Unknown," next to Stanton, a fact he learns from the movie's "good" character, played by Clint Eastwood, the character named "The Man with No Name." Cue music...

♎

Is it such a big deal if histories, purposefully or not, include minor inaccuracies and unverified, seemingly inconsequential facts and assertions? Does it matter if a woman shaves off five years from her age for the census taker, or an immigrant drops the "-insky" to create a less ethnic-sounding surname? What about completely true statements that inaccurately capture an historical moment? A farmer declares, "I'm a farmer," but he's really a revolutionary. Altered facts may matter, sometime in the future, when a historian attempts to write an accurate account of the past.

History does matter. It is a mirror society uses to gauge its health, to determine whether humanity's well-being is evolving in a positive or negative direction. It is our past behavior writ large. Reflecting on those past behaviors and their consequences guides future actions. Inaccurate history can only distort and blur that reflection, and, by extension, skew conclusions drawn from the review of the past. Accurate history educates society on how to replicate past positives and avoid past mistakes. The more accurate the historical record, the better the prospects for a brighter future.

# Chapter 31

## A TRUE LEGEND

*Dissect him how I may, then, I but go skin deep; I know him not, and never will.*

In the early years of America's Gilded Age, in the 1870s and 80s, traveling show men and show women, actors, lecturers, human oddities, preachers, and itinerant entertainers like Corsicana's Rope Walker had the potential to attain national celebrity. Some even became household names. The highly talented were praised in newspaper reviews, their shows or appearances recommended, and they became famous. For fifteen years the one-legged rope walker thrilled audiences from coast to coast and border to border. His reviews, like the man himself, were up and down, but his unique act was memorable, his talent commendable, and his national acclaim more than a trifle.[763]

The legend lives on. No longer an inscrutable story veiled in the mist of one and a third centuries of unanswerable riddles, Rope Walker is now a man with a name (or two) and a singular talent. Professor Daniel De Houne should go down in the annals of tightrope walking alongside other famous funambulists. He may not belong in the same class as The Great Blondin, The Flying Wallendas, or the peerless Philippe Petit, but he did entertain many thousands with his one-of-a-kind skill, putting on hundreds of exhibitions all over the country.

He never used a net or other safety device and predictably met his end the same way many of his contemporaries did who followed the same line of work. Despite the obvious hazards of his profession and the life-threatening injuries he suffered on more than one occasion, some obsession drove him time and time again to return to his perch, high above the crowd, showing off, tempting fate, earning a living his way.

One of Rope Walker's most exciting performances occurred at the Milwaukee Garden in 1869. The transcription back at page one had been gently, surreptitiously revised to obscure his name. Here, unadulterated, is the actual article:[764]

AN EXCITING TIME.—Visitors to the Milwaukee Garden yesterday were treated to
an excitement not on the bills.    Dehoune,
a one-legged acrobat—or rather with one
real and one wooden leg—was giving exhibitions in rope walking.    His wire was
suspended some thirty feet in height and
over this the sound leg and the wooden leg
gaily went much to the delight of all.    In
the midst of the scene, Dehoune was seen
to drop his pole and to stand for a few
seconds trembling and then to fall upon
the rope.    This was supposed for a few
seconds to be a part of the play, but it was
not.    The daring acrobat had overtaxed
his strength and was in great danger of
falling to the ground.    In coming down he
managed to get his wooden leg twisted
about the rope and for some seconds
this alone kept him from falling.    The
crowd,    now    realizing    the    state of
affairs,    stood spell-bound, expecting every
moment to see the reckless man dashed to
his death below, but that wooden leg was
true to the last.    Dehoune twisted and
worked carefully and cautiously, clinging
the while with his leg to the rope, until he
succeeded in reaching it with his hands,
and then pulled himself up.    When firmly
on the rope his strength was gone, and he
said to those about that it was the closest
call he had ever had.    When he was in
safety the crowd yelled their joy loudly,
and Dehoune came down from his rope to
rest.

"… an excitement not on the bills"

The story of Rope Walker is forever tied to the story of Corsicana. Had
he fallen under the same circumstances in St. Louis or Cincinnati his legacy
would have been different. Corsicana, it turns out, has a history as enter–
taining as a three-ring circus with its killer elephant, royal Jesters, and an
unnamed, one-footed aerialist, six feet under. Instead of cotton candy,
there's cotton and KAN-D, and fruitcake, mailed annually to the once-
greatest show on earth.

A physical description of the high-wire hero, invented in the prologue and quickly disavowed, can be assembled from his enlistment record:[765]

> **grey eyes, brown hair, fair complexion, is five feet nine inches high.**

Physical description from enlistment record

An 1880 newspaper report of a walking race of one-legged men paints a more intimate picture:

> **Professor Berg, the tight rope performer, not only lost one leg, but there isn't much left of the other, a large portion of the bone being gone. His body is covered with wounds, thirty-five in all. "For heaven's sake what was he doing to get so riddled?" someone asked. "He was acting as a target at a prize shooting match," coolly replied a joker. Eleven rebel bullets are still buried somewhere in his anatomy. And yet he is as tough as pine knot. He is a man about forty-five years old, with gray side whiskers, and stalks around as if he was on the way to join Napoleon at Waterloo.[766]**

An alternate version reports only *thirty-four* wounds, and

> **prominent side whiskers and a look such as one would suppose Napoleon to have had on the eve of Waterloo.[767]**

The seemingly indestructible soldier was always on his way to Waterloo, whether on picket duty at the head of a Civil War battalion or crossing a wire thirty feet above some random town's Main Street.

Ω

There is no known photograph of Moses Berg. An undated photo of an unidentified man with "prominent side whiskers" suffices as a placeholder.[768]

**A thirty-five-ish man with light-colored eyes and prominent side whiskers, ca. 1878**

Ω

*One-legged tightrope walker* sounds like a down-home, folksy expression.

… *with a notch on the bottom of his peg leg* makes him sound more believable.

… *with a stove on his back* takes him back to unbelievable.

… *who was Jewish* is so unexpected, it just might be true, after all.

Well, it is true. He fell from his tightrope and died in Texas in 1884 (wink).

Ω

"The One-legged Rope Walker of Corsicana" is more than history and more than legend. It is almost fable:

### The One-legged Rope Walker
### Of Course I Can —

All that's missing is a dangling schwa,[769] like Daniel De Houne's *A* dangling from a wire suspended above the Milwaukee Garden. With the right inflection, with the proper aspiration, this schwa can do tricks:

**AHH**—Ok, now I see.

**UHH**—Let me think about this.

**EH?**—Do you agree?

**AAH!**—Yikes!

Ω

A "rope walker," in the sense of a forty-two-year-old immigrant Jewish amputee Jayhawker veteran carrying a stove across a tightrope thirty feet above a street, may be defined more generally as: "someone with indom‐itable drive who excels in spite of a personal disadvantage."

The disadvantage need not be a physical disability. It could be something environmental, like a troubled home life while growing up. It could be something psychological, like a phobia, or something in the personality, like intense shyness or insecurity. It could be an absence of common sense. Examples: an obese ballerina or a business leader with a stutter. For those who use their strengths and advantages to succeed, good for them, but they are not Rope Walkers. Those who misuse or ignore their strengths and advantages, they are certainly not Rope Walkers.

- Eva Britton was glib, pretty, and fearless, descended from a family of newspaper publishers. That's who she was, so the fact that she became an editress, actress, singer, and a super saleswoman makes sense. Not a Rope Walker.

- Sandy Jenkins was a quiet introvert who got caught with his hand in a $17,000,000 cookie jar. That's a Rope Walker.

- Robert C. Campbell and John Sam Haslam were skilled at their craft, which did not seem difficult for them. Not Rope Walkers.

- David Cerf and other suiciders, not Rope Walkers.

- The early pioneer citizens of Corsicana, including an agnostic Jew and a citrus-selling Syrian, were Rope Walkers—at least most of them. The definition of a pioneer is very close to the definition of a Rope Walker.

- Abe Mulkey, uneducated and bankrupt—a Rope Walker.

- The Londons, Max, Mary, and Julia, were not Rope Walkers.

- Eva Donohoo, plantation owner, not a Rope Walker. Black Diamond, nine-ton martyr for emancipation, Rope Walker.

- Rabbi Ernst Joseph, yes, Rope Walker.

- August Blum, not sure, maybe a Rope Walker.

- An amputee, itinerant aerialist: Rope Walker.

# TEMPLE & SYNAGOGUE

*the same ancient Catholic Church to which you and I … and every mother's son and soul of us belong; the great and everlasting First Congregation of this whole worshipping world; we all belong to that; only some of us cherish some queer crotchets noways touching the grand belief; in we all join hands*

Many people during the pioneering days of Texas had foreign accents, as elsewhere in the U.S., clearly immigrants from abroad. Many were also Jewish, although nothing, neither accent nor appearance, signaled their Abrahamic ancestry and Mosaic beliefs. And so it was with the early Hebrew arrivals in Corsicana. They bore none of the outward traditional trappings of Judaism; nothing betrayed their race except their absence from Sunday church services, perhaps some dietary anomalies, and sometimes their surnames. Eventually, a large, stained-glass Star of David window on a new building on Church Street (aka 15th Street[770]) announced: "Hebrews live here!" Later, every year, more and more Beaton Street businesses closed on the two High Holy Days—Rosh Hashanah and Yom Kippur, the Jewish New Year and Day of Atonement, which occur ten days apart in the fall[771]—that became noticeable, too.

The first milestone for a nascent Texas Jewish community was typically the establishment of a cemetery. Next, it defined itself as a congregation—a group to worship together and celebrate and perpetuate ancient rituals and customs. Then maybe a B'nai B'rith lodge—a surprising number of them existed in Texas in the 1880s.[772] Ultimately, a house of prayer was built. In Corsicana, that was Temple Beth El, completed on Rosh Hashanah in the 1900th year after the execution of a certain Nazarene rabbi, a holy man from antiquity for whom other houses of worship in town had already been built.

Before 1900, groups of Corsicana's Jews gathered at various locations to recite prayers and practice rituals according to their particular version of Judaism. As the town's Jewish population grew, in the 1870s and 1880s, views about what was proper religious observance diverged as each new Jewish resident brought his or her own preferred Jewish traditions and philosophies, a phenomenon which occurred in all expanding American Jewish communities. The earlier arrivals tended to be from Alsace-Lorraine, Prussia, and other Western and Central European areas where Jewish Enlightenment ("Haskala"), a pronounced liberalization of religious prac–

tice, had taken root in the eighteenth century when Jews acquired greater acceptance in the general, Christian culture. These "reform" Jews identified as Jewish and practiced their ancient faith, but didn't adhere to many of the stringent, millennia-old biblical requirements held by their Polish and Russian cousins. Division between reform (liberalized) and orthodox (traditional) Jews existed in Corsicana as early as 1890, when the "Orthodox Hebrews" organized its own congregation.[773]

Building a house of God required a commitment by like-minded individuals to perpetuate Jewish identity and traditions, and money—a mix that didn't come together in Corsicana until the turn of the century.

Differences within Beth El's congregation relating to methods of devotion were evident right from the start, as discussed further on. The most orthodox Jews continued to meet separately, unable to accommodate themselves to the reform practices of Temple Beth El. They met at various locations, including the second floor above Freedman's Dry Goods store,[774] at the IOOF (and Woodmen of the World) Hall,[775] at City Hall,[776] and in the Red Men Hall on Beaton Street.[777] Then, sixteen years after Beth El opened, they built their own place of worship, Agudas Achim (translated: united brothers).

Temple Beth El, a Corsicana landmark

## Beth El

Temple Beth El is a remarkably pretty building, a Texas Historical Landmark (1981) and on the National Register of Historical Places (1987). It is located on South 15th Street close to the corner of 7th Ave., a short, five-block walk from the Corsicana Visitor Center just past Collin Street Bakery.

Beth El Congregation was organized in October, 1898. At the time, Rabbi **Solomon Solomon**—no discernable relation to other Solomons then living in town—was conducting religious services at the Red Men Hall.[778] He was still rabbi on September 5, 1899, when he conducted Rosh Hashanah services at City Hall.[779] Solomon's participation in the building of the temple is not known. He was living in town at the time and was leading services, but he was never mentioned in connection with Beth El's founding, its construction, or its dedication.[780]

Solomon Abraham, bartender J. Salinger,
     h. I. Solomon.
Solomon Bertha [wid M. H.] h. Simon
     Fox, 325 N. 11th.
Solomon Eugene, clk A. Fox & Son, h.
     I. Solomon.
Solomon Isidore, clk, r. 705 W. 4th ave.
Solomon Solomon Rev., rabbi Jewish
     synagogue, r. 708 E. 3d ave.

Solomon Solomon and other Solomons, Corsicana, 1898

**Julius W. Friedlander** (1853-1908) was one of the lead organizers for building the temple. He was a traveling representative for Woodmen of the World (WOW), an Omaha-based charitable and fraternal organization still in operation as WoodmenLife. WOW's objective then, as now, was the sale of affordable life insurance. Friedlander arrived in Corsicana by way of South Carolina, Georgia, Florida, and Alabama.[781] He showed up in Dallas in 1884 and subsequently lived in Corsicana from at least 1895 to 1901.[782] Despite being a relatively recent community member, he became the chair of the temple's by-laws committee. Insurance salesman are renowned for their powers of persuasion, and Friedlander used his exceptional sales skills to successfully raise money for the temple.[783]

## A SYNAGOG FOR CORSICANA, TEX.

Corsicana, Tex., October 15.—Mr. J. W. Friedlander, who is chairman of the committee on by-laws, says:

"I am truly proud of the citizens of Corsicana. The soliciting committee have been at work and have done remarkably well, and the synagog is an assured success. The citizens, both Jews and Gentiles, have subscribed liberally, and treated the committee with the greatest success. The by-laws for the order have all been drawn up, and will be submitted at the next meeting, and the application for a charter will be sent to Austin in a few days. The Knights of Honor lodge at their last meeting donated liberally, and there is hardly anything else to do but to commence building."

Mr. Friedlander is very enthusiastic on the subject, and while the funds are not all raised, it is very likely that arrangements to build will be made at the next meeting.

Ready to commence building, October 1898

He was an active member of the community. In July 1897, for example, the Friedlanders threw a party for Ida Israel, who was relocating to San Antonio.[784] Fundraising responsibility for an "Annual Installation and Ball," in January 1898, was given to

*Mr. J.W. Friedlander, an enthusiastic Knight of Honor, and in less than a half hour he had secured all that was necessary to insure a grand success.*[785]

Friedlander died in 1908 and was buried in Oklahoma, where his son lived. It is not clear why, as something of an outsider, he became so involved in the movement to build the temple. Perhaps he was the connection between the congregation and Beth El's unidentified architect.

In November 1898, **S.S. Freedman**, **Louis Cerf**, and **Ralph Costa** filed a corporate charter with the state, legally registering the "Jewish Congregation of Temple Beth-El of Corsicana."

The charter of the Jewish Congregation of Temple Beth-El of Corsicana
has been filed with the Secretary of
State. No. capital stock. Incorporators: S. L. Freehman, L. Cerf and
Ralph Costa.

Beth El charter filed, November 1898

The Hebrews of Corsicana, says a
Dallas News, are determined to have a
suitable temple of worship and the
movement started some weeks ago will
soon bear good fruit. A committee has
been appointed by the permanent organization with instructions to secure
a suitable lot on which to build a synagogue and it is expected the lot will
be selected and purchased in a short
time. One of the leading Hebrews in
the city who is a prime mover in this
matter stated to The News correspondent today that the cost of the synagogue, including the lot, would not be
less than $12,000. Considerable money
has already been raised by subscription among the Jews and there are
Gentiles who will cheerfully contri-
bute to help along the cause.

Lot to be chosen for Temple, November 1898

Freedman (Chapter 24) and Cerf (Chapter 3) were well-established
townsmen, but Ralph Costa (1864-1948),[786] like Friedlander, was a recent
arrival. No Costas are in the cemetery and the name doesn't appear on any
historical plaques. Costa's connection to Corsicana was through his wife,
the former **Minnie Frank**, and Minnie's sister, **Carrie (Frank) Freedman**,
and Carrie's husband, **S.S. Freedman**, the Freedmans being in Corsicana
since 1875.[787]

A third Frank sister, also in Corsicana, was **Cornelia Polasky**, who
married **Louis Polasky** in Dubuque in 1880.[788] It is not known when the
Polaskys came to Corsicana, but their daughter, Lillie, who died on Aug. 3,
1883, was buried in the Hebrew Cemetery, so the couple were already living
in Texas, if not Corsicana, by that date.[789] A fourth Frank sister, **Rachel
"Ray" Goldsmith**, married **Moses A. "Mose" Goldsmith**[790] and also

lived in Corsicana. All four Frank sisters were born in Syracuse, N.Y., daughters of **Moses N. and Betsy (Blum/Bloom) Frank**, who, like their daughters, emigrated from Syracuse to Corsicana.[791]

Following Cornelia Polasky's premature death, in 1904, her husband Louis relocated to Des Moines and their four children were adopted by their uncle and aunt, the Goldsmiths. The Goldsmiths and Polasky children left Corsicana in 1909 and ended up settling in New York City, arriving there in 1912.[792]

Minnie and Ralph Costa, both native-born Americans, were Corsicana residents when they married, March 12, 1890, in Marshall, Texas.[793] Ralph was born in New York as "Raphael," youngest child of John and Julia (Barnett) Costa, a couple with deep English roots. His earliest known ancestors were Raphael and Ester Da Costa, presumed Conversos who came to London from Portugal in 1746.[794] In the 1920s, the "Ralph Costa" store sold ready-to-wear women's clothing, at 215 N. Beaton Street.[795] Before that, Costa was with the Marks Bros., for fifteen years,[796] and before that he ran a dry goods and furnishings store, from at least 1898.[797] In 1928 the Costas moved to Dallas, where Ralph died in early 1948, aged eighty-four, eight months after Minnie's passing.

The land on which Beth El was built was purchased by the congregation on May 3, 1899, for $1,750 from Moses and Ray (Frank) Goldsmith. The Church Street (now 15th Street) lot, just off of Confederate Ave. (now 7th Ave.), was bought by the Goldsmiths from Captain Charles H. Allyn, who bought it from Charles and Clara Rose, who bought it from Levi L. Jester, who bought it from Arthur Sutherland, the town undertaker, who bought it from Corsicana Commissioners Alex Beaton and S.H. Kerr, who had title by virtue of a land donation by Texas Ranger Col. James Buckner "Buck" Barry.[798] Within two months, construction began.[799]

## CORSICANA, TEXAS.

Dr. Julius M. Magil, of Indianapolis, Ind., has been elected rabbi in charge of the Congregation Temple Beth-El in Corsicana and arrived here on the 4th inst. The new synagog building is completed with the exception of the furnishing, which will be all done in a short time, and inside of two weeks the dedication of the new house of worship will take place.

Congregation Beth El has a rabbi and a synagogue, September 1900

The building where Jews worship is called a "synagogue," but from its earliest conception the founders of Beth El (literally, "house of God") called their synagogue a "temple," the designation used by reform Jews. It was completed in early September, 1900. Rabbi Magil arrived on Sept. 4, and an elaborate dedication ceremony and celebration came off on the 21st.

Jew and Gentile alike attended the temple's christening, including pastors from five Corsicana churches. Solos were performed by young Lillian May Freedman and two of the town's most respected matrons, Mrs. Percy C. Townsend, daughter-in-law of Corsicana's schoolmaster Capt. Townsend, and Mrs. Edward M. Polk. Thirteen-year-old Lena Goldberg,[800] the key bearer, accompanied by flower girls Leona Goldman, Bella Costa, Sophia Levy, Sadie Cahn, Fannie Lustig, and Beatrice Horvets presented the temple key to President Costa.[801] Vice President J. Goldberg[802] brought in the Torah scrolls and together with Costa placed them in the holy ark. Young Uriah Cerf was lifted by his father to light the perpetual lamp. Carrie Freedman then made a formal presentation of the interior furnshings to President Costa, who in turn delivered a statement of gratitude. Rabbi Magil made a benediction and delivered a sermon. Following another musical selection, Rabbi Magil called Mrs. Freedman, leader of the Ladies Hebrew Society, back to the *bimah* (pulpit),[803] and

> *... in the name of the temple, the congregation and "all Jews who have not malice or envy in their hearts" thanked her ... "Had it not been for you, madam," said he, "this synagogue would not be here. You built it and in the name of all I desire to thank you."* [804]

-Then followed a scene not often seen in a church: The women rushed to Mrs Freedman, kissed and hugged her, the men shook her hands and tear-dimmed eyes but glad, were the order.

Carrie Freedman built Beth El

The Jews with "malice or envy in their hearts" are not named, but only eight months later, in May 1901, S.S. Freedman *et al.* sued Kal Shwarts *et al.* to enforce the temple's by-law which dictated that annual elections be held in September.[805] The less-orthodox faction, Shwarts *et al.*, had elected a new spate of officers on May 5, choosing Shwarts as president, Jacob Herman as v.p., Louis Polasky as secretary, I. Goldberg as treasurer, and August

Levy, Edmund Raphael, and Louis Cerf as trustees. Freedman *et al.* asserted that the initial office holders (respectively: Costa, I. Goldberg, Shwarts, and Cerf, and trustees Freedman, Louis Cohen, Abe Levine, Ben Marks, and Ben Rosenberg, a more orthodox lineup) should continue to serve until the constitutionally mandated anniversary, in September, and that the May election was therefore invalid. Freedman, who was voted out of his position as trustee, was most likely the man who spearheaded the lawsuit, and not just because he was the lead, named plaintiff; he was also an experienced litigant.[806]

Congregation divisions due to differences in worshipping styles were a frequent occurrence in developing Jewish communities. The divisions amongst Corsicana's Jews were evident early, even at the planning meeting to draw up organization papers for the temple in September 1898. Hearty debate at the time on whether to utilize a reform or orthodox liturgy was amicably resolved, if only temporarily, in favor of the proponents of the reform style of devotion.[807] The eventual fallout of the schism was the creation of a second synagogue, sixteen years later, an orthodox house of worship. At least two of the Beth El trustees who were in the orthodox camp, Ben Marks and Ben Rosenberg, became strong supporters of Agudas Achim.[808]

## Agudas Achim

This history of the founding of "the synagogue" is briefer and simpler than that of "the temple." The synagogue also had far fewer rabbis over the years than the temple. Sometime following Beth El's construction the most-religious Jews moved from the floor above Freedman's store, where all of the observant Jews had once worshipped, to the second floor of the IOOF building.[809] The Hebrew Orthodox Church worshipped there for six years,[810] at least, until one year the Odd Fellows hosted a funeral on Yom Kippur, the holiest day in the Jewish calendar, forcing worshippers to find another venue for their services, which they did at the American Legion Hall.[811] The Ku Klux Klan also met in the IOOF building, but it is unlikely both groups met there during the same years.[812]

The Texas State charter for Agudas Achim was filed March 19, 1915, and that month the congregation purchased a lot next to the Cumberland Presbyterian Church on N. 12th Street, between 5th Ave. and Collin Street. They were only waiting to sell and remove a house on the property so they could build their synagogue.[813] Nearly $6,500 was raised for the building fund and a lengthy list of donors, below, was published in the *Sun*. Benjamin Marks contributed the most, $525. The typical amount was five dollars, and many contributed one dollar. Most donations, although modest in size, were received from the Christian citizens of Corsicana. The slate of officers in 1916 were: Jacob Goldman, president; Harry Miller, vice president; Benjamin Marks, treasurer; and Sol Gottlieb, secretary. Trustees were Ben Rosenberg, Jacob Dreeben, and K. Wolens.[814]

When the congregation outgrew the small brick building, in 1932, they bought a church building on the corner of N. 15th Street and W. 4th Avenue. In 1957 they needed a still larger building and put up a modern-style synagogue at the corner of N. 19th Street and W. Park Avenue.[815] That building today houses Corsicana's Senior Center, directly across the street from Pioneer Village,[816] Corsicana's museum of historically preserved buildings and artifacts on the edge of Jester Park.

# PUBLISH LIST OF DONORS

## Agudas Achem Congregation Is Grateful to All Who Aided

The Congregation Agudas Achem wishes to thank every one who was kind enough to help towards the erection of our synagogue. To the few who have not paid their donations the congregation asks that they please remit to Mr. B. Marks, president.

Following is a full list of contributors:

| Donor | Amount |
|---|---|
| B. Marks | $525.00 |
| K. Wolens | 475.00 |
| Will Goldman | 375.00 |
| Jake Goldman | 325.00 |
| Ben Rosenberg | 275.00 |
| Jake Dreeben | 250.00 |
| E. Golden | 225.00 |
| Harry Miller | 200.00 |
| J. Jacobs | 175.00 |
| Mendel Marks | 150.00 |
| Harry Kaufman | 150.00 |
| Sam Goldman | 115.00 |
| P. Samuels | 110.00 |
| M. M. Miller | 100.00 |
| Robert Jarett | 100.00 |
| Capt. Garitty | 100.00 |
| Sol Gottlieb | 85.00 |
| S. Katz | 75.00 |
| A. Goldberg | 75.00 |
| W. M. Herman | 70.00 |
| Chas. Simon | 70.00 |
| Mrs. Newberg | 60.00 |
| L. Levine | 50.00 |
| Whiteselle Lumber Co. | 50.00 |
| Abe Hayman, Dallas | 50.00 |
| Southern Junk Co. | 40.00 |
| Ben Brown | 35.00 |
| First State Bank | 25.00 |
| Jake Ansel | 25.00 |
| I. Richter | 25.00 |
| A. E. Marks | 25.00 |
| M. L. Levine | 25.00 |
| Mrs. J. E. Whiteselle | 25.00 |
| Rev. Dow | 25.00 |
| Mose Levi | 25.00 |
| Ben Miller | 25.00 |
| S. A. Pace | 25.00 |
| J. A. Thompson | 25.00 |
| E. H. Church | 25.00 |
| Chas. H. Mills | 25.00 |
| Isaac Levy | 25.00 |
| McCammon & Lang Lbr. Co. | 25.00 |
| Central Texas Grocery Co. | 25.00 |
| C. H. Allyn | 25.00 |
| C. King | 25.00 |
| Jerry Scott, Frost | 25.00 |
| G. E. Jester | 25.00 |
| Sam Goldman | 25.00 |
| Callicutt & Johnson | 20.00 |
| Morris Jarett | 20.00 |
| Ed M. Polk | 20.00 |
| Jarrell-Elliott D. G. Co. | 20.00 |
| Texas Paper Co., Dallas | 20.00 |
| Pace Golden, West | 20.00 |
| Bank Sutherland | 15.00 |

J. M. Standing
Dr. Trim Houston
W. T. Parker
W. E. Slaughter
Robert Stell
Arthur Levi
J. W. Hornbeak
L. Treadwell
W. H. White & Son
A. S. Vann
Nat Pinkston
E. O. Vaughan
R. B. Munsey
L. Miller
J. E. McClung
Dr. Burnett
J. O. Burks
Young Bros.
Dr. Polk
J. C. Christian
A. G. Elliott
C. M. Thornall
Brooks Bros.
Jack Hays
P. Mayer
J. Alderson
Rufus Hardy
R. E. Hughes
Drane Co. (by Hoskins)
Z. R. Christian
Will McNutt
A. B. Walker
J. T. Berry
Williams Drug Co.
Corsicana Electric Co.
A. P. Wood
W. C. Knox
Will L. Kerr
C. C. Walker
Gus Weidemann
D. N. Rice
Beckett Electric Co.
J. M. Dyer
Wareing Bros.
Coulson Drug Co.
Johnson Clothing Co.
H. E. Prince
Davidson Electric Co.
W. F. Colquitt
A. M. Milligan
H. L. Porch
J. D. Carroll
J. E. Butler
J. B. Cooksey
J. R. Anderson
L. Hashop
Royall Coffee Co.
Dr. O. L. Smith
Dr. Jester
Joe Lunn
H. Iverson
H. M. Whitten
A. W. King
J. L. Lunsford
Lipshitz Refining Works, of Waco
Mr. Abbott, Fort Worth
A. Aaron, Elmhouse
Mr. Levinson, Ennis
Samuel Rothfof, Ennis
Potts Lea Co., Dallas
Jack Johnston
Nevins Bros., New York
A. Weil, Chicago
Sam Fleishman
Froth, Grey
J. A. Bonner

| | |
|---|---|
| Davis & Jester | 15.00 |
| J. J. McClellan | 15.00 |
| H. Silbert, Dawson | 15.00 |
| C. R. Terry | 20.00 |
| C. L. Matthews | 10.00 |
| I. Mohilner | 10.00 |
| Oil City Iron Works | 10.00 |
| L. E. McCormick | 10.00 |
| Walter Salm | 10.00 |
| L. Halbert | 10.00 |
| Doak Roberts | 10.00 |
| Richard Mays | 10.00 |
| R. Grossman | 10.00 |
| M. Wolens | 10.00 |
| Woods & Kerr | 10.00 |
| Chas. H. Delafosse | 10.00 |
| Ike Carr | 10.00 |
| F. P. Wood | 10.00 |
| H. Grossman | 10.00 |
| H. D. Johnson | 10.00 |
| H. B. Davis | 10.00 |
| Garrett & Holloway | 10.00 |
| R. L. Miller | 10.00 |
| Southland Cotton Oil Co. | 10.00 |
| J. N. Edens | 10.00 |
| Max Brunstein | 10.00 |
| J. N. Garitty | 10.00 |
| Corsicana Ice Factory | 10.00 |
| American Well & Pros. Co. | 10.00 |
| Ike McFadden Lumber Co. | 10.00 |
| Stroud-Dockum Gro. Co. | 10.00 |
| W. Burgess | 10.00 |
| Josh Halbert | 10.00 |
| Byron Cheney | 10.00 |
| Fortson Grocery Co. | 10.00 |
| T. J. Worthington | 10.00 |
| O. E. Hyndman | 10.00 |
| Ashmore Bros. | 10.00 |
| E. A. Johnson | 10.00 |
| Collin Street Bakery | 10.00 |
| Sowell Bros. | 10.00 |
| A. W. Levermann | 10.60 |
| A. H. Kerr | 10.00 |
| R. L. Hamilton | 10.00 |
| Alex Freedman | 10.00 |
| Sons of Herman | 10.00 |
| Sun-Light Pub. Co. | 10.00 |
| R. S. Neblett | 10.00 |
| Dr. Miller | 10.00 |
| Ralph Beaton | 10.00 |
| J. F. Stout | 10.00 |
| Walton Furniture Co. | 10.00 |
| Nat Goldberg | 10.00 |
| Harry Jacobs | 10.00 |
| L. & M. Golden | 10.00 |
| Jake Miller | 10.00 |
| I. Frankfort | 10.00 |
| E. E. Gray | 10.00 |
| Sanger Bros., Dallas | 10.00 |
| H. P. Hayman, Dallas | 10.00 |
| Missouri Metal Co., Ft. Worth | 10.00 |
| Congregation Agudas Achem of Fort Worth | 10.00 |
| Congregation Asavoth Sholom of Fort Worth | 10.00 |
| I. & I. Cerf, Ennis | 10.00 |
| H. Burk, Ennis | 10.00 |
| S. Stein, Ennis | 10.00 |
| A. Cohn, Waco | 10.00 |
| Joe Coplan, Kerens | 10.00 |
| Higginbotham Millinery Co., Dallas | 10.00 |
| Crescent Clothing Co. | 7.50 |
| J. N. Tinkle | 5.00 |
| L. M. McGill | 5.00 |
| Corsicana Cotton Mills | 5.00 |
| John Colvin | 5.00 |
| F. N. Drane | 5.00 |
| S. Mc Kerr | 5.00 |
| J. K. Collins | 5.00 |
| R. F. Irvine | 5.00 |
| Harper Drug Co. | 5.00 |
| H. Grossman | 5.00 |
| J. M. Stell | 5.00 |
| Will Thompson | 5.00 |
| S. McElroy | 5.00 |
| Tom Lovett | 5.00 |
| James Megarity | 5.00 |
| J. B. Redden | 5.00 |
| Mike Howard | 5.00 |
| J. R. Neese | 5.00 |
| Clay Nash | 5.00 |
| Dr. Shell | 5.00 |
| J. A. Harper | 5.00 |
| Albert Levi | 5.00 |
| Joe Herman | 5.00 |
| Hay Herman | 5.00 |
| Ed Baum | 5.00 |
| Sylvan McDaniels | 5.00 |
| B. L. Finch | 5.00 |
| T. J. Steele | 5.00 |
| Weiler Mfg. Co. | 5.00 |
| W. Z. Herman | 5.00 |
| W. M. Peck | 5.00 |
| J. H. Wooley | 5.00 |
| Robert Werner | 5.00 |
| W. B. Sweatman | 5.00 |
| B. Tinkle | 5.00 |
| J. E. Christian | 5.00 |

| | |
|---|---|
| T. J. York | 2. |
| Hawkins Scarborough | 2. |
| P. P. Hedrick | 2. |
| Drane & McKee | 2. |
| T. R. Chandler | 2. |
| Bud Epps | 2. |
| E. H. Powell | 2. |
| Pat McAllister | 2. |
| R. C. Townsend | 2. |
| R. P. Blanding | 2. |
| A. M. Crumbley | 2. |
| W. C. Clements | 2. |
| Thomas Cash Grocery | 2. |
| Conner & Harrison | 2. |
| Cash | 2.5 |
| N. L. Benson | 2. |
| R. L. Reed | 2. |
| J. L. Marshall | 2. |
| J. A. Jarrell | 2. |
| Corsicana Steam Laundry | 2. |
| R. M. Lockhart | 2. |
| Corsicana Garage | 2.5 |
| J. M. Pugh | 2.5 |
| Mr. Gold, Fort Worth | 2.5 |
| Jolesch D. G. Co., Ennis | 2.5 |
| E. Raphael, Ennis | 2.5 |
| Moise Cerf, Ennis | 2.0 |
| W. T. Hipps | 2.0 |
| Brown & Johnson | 2.0 |
| Brown Planing Mill | 2.0 |
| D. Molloy | 2.0 |
| Uriah Cerf | 2.0 |
| C. E. White | 2.0 |
| George Baum | 2.0 |
| Famous Shoe Store | 2.0 |
| G. W. Martin | 2.0 |
| J. W. Curington | 2.0 |
| J. M. Kerr | 2.0 |
| F. A. McKnight | 2.0 |
| Dr. Watson | 2.0 |
| F. W. Woolworth | 2.0 |
| W. T. Johnson | 2.5 |
| Ray Kerr | 1.5 |
| T. D. Garner | 5.00 |
| J. A. Pike | 5.00 |
| Joe Schwartz | 5.00 |
| Ed Call | 5.00 |
| Cash | 1.00 |
| Spank Reed | 1.00 |
| J. B. Fassaire | 1.00 |
| J. J. Sullivan | 1.00 |
| Dexter Hamilton | 1.00 |
| J. E. Norwood | 1.00 |
| E. Connely | 1.00 |
| T. Burke | 1.00 |
| Stokes & Morton | 1.00 |
| T. D. Dickson | 1.00 |
| Aaron Levine | 1.00 |
| Tony DeGeorgio | 1.00 |
| S. M. Roughton | 1.00 |
| E. N. Johnson | 1.00 |
| A. Hanks | 1.00 |
| Henry Warren | 1.00 |
| M. S. Karmany | 1.00 |
| City Book Store | 1.00 |
| H. F. Miller | 1.00 |
| W. W. Elliott | 1.00 |
| George Boyd | 1.00 |
| J. T. Stewart | 1.00 |
| Ben Boltz | 1.00 |
| Chas. Bee | 1.00 |
| A. O. Smith | 1.00 |
| Griffen & Gregg | 1.00 |
| Miss Porter Rice | 1.00 |
| J. S. Roderick | 1.00 |
| R. B. Mitchell | 1.00 |
| J. H. Jewett | 1.00 |
| Mr. Johnson | 1.00 |
| C. A. Baker | 1.00 |
| Walter Hays | 1.00 |
| A. N. Justiss | 1.00 |
| O. E. Redden | 1.00 |
| C. B. Hill | 1.00 |
| A. B. Cobb | 1.00 |
| A. Salkberg, Fort Worth | 1.00 |
| A. Gordon, Fort Worth | 1.00 |
| The Globe, Fort Worth | 1.00 |
| M. Freyer, Houston | 1.00 |
| Shoe Shop, Ennis | 1.00 |
| V. T. Wright | 1.00 |
| Rev. Wallace | 2.00 |
| Tatum & Cunningham | 12.50 |
| John Cunningham | 5.00 |
| Mr. Brillhart | 15.00 |
| T. Brooks | 5.00 |

Total ........................ $6,457.00

NAT GOLDBERG,
Secretary.

THE WAR IS A SERIOUS PROPOSITION. IN FRANCE EVERYONE IS DRESSING IN BLACK. WE MUSE BE SERIOUS INSTEAD OF STAYING IN BED OR READING YOUR NEWSPAPER COME TO SUNDAY SCHOOL AND LEARN OF GOD.

Donors who funded the building of Agudas Achim in 1916

## Temple and Synagogue Closings

Corsicana's Jewish population peaked in the 1920s, due in large part to a general increase in the town's population because of an oil boom during the early years of that decade. By the mid-fifties, however, it began a serious decline. In a paper researched by Babbette Samuels, she noted that in 1968 the Jews of Corsicana had thirty-eight funerals, but only three births.[817] Sandra Palmer, who gave tours of Beth El after it ceased to operate as a synagogue, noted, "In 1978 the Synagogue had twenty-five family memberships that consisted of fifty-five people. The Temple had twenty-two family memberships of forty-one people. Four families belonged to both the Synagogue and Temple, so there was a total of forty-seven families and eighty-seven people."[818]

By 1982, Beth El only had ten families, so the congregation decided to disband. Ritual objects, including the Torah scrolls, were given to Agudas Achim, and Beth El's remaining members joined Agudas Achim. At the same time, Agudas Achim moved to a less orthodox brand of worship, something akin to Conservative Judaism, midway between Reform and Orthodox. Beth El was in such poor shape that the wrecking ball seemed an inevitability.[819] Despite its terrible condition, and no interested buyers, it was nonetheless deemed worthy of saving because of its distinctive architecture and historical significance. A "Save the Temple Committee," formed by the Navarro County Historical Commission, purchased the building in February 1982 for $30,000, paid in part by a Texas State Historical Commission grant of $10,000. Extensive repairs made in 1983 and 1984 restored the temple to its original grandeur and on March 29, 1987, it was formally rededicated as a community center.[820]

Rabbi Joseph, who at one time was leading both congregations, and then served the remnant of Corsicana's Jews at Agudas Achim, died in 1999. The Jewish population of Corsicana continued to fall. When it became too costly to maintain their one remaining house of worship, Congregation Agudas Achim sold their building as well. The Jews of Corsicana then gathered in members' homes for Friday night services and traveled to nearby cities for major holidays. Today, Babbette Samuels is the only old-timer from Corsicana's once-thriving Jewish community who still lives in town. A once-a-month gathering at Beth El[821] reunites former Corsicana Jews. They come from Dallas, Fort Worth, and elsewhere to worship under the leadership of Rabbi Frank Joseph, son of Corsicana's last rabbi.[822]

## Beth El's Architect Unknown

The East Texas Historical Association bestowed its Terry Award for historical preservation on Temple Beth El in 1992.

> *Begun in 1898, Temple Beth El represents Nineteenth Century Moorish Revival synagogues built by Reformed Jews in the United States. Similar structures with the large Rose window, flanking arched windows, twin octagon towers and onion domes, also exist in Charleston, West Virginia, and Butte, Montana. These three, designed by an unknown architect, resemble a synagogue near Warsaw, Poland. The Moorish Revival style first appeared in 1839 in Leipzig, Germany, and immigrants carried the style to the United States in the 1850s.*[823]

Opposite the Navarro County Community Center, "The Temple," is an H-E-B supermarket. Any relation to the anti-Semitic slur, usually spelled "Hebe" or "Heeb," is purely incidental; H-E-B are the initials of the grocery chain's founder. Out-of-staters might do a double take, but in Texas, H-E-B markets are ubiquitous.

Temple Beth El's across-the-street neighbor

# CORSICANA RABBIS

*All is vanity. ALL. This wilful world hath not got hold of unchristian Solomon's wisdom yet. But he who dodges hospitals and jails, and walks fast crossing grave-yards, and would rather talk of operas than hell ... not that man is fitted to sit down on tomb-stones, and break the green damp mould with unfathomably wondrous Solomon.*

Corsicana's first rabbi was Abraham Israel (ca. 1859-1926).[824] His wife, Rachel (Efron) Israel, had Efron relatives residing in Waco, Tyler, Gonzales, and other Texas towns long before she and the rabbi arrived in Texas. One of her cousins was Ray Rosenberg, wife of Corsicana's Ben Rosenberg.[825]

Rabbi and Mrs. Israel, along with Ray Rosenberg, were Corsicana res–idents when they attended the January 1891 wedding of the two women's cousin-in-common, Abe Efron, and his betrothed, Sarah Lewis, at the Mexia Opera House.[826] Rabbi Israel had not been in Corsicana long because half a year earlier, in July 1890, he was living in Brenham when he travelled to Corsicana to circumcise Louis Marks, a son of Sam Marks and cousin of a future leading Corsicanan, Sydney Marks, who was then only three years old.[827]

The ancient right of circumcision was on Sunday last performed on the little son of Mr. and Mrs. Marks at their residence on West Ninth street by Rabbi Israel of Brenham in the presence of a large number of friends. The ceremonies were terminated by an elaborate feast. The Hebrews of this city are a numerous and thrifty element in the community, sufficiently so, to maintain a synagogue, which they soon propose to have, so THE NEWS correspondent was informed by one of their number recently.

Circumcision of Louis Marks, 1890

Thirty years later, in 1920, Sam Marks was one of the guests at a like occasion for his great nephew, in Corsicana:

**The beautiful home of Mr. and Mrs. Sydney Marks on West Fourth avenue was a scene of happiness on last Sunday**

*during the eventful occasion of the christening of their new born babe, Alvin J. Marks.*[828]


Prior to Brenham, Rabbi Israel lived in Waco, in the mid-1880s, where at least two of his children were born. Eight of his nine children were born in Texas, from 1880 through 1895,[829] and then, before the close of the '90s, he and his family left and moved east, eventually landing in Worcester, Massachusetts and finally New York City. In the 1900 federal census, in Worcester, Rabbi Israel was a "drummer," which usually means a peddler, as in "drumming up business." A few of his sons, however, were musicians, operating music schools in Providence, Worcester, and other New England locations, so maybe he was that other kind of drummer.[830] One source identified him as a cotton speculator.[831]


Ω


Another Corsicana rabbi pre-dated the erection of Temple Beth El. Solomon Solomon (ca. 1859-1927) was in Corsicana as early as August, 1897, when he circumcised August Levy's son, Louis.[832] He remained there until at least June, 1900, a span that included the legal incorporation of the temple's congregation, the building's design and construction, but not its completion. He subsequently moved to San Antonio and lived there for the rest of his life.[833] Solomon was described as a one-man, do-it-all Jewish leader: cantor, *shochet* (ritual slaughterer), *mohel* (ritual circumciser), prayer leader, and Hebrew tutor.[834] One of his several children, Eli, changed his name to Elliot Sullivan and had a number of supporting roles in major Hollywood productions. He was one of the scores of actors and directors (many of them Jewish) blacklisted in the 1940s as suspected communists. Arrested and convicted, Sullivan was eventually acquitted because of a tech–nicality.[835]

The extent to which Rabbis Israel and Solomon participated in the religious affairs of Corsicana's Jews is unknown. Nor is it known whether they catered to one segment along the spectrum of Jewish religious ortho–doxy more than another.


## Temple Beth El Rabbis

Rabbi **Julius M. Magil**, the first rabbi of Temple Beth El, resigned a position in Ligonier, Indiana and began his tenure at Beth El on Sept. 4, 1900.[836] He was born in Latvia, Dec. 29, 1871,[837] and died in Michigan on May 28, 1958.[838] Educated at Zurich and Leipzig Universities, the scholarly

Magil was chosen as one of three hundred rabbis to edit the twelve-volume Jewish Encyclopedia, the only one from Texas.[839]

Dr. Magil led the congregation for three years. He was elected for another three-year term, in January 1903, but didn't stay. Within a few years he would be the director of the National Travelers Association, based in Milwaukee. In 1910, back in Ligonier, he ran a wholesale grocery and in 1930 he was a real estate salesman in Muskegon, Michigan. When he was "Rabbi Magil," he received high praise for his eloquent sermons. In later years, as "Dr. Magil," his oratory continued. In a lecture delivered in early 1935 about brewing international troubles, he labelled Hitler an "arch-fiend," the "world's greatest menace."[840] In 1937 he spent hours with President Roosevelt talking about his fabulous stamp collection.[841]

## HAVE YOU FOUND YOUR PLACE IN LIFE?

Do you long for complete success in business, in love, in personal living? Send at once for your free copy of Dr. Julius M. Magil's new booklet, "Finding Your Place in Life," which will point the way to realization of your fondest dreams. Dr. Magil is a vocational authority, a keen analyst of human nature, who can help you to achieve life's richest gifts. A student of Universities of Zurich, Berlin, and Leipzig; graduate in philosophy; lecturer and professor in United States and foreign colleges and universities; and authoritative adviser; Dr. Magil can help you to realize your life's ambitions. Send today for free booklet, addressing:

### Dr. MAGIL'S STUDIO of SCIENTIFIC THOUGHT-ANALYSIS
Dept. 1034-PM          MUSKEGON, MICHIGAN

*Finding Your Place in Life*

Rabbi, grocer, lecturer, executive, and philatelist, Dr. Magil fittingly was the author of *Finding Your Place in Life*.

**Henri Sande Stollnitz**, the temple's second rabbi, was a witness in *Church v. Bullock*, a 1908 Texas Supreme Court case about banning Bible recitations in Corsicana's public schools. The school system's super-intendent asserted that passages, frequently taken from the old testament, were non-sectarian and not forced on students. Rabbi Stollnitz testified that his objection to the singing of Christmas songs was acceded to by school administrators, a fact presented as evidence of the school board's sensitivity to religious differences.[842]

The *Church* in the case name does not refer to Temple Beth El:

*The evidence shows that E.H. Church does not believe in the inspiration of the Bible, that J.B. Jackson and Mrs. Lita Garrity are Roman Catholics, and that M. Cohen and Abe*

*Levine are Jews. All of said parties have children and are patrons of said school. Mrs. Garrity and E.H. Church had protested to said trustees and teachers against the conducting of said exercises. Jackson, Cohen and Levine had made no protest.*

Plaintiffs objected to the system-wide practice by protesting to the superintendent and later to the school district trustees. Failing that, they sued in the local district court, lost, appealed, and lost again. Their final appeal, to the Texas Supreme Court, also failed.

After Rabbi Stollnitz took over from Rabbi Magil, in 1903, the congregation presented their new, forty-seven-year-old rabbi with a "handsome dining room set,"[843] even though he had been there less than a year. Perhaps it was not handsome enough because he left soon after.

He was previously the longtime cantor of Eden Street Synagogue, in Baltimore, a position he first held in the mid-1880s.[844] Then, in 1889, amid accusations of infidelity, his wife divorced him[845] and he left Eden Street. He took a trip to Europe and returned to Baltimore as the cantor for the Har Sinai Temple.[846] He left there for San Francisco, via Chicago, giving cantorial performances along the way.[847] He married again in San Diego in the late 1890s to Colorado native Rebecca Brown. His prior marriage may have been a secret from his new family—in several census records he stated he had immigrated to the U.S. after 1889, the year of his divorce, even though he had first arrived in 1881 and had married in New York City in 1883.[848] At the turn of the century he was living in San Francisco with his second wife and their daughter, singing and giving singing lessons as "Professor Stollnitz."

Rabbi Stollnitz served several synagogues,[849] but never for very long because he was frequently at odds with his congregations.[850] His last-known synagogue posting was in Tampa, Fla., at Cong. Schaarai Zedek, 1905-1907.[851] He probably then worked on writing and selling his books, of which the most popular, completed in 1908, was *Glimpses of a Strange World*.[852] In 1910, in Tampa, following the addition of Henry Sande Stollnitz, Jr., born in 1906, he was a dry goods merchant. During the 1920s and '30s the family lived in New York City, and that's when he first described himself as a "Doctor of Literature" and an author.[853]

Like Dr. Magil, his Corsicana predecessor, Dr. Stollnitz was a man of letters and multiple talents. Although it doesn't appear that he was actually an ordained rabbi, he was a doctor of literature, author, and professional singer. But no matter his acclaim, it paled in comparison to that of Hortense, his daughter. Born in San Francisco in 1898, while yet a teenager she became a champion typist. While others clickety-clacked, she produced a melodious hum, clocking in at a blistering 159 words per minute, 142 after deducting for errors, setting a record in October 1917.[854] Hortense was engaged in this singular activity for several years. Remington Typewriter Company hired Frank & Lillian Gilbreth, the fa-mous efficiency scientists, to study her technique.[855] Hortense mar-ried later in life, when she was in her fifties.

Hortense Stollnitz

After Dr. Stollnitz finally settled in one place, New York City, he would still occasionally travel, including visits to Hawaii where Hortense participated in typing exhibitions and competitions. The family summered on Nantucket, where they ran an antique shop.[856] Henry Sande Stollnitz died in Queens on July 30, 1935.[857]

**Max Bachrach** appears to have been the only rabbi to serve Beth El between Rabbi Stollnitz's departure in 1903 and David Goldberg's arrival in 1914.[858] Bachrach was rabbi around 1910, but for no longer than a year.[859] Bachrach returned to Corsicana in 1924 as a rabbi at Agudas Achim (see below). Other rabbis made appearances during those lean years, as necessary, like **William H. Greenburg**, Ph.D., of Dallas's Temple Emanu-El, who conducted Beth El's confirmation class ceremony in June, 1909.[860] Moses Hirsch, a leading member of the community, conducted evening services on Rosh Hashanah, October 3, 1910, featuring choral renditions by a quartet led by Mrs. Huberta Nunn, a young widow, and three other non-Jewish Corsicanans: Methodist Pastor Waller Boggs's wife, Jean; Sam Burdine; and Douglas Johnson.[861]

**David Goldberg**, of Fort Worth, a recent graduate of Texas Christian University, filled the vacant rabbinical post in 1914. He emigrated from Russia at the age of twenty-two, around 1908, and already had a mastery of English by the time he moved to Corsicana five years later. He had visited, before then, to preside at select Jewish occasions. He officially arrived on New Year's Day and was ordained and installed as rabbi on January 2. The temple trustees extended an open invitation to all Corsicanans to attend.[862] The investiture sermon was delivered by Max London, the topic of his address, fittingly, Exodus 28:30.[863]

**Rabbi David Goldberg**

Dr. Goldberg's three-year stay ended after he was selected by Texas's U.S. Senator Morris Sheppard to be the first-ever Rabbi chaplain in the U.S. Navy. The venerable Rabbi Dr. Henry Cohen of Galveston recommended him and he was appointed on Oct. 30, 1917. The navy at the time issued only one insignia for its chaplains, the crucifix. Although Goldberg wore the cross, he tried to get it changed to a symbol more appropriate for Jews and other non-Christians. A May 1918 request to the Bureau of Navigation, asking that his insignia be changed to a Star of David, was rejected. Goldberg suggested the shepherd's crook; it was once used in the army, at the end of the nineteenth century, and was sufficiently non-sectarian. The exception was allowed and Jewish naval chaplains proceeded to wear the not-quite-so-Christian insignia. In 1941 the insignia for Jewish chaplains was officially changed to the *luchos*—the two tablets of Moses—superimposed by a Star of David.[864]

Beth El's congregation gave Dr. Goldberg a good send-off and a "handsome boudoir set" in mid-November 1917, and once again was in need of a rabbi.[865] **Arthur S. Montaz** (1888-1946) and **Nathan E. Barasch** (1888-1959), two Hebrew Union College (HUC) students, each had a six-week temporary post in Corsicana, together covering the first three months of 1918.[866]

Lieutenant Commander Rabbi Goldberg retired in 1941 and passed away in 1977 at the age of ninety-one.[867]

**Lt. Rabbi David Goldberg,
with his crucifix**

**Joseph Henry Stolz** came to Corsicana as Beth El's newest rabbi in the fall of 1918. He was there until, two years later, he accepted the rabbinate of Fort Smith, Arkansas—a "larger field where his power for good will be the more greatly felt."[868]

Stolz was born in 1878 and grew up in Syracuse, N.Y., the oldest of three sons of Jacob and Yetta (Marshall) Stolz.[869] The elder Stolz was "a public spirited,

**Rabbi Joseph Stolz of Corsicana**

enterprising, and upright citizen, and in every capacity in life is highly respected and greatly esteemed."[870]

Rabbi Stolz graduated from Syracuse University, received an advanced degree in history from the University of Chicago,[871] and underwent rabbinical training at Hebrew Union College. Just prior to leaving Corsicana he married Rosa Miller,[872] sister of Harry and Mose Miller. The latter, Mose, was Beth El's president at the time. Rabbi Stolz died in Los Angeles in 1953 at the age of seventy-five, leaving his wife, his son James, and a grandson. He had lived in the L.A. area for twenty-three years.[873]

א

Before and after Stolz's tenure, rabbinic duties were occasionally conducted by local rabbis **Maurice Faber** of Tyler and Dr. **William H. Greenburg** of Dallas.[874] Corsicana's Jewish population was then around two hundred. Beth El's membership consisted of twenty-six families and the new, second synagogue, Agudas Achim, had twenty-one families.[875]

In January, 1921, Beth El voted in **Michael G. Solomon** (1868-1927?)[876] as its next rabbi and he started the following month. A native of Posen, Rabbi Solomon, like those before him, was highly educated.[877] He was previously rabbi in Youngstown, Ohio, Los Angeles (where he succeeded Abraham Blum, a rabbi who had been in Texas for decades), and Newark, N.J.[878] In 1905 he became Victoria, Texas's Temple B'nai Israel's first rabbi.[879] He once lived in Lake Charles, and near the end of his career in Lexington, Kentucky and San Diego.[880] In addition to being a pulpit rabbi he gave lectures, engaged in "sociological studies," and was licensed to practice law in California.[881]

He was one of nine rabbis to preach at Beth El who had graduated from the prestigious Hebrew Union College, which began turning out graduates in 1883. Michael G. Solomon graduated in 1893; David Lefkowitz of Dallas, a frequent guest rabbi, in 1900; Joseph H. Stolz in 1904; Israel J. Sarasohn in 1916; Wolfe Macht of Waco, another guest rabbi, and temporary rabbis Nathan E. Barasch and Arthur S. Montaz, in 1918; Charles B. Lesser in 1935; and Theodore Wiener in 1943.[882]

Rabbi Solomon married in Savannah in 1898 to Miriam Silverman[883] and in the next few years she gave birth to two boys, Jacques "Jack" and Leon. After his

Los Angeles stint, while briefly living in New York, Michael and Miriam Solomon separated. He returned to Los Angeles and she and the children went to

Savannah to live with her parents. She obtained a divorce, in April 1904, claiming desertion. No specific catalyst for their breakup was given, but she did testify at the divorce hearing that "she had a decided objection to the humdrum burdens of housekeeper,"[884] and by 1920 she had resumed her maiden name.[885]

The eloquent, intelligent Solomon gave thoughtful sermons, each advertised in advance in the *Sun*. The first was "The Martyr of Martyrs—the Jew."[886] Another was a three-part discourse, "What is Judaism?" At the end of his first, partial

**Rabbi Michael (Moses) G. Solomon**

term, in May, 1921, he was unanimously elected for another term, to start in September,[887] but by June 1922 there was no further mention in the *Sun* of Rabbi Solomon or his "Divine Services." His last discourse was "Sinai's Message—the Law," and his next to last sermon asked, "Who is to Blame, the Pulpit or the Pew?" For more than a year, while the temple was without a rabbi, Sydney Marks conducted Friday night services.[888]

Rabbi Solomon's relationships with his congregations were temperamental, if not downright antagonistic, emblematic of the strife that forced rabbis to move on—voluntarily or involuntarily. An 1899 incident in Los Angeles shines a spotlight on the balancing act performed by rabbis:

*"I have had but one method," said Dr. Solomon today, "and that has been based upon the principle of impartiality, justice and fairness to all. I have treated the rich and the poor alike. Those who are dissatisfied always have been so. Long before my ministry here, whenever things would not suit their own views they made a point to lead their spiritual leader and not to be led by him."* [889]

During an introductory speech to his new congregation in Victoria,

*He dwelt upon the necessity of co-operation on the part of the membership in order to make a minister's work effective; that without mutuality and that co-operation so essential in religious affairs, a minister would be a luxury, in one sense superfluous.*[890]

In November, 1923, Dr. **Carl Schorr** (1895-after 1930)[891] and his wife arrived from Greensboro, N.C.[892] Born in Dayton, as a child he lived in Reading, Utica, Winnipeg, and Sheboygan before arriving in Fort Wayne in 1917,[893] at which point his father, Rabbi Saul Schorr, died, and Carl took over his father's rabbinic responsibilities.[894]

The multi-talented Schorr graduated from Western Reserve College (now Case Western Reserve University), Winnipeg's Dominion Business College, and in 1917 was ordained following his graduation that year from the Edelson Jewish Seminary of New York.[895] He was a choir director, violinist, and possessed "a well trained baritone voice."[896]

CARL SCHORR

**Carl Schorr**

In May, 1924, the Beth El congregation voted to retain him for another year.[897] Nevertheless, six weeks later, there was a new rabbi.[898] The reason Schorr didn't continue is not known. It may have been that his next position, in Monroe, La., paid better, or might have been the practical application of a lesson he learned from his father borne of a synagogueal struggle in 1898 when Schorr was an infant and his father was up for renewal as rabbi of Reading, Pennsylvania's Shomro Habrith Congregation.[899]

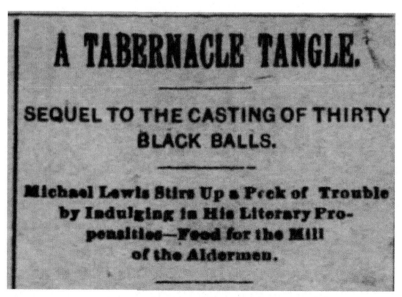

Rabbi Saul Schorr's reelection run awry

*The members of the church voted 39 to 30 to retain him. While the Rabbi was debating whether to continue or not Lewis [a member of the congregation] walked into the room and handed him a note on a postal which ran:*

*"RABBI SCHORR: – You are elected with a majority of the congregation. There were 39 votes in your favor and 30 against you. If you remain in Reading there will be a big disturbance. For the thirty black balls are not your friends. I look at it as best that you leave Reading. If you remain here don't think that you are a fine man. You are only a money-making machine.            FROM THIRTY BLACK BALLS"*

*After reading this note the rabbi was afraid to remain in Reading and, much against the demands of his friends, accepted a position at Utica, N.Y.*

Selecting and retaining a rabbi, subject as it was to a vote, put rabbis directly in the middle of congregational infighting.[900]

**Louis Brav** (1885-1950)[901] was selected rabbi of Beth El in July, 1924, and started that September.[902] He remained until the end of his 1926 summer break and then left to become rabbi of Temple Sinai, in Lake Charles,[903] though not before he married Viola Gernsbacher, a native of the Bayou State.[904]

Brav was born in Hungary and grew up in Philadelphia. He was well-educated and an eloquent speaker, like so many Beth El rabbis.[905] He received his diploma in 1906 from Gratz College, in Philadelphia, one of seven students in the school's fourth graduating class.[906] He also graduated from Columbia, where he studied German literature, and was ordained at the New York Jewish Theological Seminary. He was fluent in Hebrew and German.[907]

Between 1910 and 1920 he was rabbi in Pennsylvania at Williamsport, McKeesport, and Philadelphia, also at Pensacola, Fla. and Raleigh, N.C.[908] In February 1920 he became the first rabbi of Temple Israel in Pine Bluff, Arkansas, a new reform temple which had broken from the town's already-established congregation.[909] Following only a brief stay in Lake Charles, in 1927, he went to Temple Beth Israel in Natchez.[910]

☧

There was no permanent rabbi following Rabbi Brav's departure until Rabbi Zielonka arrived, three years later. In the meantime, every other

Rabbi Wolfe Macht

weekend, **Wolfe Macht** (1890-1952) of Waco presided.[911] Rabbi Macht was Beth El's occasional, *ad hoc* rabbi from the late twenties into the early fifties, when–ever the temple's pulpit was vacant.[912] Born in Leeds, England, he was rabbi in Waco from 1919 until his death. His only other permanent rabbinic post was for one year at Trinidad, Colorado. He held degrees from U. of Cincinnati, Hebrew Union College, and Baylor University.[913]

Rabbi **David Lefkowitz** of Dallas also filled in during this interim period,[914] just as he had done many years previous and would continue to do into the future.

Sometime around Oct. 1, 1929, **David L. Zielonka** (1904-1977) took a turn as Beth El's rabbi,[915] but he was there for not even a year.[916] Right after he left he married in Cincinnati and became rabbi at the same Tampa synagogue where Rabbi Stollnitz had gone to when he had left Corsicana twenty-five years earlier. Rabbi Zielonka served Tampa's Temple Schaarai Zedek for forty years, from 1930 until 1970.[917] His father was Martin Zielonka, rabbi of El Paso's Temple Mt. Sinai for nearly fifty years, from 1890 until his death in 1938.[918]

Rabbi David Zielonka

Ω

During the early '30s, once again there was no rabbi for Beth El. Services were provided, as needed, by either Rabbi **Leibson** of Agudas Achim, Rabbi **Macht** of Waco, or Rabbi **Lefkowitz** of Dallas.

A few months before **Charles B. Lesser** (1909-1982)[919] received his ordination from Hebrew Union College, in May, 1935,[920] he agreed to lead Beth El for a brief period before summer started.[921] He stayed on through January 1937, though, and then left for a position in Jackson, Michigan.[922]

Rabbi Lesser also attended Southwestern Univ. in Texas, U. of Cincinnati, did some post-graduate work at SMU, and received a master's degree in Hebrew literature at HUC.[923] He went on to serve congregations in Pittsburgh, Wheeling, Roanoke,[924] and Colorado.[925] He was rabbi of the Hillel at U. of Oklahoma, in Norman, and chaplain at the James Connally Air Force Base in Waco and at the McCloskey Veterans Hospital in Temple, Texas.[926] In 1953 he was serving Waco's Rodef Sholom synagogue when one Sabbath he swapped pulpits with Beth El's then-current leader, Rabbi Sarasohn.[927] Lesser later led Temple Beth Israel in Florence, S.C., from 1961-1970.

Immediately taking the place of Rabbi Lesser was Rabbi **E. Louis Neimand** (1912-1976),[928] who stayed for not quite four months, from February to mid-May, 1937.[929] Rabbi Neimand was the rabbi for Syracuse University, starting in 1958,[930] and later presided at Temple Beth Israel in Eugene, Oregon, from 1963 until his death.[931]

Col. Rabbi Edward
Ellenbogen

Rabbi **Edward Ellenbogen** (1912-1988) began at the temple on August 30, 1937.[932] He left in June, the following year, ostensibly for a summer vacation, but he didn't return.[933]

At one time he was the highest-ranking Jewish chaplain in the U.S. armed forces. He served in Omaha and Tacoma, was in North Africa during WWII, and continued to serve overseas after the war. He retired in 1965 and died at Mercer Island, Washington, in 1988 at the age of seventy-six.[934]

Rabbi **Albert A. Michels**[935] (1902-1995)[936] came to Corsicana from Natchez, Mississippi, and stayed for five years, from the fall of 1938 until the spring of 1943, easily the longest-serving rabbi for Beth El up to that point. In the summer after his departure he attended Harvard University Chaplaincy School, and, as First Lieutenant Michels, was assigned to Shenango Camp in Pennsyl–vania, a personnel depot for soldiers on their way to eastern ports and overseas deployment.

Following his military service Michels was rabbi at the U. of Miami Hillel and in St. Petersburg, Florida. He went to Cong. House of Israel in Hot Springs, Arkansas, serving that congregation from 1956 through 1974,[937] and was the first full-time rabbi at Temple Beth Shalom in Sun City, Arizona, that shul's guiding light from the mid-1970s until his death.[938] He was a popular speaker in many southern congregations and an active participant in numerous Jewish and non-secular organizations.[939]

Albert Abraham Michels was born in the Bronx and grew up first in Boston, where he attended Boston Latin, and later in Michigan.[940] He attended U. of Michigan and did graduate work at U. of Wisconsin. He was ordained at the Jewish Institute of Religion in New York, in 1934, where he received an M.H.L. degree, and later obtained his doctorate at U. of Colorado.[941] His family's U.S. roots extend back to his grandfather, Max Michels, born in 1841, a Corry, Pennsylvania merchant who, as an orphan, emigrated from Prussia around 1853.[942]

There was no rabbi to lead services celebrating Corsicana's Jewish New Year, Rosh Hashanah, 5704 (Sept. 30, 1943), but by New Year's Day, 1944 (5 Tevet, 5704), Dr. **Ernest S. Grey** (1912-1972) was the new rabbi. Erno

Szrulyovics, his original name, was born in Nagyruszka, Czechoslovakia, and arrived in the U.S. in 1939.[943] He attended El Paso's College of Mines before coming to Corsicana. At the end of May, 1944, he returned to El Paso to lead services at Temple Mount Sinai and that September began at Fort Worth's Temple Beth El. His initial stay in Corsicana was less than half a year,[944] but he returned in early September, 1946,[945] and was the regular Friday night rabbi until the spring of 1947. From Fort Worth he went to Fort Smith.[946]

**Rabbi Ernest Grey**

Ernest Grey was "gentle, soft-spoken, and knowledgeable."[947] He earned his Ph.D. in Medieval Spanish from Harvard where his wife, the former Alice Seldin, helped him to edit and type his dissertation. From Harvard they went to Denver, her hometown. Grey's research and professorships called for frequent European trips, which the couple relished.[948] They had been living in Canada for seven years when he was killed in an automobile accident in London, Ontario.[949] They did not have children.

**Theodore Wiener**[950] (1918-2006)[951] was a temporary rabbi for Beth El's High Holiday services in September, 1947, but he stayed to provide religious leadership, periodically, possibly on a regular basis, and was still there in April of 1948 when he brought in from Dallas Rabbi J. Aaron Levy as a guest rabbi.[952] He then left Corsicana.

Wiener was a graduate of Hebrew Union College, class of 1943,[953] and returned to the school in 1959 as librarian of its Jewish Institute of Religion.[954] Prior to that he served various reform congregations. He published biographies of Leo Baeck, Samuel Cohon, and Solomon B. Freehof, and was co-translator of

B. Felsenthal's letters to J.H. Schorr. Starting in 1964, Wiener supervised entries in the Library of Congress's Hebrew Language catalog.[955] His father, Rabbi Max Wiener, was an eminent scholar.[956]

♎

There is no further mention in the *Sun* of a Beth El rabbi until November 1949 when the paper reported that Rabbi Harvey E. Wessell of Beth El would be the principal speaker at a Thanksgiving event at the high school. Subsequent articles, however, show that Wessell was the rabbi of Temple Beth El in Tyler, not Corsicana.[957] There were many temples named Beth El in Texas, and elsewhere. In addition to Corsicana and Tyler, they could be found in Odessa, Brownsville, Austin, Missouri City, San Antonio, Fort Worth, Houston, and Fort Myers. Austin and San Antonio, for that matter, also had, and still have, an Agudas Achim, as Corsicana once did. Corsicana has a Bethel Church, for Methodists, and town of Temple has a Bethel, also a church of the Christian variety. Temple has no temple, but at one time did have Beth El's Rabbi Lesser.[958] Bethel, a small settlement not far from Corsicana, on the road to Palestine, never had a temple.

Rabbi **Israel Joshua Sarasohn** (1891-1972) had a long and varied career

Rabbi Israel J. Sarasohn

before arriving in Corsicana, July 1952, at the age of sixty-one. He had, since 1946, led Temple Moses Montefiore in Marshall, Texas.[959] During his time at Beth El, in 1953, Sarasohn was elected head of the *Kallah* (convocation) of Texas rabbis.[960] His last Beth El sermon was on June 29, 1956, at the end of the congregational season,[961] and he then moved on to Oheb Sholom, in Goldsboro, North Carolina.[962] His earliest known rabbinic post was in 1917, at Cong. B'nai Israel, in Natchez.[963] A year after that he was a chaplain at Camp Pike, Arkansas, and subsequently he served at: Children of Israel, Augusta, Georgia (1919);[964] Beth El, Pensacola, (1920);[965] and B'er Chayim, Cumberland, Maryland. (1921). He was at Temple B'nai Jeshurun, Leavenworth, from 1928 until 1943, and then took over at Beth Hillel Temple in Kenosha for the duration of the war—the regular rabbi there was serving as a military chaplain.[966] He next became East Liverpool, Ohio's rabbi, in 1944.[967]

Sarasohn was born in Vilnius, Lithuania[968] and died in Clemmons, North Carolina.[969] He did undergraduate work at Clarke University, in Massa–

chusetts, received his master's degree from U. of Cincinnati in 1914, and graduated Hebrew Union College in 1917.[970]

**Joseph David Spear "J.D." Spear** (1878-1958)[971] became Corsicana's rabbi at the age of seventy-eight, on Aug. 31, 1956.[972] The German native emigrated in or around 1903 and initially lived in New York for many years. He was a graduate of Heidelberg University and earned a Ph.D. at Columbia.[973] In 1907 he married Theresa (Konigsburger) Reinach, a widow twenty-five years his senior who had four children from her first marriage. She died in 1921.[974]

He was rabbi at the Ahawath Achim Temple, Quincy Street, Brooklyn, from 1911 to 1913,[975] and at Temple Israel, West Farms Rd., Bronx, from at least 1918-1920.[976] "During World War II, Dr. Spear was stationed at Columbus, Miss., serving as chaplain to military personnel at Columbus Army Air Field, Starkville College, and the prisoner of war camp at Aliceville, Ala."[977] In August 1952, following a two-and-a-half-year stint at Rome, Georgia, he took charge of Temple Beth Tefilloh in the Georgia town of Brunswick.[978] On August 1, 1955, he took the pulpit of Cong. Children of Israel, in Athens, Georgia.[979] He was the rabbi of a Columbus, Georgia congregation just prior to his arrival in Corsicana.[980]

Dr. Spear died from a heart attack on December 12, 1958, and was interred in Corsicana's Hebrew Cemetery.[981]

Seventy-one-year-old Dr. **Harry A. Merfeld**[982] arrived in Corsicana as Beth El's newest rabbi in June, 1959. "The Corsicana congregation could not afford a rabbi at the time, but a benefactor from Fort Worth quietly supplemented the rabbi's

**Rabbi Harry Merfeld**

paycheck."[983] He had extraordinary educational cred–entials, including rabbinic training at HUC and a law degree from Johns Hopkins.[984] He was the rabbi of Fort Worth's Temple Beth El from 1922 to 1936, before that at Temple B'nai Israel, in Monroe, Louisiana, and at a number of other southern synagogues.

He was very active in social and fraternal groups.[985] While rabbi in Fort Worth he was manager of its Little Theater. His dedication to the dramatic arts and high-society schmoozing eventually resulted in a warning

from that temple's board: spend more effort on your rabbinic duties—or else. Sure enough, three years later he left Fort Worth for Temple Israel in Hollywood, California's. He also served congregations in Brownwood, Texas, in Alabama, and for eight years in the Panama Canal Zone, all before arriving in Corsicana.[986] Rabbi

Merfeld died in Corsicana on Jan. 10, 1961, at the age of seventy-three, and was buried in Fort Worth.[987]

Ω

There was no permanent rabbi for the next several years. Rabbi **Gustave Falk** of Dallas officiated at High Holiday services in the mid-1960s and Sydney Marks also led the congregation.[988]

> *Beginning in 1969, Rabbi Ernest Joseph of Agudas Achim, the town's orthodox synagogue, was also leading services at Beth El. He was the temple's last full-time rabbi, leading services for Beth El on Friday nights and Agudas Achim on Saturday mornings.*[989]

Rabbi Joseph's profile is presented with the rabbis of Agudas Achim, below.

## The Rabbis of Agudas Achim Synagogue

The members of Corsicana's Orthodox Hebrew congregation, Agudas Achim, had rabbis conducting services long before their first synagogue was built. Although several of AA's rabbis are known, there may have been others who came and left without a trace. Some of the men, it seems, were not ordained, not rabbis *per se*. Kalman "K" Wolens, for one, a leading Corsicana businessman, had studied for the rabbinate before arriving in the U.S. and was able to lead the congregation during some of the periods when there was no rabbi.[990]

The first Agudas Achim rabbi, **Louis Ratner** (1860-after 1940),[991] was in Corsicana as early as 1901 and left at the end of May, 1907.[992] No information about his stay in the community is known except that he served as rabbi for the orthodox congregation. Before he arrived he was a rabbi in Dallas for about a decade, in the 1890s, and after he left Corsicana he was the rabbi of Cong. Emanuel in Oklahoma City.[993] He returned to Corsicana at least once, in 1909, possibly on official business.[994]

Unfortunately for the Ratner family, the rabbi and his second wife, Dina (his first wife died in 1897[995]), went through a very public and messy divorce in the summer of 1909. Oklahoma City's *Daily Oklahoman* spewed out a front page headline, "Rabbi Cruel, is Wife's Charge," and subsequent issues continued coverage of the sensational trial.[996] Mrs. Ratner's principal charge, in addition to other hurtful and destructive behaviors she alleged, was that the rabbi granted greater household authority to Celia, his daughter by his first wife, than he did to her.[997] The divorce action was filed shortly after the birth in Corsicana of the couple's only child, Ethel,[998] two or three years before it became public fodder, and ended in November 1909 with a divorce decree from Referee Stringer.[999] In 1912 Ratner moved with Celia to Chicago.[1000] Rachel, who seems to have been a third wife, died in 1929, in Chicago.[1001] His last wife, Ella, brought to the marriage children from her prior marriage and she also predeceased him, in 1941.[1002]

Rabbi **Isaac Mohilner** (ca. 1872-1924) was born in Shklov, Mogilev, arrived in the U.S. in 1904, and lived in Corsicana from about 1911 to 1920.[1003] What portion of his time was spent as rabbi for the orthodox congregation is not known. The historical record on this point is thin. It is entirely possible he was more of a *shochet* than a pulpit rabbi because his name is not connected to any synagogue history—he is not associated with any congregation except in a 1911 Corsicana city directory he is listed as the rabbi for the town's "Orthodox Hebrew Church."[1004] Just prior to coming to Corsicana he lived in Topeka, where he identified himself as proprietor of a meat market,[1005] and he was listed as a butcher on his 1904 ship arrival manifest and in the 1910 federal census.[1006] In 1909, in Kansas City, before he went to Topeka, he described himself as a Hebrew teacher.[1007] Although records indicate he was a Corsicana resident in 1911, 1917, and 1920, during those last four years, 1917 to 1920, Agudas Achim, with its new building, had a full-time leader—Rabbi Dow.

**Ydel** (also spelled Yidel) **Gedalia Dow** (1887-1956) was born in Vilnius, Lithuania, and came to the U.S., landing at Galveston, in 1910.[1008] He was in Corsicana as early as January, 1916.[1009] Prior to that, in 1914, he was in Brenham—the date and place of birth of his first child, Esther.[1010]

Rabbi Dow officiated at the dedication Agudas Achim's first synagogue in September, 1917.[1011] He was still in Corsicana a year later, in October 1918,[1012] but by the summer of 1920 he had moved to Fort Worth.[1013] He served B'nai Zion in El Paso from 1921-1926,[1014] next moved to Tucson, and within another year moved again to Phoenix[1015] where he served its Jewish community and ran the Reliable Kosher Market.[1016] He spent his final thirty years in Phoenix.[1017]

Dow, a *mohel*, circumcised the third child of Mose M. (Myer) and Rose (Daniels) Miller in Corsicana on June 15, 1916. The infant was "christened, Sidney Harrold":[1018]

**Rabbi Ydel Dow and family**

*...the ceremony was performed by Dr. Dow, who was serious in the spoken words, impressive at all times and skillful when skill was necessary. The earnestness of the entire proceedings was impressed upon all and particularly the gentiles present.*

♎

According to a brief note in the October 15, 1920 issue of the *Jewish Monitor*, a Dallas paper,[1019] a "Rabbi Horowitz" had moved to Corsicana from San Augustine, Florida with his family and would make it his new "permanent home." Herman Horowitz, an itinerant "clergyman" who did live in St. Augustine, and who did come to Texas around that time, never served either of Corsicana's congregations.[1020] He is not to be confused with Rabbi Henry Jacob Horowitz, who also relocated with his family to Texas, in 1919, and who likewise did not go to Corsicana.[1021]

In the fall of 1924 AA hired Rabbi **Max Bachrach** (1874-1943)[1022] of Kansas City, Mo.,[1023] who had previously served as Beth El's rabbi in 1909 and early 1910 (see above). His second stay in Corsicana was very brief, no more than a year.[1024] Between those two dates he lived at various locations, including Wichita, Dubuque, and Kansas City.[1025] In 1913, when he was a kosher meat dealer and rabbi in Wichita, his wife died and he was left on his own to care for his three teenage daughters.[1026] In 1930 he returned to Corsicana to visit with Harry and Sarah Golda Rothkopf.[1027]

Rev. **Morris Renov** (1883-1964)[1028] served Agudas Achim for a brief period in the 1924/1925 time frame.[1029] It is not known when he left, but by 1928 his family had relocated to New York City.[1030] Renov arrived from his native Gomel, now in Belarus, in the summer 1914, landing at Galveston en route to his brother, Elias, who had settled in Shreveport.[1031] The rabbi's wife, May, and their two young children came three and a half years later, in 1917, joining him at Montpelier, Vermont.[1032] Around the start of 1918 the family moved to Westfield, Massachusetts, where he had charge of the local synagogue until August 1920 when he left due to health problems.[1033] He then spent a year or so in Anderson, South Carolina, where he was a *shochet* and Hebrew teacher.[1034] From Anderson he went to Corsicana, probably via Shreveport where his parents, Kalman and Rivka, his brother, Elias, and Elias's large family lived. In New York, where he spent his later years, he lived in the Bronx and Tannersville, a Jewish resort community in New York's storied Catskill Mountains.[1035]

Rabbi **Baruch Lebovits**[1036] (1893-1962)[1037] was in Corsicana as early as February 1927 when the *Sun* mentioned him as part of a small land transaction.[1038] In September that year a notice in the *Sun* advertised he would be giving lectures at Agudas Achim during Rosh Hashanah—one day in English, the other two in the "Jewish language," presumably Yiddish.

Lebovits came to the U.S. in 1922 from Czechoslovakia at the age of twenty-nine with his wife, Leah, and three-year-old son, Israel.[1039] Another son was born in Texas. He later moved to San Diego, lived there into the late 1930s,[1040] and then moved to Los Angeles where he passed away.[1041]

The next mention of a rabbi for Agudas Achim was in March, 1928.[1042] **Moses J. "M.J." Leibson** (1881-1951) was rabbi until November 1935, when he left for Fort Worth's Congregation Ahavath Sholom.[1043]

Leibson, his siblings, and his parents, Rabbi Leib "Louis" and Minnie (Saltzman), came to the U.S. in the early 1900s, settling in St. Louis.[1044] Rabbi Leibson married but did not have children. He passed away in Fort Worth.[1045]

Rabbi **Harry Shapiro** (1905-1996) came from Austin to immediately assume the Agudas Achim pulpit following Rabbi Leibson's departure and remained there for

ten years. He was the first of two consecutive Shapiro rabbis and he promoted a more visible profile than his predecessors. Frequent notices of upcoming synagogue events, including sermon titles, appeared in the *Sun*. He opened his home to guests and participated in interdenominational programs with other Corsicana clergy. He even took a turn as president of the Corsicana Ministerial Association.[1046]

The public was invited to attend his Feb. 9, 1936 installation as Agudas Achim's newest rabbi. Among those attending were: former Corsicana

Rabbi Harry Shapiro

rabbi, M.J. Leibson, of Fort Worth; Rabbi Lesser, Beth El's then-current rabbi; and two Dallas rabbis.[1047] Agudas Achim's new building, a former Presbyterian church, was dedicated at the same time.[1048]

Rabbi Shapiro was born in Jerusalem and studied at the holy city's renown Etz Chaim and Rabbi Kook Yeshivas (schools for advanced Jewish studies).[1049] He came to the U.S. in 1923 and graduated from the Hebrew Theological Seminary of Chicago four years later. He was rabbi in Bismarck, North Dakota in 1927 and in Fond du Lac, Wisconsin, at Khiloth Jacob Cong., in 1928.[1050] He attended U. of Wisconsin and U. of Texas, Austin, and taught Hebrew and Jewish history at UT's Hillel. He also received a degree from Baylor U., in Waco.[1051]

Harry and Alice (Laebovitz) Shapiro had two children, Lionel David "Davis" and Judith "Diana," both born in Corsicana.[1052] Alice died young, in 1944. The rabbi and his second wife, Sadye, lived their final years in Phoenix, both passing away in 1996.[1053]

Rabbi Shapiro, the first, left Agudas Achim at the end of May, 1945, returning to Wisconsin to take the pulpit at Cong. B'nai Zedek in Kenosha.[1054]

In May, 1946, a year after Harry Shapiro's departure, **Joseph N. (Nathan) Shapiro** (1894-1976)[1055] became the new Agudas Achim rabbi.[1056] He led the orthodox congregation for eighteen years, retiring in October 1964 after a rabbinic career of fifty-one years.[1057] He and his wife, Tillie (Menkov), moved to Miami. Like his predecessor, he kept the synagogue in the public eye with frequent notices in the *Sun*.

Rabbi Joseph N. Shapiro

The second Rabbi Shapiro was a fourth-generation rabbi. Born in Mozyr, in the Minsk district of Belarus, he was admitted to the highly respected Slutsk Yeshiva at the age of thirteen. Five years later, in 1913, he came to the U.S., motivated by a keen interest in the country and its history, joining his brother and sister in New York.[1058] His first work as a rabbi was in the Roxbury section of Boston. Just prior to Corsicana he was rabbi of Little Rock's orthodox synagogue, also named Agudas (or Agudath) Achim, where he also served for eighteen years, from 1929 to 1946.[1059] His grown children, two sons and two daughters, lived in the South.[1060]

Rabbi Shapiro's health declined during his last few years in Corsicana and he lost his sight. Ernest Joseph, a Corsicanan with a good Jewish edu–cation, became his assistant.

**Ernest Joseph** took over leadership responsibilities at the synagogue when Joseph Shapiro retired and by the end of 1965 Joseph was the acting rabbi.[1061]

Born in Germany, at the age of nine, in 1939, he and his family went to Shanghai to escape Nazi tyranny. They spent the next eight years in China along with thousands of other Jewish refugees, much of the time in a ghetto created by the occupying Japanese forces. In 1947 the Joseph family was sent to Dallas, via San Francisco, as part of a program to resettle the Jewish refugees of China.[1062]

Prior to his arrival in Corsicana, Joseph worked for seven years at the Dallas Home of the Jewish Aged. When he first moved to Corsicana, in 1956, he worked for K. Wolens and was able to assist the aging Rabbi Shapiro because he had learned to read from the Torah during his Jewish education in Shanghai. He attended the St.

**Rabbi Ernest Joseph**

Louis Rabbinical College with financial help from the Wolenses and was ordained by the Rabbinical Academy of America. Once ordained, in 1966, he officially became rabbi.[1063]

In 1969, about five years after formally taking on rabbinic responsibilities at AA, he started to also conduct services at Temple Beth El, thereby becoming rabbi to all of the observant Jews of Corsicana—Reform, Conservative, and Orthodox.[1064]

Ω

Rabbi Joseph's ministry continued, even after his 1999 death, thanks to his son, Rabbi Frank Joseph. Rabbi Frank serves some of Texas's congregations which do not have a resident rabbi, including Corsicana. His business card carries the slogan, "Have Torah—Will Travel," a pun on the late 50s/early 60s TV western, "Have Gun—Will Travel," and *Haftarah*, the collection of readings from *The Profits* (the biblical books Joshua through Malachi) which follow the *Torah* (the first five books of the Bible—*Genesis* through *Deuteronomy*)—perfect for a circuit riding Texas rabbi.[1065] He conducts services at the temple (now a community center) for Corsicana-area Jews about once a month. Babbette Samuels and former Corsicana Jews from surrounding areas gather for prayer, fellowship, and fond memories.

# BURIALS TO 1890

*And this empties the decanter.*

The twenty-seven burials prior to 1890 identified in the Corsicana Hebrew Cemetery Association's record book, Rope Walker excluded, are presented in chronological order on the following pages. For several decades, up until 2020, the cemetery property, on the west side of Corsicana, was under the stewardship of CHCA board member Babbette Samuels. Until recently she oversaw maintenance work on the five and a half acres of beautifully landscaped grounds and kept up CHCA's record book of over four hundred burials. Now, having entered her tenth decade, she decided to turn over those duties to younger board members.

The current record book was created in 1951 by Ivan Rosenberg and was subsequently maintained by Wally Levy, Jay Silverberg, Bernard Rosen, James Cerf, Irvin Samuels, and most recently, by Babbette and other current members of the cemetery association.[1066]

**With a Jewish community in the single digits,**
**Corsicana's beautiful Hebrew Cemetery**[1067]

Bayside Jewish Cemetery, Queens, N.Y.

In contrast, New York City's Jewish community, numbering in the millions, has permitted some of its cemeteries, with tens of thousands of burials, to decline into unnavigable jungles.[1068]

ᴖ

It's possible that one or more burials took place in Corsicana's Hebrew Cemetery during the fifteen months between December 1875, when the grounds were purchased, and March 19, 1877, when Leo Fox, the first "known" burial, died.[1069] If there were earlier burials, nothing about them is known.

The formation of the Ladies Hebrew Cemetery Association in 1891 coincided with improved cemetery administration. Very few burials after that date, or just prior to it, were poorly memorialized in stone or in record, whereas many before then have all manner of missing information and errors.[1070]

Just missing the 1890 cutoff chosen for this supplement was Jonathan Tobias London, son of Max and Bertha London. He died on Jan. 20, 1890 at the age of twenty-two, kicked by a horse.[1071] He was memorialized with a proper gravestone. The next death was Sarah Golden, who died Aug. 6, 1890. She has a *matzevah* (gravestone, in Hebrew) with extensive information, both in English and Hebrew. Louis Lustig, the "infant" child of Mr. and Mrs. Albert Lustig, according to the record book, died on Aug. 20, 1890 and is remembered with a plain tombstone similar to other early memorials for children. His epitaph is "Louis, son of A. & D. Lustig," and nothing more. Joshua Cahn's gravestone has basic information, including his date of birth, May 1, 1890, his date of death, Sept. 11, 1890, and his and his parents' names, "Joshua son of A. & M. Cahn." The memorial stones for Joseph Solomon and Bettie (Shwarts) Baum recall their lives appropriately and include their dates of death, Jan. 25, 1891 and July 3, 1891, respectively. The LHCA was formed two weeks after Bettie's death. One week later, the group's first fundraiser was held, netting $260 for cemetery upkeep.[1072]

## March 19, 1877

***OUR LEO***
***A BUD ON EARTH***
***TO BLOSSOM IN***
***HEAVEN***

**Leo Fox**, age eleven months, twenty-two days, is the earliest known burial. He was the son of cemetery co-founder and CHCA original trustee Alexander Fox. The traditional epitaph has Leo and his father's given names in Hebrew: Ari Leib, son of Sender Fox (transliterated). Sender, a common nick–name for Alexander, doesn't sound very Jewish, but it is, carried by Jews since the time of, and in tribute to, Alexander the Great.

## 1878

**Morris** twins, no given names, ages unknown. "Twins, Infants of C. Morris" says the record book, with "1878" as their date of death. "C. Morris," presumably the father, has not been identified.[1073] One Charles Morris was "dangerously stabbed" in Corsicana on May 27, 1875, but nothing more is known of that incident or the victim.[1074]

## April 13, 1878

**Anna Wolf**, age seven months, was the "infant child of Mr & Mrs Wm Wolf of Ennis," according to the record book. No such family was found in historical records, but there was a William C. Wolf family in the 1880 census in Corsicana. That William Wolf was born in Prussia, and his wife, Nanny, was born in Tennessee, where the two were married in 1868.[1075] In Sherman, in 1884, "W.C. Wolf" of Corsicana ended his earthly woes with strychnine. The Fort Worth newspaper reporting his suicide said a note he left gave as the cause his inability to support his destitute family.[1076] If not for the record book's reference to Ennis, the 1880 "William C. Wolf" and the 1884 "W.C. Wolf," both of Corsicana, would convincingly be one and the same and the father of Anna Wolf. Even though there is no indication in that census record or that news item that he was a Jewish man, the 1880 "William C. Wolf" was born in Prussia and the name "Wolf" is frequently a Jewish surname, both evidence that Corsicana's William C. Wolf was indeed Jewish, and by extension, Anna was his daughter.

## May 13, 1878

**Freeman**, no given name, age one day. The stone is entirely illegible, but the record book has the child's date of death and says he or she was born the prior day: "Still born child of Mr & Mrs Pete Freeman, Ennis, Texas." Philip "Pete" Freeman was one of Ennis's leading citizens.[1077]

# June 28, 1878

**Fannie Freeman**, eighteen months. This stone is also entirely illegible. She was another child of Phillip and Theodosio (Rushing) Freeman, of nearby Ennis.[1078]

# May 14, 1879

*MAMA TAKE ME I HAVE GONE TO MEET YOU*

**Saul Harris**, age four months, fourteen days. The entry for him in the record book, "Infant Child of Mr & Mrs R.L. Harris - New York," supplements the biographical information about him on his gravestone. The location of Sarah Harris's burial—the heartfelt epitaph indicates that Saul's mother, Sarah, predeceased him—is unknown.

There was an "R.L. Harris," probably the same R.L. Harris, a widowed merchant, born in New York, who was enumerated in Tyler, Texas in the 1880 census, residing with one "S. Fox."[1079] Additionally, there was a Robert L. Harris who married Carrie Senfeld (Schoenfeld) in New York City in 1883, went to Texas with his new wife, and had their first three children born in Texas. The oldest, Minerva, was born in 1888 in Hillsboro. By 1900 the family had moved back east, to Paterson, N.J.[1080]

# July 7, 1880

**Rosalie Zadek**, age seventy-five. Her husband was a merchant who died in Poland in 1849.[1081] Her only known descendants today are through her son Oscar, aka Major Emil Zadek, a successful jeweler in Mobile, Alabama and a confederate veteran. Adolph and Bertha, her two other children, were longtime, prominent citizens of Corsicana.[1082]

# March 23, 1881

**Louis Morris**, age two days.[1083] Like the "Morris" gravestone above, the record book for this burial says the deceased was a child of "C. Morris." The original grave–stone no longer exists.

# September 18, 1882

*Beautiful, lovely, she was but given,*
*A fair bud to earth to blossom in heaven.*

**Mabel Freedman**, age ten months, was a child of S.S. and Carrie (Frank) Freedman.

Another child of theirs, a fifteen-month-old infant, died in Michigan on July 7, 1875. Carrie, her parents, and a Mr. Harris of Chicago were riding in a wagon in Flint when the two left wheels gave out and the child, sitting on Carrie's lap, fell to the ground. Moses Frank, Carrie's father, who was also injured, picked up the baby and ran to a local doctor. The child, whose name is not known, suffered a fractured skull and could not be saved.[1084]

## February 20, 1883

**Elkan London**, age about two years. The record book says he was born in 1881 and died Feb. 20, 1883. He was the son of Max and Bertha (Simon) London. Family plots were not laid out at the time, so the grave is not with the rest of the London family; instead, he was buried in the old section, near Rope Walker and other early burials.

## March 9, 1883

**Harriett or Henrietta Rich**, age fifty-one. The spelling on the gravestone, "Herriet," is not a spelling which was used for her when she was alive. One side of the stone says "Herriet, Wife of Isaac Rich, Died Mar. 9, 1883, Aged 51." The other side, written in Hebrew, gives her Hebrew given name, Hinde, her father's given name, Moshe (Moses), and says she is the wife of Izik Ritz (transliterated). One of her children, Charles (see below), and her husband Isaac, who died in 1908, were also buried in the cemetery.

Her gravestone is clearly visible in the photograph that accompanied Robert C. Campbell's 1949 "Walk into Oblivion" newspaper story, the earliest known photograph of Rope Walker's gravestone, and for that matter, the earliest photograph of any part of the Hebrew Cemetery.

Detail from photograph
in "Walk into Oblivion"

## August 3, 1883

*Thou art gone little Lillie*
*Sweet child of our love;*
*From earth's fairy strand,*
*To bright mansion above.*

**Lillie Polasky**, age one year, eleven months, seven days, was a daughter of Louis and Cornelia (Frank) Polasky.

## December 1, 1883

*Sleep on, sweet babe, and take thy rest,*
*God calls away when He thinks best.*

**Daisy Freedman**, age three months, was another daughter of S.S. and Carrie (Frank) Freedman. Her stone lies next to her cousin, Lillian Polasky, who died four months earlier, and alongside her sisters, Bessie and Mabel, who also died in their first year of life.

## August 11, 1884

**Joe Goldberg**, age unknown. The record book says he was the nephew of Joe Reisman of Ennis and that he died on Aug. 11, 1884. He must have been the son of a sister of Joe Reisman because Reisman's wife, Sarah, was a member of the Shwarts family of Corsicana, and the deceased would have been described that way if he was the son of one of Sarah's siblings. Reisman's sister, purportedly Joe's mother, could not be identified.

| Name | Plat | Size | Secti- |
|---|---|---|---|
| Goldberg Joe | | | F G |
| | Born | Died | L |
| | | 8/11/1884 | |

History
Nephew of Joe Reisman, Ennis Texas

A search of Ennis records, where Joe Reisman was a longtime resident, located only one Goldberg from around the time Joe Goldberg died. A newspaper article dated Nov. 1, 1886, described the fiery death in Ennis of "S. Goldberg,"[1085] while two other papers on the same date said the victim's name was "S. Goldsburg"[1086] All of the articles said the body would be buried in Corsicana, and the two that called him *Goldsburg* said burial would be in the Jewish Cemetery. The only burial in Corsicana's Hebrew Cemetery with a name and date of death remotely close to that of the man killed in Ennis is that of Joe Goldberg.[1087]

The Coroner's jury, presided over by 'Squire Higginbotham, rendered a verdict in the case of Goldsburg of, "Come to h s death by the flames." His remains will be shipped to Corsicana to-morrow morning for interment in the Jewish Cemetery.

"Goldsbusg" (Goldsburg) to be buried in Corsicana Jewish Cemetery

Joe Goldberg, buried in 1884 according to the record book, and S. Goldberg/Goldsburg, who died in an 1886 fire, appear to be one and the same, despite the differences. Stated another way, in 1886 a Goldberg/Goldsburg of Ennis was brought to the Hebrew Cemetery for burial, but no grave for him exists, and yet a record book entry states that a Goldberg from Ennis was buried there in 1884.

## October 15, 1884

**Annie Levy**, age four. She was the daughter of L. Levy, from Ennis, according to the record book. Louis and Amelia (Samuels) Levy had a large family living in Ennis in 1880.[1088] Most of the family, including Annie's many siblings, relocated to Oklahoma City.

## 1885

**Charles Rich**, age thirty-one, was the son of Harriett and Isaac Rich. He died in 1885, according to the record book.

## September 29, 1885

**Rebecca Blumrosen**, age fourteen months. A recently placed granite marker next to her entirely illegible gravestone has the same information found in the record book, identifying her as the daughter of Jacob B. and Esther (Freedman) Blumrosen and gives her date of death.

## December 5, 1886

**Isadore Marks**, age twenty-one months. No gravestone exists for him, but his death is included in the record book, which says his parents were "B. and Mrs. Marks," that he was born Feb. 28, 1885, and that he died Dec. 5, 1886.[1089]

## June 1, 1887

**Moses M. Cerf**, age six and a half months, was the son of Henry Cerf of Waxahachie. A published death notice for a young child is unusual today, and a rarity then.

> The infant son of Mr. Henry Cerf died this afternoon; also the infant son of Mr. Henderson died to-day. The remains of Mr. Cerf's child will be removed to Corsicana to-morrow for burial.

## 1887

**Brin**, no given name, age unknown. According to the record book he died in 1887 and "At time of death his father was reported to live in Ennis Texas—but later moved to Chicago."

The parents were most likely Barney and Lena (Freedman)[1090] Brin. They and their children were longtime Dallas residents before moving to Chicago and Iowa, although there is no record that they ever lived in Ennis. Lena died in 1895, so she does not appear in the 1900 or 1910 censuses where it is reported for women the number of children born and how many remain alive.

Hyman Brin, on the other hand, did live in Ennis, according to the 1880 census, and subsequently in Waxahachie and Dallas.[1091] His wife, Jennie (Edloff), died in 1884, and as it does not appear that Hyman remarried[1092] it doesn't seem possible this was his child. In any case, Hyman did not move to Chicago.

This "Brin" burial also might be a child of David and Josephine "Josie" (Blum) Brin, longtime residents of Waxahachie, which is close to Ennis and not far from Corsicana. Josie had four children born to her between 1880 and 1900, and during that time one had died, according to census records.[1093] This Brin family likewise never lived in Chicago.

Barney, Hyman, and David Brin were Jewish, but none of them, it appears, lived in Ennis and then moved to Chicago.

## 1887

**Abraham.** The record book lists a death date of 1887 and says "No other information available." It is not known if Abraham is a first or last name. There were no Jewish families with this surname living in the Corsicana area.

## January 9, 1888

**Ben Gottlieb**, age thirty-two. His traditional gravestone gives his Hebrew given names, Dov Ber (thus "Ben," which sounds like "Ber"), son of Nehemiah. He was married to Sarah (Simon) and they had two sons, Sol and Jack. After Ben's death, Sarah remarried to William Herman and had five more children, two of them surviving past infancy.[1094]

## February 8, 1888

**Louis Shwarts**, age fifteen. The very top of his gravestone, barely legible, says:

*In loving remembrance of*

The epitaph at the bottom is unreadable. He died of "congestion of the brain."[1095]

## October 27, 1888

**Benedict Lissauer**, age about sixty-five. His 1823 birth date and his death date are noted in the record book. His name does not appear in any Texas records, but only one person in the U.S. prior to his date of death (and no one after) had this unusual name combination. Occasionally spelled *Lessauer*, all occurrences in records, with either spelling, presumably refer to this one

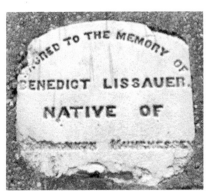

individual. He was naturalized in New York City in 1860, renouncing allegiance to the "Elector of Hesse Cassel,"[1096] and was listed in New York City directories for several years in the 1870s and early 1880s. An 1885 St. Louis city directory listing, occupation peddler, is the last record of him prior to his death.

His birthplace, carved into the gravestone, is damaged and mostly illegible, but the record book made a note of it, presumably when it could still be made out: "Ungedanken, Kahrhessen." Kurhessen was part of the Prussian electorate Hesse, now the German state of Hesse, north of Frankfurt along the Eder River, thus matching up to the New York naturalization.

A family history researcher who posted her family tree on www.geni.com published a set of vital records from Ungedanken, one of them a birth record for a Bendix (a common variation of Benedict) Lissauer. Unlike other Lissauers from the town, whose birth records could be matched to a subsequent marriage and/or death record in the town, there were no additional records for "Bendix Lissauer," suggesting he had moved from Ungedanken. *Bendix* Lissauer was born in 1828, not too far off from the 1823 birth date given for *Benedict* in the record book (especially if an "8" was misread for a "3," or vice versa, a popular transcription error). In conclusion, this was probably one and the same person.

One month after Benedict Lissauer's death, one "M. Lissauer" of New York was a guest at a Galveston hotel.[1097] The rarity of this surname suggests he was a relative of Benedict who had travelled to Texas to attend to Benedict's affairs, including, no doubt, the procurement and installation of a grave marker.[1098]

## October 31, 1889

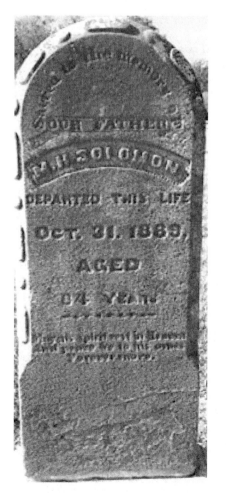

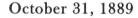

*May his spirit rest in Heaven*
*And peace be to his ashes*
*Forevermore.*

**Michael Hirsch Solomon**, age eighty-four. He and Rosalie Zadek (she died July 7, 1880; see above), both born about 1805, were the earliest-born Corsicanans whose final resting place is in the Hebrew Cemetery. His given names, "Michael Hirsh," represented by only initials on the gravestone, are spelled out in the record book. M.H. Solomon and his wife, Blouma,[1099] who died in 1908 at the age of ninety-one, had seven children, five of them known:[1100] Bertha, Joseph "Joe," Isadore, Abraham "Abe," and Lena.

- **Bertha (Solomon) Fox** (1842-1906)[1101] married Alexander Fox in New Orleans in 1864.[1102] Alex Fox was a leader in Corsicana's civic life for many years and a leading member of its Jewish community. Their son, Leo, is the earliest known internment in the cemetery.
- **Joseph Solomon** (1846-1891)[1103] also lived in Corsicana. In 1884, the *Dallas Daily Herald* noted,

> *Joseph Solomon, Corsicana's gigantic Israelite, has been absent for a week at Vermillionville [Lafayette, Louisiana], from whence he was expected to-night with a bride.*[1104]

In 1888, Joe operated the People's Store on Beaton Street. It had "no less than six separate departments of merchandise," all at bargain prices.[1105] He was about forty-five when he died, in Corsicana, and he was buried near his parents in the Hebrew Cemetery.

> *Joe Solomon who, for several years, has merchandised in this city, dropped dead Sunday from Heart failure and was buried with masonic honors from the residence of his brother, Mr. I. Solomon, this after-noon.*[1106]

- **Isadore Solomon** (1851-1907)[1107] of Corsicana appears to have been another child of M.H. and Blouma Solomon, the "I. Solomon" referred to as Joe Solomon's brother. Corsicana directories from 1898 and 1901 show Eugene Solomon, Isadore Solomon's son (according to censuses), was working for Alex Fox, i.e. Isadore's brother-in-law and Eugene's uncle. Another son of Isadore, Mitchell, born sometime in October of 1889,[1108] was given essentially the same name as Michael, his grandfather, who died that month, strongly suggesting that Mitchell was named after Michael.[1109]
- **Abraham Solomon** (1856-1900).[1110] In 1892, Simon Fox, husband of Lena (Solomon) Fox (listed next), was a clerk in Abe Solomon's Corsicana store,[1111] suggesting that Abe was also a child of Michael and Blouma Solomon. Additional evidence is that Abe's gravestone is next to the M.H. and Joseph Solomon gravestones in the cemetery. Abe does not appear to have married because his epitaph doesn't refer to him as a "husband" or "father," but instead is "our departed brother."
- **Lena (Solomon) Fox** (1863-1925)[1112] married Simon Fox,[1113] brother of Alexander Fox, who was Lena's brother-in-law.[1114]

The common occurrence of the surname "Solomon" makes it difficult to identify M.H. and Blouma Solomon's two other children, at least one of whom was still living as of 1900.[1115] To illustrate, there were two rabbis in Corsicana named Solomon, and, for good measure, there was Rev. Emmett W. Solomon, pastor in 1900 of Corsicana's M.E. Methodist Church (South).[1116]

Further Solomon family connections might be found in the records of Vicksburg, Miss. That's where Isadore married Alice Kahn, in 1872, and where their first two children were born. There was an Abraham Solomon in Vicksburg who married a Mary Fox of that town, but this is not the same as Abraham Solomon of Corsicana, and no connection between the Solomon/Fox families of Vicksburg and the two Solomon/Fox families of Corsicana could be puzzled out.[1117]

## Undated

**Morris Rosenbaum.** No date of death is noted on this gravestone or in the record book. Located adjacent to gravestones of others who died before 1890, it seems likely he did as well.

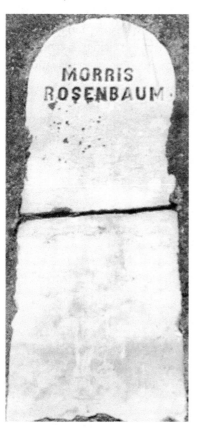

Families with this common though not exclusively Jewish surname lived in the vicinity of Corsicana at the end of the nineteenth century, but without knowing anything else about him, such as his date of birth or death, identification of Morris Rosenbaum is not possible. He may have been related to the large family of Simon and Ella Rosenbaum, who lived in Marshall, east of Dallas, in the 1860s.[1118] Simon was postmaster at Hallville (aka Ash Spring), near Marshall, in the mid-1860s.[1119] After Simon's death his family lived in Woods County, also east of Dallas, but closer to Dallas and Corsicana, where they were enumerated in the 1880 census.[1120] Later still, the family moved to Dallas.[1121] There was no known family member named Morris. Brothers Abra—ham, Eugene, and Isaac Rosenbaum, sons of Simon and Ella, lived in Hillsboro for a number of years, during the late 1880s and early '90s,[1122] when the closest Jewish cemeteries, equally distant, were in Corsicana and Waco.

Morris Rosenbaum may have been a shoot from that family tree who died in Hillsboro and was buried in nearby Corsicana. Eugene and Isaac, of Hillsboro, never married,[1123] but Abraham, who did marry, and lived in Hillsboro, or even one of the other brothers, David and Sidney, who seemed to have lived elsewhere in the vicinity, could have been the father of Morris Rosenbaum, another forgotten soul buried in Corsicana's Hebrew Cemetery.

Abraham Rosenbaum married Minnie Marcus in 1895 in Hillsboro, but they do not appear to have been Morris's parents because the 1900 and 1910 censuses state that only one child was born to Minnie,[1124] and that would be her daughter, Ervill, who was still alive in 1900 and 1910.[1125]

Simon and Ella also had three daughters: Hattie, Ophelia, and Ella. Maybe Morris was a ninth child of Simon and Ella Rosenbaum, a child who died young, who was never recorded in any census or other record.[1126]

It is also possible that the stone identifies a plot jointly owned by the Morris and Rosenbaum families—families with those surnames concurrently lived in Hillsboro and there was a business partnership bearing those two surnames. In other words, the stone bears two surnames and simply marks the ownership of the lot, a common practice in cemeteries, typically done with low granite markers. Morris was a Jewish surname for at least one family in the vicinity, as shown by the Morris burials in the cemetery previously shown. Accordingly, it may turn out that no one is buried beneath that gravestone.

# Abbreviations

# Notes

# Acknowledgements

# List of Illustrations

# Abbreviations

*AMB1* Abe Mulkey, Abe Mulkey's Budget (1897)

*AMB2* Abe Mulkey, Abe Mulkey's Budget No. 2 (1909)

**Anc.** www.Ancestry.com

*CSWL* Corsicana Semi-Weekly Light, www.Newspapers.com

**Census** U.S. Federal Censuses, Anc., unless indicated otherwise

*DDH* Dallas Daily Herald

*DMN* *Dallas Morning News*, www.GenealogyBank.com

**FAG** Find A Grave burial site database, www.FindAGrave.com

*FWDG* *Fort Worth Daily Gazette*, www.Newspapers.com

**GB** www.GenealogyBank.com

*GDN* *Galveston Daily News*

*HP* *Houston Post*, www.Newspapers.com

**ISJL** Goldring/Woldenberg Institute of Southern of Jewish Life, Encyclopedia of Southern Jewish Communities, www.isjl.org/encyclopedia-of-southern-jewish-communities.html

**LDS** www.FamilySearch.org

*Love* Annie Carpenter (Mrs. W.F.) Love, *History of Navarro County* (1933)

*Memorial* *A Memorial and Biographical History of Navarro, Henderson, Anderson, Limestone, Freestone and Leon Counties, Texas* (Chicago: The Lewis Publishing Company, 1893)

**NP** www.Newspapers.com

**PTH** The Portal to Texas History, texashistory.unt.edu/ (landing page) and texashistory.unt.edu/explore/collections/TDNP/ (Texas Digital Newspaper Project)

**RWeb** RootsWeb, Navarro County, Texas, www.rootsweb.ancestry.com/~txnavarr/

*Sun* *Corsicana Daily Sun*, www.Newspapers.com

**THB** Texas State Historical Society, Texas Handbook Online, https://tshaonline.org/handbook/online/articles

## 2. Written in Stone

1 "Abe Weiss" was not Rope Walker's real name.

2 The purpose was to reduce theft by vandals (Babbette Samuels, personal correspondence with author, Jan. 4, 2018). More than a dozen other old gravestones, most of them for infants or young children, were similarly planted in beds of concrete.

3 Samuels, personal correspondence.

4 ISJL, "Corsicana, Texas." Philip and Esther (Goodman) Samuels came to Corsicana just before the turn of the century and spent the rest of their lives there.

5 Nancy Roberts, "He was in Temple Beth-Els's First Confirmation Class," *Sun*, Sept. 22, 1974.

6 ISJL, "Corsicana."

7 In Corsicana, Beth El is the "temple," while Agudas Achim is the "synagogue." Both, in fact, are synagogues, which is to say, Jewish houses of worship. Synagogues referred to as "temples" conduct a more liberal, progressive, "reform" liturgy than other, more orthodox synagogues.

8 Referenced as "the old Levine store," a directory from 1898 (*Morrison & Fourmy's General Directory of Corsicana, 1898-1899*, City Directories, Waco (sic), Tex., Anc.) indicates the store at this intersection was in fact a saloon, run by Louis Levine.

9 See *Sun*, June 29, 1976 (full page advertisement with company history); Oral interviews of Louis Wolens (son) and Jay Silverberg (son-in-law), discussed in Chapter 4.

10 ISJL, "Corsicana"; Bud Silverberg, telephone interview with author.

11 "Observance of Memorial Day: Veterans and Daughters Pay Tribute to Fallen Heroes," *Sun*, Apr. 27, 1918.

12 Joseph Levy was an Alsatian. His daughter Celia (Levy) Amsel resided in Corsicana for many years. He was probably a Confederate soldier because he was born about 1828 and lived in Louisiana just prior to the Civil War. (Louisiana Marriages (abstracts), Ascension, La., for Joseph Levy and Pauline Levy, Oct. 30, 1856; 1860 Census, Ascension, La., for Joseph and Pauline Levi with children Flora and Cele). Due to the commonness of his name, no Civil War record, certain to be for this "Joseph Levy," could be identified.

13 Louis Niveth "was a Lieutenant in the Russian army, and served through the Polish insurrection of '64, was wounded thirteen times. ... He was also at the assaults on Plevna, during the Turkish war ..." (*Centerville Citizen*, (Centerville, Mo.), May 12, 1881, NP). He was Adjutant of the Tex. 5th Reg., 1st Battalion, carrying the rank of Lieutenant, in 1893 ("The State Encampment: List of the Troops in Attendance Sunday Night," *GDN*, July 24, 1893). It does not appear that he was in the Civil War.

14 "M. Hirsh," according to the 1918 article about Jewish veterans. He was born Nov. 28, 1843, in France. (Tex. Death Certs., Corsicana, for Mise Hersch (sic), Aug. 25, 1914, Anc.). He and his wife, Hannah, brought up their granddaughter, Sadie Cohen (who later married Abe Marks, Sydney's brother), following the early (1903) death of Nora (Hirsch) Cohen, Moise & Hannah's daughter. (*Sun*, Sept. 28, 1918; "Venerable Lady Passes Away," *CSWL*, Sept. 27, 1918). No Civil War records could be found for Hirsch.

15 "To Celebrate 82D Birthday: Max London Has Lived in Corsicana for Forty-Three Years," *Sun*, July 19, 1920; "Max H. London Died at Home Here Just After Noon Today: Long Time Resident of Corsicana and Prominent Mason," *Sun*, Dec. 24, 1925.

16 "To Celebrate 82D Birthday."

17 Now called Main Street.

18 England & Wales, Civil Registration Death Index, 1916-2007, for Elkan London, 1922 Q4-Oct-Nov-Dec (Anc.).

19 Ancestry index.

20 *The American Jew as Patriot, Soldier and Citizen* was a rebuttal to allegations published some years earlier labeling American Jews as unpatriotic because they didn't serve in the military. The allegations received a lot of attention due in large part to anti-Semitic currents then prevalent in Russia, Germany, and especially France, where the Dreyfus Affair was simmering. Wolf's lofty goal was to

list all Jews who had served in the U.S. military. Most of the Jews Wolf listed served in the Civil War, by far the war which engaged the most Americans up to that point. He listed soldiers on both sides of the conflict and acknowledged up front that his compilation would be imperfect and incomplete, despite his best efforts.

21 Alexander Fox's Confederate service record on www.Fold3.com confirms that "A. Fox" of Waul's Legion is Alexander Fox.

22 ISJL.

# 3. Cerfs

23 "Circus Blumenfeld: Overview & General History," Circus Blennow & Blumenfeld Genealogy (blog) www.blennowgenealogy.wordpress.com/circus-blumenfeld-overview-general-history/.

24 "Jewish Children Treated to Real Circus in Berlin," *Wisconsin Jewish Chronicle*, Oct. 18, 1946, NP.

25 Both names are referenced in the Circus Blennow & Blumenfeld Genealogy blog.

26 The deer is symbolic of the Hebrew tribe Naphtali. A son named Naphtali, after one of biblical Jacob's twelve sons, would also get a familiar name meaning "deer." Jacob's deathbed blessings upon his sons are the source for the animal nicknames—Naphtali was compared to a deer (Gen. 49:21). The Hebrew name added to the name Naphtali would be Tzvi, Hebrew for deer, along with the name Hirsch, in Germany, or Cerf, in France. "Naphtali Tzvi Hirsch" (in English, frequently resulting in "Harry") is a common given-name combination for Jewish boys; similarly, "Yehudah Aryeh Leib" (aka Judah, associated with the lion, frequently "Louis" in English) and "Benjamin Zev Wolf" (associated with the wolf, frequently "William" in English).

27 One factor complicating the analysis of Jewish family connections is that surnames for most Jews were first acquired in the early nineteenth century. The older custom, outlawed by the Napoleonic Code, was to use the given name(s) of one's father as a second given name (a patronymic) and people did not have inheritable surnames passed down from one generation to the next. The paternal grandfather's given name might be added as an additional given name, following the father's name. Furthermore, the founder of the Blumenfeld Circus might have changed his name when he acquired an official surname. When surnames were first adopted, frequently the father or paternal grandfather's given name became the new surname, or a surname used by the wife's family would be adopted.

28 In Jewish genealogy, "spelling doesn't matter" is frequent refrain.

29 Circus Blennow & Blumenfeld blog; Kultur-Büro AHB, Dr. Wolfgang Fritzsche: Kulturwissenschaftliche Dienstleistungen, Name adoption list of the Department of Bonn, 1846, http://www.a-h-b.de/AHB/Listen/Bonn.htm.

30 Names are just one challenge to tracing Jewish ancestry. Other challenges result from frequent migrations and the abuses visited on the vulnerable, minority Israelites by their hosting nations. Each new generation might use a whole new set of familiar given names, adapted to a new homeland.

31 JewishGen Online Worldwide Burial Registry, at Phalsbourg, France, https://www.jewishgen.org/databases/cemetery/: Plot N-03, Jeannette KAHN, wife of Moise CERF, 1817-Feb. 4 1911, husband in S-03, daughter in N-05; Plot S-03, Moise CERF, June 26 (or July 15), 1803-July 1, 1874, b. and d. in Mittelbronn, husband of Jeannette KAHN and son of Lazard and Gittel (MAY), wife in N-03, parents in V-03 and V-33; Plot V-03, Lazare CERF, 1774-Sept. 12, 1842, d. at Mittelbronn, husband of Gittel MAY and son of Moise, wife is in V-33; Plot V-33, Gittel MAY, 1782-Apr. 30, 1852, d. Mittelbronn, wife of Lazare CERF, husband in V-03, son in S-03. MAY was a common surname in the area based on its preponderance in cemetery records.

32 *Typical?* A study of Alsatian Jewish families in late-nineteenth-century Texas (and Louisiana) would make a tidy monograph. Mose Levi (1851-1919) and Joseph, August, and Isaac Levy are other Jewish Corsicanans with Alsatian origins.

33 New Orleans Passenger Lists, Dec. 15, 1855, Arrivals, SS *Wurtemberg*, for Henry Cerf, age 15, Anc.; 1900 Census, Waxahachie, Tex.; 1910 Census, Manhattan, N.Y.

34 "Henry Cerf Dies in New York," *Waxahachie Daily Light*, Mar. 1, 1911, NP. In Galveston, in 1872, he was in business as "Cerf Brothers," selling groceries wholesale. A Galveston business

directory for that year listed a "D. Cerf," who is likely Henry's brother David, who was also in the wholesale grocery business, but based out of New Orleans (1860 Census for David Cerf, New Orleans, Anc.).

35 Jules Cesar, Joseph, Rosa (wife of Samuel Lipsit), Jasmine (wife of Morris Schector), Madeline (wife of Augustus Davis), Albert A., and Lillie (wife of Joe Cohn).

36 Morton, Rebecca, Eugenia (wife of Isaac N. Cerf), Leonie (wife of Max Schneider), Louise (wife of Coleman Roddy), Morris, Alexander "Lexie," Josephine (wife of Barner Goldberg), and Walbert "Wally." The family initially lived in Jefferson, Texas. After U.P. Levy died, Sophia and the children moved to Corsicana, and later she lived in Waco.

37 The burial registry for the Jewish cemetery in Lixheim, France, lists an Ester Raphael, born in Mittelbronn, daughter of Moises and Jeanne (Kahn) Cerf, the same parents listed for the other Cerf siblings. The burial register identifies her husband as Moises Raphael (JewishGen Online Worldwide Burial Registry, at Lixheim, France, https://www.jewishgen.org/databases/cemetery/, Ester Cerf, b. Mittelbronn, died 3 Oct. 1916, wife of Moises RAPHAEL, daughter of Moises CERF and Jeanne KAHN; JewishGen Online Worldwide Burial Registry, at Phalsbourg, France, Plot M-07, Esther CERF, wife of Moise RAPHAEL, 1846-Mar. 10, 1916). The discrepancy in the day and month of burial is undoubtedly due to confusion between European and American styles of recording dates—one is 3/10 and the other is 10/3.

38 Nonnie (Raphael) Levine died in Corsicana on Nov. 19, 1947, at the age of seventy-eight. Her husband was Abe Levine of Corsicana. Her Texas death certificate (Anc.) says she was born in Loraine, France, on Feb. 14, 1869, the daughter of David (sic) Raphael & Esther (Cerf) Raphael.

39 He was born in 1882 and died in 1947 (Tex. Death Certs., for David A. Raphael, Ferris, Tex., Anc.).

40 "Pioneer Citizen Passes Away," *Sun*, Mar. 12, 1917. He first arrived at New Orleans. In 1869 he relocated to Bryan, Texas, and a few years later came to Corsicana when it became the newest terminus of the railroad.

41 "Pioneer Citizen Passes Away."

42 "Heard Very Fine Lecture," *Sun*, Feb. 11, 1918.

43 Tex. Death Cert., Navarro Cty., for Isaac N. Cerf, Anc.

44 Tex. Death Cert., Isaac N. Cerf, Anc. Cousin marriages were not unusual in Jewish families. Isaac and Eugenia's children were: Uriah M. (Moise), Idalia, Robert, and James. Only James married (L. Garner, interview with author). Eugenia was the daughter of U.P. and Sophia (Cerf) Levy.

45 Tex. Death Cert., Anc.

46 "Pioneer Corsicana Resident Found Dead in Home Here Today," *Sun*, Aug. 24, 1927; FAG; Texas Death Cert., Anc.

47 FAG.

48 Their children were Ernest, Raymond, Wilhelmina, Allen, and Julia.

49 Edmond Raphael of Corsicana "was the only member of his immediate family who came to America but it is thought that all of his brothers and sisters in France have died" ("Pioneer Corsicana Resident Found Dead"). His father was "Leon Raphael" (Texas Death Cert., Anc.). This was probably the Leon Raphael, married to a Sophie Cerf, who lived in Mittelbronn, where Edmond was born. Whether this Sophie (Cerf) Raphael, Edmond's mother (possibly), was related to the Corsicana Cerf family could not be determined; her father was Jacob, not Moises. There were many families with the name CERF and not a few named RAPHAEL in Mittelbronn and nearby. (JewishGen Online Worldwide Burial Registry, Phalsbourg, France: Plot X-10, Lion Jehuda RAPHAEL, 2 Jan. 1799-6 July 1866, died Mittelbronn, husband of Sophia CERF and son of Seligman RAPHAEL and Gouttel (KAHN); Plot X-13, Sophia Zepho CERF, 1810-27 Oct. 1866, died Mittelbronn, wife of Lion Jehuda RAPHAEL and daughter of Jacob CERF; Plot V-20, Seligmann RAPHAEL, born 1764, St. Jean Kourtzerode, died 19 Jan. 1849, Mittelbronn, husband of Odile Goutel (KAHN) and son of Jacob RAPHAEL and Jeanne (MATZ). St. Jean Kourtzerode is close to Mittelbronn and Phalsbourg.)

50 Tex. Death Cert., Anc.

51 Jewish custom encourages remarriage to a deceased spouses' brother/sister.

52 "Isadore Cerf, Veteran Ennis Merchant, Dies," *Sun*, Oct. 10, 1923.

53 Social Security Death Claims (abstract), for Rosa Cerf Berger, Anc.

54 Leon Cerf's children were Moise, Mamie Jolesch, Sadie (Sophie) Epstein, Rosa Berger, and Corinne (FAG; U.S. Passport Applications, Anc.; 1900 Census).

55 1900 & 1930 Censuses, Ennis, Tex.

56 JewishGen Online Worldwide Burial Registry, Phalsbourg, France, Plot N-05, Sara CERF, 1858–12 Mar. 1910, wife of Edouard BEHR and daughter of Moise CERF and Jeannette (KAHN), first wife of husband in O-01, parents in S-03 and N-03.

57 "Isadore Cerf, Veteran Ennis Merchant, Dies."

58 Nor has a connection been made from either of those two Cerf families to the large family of Alsatian Cerfs reaching well back into the eighteenth century, documented by genealogy hobbyist Rémi Klotz. The head of Rémi's family tree is a Neftali Moyse CERF, born about 1700. (http://gw.geneanet.org/rklotz1?lang=en&pz=remi+charles&nz=klotz&ocz=0&m=D&p=jacob+moyse&n=cerf&sosab=10&color=&t=A&v=10). One of his many grandchildren was a Moyse Salomon CERF, who in turn was the grandfather of certain early CERF settlers in California, a family documented by blogger Dawn Cerf (http://cerfancestry.blogspot.com/).

For the curious, Bennett Cerf (1898-1971), a founder of Random House publishers, public wit and raconteur, cannot be connected to any of these CERF families. His Alsatian Cerf line is Gustave (1868-1941), Benoit (1835-1895), and Lazard (ca. 1785-ca. 1845). In sum, there was a surfeit of Cerfs in Alsace.

59 See JewishGen Online Worldwide Burial Registry, at Phalsbourg, France, and naturalizations from Alsace-Lorraine, Anc.

60 "Grand Jury Will Probe Kidnaping: Judge Scarborough Orders Reconvening Body Next Monday: Thorough Investigation to be Made in Robert Cerf Case," *Sun*, Jan. 16, 1931. The kidnappers were caught several months later.

61 Solomon (1932-33 obituaries, for Sol Branch Cerf, Ph.B., 1897, Yale University, posted to family tree of "BRegenstein," Anc.) and Frederick (WWII Draft Reg. Cards, Anc.). In 1876, Dave Cerf was living in Corsicana when his store on Beaton Street was the origin of a devastating fire ("Corsicana: Extent of Wednesday Night's Fire—Loss, $30,000; Insurance, $20,000—Names of the Losers, Etc.," *GDN*, Nov. 10, 1876).

62 Louis Amadee, Achilles A., Harry, Edgar Allen, Madelaine (married to Harry Kahn), Solomon "Sol" Branch, and Frederick D. (1870 Census, New Orleans, for David Cerf; 1880 Census, Evansville, Ind., for David Cerf; 1932-33 obituaries, for Sol Branch Cerf).

63 *Texas Agricultural and Mechanical College Annual Catalogue* (College Station, Texas: 1876), 8-10 (Courtesy of Cushing Library, Texas A&M University). There were 106 students. Also listed from Corsicana was Meyer Cohen, son of Louis and Rosa. No other names in the list seemed obviously Jewish.

64 "Former Resident Oldest Living A&M Graduate," *Sun*, July 24, 1953. His birth date is from a 1922 passport application (at New York, for Louis A. Cerf, Anc.). The *Sun* article said he was thirteen, but the school session started on October 2, 1876 ("State Agricultural and Mechanical College: Bryan, Texas," *DDH*, Sept. 29, 1876, NP). Based on his known birth date, he would have been a month shy of his thirteenth birthday. His date of death is taken from several family trees posted to Ancestry.com.

65 "He Shot Himself to Death: D. Cerf, a Methodical Business Man, Puts a Period to His Career in a Business-Like Way," *Times-Picayune* (New Orleans), May 13, 1881, NP; "The Curse of Poverty: Drives Drummer to his Death: A Deliberate Suicide," *Times-Democrat* (New Orleans), May 13, 1881, NP; David Cerf, Hebrew Rest Cemetery, New Orleans, FAG.

66 "Simon Hernsheim's Death Deplored," *Times-Picayune* (New Orleans), Jan. 6, 1898, NP.

67 John Steinbeck, *Travels with Charley: In Search of America* (New York: Viking Press, 1962).

# 4. Histories of the Jews of Corsicana—Texans

68 Song title, Kinky Friedman. The song was recorded by Kinky Friedman and the Texas Jewboys, by Willie Nelson, and performed by Bob Dylan.

69 Gene Fowler, *Mavericks: A Gallery of Texas Characters* (Austin: University of Texas Press, 2008), xii ("Active from the frontier era to the space age, these one-of-a-kind Texans inhabited the worlds of oil, ranching, real estate, politics, rodeo, metaphysics, show business, folklore, and art.").

70 T.R. Fehrenbach, *Seven Keys to Texas* (Texas Western Press, UT, El Paso, 1983), vii.

71 Fehrenbach, vii.

72 Fehrenbach, vii.

73 Rabbi James L. Kessler, "Jews," THB,
https://tshaonline.org/handbook/online/articles/pxj01.

74 Henry Cohen, *One Hundred Years of Jewry in Texas* (Dallas: Texas Centennial Exposition, 1936); *The Jewish Texans (Texian and Texans* pamphlet series) (San Antonio: UT Institute of Texan Cultures, 1974); Natalie Ornish, *Pioneer Jewish Texans* (Dallas: Texas Heritage Press, 1989); Hollace Ava Weiner and Kenneth D. Roseman, *Lone Stars of David: The Jews of Texas* (Lebanon, N.H.: University Press of New England, 2007); Ruth Winegarten and Cathy Schechter, *Deep in the Heart: The Lives and Legends of Texas Jews, a Photographic History* (Austin: Eakin Press, 1990); "Trail Blazers of the Trans-Mississippi West," 8 *American Jewish Archives* (Oct. 1956), 59-130.

75 The insulting term "Marano" was doubly insulting because eating pork is contrary to Jewish dietary law.

76 For an honest, untraditional perspective of Columbus, see James W. Loewen, *Lies My Teachers Told Me: Everything Your American History Textbook Got Wrong* (New York: Simon & Schuster, Touchstone edition, 2007), 31-69.

77 See, e.g., *Jewish Encyclopedia*, Cyrus Adler & George Alexander Kohut, "Carabajal" (1906), reproduced at www.jewishencyclopedia.com.

78 Amanda Lipsitt, "The Secret Society: Descendants of Crypto-Jews in the San Antonio Area," *Texas Undergraduate Research Journal* (UT, Austin), texasurj.com/archives/2007.pdf; Mercedes Olivera, "Latinos Along Border Discover Sephardic Jewish Heritage," *Dallas Morning News*, www.dallasnews.com.

79 "DNA Clears the Fog Over Latino Links to Judaism in New Mexico," *Los Angeles Times*, Dec. 5, 2004, http://articles.latimes.com/2004/dec/05/nation/na-heritage5/2.

80 See, i.e., Simon Romero, "Hispanics Uncovering Roots as Inquisition's 'Hidden' Jews," *New York Times*, Oct. 29, 2005, www.mobile.nytimes.com.

81 Kessler, "Jews," THB.

82 William Groneman III, personal correspondence with author, Mar. 4, 2018. The four were: Anthony Wolfe, his two young sons, and one Galba Fuqua. See also *Pioneer Jewish Texans*.

83 It should not pass notice that Santa Anna, a colorful subject for biographers, was a one-legged man who danced a political jig for years as he fell in and out of power.

84 Kessler, "Jews," THB.

85 A concise history of early Jews in Texas is also found in *Jewish Encyclopedia*, Cyrus Adler & Henry Cohen, "Texas" (1906), reproduced at www.jewishencyclopedia.com.

86 Natalie Ornish, "De Cordova, Jacob Raphael (1808-1868)," THB,
https://tshaonline.org/handbook/online/articles/fde03.

87 C.T. Neu, "Annexation," THB,
http://www.tshaonline.org/handbook/online/articles/mga02.

88 *Memorial*, 106-07, 113, 148, 150-51, 164.

89 "A Brief History of the Corsicana Jewish Community," *Jewish Monitor*, Dec. 17, 1920, NP. Herman Dessauer was the newspaper's Corsicana correspondent.

90 It can be inferred that the reporter was referring to Alsace-Lorraine and German states, where Jews were highly assimilated.

91 Other officers of Beth El elected in 1913 were: Robert Jarret, V.P.; Moise Hirsch, Recording Secy.; Kal Shwarts, Financial Secy., and Alexander E. Marks, Treasurer. Trustees at the time of the reorganization were Louis Cerf, Morris Jarret, M. (presumably Meyer, who later moved to Sherman) Cohen, Edmond Raphael Jr., and Moses Myer Miller. Ben Goldsmith became secretary as of Jan. 1915 ("A Brief History of the Corsicana Jewish Community").

92 More about Rabbi Goldberg is found in Supplement II.

93 The history of Corsicana's two synagogues is treated in detail in Supplement I and Corsicana's rabbis in Supplement II.

94 The 1920 article also says the IOBB lodge was organized in 1919, but IOBB Lodge 275, Corsicana, was in fact established in the 1870s, as discussed in a later chapter.

95 Other officers of the lodge in 1915 were Ben Goldsmith, M.M. Miller, Harry Kaufman, and M. Hirsch. In 1920 the officers were Robert Werner, Moses Goldsmith, S. (should be P., for Philip?)

Samuels, Ben Brown, Sol Gottlieb, and Ben Goldsmith. Ben Goldsmith was secretary of Temple Beth El, the IOBB lodge, and the Cemetery Association.

96 Tommy Stringer, "Corsicana, Texas: An Unlikely Promised Land," paper presented at the annual meeting of the Texas Jewish Historical Association, held with the Texas State Historical Association, Austin, Mar. 1990 (Briscoe Archives, University of Texas, Austin). A courtesy copy was received from the Goldring/Woldenberg Institute of Southern of Jewish Life. The 1920 *Jewish Monitor* article says services were held in a "large hall in the city." See Supplement I.

97 Golden's first name was seldom spelled out, but was recorded as "Edward." Other building fund committee members were Nathan Goldberg, J. (Jonas) Jacobs, Will and Jacob Goldman, Philip Samuels, Kalman Wolens, Max Wolens, Sol Gottlieb, Jacob Dreeben, Max Brustein, S. (Samuel) Katz, H. Grossman, and I. Rothkopf.

98 Wikipedia's "Sanger Brothers" entry; Ornish, *Pioneer Jewish Texans*, 150-52; Christopher Long, "Corsicana, TX," THB, https://www.tshaonline.org/handbook/entries/corsicana-tx; Diana J. Kleiner, "Sanger Brothers," THB, https://www.tshaonline.org/handbook/entries/sanger-brothers.

99 *Love*, Chap. VI.

100 1880 Census, Navarro Cty., E.D. 138 (hereinafter E.D. 138), 4. Mary, better known as Nancy (or Nanny) M., was born in Tennessee and does not appear to have been of Jewish ancestry. The Wolfs are included here as Jews because of the 1878 Hebrew Cemetery grave of Anna Wolf, recorded as the child of "William" (Supplement III).

101 E.D. 138, 13.

102 E.D. 138, 20. Alternatively, Cecelia's maiden name was Jacobs (Tex. Death Cert., Corsicana, for Nannette Goldstein, Anc. (Cecelia's daughter)). Her gravestone has her name as "Cecelia," but the 1880 and 1900 Censuses list her as "Celia."

103 E.D. 138, 20. Her maiden name is from Death Cert., Dallas, 1914, Anc. The nieces are both from Ennis families, daughters of Rosa's sisters: Hattie Levingston was the daughter of Frances (Samuels) Levingston and Sallie Levy was the daughter of Amelia (Samuels) Levy.

104 E.D. 138, 21. The census spelling is "Newburgh," but other sources leave off the "h."

105 E.D. 138, 21.

106 E.D. 138, 21. Her maiden name is from her Death Cert., Corsicana, 1926, Anc.

107 E.D. 138, 21.

108 E.D. 138, 21.

109 E.D. 138, 38.

110 E.D. 138, 39. Lena Solomon and Bertha (Solomon) Fox were sisters, married to brothers Alex and Simon Fox. In 1880, Lena and Simon had not yet married.

111 E.D. 138, 44.

112 E.D. 138, 41.

113 E.D. 138, 44. Isaac "Ike" Levy's obituary identifies August as a brother, and both their obituaries name their sisters. ("Funeral Services Held Friday For Pioneer Resident," *CSWL*, Dec. 17, 1929 (Isaac); "Pioneer Resident of Corsicana Dies Here on Monday," *Sun*, Jan. 4, 1932 (August)).

114 E.D. 138, 45. Her family name is based on Lottie Obright's New York City birth record, LDS.

115 E.D. 138, 43. This Morris Sterne might be the same as Morris E. Sterne of New York. They have the same year of birth. Morris E. Sterne of New York invented the school fire drill. Morris Sterne of Corsicana's wife Laura died in 1886 and was buried in Corsicana's Oakwood Cemetery (FAG). Morris Sterne was Jewish because he was a member of Corsicana's B'nai B'rith in 1877 and 1883 (*American Israelite*, Oct. 12, 1877; "B'nai B'rith," *DDH*, May 8, 1883, NP). He was possibly related to the Frank family because he was included at a "family reunion" that took place with the Franks in Corsicana on May 24, 1891 ("The Whirl of Society," *DMN*, May 25, 1891, NP).

116 1880 Census, Navarro Cty., E.D. 129, 13. The location is probably in the Chatfield area, ten to fifteen miles northeast of Corsicana. In Ancestry.com, the parents' names were transcribed as they appeared, as "Ivey" and "Mattie," but based on other information the enumerator probably wrote "Izey," hardly legible, and "Mattie," which should have been "Hattie." Their names were Isaac and Harriett Rich, and they are discussed in later chapters.

117 William and "Mary" (should be Nanny) Wolf were residents of Corsicana, according to the 1880 and 1900 censuses only, not later.

118 E.D. 138, 21. The Blums are discussed in greater detail in a later chapter. The name Blum is a common (but not exclusively) Jewish name, and other Blums in Corsicana early on are believed to be Charles Blum's brothers. Several of these Blums were buried in the Oakwood Cemetery, including Charles and "Lou."

119 E.D. 138, 62. Lizie is twenty-three and Corine twenty-six. Lizie and her parents were born in Texas. Nothing further could be learned about these two, who boarded with two other young women, all four of them listed as having "no occupation."

120 Myers and his son were both named Benjamin, an indication they were not Jewish because naming a child after a living family member, according to the more-common Ashkenazic tradition, is not done (Sephardic Jewish tradition does permit it). Her pre-marriage name does not ring Jewish— Frances Emaline Thashley. Enumerated with them are their daughter and son-in-law, Katie and John O. Dalton. John Dalton was murdered in a Houston bar on Jan. 28, 1896 ("Died with His Boots On: John O. Dalton Shot and Killed by Mike Ryan," *HP*, Jan. 29, 1896; FAG, Washington Cemetery, Houston, Tex. (includes substantial transcription of the *Houston Post* article)).

121 *Logan's Railway Business Directory* (A.L. Logan & Co., 1873), 96-99, Archive.org/stream/logansrailwaybus00loga.

122 South Side (of the public, e.g., courthouse) Square.

123 Alexander Fox was a fixture in Corsicana for many years, dying in 1922 at the age of eighty-four. His brother in the dry goods business was Abraham L. Fox, of New York City. Their 1873 store was on Beaton Street, and they also had a store on Elm Street, in Dallas (*DDH*, June 25, 1873, NP (advertisement)).

124 Aaron's early use of the given name "Abraham" explains why his son was occasionally known as "Abraham Shwarts, Jr."

125 Also listed is "Caplen & Bro., Dry Goods and Notions." This does not seem to be a Jewish family, nor are they related to Zipporah Caplan, who is buried in the Hebrew Cemetery.

126 "T.D. Solomon" had recently lived in Ennis, until he lost his place due to a fire ("Roasted Alive," *FWDG*, Nov. 1, 1886).

127 The twelve-page transcription of his talk, "Corsicana's Early Jewish Settlers," appeared in the 1977 issue of *Scroll* (Navarro County Historical Society). Much of the *Scroll* article was condensed and repeated in "Early Jewish Families Helped Build City," *Sun*, Nov. 20, 1977. References here to Silverberg's history are based on the *Scroll* version, which was more complete (and accurate) than the *Sun* article.

128 In most records, Golden is referred to with an initial "E" or as "Edward." He is listed in the 1900 Census in Corsicana with the first name "Harris," which probably was derived from his Hebrew name, Naphtali Hertz (his son Pace's gravestone includes that as E. Golden's Hebrew name).

129 See, e.g., 1900 Census.

130 Sarah's date of death is taken from her gravestone in the Hebrew Cemetery; "Store Burned at Corsicana," *FWDG*, Aug. 11, 1890. There is no known connection between the two events.

131 1900 and 1910 federal censuses show Jacob born in 1864 and the same age as his wife, Flora, but later censuses (1920 Census; 1930 Census) show he was five years younger, possibly dropping a lie in later years which they had perpetuated in their youth to hide an embarrassing age difference. Their gravestones in the Hebrew Cemetery agree: she was born in 1858 and he in 1864.

132 Census records; Hebrew Cemetery gravestone. Records of when he arrived range from 1881 to 1886, but most say 1885 or 1886.

133 He arrived in 1881 (1930 Census) or 1890 (Naturalization Petition, Anc.). The naturalization petition is probably a more reliable document.

134 She was Razel "Rosa" (Solinger) Goldman. (Death Cert., Texas, for Sam Goldman, Anc.; Hebrew Cemetery gravestone).

135 Sarah Ida (Goldman) Golden, second wife of Edward Golden, was buried next to her husband. Her death certificate (Anc.) erroneously records her father's surname as Golden and the informant is written as "Will Golden" when it was almost certainly Will Goldman. The name of the mother on the certificate, Rachel Solinger, is the same mother listed on Sam Goldman's death certificate. As previously mentioned, inter- and intra-family marriages in Jewish family histories are not uncommon.

Isaac and Fannie (Friedman) Golden, no known connection found to the Corsicana Golden family, lived in Ennis in 1880 (Census), and had a daughter, Sarah, who married a Robert Goldman of Chicago, also no discernable connection to Corsicana.

136 The *Scroll* article spells the last name as "Rayfield." It is unclear if this was the spelling used by Silverberg or a mis-transcription from his oral presentation.

137 U.S. Census records, as discussed in Chapter 3.

138 U.S. City Directories, *R.L. Polk's Corsicana City Directory*, 1908, Anc. An "L. Newburg" and a family of Flonachers were enumerated together on the same page in the 1860 Census in Feliciana, La. In 1870, D. Cerf, Ed Raphael, and L.H. and Henrietta Newburg were enumerated together in Calvert, Tex. (1870 Census). Henrietta was born in 1846 in Charleston, S.C., daughter of Isaac, a Frenchman. (1870 Census, Anc.; Tex. Death Cert., Aug. 23, 1918, Anc.).

139 This is a common story told about Jewish merchants in Texas.

140 Malcolm Stern, *First American Jewish Families: 600 Genealogies, 1654-1988*, 3d Ed. (American Jewish Archives, 1991), 159, www.AmericanJewishArchives.org.

141 FAG, Mount Sinai Memorial Park, Texarkana, Ark., for Uriah P. Levy; "Knocked Down and Robbed of His Money and His Shoes," *DMN*, Feb. 26, 1889.

142 Uriah P. Levy was born Jan. 14, 1842 and died May 15, 1891. The *Sun* version of Silverberg's talk failed to explain the commodore's relation to the Cerfs, making the comments about "U.P. Levy" oddly out of context. (See also: 1850 Census, New Orleans, for "Widow Levy" and eight children, ages 2-17; "Married," *New Orleans Times*, Mar. 17, 1867, GB (marriage of U.P. Levy and Sophie Cerf); 1880 Census, Jefferson, Tex., for U.P. Levy.).

143 The statue honors deceased firefighters. It was not erected "in memory of the beloved fire chief," but it was dedicated to his memory. Freedman had been a driving force in raising funds to get the memorial created but passed away before its completion. ("Firemen Had Great Time," *Sun*, Jan. 17, 1918; "Monument Will be Unveiled," *Sun*, July 19, 1918; "Fireman's Monument Unveiled Yesterday," *Sun*, June 16, 1919). Rube Freedman is also discussed in Chapter 24.

144 Her mother was Sophie (Cerf) Shwarts and her father Kal Shwarts. See Chapter 3.

145 Or, they were married in New York City (probably Manhattan), on or about March 25, 1871 ("Corsicana Couple Celebrates 50th Wedding Anniversary," *Jewish Monitor*, Mar. 25, 1921, NP). Their marriage record could not be located. Daughter Susan's marriage record lists her mother's surname as "Reffischkowsky" (NYC Marriages, abstracts, for Susie Marks and Jusman Epstein, June 15, 1892, LDS), while other records list it as Levy (e.g., Texas Deaths, for Jennie Marks, 1926, Anc.).

146 The Corsicana store started as the "New York Store," then became "B. Marks," and after his sons became involved, "The Marks Brothers." At the time of his retirement, Sydney owned fourteen buildings in Corsicana and three farms. ("He Does His Part," *Corsicana Weekly Light*, Dec. 16, 1971, NP (Sydney Marks tribute).).

147 The Corsicana store was sold in the early 1950s and the Sherman store in 1958. The fifth son, Harry, was not mentioned by Silverberg.

148 "Corsicana Store Rounds Out Fifty Years of Service," *Sun*, May 5, 1931; "Dry Goods Business Started 69 Years Ago in Corsicana is Moving Back Same Location," *CSWL*, July 11, 1939 (should be "59 years"; the article was off by ten years); Bob Campbell, "History of Marks Bros. Store, Observing 67th Anniversary, is Recalled from Earliest Days," *CSWL*, June 13, 1947; "He Does His Part."

149 Benjamin Marks came to Corsicana on July 31, 1880, after spending two years doing business in Austin ("Marks Brothers Established Here 69 Years Ago," *CSWL*, Aug. 2, 1949, quoting an article from the *Austin Statesman*, dated July 31, 1880). In 1880, Ben was living with his family on Hester Street, the archetypical New York City Jewish neighborhood, on the Lower East Side of Manhattan, according to the census of that year. He was enumerated again in 1880 in Austin, without his family, as "B. Marks," living with "J. Jacobs," both dry goods clerks. In New York he was enumerated with his wife "Jane" and children Susan, Elias, and Mendel. Jennie Marks gave birth to eleven children, although four had died before 1900 (1900 Census, Corsicana). Ben Marks died in Corsicana on Aug. 30, 1929. His survivors included a brother in Waco and family in Cleveland (*CSWL*, Sept. 3. 1929). Ben's son Harry Marks was born in Corsicana on April 3, either 1883 or 1884 (1900 Census (1883); WWII Draft Reg. Cards, Anc. (1883); Death Cert., Bell County, Feb. 1, 1945, Anc. (1884)). This is ample evidence the family had relocated from New York City to Corsicana before Rope Walker's accident.

150 The family's legacy also includes K. Wolens's great-grandson, Steven Wolens, a Texas State Representative for twenty-four years.

151 Stringer, "Corsicana, Texas: An Unlikely Promised Land," (see note 96). Dr. Stringer also published "Corsicana, Texas: A Most Unlikely Canaan—A Brief History of the Corsicana Jewish Community," *Journal of Regional Cultures*, Vol. 1 (Bowling Green State University, Spring 1981).

152 Stringer lists thirteen taped interviews, of which five transcripts are available and were reviewed: Morris Evans, Mar. 20, 1978 (his in-laws were the Haymans, who were Corsicana residents before 1923, the year Morris arrived there); Louis Wolens, Nov. 1977; Jay Silverberg, Mar. 16, 1978; Irvin Samuels, May 7, 1982; and Rabbi Ernest Joseph, Jan. 10, 1978. Other interviews of Corsicana community members were not reviewed: Louis Shwarts (a grandson of the family patriarch, Aaron Shwarts), Audrey Kariel, Julius Jacobs, Gabe Goldberg, and Dean Milkes. Another three tapes are listed, of Holocaust survivors, distinct from the Corsicanans. (Application submission for registration of Texas Historical Landmarks.).

153 Evans's opinion may be a little exaggerated. Any look at a business directory shows there were many non-Jewish businesses.

154 Thirty-one pages transcribed, single-spaced.

155 Coming of age ceremonies for boys and girls, usually at age thirteen.

156 Joseph identified for Stringer three historical sources for his research of Corsicana's Jewish history: *Love*; Yvonne Putnam, *Navarro County History*; and Alva Taylor, "Navarro County History and Photographs."

157 This is incorrect, and will be rectified in a later chapter.

158 Sources identified were the three previously noted county histories, the Hebrew Cemetery Association's records and its constitution, and the bylaws of Temple Beth El.

159 The Wolens store was originally on the corner of 5th Ave. and Beaton, and then moved one block to the intersection with 4th Avenue. Silverberg said he had purchased, prior to his interview, the building which once housed the original store. Silverberg's narrative about which store branches opened and when, and the black cow dream anecdote, differ significantly from Louis Wolens's oral history.

160 Pages 15 & 16 of the interview transcript.

161 Mary Miller Affidavit (see note 286). The oral history given by Mary Miller is discussed in more detail in Chapter 11.

162 Searches were made in *Navarro Express* issues currently available, from 1857-1860 (PTH).

163 "Dissolution of Copartnership," *Navarro Express*, Dec. 17, 1859, PTH (legal notice).

164 The notice appears in a Dec. 17, 1859 issue, but the notice itself bears a date of Sept. 12.

165 Businessmen were noted for their "business attainments," wrote Love, with one exception, a "Mr. Kuchoffer whose two beautiful daughters were known far and wide for their comeliness." (*Love*, 84) Love's spelling was slightly off—John (Johann) H. Kirchoffer, a native of Ireland, and his wife, Catherine (Allbright), had two girls, Sarah and Elizabeth "Bettie," born around 1843 and 1845, respectively. Regrettably, no photographs of these exceptionally attractive women could be obtained.

166 *Love*, 82-83.

167 Enumerated on June 20, 1860, p. 18, Corsicana Post Office, Navarro County.

168 The 1860 federal census entries for J. Michael and Jacob Michael, listed five hundred people apart on the census sheets and enumerated eight days apart, were presumably for the same person, despite the one-year difference in their ages. Information requested for the size of a person's real and personal property assets ("estate") is blank in the enumeration for "J. Michael" but reported for Jacob Michael as $12,600 of real property (it could be read as $112,600, but that would be quite unusual and probably reflects an errant mark by Mr. Love, the enumerator) and personal property of $18,000.

169 *Prairie Blade*, Nov. 17, 1855, PTH. This is probably G. Roller, a co-defendant with A. Michael, in 1861, for failing to pay a note ("Citation Notice," *Navarro Express*, Oct. 10, 1861, PTH). One George Roller was a longtime resident and dry goods merchant at nearby Fairfield.

170 *Navarro Express*, Sept. 14, 1860, PTH.

171 Anderson Cty., Tex. Marriages, Vol. 4, 124, http://www.usgwarchives.net/copyright.htm, Beverly Bailey Odom, *et al.*, transcribers, submitted by Scott Fitzgerald, http://files.usgwarchives.net/tx/anderson/vitals/marriages/Volume04.tx, East Tex. Genealogical Soc., Sept. 13, 2006. There is no certain proof that the groom, Alexander Michael, is the same as the

early Corsicana resident with that name, but the weight of circumstantial evidence and an absence of contradictory evidence are sufficient to draw the tentative conclusion they are the same.

172 The registration to vote for A. Michel in Bexar Cty. in 1867 states he has been in the county for three years, in Texas for eighteen years, that he was born in Germany, and he was naturalized in Harrison Cty. (probably the town of Marshall) in March 1855 (Bexar Cty. Voter Reg., July 11, 1867, p. 246, Anc.).

173 Some records, including his death notice, used the spelling "Michael" ("Died," *San Antonio Daily Light*, Mar. 28, 1885, GB; *San Antonio Daily Light*, Mar. 30, 1885, GB).

174 "County Arms," *Navarro Express*, July 25, 1861, PTH.

175 Muster Roll Index Cards, Tex., Anc. The index card for Henry spells his name as "Michail." No subsequent history for Jacob or Henry could be ascertained due to the commonness of their names.

176 *Love*, 83. Unquestionably, and it goes without saying, many non-Jews were also respected for their business ethics and received patronage and friendship from Navarro residents.

177 Mary Miller Affidavit (see note 286).

178 "H. Fox" was enumerated in the 1860 federal census, in Houston, then a twenty-seven-year-old merchant. Enumerated with him were: Elisabeth Fox, eighteen; A. Fox, sixteen, a clerk; and Pauline Fox, eighteen. Elisabeth was born in Mississippi and the others in Prussia. Further research indicates this would be Henry S. Fox (1832-1912), who became a leading banker in Houston; his first wife, Elizabeth (Gohlman); and Henry's siblings, Abraham and Pauline (later, Mrs. Joseph Rosenfeld). Still further research shows there were at least six Fox siblings: Henry S., Abraham L., Alexander, Pauline, Simon, and Morris (Moses), although one or more may have been related in some other way, maybe as a cousin, for example. Naming patterns in all of these Fox families support the possibility they are related to one another because the naming of their children indicates they were named after close relatives they had in common who had recently died, a common Jewish naming tradition.

179 The same advertisement appeared in other issues, i.e., *Prairie Blade* (Corsicana, Tex.), Feb. 29, 1956, PTH. The advertisement was identical in all issues and bears a date of Oct. 13, 1855. That the "Fox" in the company's name was Henry Fox is based on other sources showing that Henry Fox was in Corsicana and on a notice of the dissolution of the company ("Partnership Dissolution," *Houston Tri-Weekly Telegraph*, Jan. 23, 1863, GB (legal notice by partners Henry Fox and Manheim Jacobs).

180 *DDH*, Nov. 17, 1858, NP (reprinting an item from the *Waco Democrat* about merchants, including Fox, who were swindled by a bad check). In the brief historical notes about Waco's Jews by I. Goldstein, published posthumously (*Jewish Monitor*, Feb. 11, 1921, NP), Goldstein recounts that in "about 1865 (sic—should read "1856") Manheim Jacobs and a young man by the name of Alexander had a store here."

181 "Fox & Jacobs," *Houston Tri-Weekly Telegraph*, Sept. 18, 1860, GB (advertisement); "Partnership Dissolution," *Houston Tri-Weekly Telegraph*.

182 "Democratic Mass-meeting," *Prairie Blade*, Nov. 17, 1855, PTH. The Know Nothing party, active in the mid-1850s, was characterized by its anti-immigration and anti-Catholic, nativist rhetoric. The leader of the movement was Lewis Charles Levin (1808-1860), a first-generation Jew born in North Carolina (Wikipedia's "Lewis Charles Levin" entry).

183 Alexander Fox was enumerated with "Moses" Fox, probably the same person as Morris Fox, in the 1860 federal census at Hallandale (now, Navasota), Western Dist. Grimes Cty., Tex. Presumably, they were brothers, but their relationship to one another is not known.

184 "Short History of Navarro County and Corsicana," *CSWL*, Sept. 22, 1922 (sixth through eighth of nine installments published in issues of the *Semi-Weekly Light*).

185 *DDH*, Jun 25, 1873 (advertisement); "In Corsicana," *St. Louis Globe-Democrat*, Jan. 14, 1897, NP (fire destroyed inventory of Corsicana's A. Fox. & Bro.).

186 Proceedings, Grand Lodge of Texas Masons, PTH. The original Corsicana Lodge, No. 104, started in 1851, was suspended at the end of 1854 due to intense infighting. In 1855, W.E. Oakes petitioned for a new charter, declaring the proposed members are Masons "entirely free of prejudice on account of our former difficulties at this Lodge." No document explains the animosities present in the old lodge, but in 1855 a new lodge was chartered, No. 174, and shortly afterward two Corsicana Jews became new brethren there. ("A Leaf from the Past," a history written by R.S.

Neblett in 1915, reproduced in Jno. H. Rice, *A History of Corsicana: Lodge No. 174: A. F. & A. M. 1851 – 1920*, https://sites.rootsweb.com/~txnavarr/organizations/a_history_of_corsicana_lodge_174.htm#Pg.%206.

187 See, e.g., Jesse Bartlett-Frances Callaway Web Site, C.L. Jester, "A History of Navarro County, Texas" (Sept. 22, 1922), http://homepages.rootsweb.ancestry.com/~bartlett/tx-navarro-co-history.htm.

188 1860 Census, Richmond E.D., 26, Anc.

189 There are many U.S. records of men with the name of Sol or Solomon Weil who were born in Germany around the same time as Corsicana's Sol Weil, making it difficult to identify him in later records. Corsicana's Sol Weil may be the same as the Solomon Weil who died Oct. 7, 1907, in Dallas, even though their recorded ages differ by a few years. Both were identified as Bavarian, a somewhat atypical nativity designation ("Funeral of Solomon Weil: Services at Daughter's Residence and Internment in Jewish Cemetery," *DMN*, Oct. 9, 1907 (Alex Sanger was one of the pall bearers); "Death of Solomon Weil: Deceased was a Native of Bavaria and Eighty-Three Years of Age," *DMN*, Oct. 8, 1907). Solomon Weil of Dallas started his family in Louisville and had children living in Texas and Louisiana at the time of his death (1880 Census, Louisville, Ky., for Saml Weil; FAG, Emanu-El Cemetery, Dallas, for Solomon and Bertha Weil and their children).

190 The year of his enlistment could be read as "1863," but because he was disabled for six months, that would be two months longer than his total service based on an enlistment in July, 1863. The sensible date would be July, 1861, when the regiment was first mustered for service. (Confederate Army Service Record, Anc.; see Rweb, biographies, for Clinton McKamy Winkler and James Rodgers Loughridge. Winkler was one of the most influential men in Navarro County during its first few decades. Loughridge was a highly respected Corsicana lawyer, County Judge, and publisher of the *Prairie Blade*, Navarro County's first newspaper.).

191 The discharge certificate says he was forty-eight years old in 1863, a difference of about four years from his age according to the 1860 federal census. Despite the reported age difference, it seems unlikely there were two men with this name in Corsicana at that time, and therefore they must be one and the same.

192 Anc.

193 L.O. Dunn, personal correspondence with author, June 19, 2017, regarding title chain searched by Navarro County Abstract, courtesy J.E. McClure, Abstractor. The property at the northwest corner of Beaton and 5th Ave. was purchased by Block Brothers and Company on Nov. 28, 1872. The heirs of the owners sold to F.W. Caruthers, recorded at Vol. 27, P. 9; Vol. 27, P. 11; Vol. 27, P. 12; and Vol. 30, P. 19, transactions executed Oct. and Nov. 1874 and recorded from Apr. 6, 1875 to 1877. Mr. Caruthers sold to R.P. Goodman, Vol. 30, P. 39 (1877). Goodman conveyed to G.T. Jester, Vol. 87, P. 83, Aug. 4, 1896.

Virginius Block, a resident of Groesbeck, was running the Corsicana merchantry when he died on Oct. 17, 1871. He and his large family established businesses in Texas along the rail line from Houston to Dallas. Virginius was born about 1823 in Louisiana to Abraham and Fannie (Isaacs) Block, his parents believed to be the first Jewish settlers in Arkansas territory, arriving there in 1827. (David M. Marcus, https://encyclopediaofarkansas.net/entries/abraham-block-6306/ and https://encyclopediaofarkansas.net/entries/frances-isaiah-isaacs-8087/ (retrieved Apr. 30, 2020); "Death of Henry Block," *New Orleans Republican*, Nov. 17, 1871, NP (death of popular Corsicana merchant [corrected the next day]); *New Orleans Republican*, Nov. 17, 1871, NP (correction, previously reported decedent was Virginius Block, not Henry Block); *DDH*, Oct. 28, 1871, NP (cites to the *Corsicana Observer*, chronicling the death of Virginius Block); *Washington Telegraph* (Washington, Ark.), Oct. 25, 1871, NP.)

# 5. Walk into Oblivion

194 Babbette's husband was Irvin Samuels, one of Prof. Stringer's interviewees for his oral history project (Chapter 4). Irvin passed away in 2003 at the age of eighty-eight.

195 Babbette Samuels, personal correspondence with author, Jan. 25, 2016. An introduction in the record book by Babbette explains that she took over sole responsibility for record keeping after her husband died, that she and Irvin had taken it over from Jay Silverberg when the Agudas Achim synagogue closed, in 1999, and that Silverberg had succeeded Ivan Rosenberg after Rosenberg's

death (he died Apr. 4, 1976). A separate note in the record book, by Rosenberg, dated Feb. 5, 1952, says, "After much work and by checking thru old records and then rechecking all graves in our cemetery I have at last compiled for you a complete and correct perpetual internment record…"

196 Herbert Levene, deceased, did the illustration. Attempts to contact his family were unsuccessful.

197 *Rocky Mountain Empire Magazine, Denver Post*, Dec. 11, 1949, courtesy Denver Public Library.

198 There are gaps in the available issues of the *Sun* newspaper at Newspapers.com. There are no issues for July-Sept. 1949. The *Corsicana Semi-Weekly Light*, a sister publication of the *Sun*, carried many of the same news stories as the daily version and issues for those months of the *Semi-Weekly Light* are available on Newspapers.com, but the article was not found in those issues.

199 From 1946-1953 there are forty-six issues of the *Sun* with articles attributed to "Bob Campbell, Daily Sun Staff." There could have been many more articles written by him which did not have his byline.

200 "A Saga of Corsicana and its Pioneers," *Sun*, July 2, 1948 & June 29, 1976.

201 Helen McLure, "'With the Past Let These Be Buried': The 1873 Mob Massacre of the Hill Family in Springtown, Texas," *Southwestern Historical Quarterly* 105, no. 2 (Oct. 2001): 292, https://texashistory.unt.edu/ark:/67531/metapth101222/m1/322/, PTH.

202

> ²³ Robert C. Campbell, "When Death Danced With Eleven," *Rocky Mountain Empire Magazine*, Jan. 9, Mar. 10, Apr. 14, 1949; Campbell claimed he received the entire story from an elderly man who as a ten-year-old boy witnessed Laird's murder in Springtown.

(McLure, "'With the Past Let These Be Buried,'" 301-02).

203 McLure, 302.

204 McLure, 302.

205 Texas Death Cert., Dallas, May 12, 1965, Anc. gives his birth date as 1904. At twenty-five he was already a newspaper editor, for the *Mineral Wells Index*, and ex-editor of the *Ranger Times* ("Miller Resigns as Editor of the Mineral Wells Newspaper," *Longview Daily News*, May 6, 1929, NP). Both papers were from small towns west of Fort Worth.

206 Texas Death Cert, Anc.

207 "Miller Resigns as Editor," *Longview Daily News*; "Mrs. Conway, 85, Ex-Editor, Dies," *DMN*, Mar. 5, 1965.

208 See 1930 Census and 1940 Census.

209 1930 Census; 1933 Tex. Death Cert.

210 "Hymeneal," *DMN*, Aug. 20, 1901.

211 Claude Campbell and thirty-eight other workhouse inmates, along with nineteen prisoners from the county jail, were each given a silver dollar and liberty for Christmas Day, a tradition of good will by the authorities. Campbell predicted, correctly, that he would abuse the privilege and initially requested he be allowed to stay in the workhouse. Later that same day he was arrested for drunkenness and faced an additional term of incarceration ("Liberty and Dollar Too Much; He's in Jail Again," *Fort Worth Star-Telegram*, Dec. 26, 1915, GB). Claude's death certificate (Dallas, Tex., Anc.) states he died in the Dallas jail from "chronic alcoholism."

212 His marital status in the 1930 census is single; in the 1940 census, divorced.

## 6. A Better Memorial

213 Evelyn Oppenheimer, "Tolbert, Francis," THB, https://www.tshaonline.org/handbook/entries/tolbert-francis (retrieved Dec. 2, 2016).

214 *Love*, 143.

215 The *Blade* existed until 1858, when its presses were used to publish the *Navarro Express*, which continued through the Civil War, but only when paper was available. The *Corsicana Times* was published in the first half of 1857, the title cited as a source in articles published during those months in other papers, e.g., the *Times-Picayune* (New Orleans). Two brief article transcriptions from the *Corsicana Times* are also found on RootsWeb (RWeb, "Newspaper Extracts Index"). After the war, the *Express* was renamed the *Corsicana Observer* (*Memorial*, 163-64, quoting Judge A.B. Norton of Dallas upon the thirtieth anniversary of the *Observer*, possibly 1895). The *Index*, another early paper, started around 1876, was merged with the *Observer* in 1879. Publication dates of the *Index* are based

on articles attributed to the paper contemporaneously republished in other newspapers between 1876 and 1879 (*Southern Banner* (Brenham, Tex.), Oct. 31, 1879, GB (*Index* and *Observer* to merge/hyphenate); *Love*, 144). The *Courier* was being published in Corsicana by 1870 or so (*Love*, 144). The *Independent* began in early 1872, but by June was renamed the *Navarro Banner* (*Dallas Weekly Herald*, Jan. 13, 1872 & June 8, 1972, GB; *GDN*, June 21, 1872). The *Banner* quickly became one of Texas's leading papers, but folded within a year or two (*Love*, 145-46; *Cincinnati Enquirer*, June 24, 1872, NP). No news articles referencing the *Navarro Banner* were found after 1872. The *Corsicana Messenger* was published from 1880 to at least 1883. Two issues of the *Messenger*, from 1882, are held at UT, Austin. Catalogers surmised that the *Messenger* started in 1880, based on the numbering in the mastheads of issues (ChroniclingAmerica.org, newspapers database). The *Messenger* was quoted from in other papers as late as Nov. 1883, although the latest item referenced, in November, could have appeared in the *Messenger* much earlier (*GDN*, Nov. 28, 1883). Another reference to that paper, in April 1883, was an item which would have been referenced only in a timely manner, the "becoming obituary of the late Mrs. Mary Bains McKinney," wife of Hampton McKinney (the first permanent settlers in Corsicana) (*GDN*, Apr. 8, 1883). Thus, the *Messenger* existed at least until April, probably as late as Nov. 1883, and possibly later. In 1882, the *Corsicana Journal* was a "new moral and literary weekly" ("Corsicana," *Dallas Weekly Herald*, June 1, 1882, GB) which was "engaged in a very absurd quarrel" with the *Observer* a year later (*GDN*, Apr. 3, 1883). The *Dallas Morning News* was picking up *Journal* articles through the end of 1887 (*DMN*, various issues). In 1886 there were at least three newspapers in Corsicana, as shown on the bird's-eye view map in Chapter 14: the *Corsicana Observer*, the *Corsicana Daily Courier*, and the *Corsicana Democrat*. Two operated along the busy commercial blocks of Beaton Street, identified on the magnified view of the map as buildings 37 (the *Courier*) and 38 (the *Observer*). The *Democrat*, a weekly started in 1885 (*Love*, 145), lasted until at least 1892. The *Corsicana Cyclone* blew through town in July 1884 (*Southern Banner* (Brenham, Tex.), June 26, 1884, GB ("Corsicana has a new weekly paper called the Cyclone. A cyclone is usually of short duration and the paper may partake of the nature of the atmospheric disturbance for which it is named.")). In 1889, the *Corsicana Daily and Weekly Light*, started the previous year (*Love*, 146), bought out the *Exponent*, a political paper. In 1892, the lead paper of the city was the *Courier-Observer*, a daily which was merged with the *Light*, in 1895, to become the *Daily Courier Light*, while the *Semi-Weekly Light* was spun off as a separate paper. The *Daily Sun* began in 1897, using the printing plant of the *Weekly Light* (*Love*, 146). Still other papers and periodicals came out of Corsicana before the turn of the century. The *Texas Observer* was a religious paper started around 1880 and the *Corsicana Methodist* was also published around that time. Literary journals circulated, like *The Odd Fellow and Literature*, a monthly created in 1876, and *The Texas Prairie Flower*, begun in 1882 (*Love*, 144). The People's Party put out the *Truth* in 1891. The *Christian Advance* was also printed during that era. (*Love*, 145).

216 *DDH*, Dec. 11, 1884, NP.

217 No longer a daily, the most recent publishing schedule change occurred on May 1, 2020. Due to the economic downturn brought on by the Covid-19 pandemic, the paper ended its Thursday and Friday editions.

218 "Disastrous Fire Visits Corsicana," *Sun*, Apr. 18, 1911.

219 Newspapers.com (www.newspapers.com) has digitized issues of the *Corsicana Daily Sun* from April 1, 1909 through 1981, under *Sun* and *Light* title variations, and many gaps. The earliest issues are quite damaged, probably due to fire. Only two pages are filmed from the April 1, 1909 issue, which likely was a six-page paper. Moving ahead one month, the May 1 issue has less missing from the edges and consists of six pages. June 1 is nearly complete, with only small parts of the corners missing. The remaining 1909 issues are available on Newspapers.com, but only the last three months are there for 1910, and the papers from those dates are also damaged, although not as bad as those in 1909. For 1911, only April 1 through September issues are available. No papers are available for 1912, and only the last quarter of 1913 is available. No issues are available for 1914. 1915 issues start with March and go to the end of the year. July and August are missing from 1916. The run is then mostly complete for 1917 through 1981, with just occasional missing months, such as December 1919 and the first three months of 1920. August 1 through September 16, 1923 issues are also missing. Occasional gaps continue into the 1940s but from the 50s forward, through the entire year of 1981, www.newspapers.com's holdings for the *Sun* appear to be complete.

Newspapers.com also has the *Semi-Weekly Light*, published on Tuesdays and Fridays, from July 1915 through June 1916. The next issues are from Nov. 1917 through Nov. 1919, but are quite spotty. There is nothing for the *Semi-Weekly Light* for 1920 through 1926, except all of 1922 is there. The paper continues into 1970, at which time it was renamed the *Weekly Light*, and Newspapers.com has that paper through 1981.

220 In context, it seems the fire would only have destroyed old copies of the *Sun*, although it's possible that other titles were also held in the building. Historic newspapers could be missing for many reasons. For example, an effective effort to collect old newspapers for recycling during WWII enlisted not only every patriotic adult, but two million Boy Scouts. The War Department purchased collected papers by the ton. It may be that a large collection of Corsicana's newspapers will turn up in the future, probably not far from Corsicana. In 1884, few newspapers were sent to other cities; instead, interesting news was transmitted instantaneously by telegraph and reprinted in the local newspapers of distant communities. See "Historical Society Holds Show and Tell Program: From the Corsicana Daily Sun," *Navarro County Scroll*, 21 (1968).

221 The museum holds some issues from Apr. 1887, one issue from 1888, and a run from May 17, 1889 through Mar. 8, 1890. There is nothing from 1884. The issues are available on the Portal to Texas History website, https://texashistory.unt.edu/explore/collections/TDNP/.

222 Newspapers.com and GenealogyBank (GenealogyBank.com) both have extensive runs of the *Sun* newspapers, starting in 1909. Ancestry (www.Ancestry.com) and MyHeritage (www.MyHeritage.com) are popular genealogy websites, available by paid subscription, with sizeable historical newspapers content. Free websites besides ChroniclingAmerica.com include FultonHistory.com, which holds mostly New York State newspapers, but also from other states, including some Texas papers. Google.com once had an historic newspapers database program, and even though it was discontinued, the data is still accessible (https://sites.google.com/site/onlinenewspapersite/Home/usa).

223 *Sun*, June 29, 1976, p. 77 (Bicentennial Edition).

224 Google searches performed on Dec. 2, 2016.

225 Searches were done on newspapers.com, which appears to have a slightly more extensive run of the paper than GenealogyBank, although not by much.

## 7. The Wonderful Country

226 Frank X. Tolbert, "Tragic Saga of a Rope Walker," Tolbert's Texas, *DMN*, July 20, 1958.

227 The article is missing a closing quotation mark for the name of the record book, which I have furnished but may have put in the wrong place.

228 Frank X. Tolbert, "'The Mesmeriser' Named a Creek," Tolbert's Texas, *Dallas Daily News*, Nov. 2, 1959, GB. The creek was named for a man who claimed he could hypnotize cattle and use it as a way to coral them. His efforts met with mixed results, including his death. The legend has never been substantiated.

229 Frank X. Tolbert, "Gravestone Restored for the Rope Walker," Tolbert's Texas, *DMN*, Aug. 7, 1973.

230 Frank X. Tolbert, "Theory on 1-Legged Rope Walker'," Tolbert's Texas, *DMN*, May 18, 1968.

231 Wikipedia's "Thomas C. Lea III" entry.

232 Forty-three issues of the *Mesilla Valley Independent*, from 1878-1879, are available online at the University of New Mexico's digital repository (https://digitalrepository.unm.edu/). Issues from those years for the *Mesilla News* are available in the Readex "Hispanic American Newspapers" database, as well as on microfilm at UT, El Paso.

233 Prof. Henry Bergh (1813-1888) founded the American Society for the Prevention of Cruelty to Animals (ASPCA) in 1866 (Wikipedia's "Henry Bergh" entry).

234 The Tom Lea Institute is a "non-profit organization dedicated to documenting, presenting, teaching, and exhibiting the works of Tom Lea" (www.tomlea.com/about-us/institute/).

## 8. Identity of "Rope Walker" Remains Unsolved Mystery

235 Social Security Death Index, Anc.; P. Jamison, personal correspondence with author, Feb. 21, 2016.

236 John Sam Haslam, "Identity of 'Rope Walker' Killed Here 52 Years Ago Remains Unsolved Mystery," *Sun*, Feb. 25, 1936.

237 "Lad Seriously Injured in an Auto Wreck Late Tuesday," *Sun*, Oct. 17, 1923.

238 Jamison, personal correspondence.

239 "Corsicana Boy Wins Prize in Radio Contest," *HP*, Apr. 11, 1924.

240 John Sam Haslam, "Superintendent of Corsicana Schools Speaks to Parents," *CSWL*, Oct. 8, 1929.

241 *Sun*, Nov. 25, 1931.

242 *Sun*, Feb. 13, 1933.

243 "Rotarians Heard Talk on Printing Daily Newspaper," *Sun*, Nov. 22, 1933; "Reporters' Association," *CSWL*, Apr. 12, 1935.

244 *Sun*, Sept. 15, 1938.

245 Jamison, personal correspondence.

246 Jamison, personal correspondence.

247 "Fire Routs Toilers from News Room," *Odessa American*, Dec. 5, 1954, NP.

248 Deut. 34:4.

249 Mary was born Aug. 1869, based on the 1870, 1880, and 1900 federal censuses, Anc.

250 Tex. Death Cert., Anc.

251 "Resolution in Memory of Ben Goldsmith," *Sun*, Oct. 19, 1946.

252 "A Brief History of the Corsicana Jewish Community," *Jewish Monitor*, Dec. 17, 1920, NP; "Resolution," *Sun*, July 31, 1946.

## 9. True Story

253 June 2003 is the date of the issue of *Jewish Magazine* in which it appeared, and probably the date it was published on the internet.

254 "True Story from Jewish American History: Rope Walker," *Jewish Magazine*, http://www.jewishmag.com/104mag/ropewalker/ropewalker.htm (retrieved Dec. 15, 2016).

255 "Circus History, Message & Discussion Board," http://www.circushistory.org/Query/ Query05b.htm. The query was placed by the author.

256 Email sent by the author, Dec. 26, 2015.

257 Dave Schechter, "Here's How One Man Has Preserved the Milestones of Jewish History," *Forward*, Aug. 4, 2016, http://forward.com/culture/345517/heres-how-one-man-has-preserved-the-milestones-of-jewish-history/?utm_source=rss&utm_medium=feed&utm_campaign=Main (courtesy Jerry Klinger).

258 *War of the Worlds* (transcript), http://www.sacred-texts.com/ufo/mars/wow.htm.

## 10. Descended from a Legend

259 Sure, it's been edict that each one, minute, bedeviled detail matters. Not in this chapter. Choose. Om. Let it be.

260 Rweb, Biographies, Rope Walker (retrieved Dec. 1, 2016).

261 "True Story" does not give a birth date of Feb. 6. It is unknown how this date, which is the precise birth date of Dr. Gulick, found its way here.

262 www.findagrave.com.

263 As of Sept. 5, 2020. Additional entries are made daily.

264 E. Barbieri, interview with author, Dec. 2, 2016.

265 Dianne West Short, "Rope Walker," *Texas Escapes* (blog), June 17, 2012, http://www.texasescapes.com/Dianne-West-Short/Rope-Walker.htm.

266 Rabbi Ranaan Broderick, RFR, "Rope Walker, the Legend," *OU Kosher* (blog) https://oukosher.org/blog/consumer-kosher/rope-walker-legend/. Read on, rabbi.

267 http://www.isjl.org/texas-corsicana-encyclopedia.html (retrieved Dec. 5, 2017).

268 Ernest Joseph, "Rope Walker's Tombstone," *Texas Jewish Historical Society Newsletter* (Jan. 1989), www.txjhs.org/sites/default/files/1989_january.pdf.

269 Virginia Riddle, "L'chayim: to Life!" *CorsicanaNow Magazine* (Apr. 2012), www.nowmagazines.com/onlineeditions/editions/412corsicana.pdf.

270 Louis Davidson, "The Last Jew and the Rope Walker," *Tulsa Jewish Review* (Feb. 2013), https://jewishtulsa.org/our-work/tulsa-jewish-review/.

271 Melody Amsel-Arieli, "A Custodian of Memories," *Forward*, Nov. 18, 2005, www.forward.com/articles/2306/a-custodian-of-memories/. Melody has also written about the 1914 murder in Durant, Oklahoma, of her fourteen-year-old relative, Pauline Amsel. Pauline was born in Oklahoma, but her parents, Celia (Levy) and Jake Amsel, lived in Corsicana for many years, before and after they lived in Oklahoma. The parents and Pauline, their only child, all found their final resting place in Corsicana's Hebrew Cemetery.

272 David Searcy, *Shame and Wonder: Essays* (New York: Random House, 2016). See 100West, www.100westcorsicana.com/shop/shame-and-wonder.

273 Deeanne Gist, *The Trouble with Brides* (Bloomington, MN: Bethany House Publishers, 2011), 131 and Author's Note, https://books.google.com/books?isbn=0764208934. A Baumgartner family which has lived in Corsicana for a few generations is not Jewish.

274 Navarro Council of the Arts, Inc., *Brick Streets and Back Roads* (Taylor Publishing, 2000), 147.

275 Ruthe Winegarten and Cathy Schechter, *Deep in the Heart: The Lives and Legends of Texas Jews, a Photographic History* (Austin, Tex.: Eakin Press, 1990).

276 The Jerry Klinger (Manny Rabin) version, which also said the rope failed, was published later.

277 Joseph, "Rope Walker's Tombstone."

278 Bryan Stone, *The Chosen Folks: Jews on the Frontiers of Texas* (Austin, Tex.: University of Texas Press, 2010).

279 Stone, ix (Prologue).

280 Stone, x.

281 Stone, ix.

282 The day Rope Walker fell was beautiful, with plenty of sunshine and birds singing, the type of weather which induces the ladies to go outside and spend money—good news for Rope Walker! Sources are cited in an upcoming chapter.

283 Stone, *The Chosen Folks*, ix-x.

284 Bryan Stone, personal correspondence with author, Nov. 30, 2016.

285 Lyrics by Patty George, music by Nancy Roberts ("Parade of American Music to Feature Local Composers," *Sun*, Feb. 9, 1975). Courtesy of Byron Haynie, who first performed the song in 1977. Patty George was a local who enjoyed writing parodies for local theater productions and occasionally wrote for the *Sun*. Nancy (Mize) Roberts (1931-2009) was a talented and enthusiastic musician who frequently performed at Temple Beth El. Roberts was not Jewish, but her rendition of "*Kol Nidre*," the sorrowful Hebrew song performed each year on the eve of Yom Kippur, during what is called the *Kol Nidre* service, was wonderfully heartfelt. ("Nancy Mize Roberts," *Sun*, Aug. 12, 2009, https://obituaries.corsicanadailysun.com/obituary/nancy-roberts-728998962 (retrieved Feb. 23, 2020); L. Garner and R. Rosen, interview with author, Oct. 29, 2019). "Rope Walker" was performed in a theatrical production, "Tuckertown, U.S.A.," part of a pageant created by George, Roberts, Jewel Gibson, and Billie Carroll for Corsicana's Chamber of Commerce's Festival '76 Committee, a bicentennial celebration, through a committee chaired by Herb Silverberg, an accomplished pianist and son of Jay Silverberg ("School Skit First Glimpse of Bicentennial Pageant," *Sun*, Feb. 2, 1975). See also, "'Tuckertown, U.S.A.,'" *Sun*, Nov. 17, 1976; "Annual Talent Show is the Next Clubhouse Event," *Sun*, Mar. 20, 1977.

# 11. Jesters

286 "Sketch of the McKinney family and descendants as told by reminiscences of Mrs. Jane Beaton and Mrs. Mary Miller of Corsicana, Texas. Elicited by questions propounded to them by their great nephew C.L. Jester and reduced to narrative form" (title from introductory paragraph). The two affidavits were "Sworn to and subscribed before me this the 10th day of Feb. A.D. 1921-Lucille Bonner, Notary Public for Navarro County" (final paragraph), http://freepages.genealogy.rootsweb .ancestry.com/~teaster/affidavits.htm. Also republished at RWeb, "Rev. Hampton McKinney." Hereinafter, "Jane Beaton Affidavit" and "Mary Miller Affidavit." A concise history of Corsicana origins was published as "Corsicana was Midway Point, Good for County Seat," *Sun*, June 29, 1976.

Jane (McKinney) Beaton's narrative is a rich historical record of early Corsicana. Born in 1832, in Illinois, not far from St. Louis, she was fifteen when her family travelled to Texas by wagon, a trip of two or three months, which she described, apparently without sarcasm, as "one long picnic." In

Texas she married Alexander Beaton. It was Beaton's leadership which helped bring the railroad to Corsicana in 1871, one of the most important events in the town's history, the discovery of oil being another. Beaton Street was named in his honor.

Mary Miller gave an equally detailed and informative history, but with a different perspective because she was only eight when the family came to Texas. She married John L. Miller, another early settler and prominent citizen.

287 Jane Beaton Affidavit. Land transfers were more complicated than the simplistic version presented here.

288 The *Memorial* and *Love* histories tell the same origination story. Both erroneously say Levi died in 1858, but it was 1851 (Jane Beaton Affidavit; FAG, Waverly East Cemetery, Waverly, Morgan Cty., Ill., for Levi Jester).

289 Charles Wesley Jester (Apr. 3, 1841-1909) had nine children. His wife was Eliza Rakestraw, from a local, well-established family. Their nine children were George Ernest, 1869-1935; Charles Lee, 1871-1942; Homer Bates, 1876-1943; Walter Beaton, 1877-1878; Ida, 1879-?; Hugh Cain, 1881-1935; Mabel, 1883-1885; Lila, 1885-1958; and Angelina Jean, 1897-1963.

290 George Taylor Jester (Aug. 23, 1846-July 19, 1922) had five children. He married Alice Bates, who died in 1875, and then Frances Paine Gordon. His five children were Claude W., 1873-1953; Charles G., 1883-?; Ruby, 1884-1888; Beauford Halbert, 1893-1949; and George Taylor Jr., 1895-1914.

291 Diadema Jester's four other children:

Martha Louise Kendall (Dec. 5, 1842-Dec. 19, 1871) had two children. She married Thomas Jefferson Kendall and resided in Ennis. Their two children were Edgar Jester, 1865-1945, and Charles Paul, 1869-1940. Martha was buried in the Myrtle Cemetery in Ennis.

Mary Diadema Hamilton (Feb. 11, 1844-Nov. 11, 1903) had two children. Mary married James Daniel Hamilton. Their two children were Lillie D., 1870-1923, and James Mackey, 1881-1883.

Vina Cordelia Bates (Aug. 10, 1848-June 9, 1916) had one known child. She and Robert Patrick Bates were the parents of Robert Patrick Bates, Jr.

Levi Leven Jester (Jan. 6, 1851-Mar. 11, 1938) had five children. He married Mary Eliza Cain of Tyler. Their five children were Stanley Cain, died at age six in 1888; Herbert Whiteselle, 1884-1974; John Cain, 1891-?; Levi Leven, 1892-1951; and Ralph Kouns, 1901-1991.

292 The Jester family genealogy is summarized in a Public Family Tree, developed by walter9800, Anc.

293 *Love*, 261-64.

294 Tommy W. Stringer, "Jester, Beauford Halbert (1893-1949)," THB, https://www.tshaonline.org/handbook/entries/jester-beauford-halbert.

295 A few small buildings have other historical themes, like the Lefty Frizzell Museum. Lefty Frizzell was a country star who spent a portion of his boyhood in Corsicana.

296 Most Jester families in the U.S. trace their lineage to Delaware and other mid-Atlantic states (U.S. federal census records in Ancestry.com were queried for people with the surname spelled exactly as "Jester.").

297 Beatrice K. Otto, *Fools are Everywhere: The Court Jester Around the World* (Chicago: The University of Chicago Press, 2001), 49, 53, 64.

298 Otto, 49.

299 Otto, 49. *Fools are Everywhere* has an appendix, "Table of Named Jesters," which states that Zuñiga flourished from ca. 1490-ca. 1532.

300 Kaye (née Kaminsky) and Sylvia Fine, his wife, penned the movie's script.

301 The interviews were ostensibly about John McKinney, who served in the Revolutionary War and was the father of Hampton McKinney and grandfather of Jane and Mary. The interviews covered many other topics as well. See note 286.

302 According to the index to marriages of Madison Cty., Ill., Anc., Levi and Diadema Jester were married there Oct. 14, 1839.

303 Jane Beaton Affidavit.

304 Otto, *Fools are Everywhere*, Appendix.

305 World War I draft registration cards (Anc.) for Levi Jester's descendants shows some of them checked off the box for "tall," some for "medium," and only a few for "short." His youngest child, also named Levi, was 5' 11". (Passport Applications, for Levi L. Jester, Feb. 20, 1912, Anc.).

306 His gravestone in Waverly, Ill., shows a date of death of Apr. 30, 1851, aged thirty-one years, six months, and three (?) days (FAG).

307 In 1840 Levi Jester was enumerated in Ridge Prairie, Madison Cty., Ill., aged between twenty and thirty, with two other men (unnamed), same age range (possibly brothers?), and a female, aged fifteen to twenty, also unnamed, presumably Diadema, who was then nineteen or twenty (in the 1840 Federal census only the head of household was named and others were categorized by sex and age range). In the 1850 Census, Levi, Diadema, and their five children (son Levi was not yet born) were living in Morgan Cty., Ill., where he was a peddler. In that enumeration, for place of birth, all children were born in Illinois, but the parents have a designation of "unknown."

308 1880 Census enumerations of Levi's living children state that their father was born in Delaware (for Charles W., "Penn." was written, crossed out, and "Del." inserted). Martha Kendall died prior to 1880. Parents' birth places for Vina Bates in her 1880 census entry (Sherman, Tex.) are blank, but her 1900 and 1910 census enumerations (she resided in Corsicana then) say her father was born in Delaware.

309 J.M. Runk & Co., *Biographical and Genealogical History of the State of Delaware, Volume 2* (Chambersburg, Penn., 1899), 927, https://archive.org/details/biographicalgene02runk. The Hebrew People are commonly described as the "Children [i.e., descendants] of Abraham, Isaac and Jacob." If research showed the existence of those Jester brothers it would quash any notion that the reference in this biographical volume was a thinly veiled reference to their Jewish origins; however, research to find and identify the original Jester brothers of Delaware, as described in the Runk history, was unsuccessful.

310 Ralph Kouns Jester was nominated for an Academy Award in 1957 for his costume design work on *The Ten Commandments*.

## 12. Corsicana News

311 The inquiry, by the author, was fielded by Pete Shrake, Archivist, Circus World (July and Aug., 2016).

312 Reviewed by the author in July, 2016.

313 It is unlikely the performance was after sunset, in the dark, and therefore it was still *Shabbat* (Sabbath, also *Shabbos*), which lasts from sundown Friday until sundown Saturday. (The nearly hundred-foot-high light tower erected at the corner of Beaton and Collin went up in 1885, first operating on gas and then converted to electricity, in 1886, according to a brief note in the Bicentennial Edition of the *Sun*, June 29, 1976 ("Lights in 1885"). The tower, designated as an electric light tower, was erected in February 1886 according to a more contemporaneous article ("Corsicana Cullings: An Electric Light Snag," *DMN*, Feb. 16, 1886).)

A different *parashah* (portion) of the Torah is read each *Shabbat*, keyed to the Hebrew calendar. Saturday, March 3, 1883, was the twenty-fourth day of the month of Adar I in the year 5643 (5643 is a year with a leap month—an extra month of Adar—so the two Adars are designated as Adar I and Adar II (www.Hebcal.com)). The *parashah* for that *Shabbat* was Vayakhel (Exod. 35:1-38:20), which begins "And Moses assembled all the congregation of the children of Israel, and said unto them: 'These are the words which the LORD hath commanded, that ye should do them. Six days shall work be done, but on the seventh day there shall be to you a holy day, a sabbath of solemn rest to the LORD; whosoever doeth any work therein shall be put to death.'" (Exod. 35:1-2) (https://www.mechon-mamre.org/p/pt/pt0235.htm#1, visited April 23, 2020).

314 No other paper, except one out-of-state paper, gave a different date.

## 13. Professors

315 Each database employs its own search engine. Some are similar, but there can also be significant differences such as search criteria options and methods for reviewing, organizing, and saving query results.

316 In general terms, the technology is not complicated. Libraries, archives, and commercial republishers (e.g., genealogy websites) take electronic photographs of newspaper pages (and books, and other writings). These are then "read" by computer programs which turn the images into computer-readable characters—letters and numbers. The resulting text files are connected to a program that anyone with an internet connection can use to search the files. A request to find certain

words is typed in, a "query," with or without restrictions, "filters," and *presto*: the original article, ready to print, download, or send by email!

Sorta. There is an art and a science to creating just the right query. It has to be specific, but not too specific, so only a manageable number of results are returned. The results—the articles—have to be reviewed by the user to see if it one or more of them have the information being sought; just because articles contain the requested, literal text, they may not be what is being sought. A carefully constructed query uses only necessary words and/or phrase combinations so that the search finds neither too many nor too few matches. Getting too few matches means the desired article(s) might not be included. Getting too many means weeding out hundreds or more "false hits." Lastly, and most importantly, a successful search of historical newspapers requires that some library, archive, corporation, or individual has imaged the particular newspaper issues containing the desired information, has created searchable OCR files from the images, and made it all available to the public.

317 OCR text files are not user-viewable in all newspaper database websites, but they are in Chronicling America, where this article was found.

318 The illustration here was taken from the Newspapers.com database. The same article, in the PTH database, it turns out, was perfectly legible.

319 Text along the left margin was not properly photographed and is extrapolated from context.

320 A full catalog of the performances of Rope Walker with commentary will be published in *One Foot Over Main Street*, second book in the *Rope Walker* Series (projected date of publication, 2021).

# 14. Rope Walker Slipped Here

321 *Love*, 134-37. The history of banks in Corsicana could mesmerize a buffalo.

322 Navarro Council of the Arts, Inc., *Brick Streets and Back Roads* (Taylor Publishing, 2000), 115.

323 Navarro Council of the Arts, Inc., 115.

324 Janet Jacobs, "Extreme Makeover: Hashop's Getting New Look," *Sun*, Mar. 14, 2014.

325 Hashop relocated "to the corner of Beaton street and Fifth avenue in the recently remodeled Baum building on the southeast corner of Fifth and Beaton" ("Louis Hashop Has Moved Store from Former Location," *Sun*, Oct. 18, 1927).

326 "New Drug Store," *Sun*, Mar. 20, 1917.

327 The key question is: where was the building which Haslam referred to as Hashop's Confectionary? Answer: on the southeast corner of Beaton and 5th Avenue. It's interesting to note that Hashop's earlier location was where the State National Bank building was later built. A 1924 fire next door to Hashop's damaged his shop, causing him to temporarily move to a store which Charlie Simon was quitting to go into retirement ("Louis Hashop Has Purchased Simon Place," *Sun*, July 22, 1924). After another few years, Hashop moved to 125 N. Beaton.

328 *Love*, 136. The "Jesters" bought control of the bank, and Geo. T. and Geo E. became officers of the bank. George E.'s father, Charles W., had run the Corsicana National Bank before then (*Love*, 135). Charles W. Jester died in 1909. A review of real estate records for the First State Bank location confirms that George T. Jester purchased the property in 1896 (see note 193).

329 "Will Improve Building," *Sun*, Nov. 1, 1915.

330 RWeb, Maps, Sanborn Maps Index. Originals are at the Dolph Briscoe Center for American History, UT, Austin. Sanborn insurance maps exist for many years for many towns and cities.

331 Color coding indicates the construction materials of buildings, brick or wood.

332 A fire during the early morning hours of Oct. 1, 1883, burned down "the last block of wooden buildings in the business part of the city," at the "head of Beaton Street," e.g., where it meets 7th Avenue. Seven wooden houses were destroyed, five of them used as dwelling houses and two which were general merchandise businesses, one of Charles Blum, and one of Jackson & Bro. "The burn improves the looks of that quarter." ("Corsicana," *Austin Weekly Statesman*, Oct. 4, 1883, NP). The erection of brick buildings began as early as 1874, when an entire brick block of ten stores was built on the west side of Beaton Street for the businesses of Allen & Co., U.M. Lee & Co., Dr. J.T. Barton, A. Fox & Bro., R.N. White, C.W. Jester, Jos. Huey, A. Shwarts, and Garitty, Huey & Co. (*Times-Picayune* (New Orleans), June 9, 1874, NP; *GDN*, June 17, 1874; see also "Navarro County," *GDN*, Nov. 24, 1875 (buildings being put up on the east side of Beaton Street, opposite the new brick block)). Two years later, at 8:45 p.m. on November 8, 1876, a fire started in the back part of

Dave Cerf's grocery store on the west side of Beaton Street which spread and nearly burned down the entire block between Collin and White (5th Ave.) Streets. The "unfortunates" with losses were Louis Cohen, M.C. Fewell & Co., James Talley, Adolph Zadek, W.B. Edwards & W.S. Hord, W.H. McElwee, Branch Watkins, M.N. Frank, A. Aaron & P. Vogel, Saunders Murray & Hamburger, Steve Smith, L. Gamba, John Young (the barber), Wm. Wiggins, Max Miller, and U.M. Lee's unoccupied house. Most of the structures were wooden ("Corsicana," *GDN*, Nov. 9, 1876; "Corsicana," *GDN*, Nov. 10, 1876; *Austin Weekly Statesman*, Nov. 23, 1876, NP). At that time, new construction was always brick ("Navarro County," *GDN*, Mar. 13, 1877 (Corsicana has "A good brick hotel and five two story brick blocks")). Another devastating fire broke out during the morning of Dec. 23, 1880, destroying the Ferrell & Jester hardware store, A. Fox & Bros. dry goods, and J.F. Sullivan & Co. Boots and Shoes. Brick buildings were safer than wooden structures, but not impervious to fire ("Fire at Corsicana: Considerable Property Destroyed – Loss Estimated at $50,000," *GDN*, Feb. 25, 1884 (fire destroyed two two-story brick stores, Mallory & Allen, clothiers, and T.J. Stuart's Moss Rose saloon; badly damaged two others, J.P. Vance's and W.T. Van Shook's, both druggists)). A. Fox & Bro. suffered another major fire loss in 1897 ("At Corsicana, Tex.," *St. Louis Globe Democrat*, Jan. 14, 1897, NP (loss estimated at $50,000, insured for $56,000)).

333 Norris Wellge Co. (Beck & Pauli, lithographers) (RWeb, Corsicana, Old Photographs & Post Cards Gallery (Photographs and Postcards Index)). The Amon Carter Museum website (http://www.birdseyeviews.org/history.php) has additional information about bird's-eye view maps, especially for Texas localities. Bird's-eye view maps were made for cities throughout the United States in the late nineteenth and early twentieth centuries.

334 The map does not identify any other buildings at the intersection. It also does not identify buildings at the northwest and southeast corners at Beaton and Collin, endpoints of the rope according to the cemetery record book, although the other corners of that intersection are indexed, as nos. 37 and 41. At the northwest corner, 37, future site of the six-floor State National Bank, was "The Corsicana Daily Courier, Eylar & Eylar, Publishers." At the southeast corner, 41, was "C. H. Allyn, Wholesale Grocer," then known as "Allyn Corner," named for the same Mayor Captain Allyn introduced in Chapter 1.

335 *Logan's Railway Business Directory* (A.L. Logan & Co., 1873), 96, Archive.org/stream/logansrailwaybus00loga.

336 Issues of *Navarro Express* are available on PTH. See also *Love*, 149.

337 *Texas Messenger*, Sept. 1, 1882, PTH. He and his wife, Missouri, had three children: Thomas Edward, Solomon La Fayette, and William Davidson (1880 Census; Texas Probate, Navarro Cty., for T.N. Carter, Sept. 3, 1882, Anc.).

338 Ben Rosenberg was listed as a Waco resident in the 1889 Waco directory (Anc.). He married Ray Goldberg in Waco in 1893 (Texas County Marriages, McLennan Cty., Jan. 19, 1893 (abstract), Anc.). It's possible Rosenberg travelled from Waco to Corsicana to pray with Rope Walker, as Jay Silverberg said in Silverberg's oral history, but that seems unlikely—why not get a rabbi to travel to Corsicana? Couldn't one of the Jews in Corsicana at that time say a Hebrew prayer?

339 Mary was in charge of placing decorations on certain graves for Confederate's Memorial Day. ("Memorial Day," *Sun*, May 1, 1920; "U.D.C. Notes," *Sun*, May 22, 1924).

# 15. Molloy, Gulick & Mulkey

340 Hardin Street is now called Commerce Street. It was also called 10th Street. *Love* (116) said it was once called "Marshall Street," but Sanborn insurance maps show it was "Waco Street." It was named for J.G. Hardin, a circuit-riding preacher in early Texas who was the father of the notorious gunslinger John Wesley Hardin.

341 RWeb, Markers, The Molloy Hotel.

342 *Love*, 118, quoting the *American Sketch Book*, (published by "Mrs. Swisher," 1880).

343 Navarro Council of the Arts, Inc., *Brick Streets and Back Roads* (Taylor Publishing, 2000), 103.

344 William B. Vallie, son of Peter Vallie of Corsicana, was recently fired from his job as a train conductor. He and his wife, the former Laura Lewis (Louis? Louise?) of Walnut Hills, were married on Nov. 18, 1888, not quite two years prior, in Kopperl, where she lived at the time. They had separated after only a few months of marriage. Less than a week prior to the fateful night they had

reunited somewhere in northern Texas. They registered at the Molloy Hotel on Friday, having arrived there from Dallas.

On Sunday morning, Vallie bought a cheap gun in Corsicana, and that night, after paying the hotel bill, he went to their room. Late at night three gunshots were heard in quick succession. The proprietor and others forced the locked door and found that Vallie had shot his wife twice, once in the head and once in the neck, and then turned the gun on himself. He was dead, but his wife was alive, though clearly on the threshold of death. She died two days later, on Nov. 10, 1890. (Index to Texas County marriages, Bosque Cty., Anc.; "A Husband's Deed: He Shoots His Wife and Then Himself—The Cause Unknown," *GDN*, Nov. 10, 1890; *Alabama Beacon* (Greensboro), Nov. 18, 1890, NP; FAG, Kopperl, Tex., for Laura T. Vallie).

Nothing about Laura suggests she was a "working girl," but prostitution was present, and sometimes thriving in Corsicana. One indication of its persistence was the town's 1909 ordinance which restricted the practice to a "vice district" along Hardin/10th/Commerce Street between Collin and 5th Ave., close to the Molloy Hotel ("An ordinance to locate, regulate and restrain prostitutes, lewd women and women of bad reputation for chastity—to regulate persons, firms, corporations and companies renting and leasing to prostitutes, lewd women and women of bad reputation for chastity—to regulate owners, drivers and persons in charge of hacks, cabs, carriages and other vehicles carrying prostitutes, lewd women and women of bad reputation for chastity. To promote the order and good government of the city—and to punish violations of same," *Sun*, May 19, 1909).

It is a safe assumption that the Vallie murder-suicide was the source of the "Sally" story. It is the only murder known to have occurred at the hotel, it happened in the correct time period, and it was the murder of a woman. There is also the separation-then-reunion element in common to the legend and the news stories. Several newspapers reported on the event, but none of them were Corsicana papers, which are no longer extant for that time period. Most of the articles about the event are similar to the papers cited here. Some say there was no known motivation for the tragedy, while others, without being specific, say jealousy was the cause, which seems to seal the deal that Laura Lewis Vallie of Walnut Hills is the real person behind the legend of "Sally."

345 *DDH*, June 12, 1881, NP (death notice for Mary, seventy-six-year-old mother of Molloy House proprietor Henry Molloy).

346 FAG, Oakwood Cemetery. Her family name is from the death certificate of Clara Young (Tex. Death Cert., Anc.).

347 The Molloys' seven children were:

1. John, born about 1824, Ala.

2. Henry L., born about 1829, Ala.

3. Hartwell Horace, born about 1833, Ark. He was captain of Co. H, 20th Tex. Cav. (Dismounted). He was killed at the Battle of Honey Springs, July 17, 1863 (RWeb, Civil War Index, Confederate Units & Rosters (Civil War Rosters Index), Molloy's Company). *Love* (109) erroneously said his name was "Henry," confusing him with his brother.

4. Clara (aka Rose), born about 1840, Ala. She married Joseph Young Bates.

5. Ann, born about 1841, Ark. She married Alonzo Kirkendoll.

6. Robert B., born about 1843, Miss. He was referred to as "Senior" because his nephew, attorney R.B. Molloy, shared the same name.

7. David (Daniel?) D., born about 1843, Miss.

All nine family members were living in Freeo, Ouachita (pronounced like "Wichita") Cty., Ark. in 1850, recorded there as "Malay" (1850 Census). Hartwell and David were no longer living with the family ten years later, in Vineyard, Washington Cty., Ark., but newly added were Henry and John's wives and children (1860 Census, enumerated as "Malloy").

348 1870 Census, Corsicana, for H.L. Molloy; see *Dallas Weekly Herald*, July 13, 1872, GB; "Looking Back: Vintage Newspaper Reveals Corsicana of 1874," *Sun*, Sept. 26, 1971; "Corsicana Improvements," *Galveston Daily News*, Mar. 21, 1875, PTH (Molloy House near railroad depot cost $10,000 to build); "Bought Molloy Hotel, *Sun*, Nov. 25, 1916.

349 FAG, Lincoln, Ark., for John Thompson Molloy, died Nov. 13, 1862. The story of his murder is posted to his FAG page, but no source reference is given there. The gravestone's epitaph reads, in part: "Stand still and see the salvation of God." See also 1860 Census, Vineyard, Washington Cty., Ark., for John, Mary, three-year-old Henry, and half-year-old John Malloy; 1870 Census and 1880 Census of Mary and three sons at Cane Hill, Ark.; 1900 Census of Robert B. and

Eugenia Molloy, and their sons, at Corsicana; Tex. Death Cert. for Robt. B. Molloy, Navarro Cty., Mar. 16, 1946, Anc.

350 "Funeral Rites for R.B. Molloy Held on Monday Morning," *CSWL*, Mar. 19, 1946.

351 "Well Attended Funeral: Remains of David Deutschner Buried in Hebrew Cemetery," *Sun*, Jan. 6, 1916; "Funeral Services for Max London Were Held Sunday," *Sun*, Dec. 28, 1925; "Pioneer Business Man of Corsicana Died Saturday: Ben Rosenberg Passed Away Early Saturday Following Long Illness," *Sun*, May 4, 1929.

352 Roger Q. Mills was a highly accomplished early settlers of Corsicana. He was a strident supporter for Texas's secession and reached the rank of colonel in the Civil War. He served in the Texas state legislature and later as a U.S. Representative and Senator.

353 *Corsicana Observer*, July 18, 1861, quoted in *Memorial*, 139.

354 *Tri-Weekly Telegraph* (Houston), July 21, 1862, PTH.

355 See RWeb, Civil War Index, Confederate Units & Rosters (Civil War Rosters Index), Molloy's Company.

356 *Memorial*, 169-72.

357 Sons of the American Revolution Membership Application of Wiley Gulick Clarkson, (grandson of John Wiley Gulick), Aug. 23, 1947, Anc.

358 He was given a choice of any service in the Trans-Mississippi Dept., chose Forney's Infantry Division, and was assigned as senior surgeon of King's Brigade. At one time he was also a surgeon with Ochiltree's 18th Reg. Tex. Inf.

359 *Love*, 127.

360 This is according to a public family tree by Ruth Ann Davenport, Anc. The common ancestor was one John Molloy of Argyll, Scotland, born 1726, who had two children: Charles, born 1753, and John, born 1757, both in Argyll. One of Charles's nine children was Dr. Archibald Alexander Molloy, born in N.C., died in Cheraw, S.C. One of John's eleven children was David Molloy, born 1801 in Scotland Cty., N.C., the same David Molloy who came to Corsicana with his family.

361 *Memorial*, 170.

362. He died on July 21 (S.A.R. Application of Wiley Gulick Clarkson; see *DMN*, July 24, 1898). Find-A-Grave erroneously says he died on July 25, probably based on what appears to be a mostly illegible gravestone.

363 "Funeral Services Tues. Morning for Mrs. L.T. Gulick," *Sun*, May 10, 1927.

364 Spruill Cook, "Abe Mulkey, Exhorter for God and the Orphans," *Navarro County Scroll*, 1964, 12.

365 *AMB2*, 5.

366 Cook, "Abe Mulkey, Exhorter," 12.

367 *AMB2*, 93 (transcription of an undated article attributed to the *Durant Statesman*). *AMB1* says he was born in Columbus, Hempstead Cty., Ark. (page 7th (unnumbered)). Cook acknowledges the discrepancy and points out that Mulkey's Bible says he was born in Center Point. (Cook, 12n2.)

368 FAG, Waxahachie Cemetery, Waxahachie, Tex., says her maiden name was Reid and her middle name Pinkerton. Several family trees on www.Ancestry.com include Annis Mulkey, but primary records about her could not be readily identified as valid sources.

369 Cook, "Abe Mulkey, Exhorter," 13.

370 *AMB1*, Introductory.

371 *AMB1*, 121.

372 Cook, "Abe Mulkey, Exhorter," 10, 20. The lovely three-story house he built had "much fine woodwork, colored glass windows, and a wrought iron fence." The Mulkeys rented out the first and second floors of their home to help make ends meet (*Love*, 84).

373 School Yearbooks, Vanderbilt U., 1898, Anc.; 1898 Corsicana Directory, Anc.

374 "Son of Evangelist Succumbs to Tuberculosis," *McKinney Daily Courier*, Jan. 25, 1904, NP (republishing an article from the *Christian Advocate*); 1900 Census, Corsicana, Tex., for Royal R. Mulkey.

375 www.mch.org

# 16. Mary London

376 In the 1870 federal census the London family was enumerated within the Eutaw Post Office jurisdiction, near Kosse, Tex. The family was said to have lived in Springfield around that time, according to biographical information about Max London. Both locations are in Limestone Cty.

377 *Love*, 127, 131. An extensive history of Corsicana's educational institutions was prepared in celebration of the country's two hundredth birthday in "Corsicana Schools Began Almost When the City Did," *Sun*, June 29, 1976.

378 *Love*, 130.

379 *Love*, 127.

380 Elkan's date of death is from the Hebrew Cemetery record book. His gravestone only has his name.

Elkan was also the name of Max London's brother. A widely followed practice of Ashkenazic Jews (those who hailed from Germanic lands, as opposed to Sephardic Jews, who lived on the Iberian Peninsula or in Turkey), who comprise the vast majority of Jews, is that children are never named after a living relative. Since Elkan the brother was alive when Elkan the son was born, this suggests that "Elkan" was the name of someone who died prior to the birth of Elkan the brother, which was about 1830. Two family members named after the same deceased relative forty-nine years apart is very unusual and therefore suggests the ancestor was a very renowned and respected person. Alternatively, the London family has Sephardic origins, which allows naming children after living relatives. Another possibility is that Max did not follow traditional naming conventions.

381 Tobie's gravestone is in the London plot in the Hebrew Cemetery. Oral history from the family is that he was thrown from a horse. (K. Goldman, personal correspondence with author. Goldman is a distant relative of the Londons.)

382 In the London Family Collection at the National Museum of American Jewish History (NMAJH), three postcards, which are dated over the course of two decades, show family and friends expressing concerns over Julia's health.

383 Julia was not socially active and may have had a personality disorder which made it difficult for her to engage with others. Mary had some prospects for marriage, but none worked out (K. Goldman, personal correspondence with author). One Corsicanan, however, recalled that when he walked past the London home, as a boy, the sociable elderly ladies on the porch would chat him up (Bud Silverberg, telephone interview with author, 2017).

384 The most notable newspaper mentions found are about Mary being in charge of placing Memorial Day decorations in the Jewish cemetery ("Memorial Day," *Sun*, May 1, 1920; "U.D.C. Notes," *Sun*, May 22, 1924 (she participated with Mrs. Louis Cerf, according to the latter article)).

An autograph book given to Mary as a present in 1883 contains about a dozen short messages from friends, indicating some interest from young men (NMAJH, object 2011.142.15, "autograph book"). Mary may have remained at home to support her sister's needs (K. Goldman, personal correspondence).

385 Tex. Death Cert., Julia London, Feb. 11, 1951, Anc.; Tex. Death Cert., Mary London, Feb. 21, 1852, Anc.

386 Mamie (Oppenheimer) Hart was three years old on Aug. 7, 1888, when her mother, Dora (Simon) Oppenheimer, died ("Mrs. David Oppenheimer," *GDN*, Aug. 8, 1888 (transcribed at FAG, Hebrew Rest Cemetery, Waco, for Dora Oppenheimer)). Born in Houston in 1863, Dora was the youngest, while Bertha, born in Prussia around 1835, was the oldest of the children of Bernard and Mina "Mamie" (Jacobowsky) Simon. Ashkenazic Jewish tradition is to name children after relatives who are deceased. The closer the deceased relative, the more likely their name would be perpetuated in a subsequent generation.

387 K. Goldman, personal correspondence.

388 "Max H. London Died at Home Here Just After Noon Today," *Sun*, Dec. 24, 1925. At the time of his death, Grodzisk was known as Graetz. It is located about thirty-five miles southwest of the city of Poznan.

389 The ship arrival is for M. London, a native of Graetz, who arrived at Hull, England, May 13, 1852, sailing from Hamburg. (Alien Arrivals, Anc.). Arriving with him (listed one name away, on the same page) is someone else named London, also born in Graetz, first initial "K," or possibly "Ph."

This could be Max's brother Philip. Arguing that this arrival is for Max and Philip is the date of arrival, because it is later than the 1851 English census in which neither Max nor Philip was listed with their father (1851 England census, for Henry and Elkin London, St. James Dukes Place, London, Anc.). This was also prior to Max's arrival in America, in 1853. The K. or Ph. London immigrant was listed as an apprentice haberdasher (translation courtesy of Jonathan Michael Wien via ViewMate, https://www.jewishgen.org/ViewMate/, request #62545).

390 Max had two other known siblings in addition to Elkan: Raphael and Philip. These two both married women from the Berliner family, who lived next to Henry and Elkan London in 1851 (1851 England Census, St. James Dukes Place, London, Anc.). Henry and Elkan lived between the families of Benjamin Berliner, a baker, and Abraham Belize, Rabbi of the Portuguese Synagogue. Benjamin Berliner's family, like the Londons, was from Grodzisk (Biography of Bero Berliner in Mamie Yeary, Compiler, *Reminiscences of the Boys in Grey, 1861-1865* (Smith & Lamar Publishing House, 1912), 54, PTH). Bero Berliner lived with his Berliner family in London, in 1851, came to the U.S., served in the Civil War, and was a pioneer settler of Texarkana, Arkansas.

In a 1938 letter to the editor of the *Jewish Chronicle* (London, Nov. 8, 1938), George G. Jacob advocated for the acceptance of a refugee from Berlin, one Horace Berliner, explaining that Horace (aka Hirsch) had retained his family's British citizenship despite there being two generations since his last ancestor resided in England. Horace's father was Ephraim Hirsch [Berliner], son of an earlier Hirsch Berliner, a merchant who died in Jerusalem, who in turn was the eldest son of Dr. Solomon Hirschel Lewin (his surname was different than his son's), chief rabbi of London from 1802 until his death in 1842. Solomon Hirschel Lewin's father, Hirschel Loebel, was a London rabbi from 1756-1764. The letter writer notes, "one branch still bears the surname London" (J. Wolkovitch, personal correspondence with author). No direct link between Max London and this early English rabbinic family, e.g. a link to Ephraim London, who was the brother of Solomon Hirschel Lewin, could be ascertained, but it seems possible in light of the close connections between the London and Berliner families and Max London's unusual desire to retain his British citizenry (discussed in an upcoming chapter) that Max's London family was a branch of the well-known rabbinic Berliner family.

391 "Max H. London Died" ("...in March, 1854, landed in Galveston"). His obituary says he "landed in New York," Oct. 17, 1853, but it appears he was the passenger named "Manifest [?] London" who arrived on Oct. 22, 1853 (N.Y. Ship Arrivals, New York, *The Jeremiah Thompson*, line 325, Anc., indexed as "Manipst"). "Manifest London," seventeen, a shoe dealer, is a perfect match to Max London's age and likely profession—the same profession followed by his father and brother.

392 1860 Census (Calhoun Cty.). He came to Lavaca in Jan., 1859 ("Max H. London Died"). His detailed biographies in the *Sun* do not state where he lived between 1854 and 1859, but in "To Celebrate 82d Birthday: Max London has Lived in Corsicana for Forty-Three Years" (*Sun*, July 19, 1920), he said he was the only living Jew (in 1920) who had lived in Galveston before the war.

393 "Max H. London Died." At the time of their marriage, Bertha was living in Houston. She had previously lived in Springfield, and together they moved back to Springfield. Hallettsville is close to Austin. The "Springfield" mentioned (there are more than one in Texas) is probably the one located in Limestone Cty., near Mexia, which is no longer an inhabited place, although it was once the county seat. That particular Springfield is now located inside Fort Parker State Park. Bremond is in Robertson County, just south of Limestone County, the county just south of Navarro County.

394 "To Celebrate 82d Birthday"; "Max H. London Died."

395 London's military service history is based on his obituary, "Max H. London Died" and a "Statement of Max H. London" (Compiled Service Records of Confederate Soldiers, www.Fold3.com) dated Feb. 12, 1863. The obituary is at odds with the "statement." The latter was written by London himself to convince prison officials that he was a non-combatant and should therefore be allowed more freedom, while the obituary says London "participated in the battle of La Salle [a small settlement about ten miles from Victoria] and shortly afterwards went into training camp at Garacitas near Victoria." No reference to such a battle or training camp could be found. The obituary said he joined the CSA in April 1861, which seems at odds with London's own words, in the statement, stating that he enlisted in September of that year.

396 "Statement of Max H. London." A hospital steward's primary role was pharmacist, although other duties might include administration of anesthetics, dressing of wounds, and ensuring the overall proper administrative functioning of the hospital (William T. Campbell, "Seven Hospital

Stewards," National Museum of Civil War Medicine, Dec. 24, 1914, http://www.civilwarmed.org/surgeons-call/steward2/ (originally published in *Surgeon's Call* 18, no. 2, Dec. 2013)).

397 Benjamin was the most famous American Jew of the era. He was a U.S. Senator from Louisiana who served at the highest levels in the Confederate government. He went into exile in 1865 following the South's defeat.

398 Arkansas Post was once the most important European settlement in Arkansas, its history going back to the late seventeenth century, and capital of the Arkansas Territory for the first two years of the territory's existence (The Encyclopedia of Arkansas History and Culture, "Arkansas Post," http://www.encyclopediaofarkansas.net/encyclopedia/).

399 The Encyclopedia of Arkansas History and Culture.

400 He said he never bore arms, was never out on picket, in a battle, or in a skirmish. His statement is at odds with his obituary, "Max H. London Died," which said he fought in the battle of La Salle.

401 "Statement of Max H. London."

402 "Max H. London Died."

403 "Funeral Services for Max London Were Held Sunday," *Sun*, Dec. 28, 1925. Pallbearers, actual and honorary, were often listed in articles about the funerals of honored citizens, at least in Corsicana papers. Almost all of these individuals appear elsewhere in this volume.

404 Bernard Simon's gravestone in the Waco cemetery says he was born in "Witkoway, Province Posen" (FAG). Witkowo, the town's current name, is about thirty miles north-northeast of the city of Poznan, meaning the London and Simon families—those surnames may or may not have been used in Poland—came from Polish towns close to one another. The Solomon family of Corsicana (see Supplement III), according to some researchers, was also from Witkowo.

405 Ziror Simon married Abe Kiersky and lived in Waco (the "Aurora" listed in the 1860 census appears to be Ziror). Henry Simon was a merchant in Milam, died there in 1892, and was buried in Waco. Theresa (Simon) Mandelbaum was married to Asher Mandelbaum, and they lived in Dallas. (Asher was in business at one point with his cousin, Philip Sanger, of the famous Sanger brothers mercantile. Asher's sister Cornelia Mandelbaum was married to Philip Sanger, a first cousin marriage (Asher and Cornelia's father was the brother of Babette Sanger, mother of the Sanger brothers.)) Julius Simon was also buried in Waco. The fate of the other Simon children, Sarah, Hypatia "Hy" Beatrice Pollack (of Dallas), and Isaac, was not readily apparent and not ascertained.

406 1860 Census, Springfield, Limestone Cty., p. 2.

407 1870 Census.

408 "B. Simon," age fifty-five, occupation "leisure" (1880 Census, Falls Cty., Tex., precinct one (E.D. 36), p. 23, line 40). On line 24 of the page is a "Simon Henry," age twenty-eight, who is Bernard's son Henry, his name transposed by the enumerator.

409 1900 Census.

410 FAG.

411 Records indicate Charlie Simon was born in either Russia or Russian Poland. He immigrated much later than Bernard Simon, who immigrated in the early 1850s (according to the 1860 census), a factor suggesting that they were not related.

412 1900 Census (arrived in 1873); 1910 Census (arrived in 1872).

413 His wife was from Houston, and Charles's death notice was published in a Houston paper (*HP*, Aug. 20, 1924).

414 *Morrison and Fourmy's General Directory of the City of Corsicana* (1894-1895), 57, RWeb, Corsicana, Directories. *Morrison & Fourmy's General Directory of Corsicana 1898-1899* lists his business as "club room over 212 N. Beaton" (City Directories, Waco (sic), Tex., Anc.).

415 Yetta was from a large Houston family that resided in Texas by 1870 (1870 Census, Galveston; 1880 Census, Houston). Her parents, Louis and Hanna Finberg, had nine children who survived to adulthood. In 1910, Yetta's parents and her sister, Helen, lived in Corsicana (1910 Census). Yetta's brother Abraham was a sometime-magician known as "Al Landon." His children were successful entertainers, especially his daughter, Honey Bee, an actress, magician, and hypnotist with the stage name Joan Landon (See http://joanbrandon.com; "Daughter Corsicana Couple Meets Success in Motion Pictures," *Sun*, Sept. 7, 1937).

Magician Abraham Finberg/Al Landon's debut performance, at the age of eight days—his circumcision—was reviewed in the *Galveston Daily News* ("Bayou City Budget," *GDN*, Dec. 31, 1888).

416 1900 Census. In 1901 he had a "Club room over 105 N. Beaton" (1901 Corsicana Directory, Anc.), at the intersection of Beaton and 5th Avenue. In 1910 he and his wife still resided at 3rd Ave., but the Blums were gone, and his profession at that later date was confectioner—the occupation followed by Louis Blum in 1900 (1900 and 1910 Censuses).

417 Sarah was first married to Ben Gottlieb, who died young, with whom two children were born: Sol in Oct., either 1883 or 1884 (WWI and WWII Draft Reg. Cards, Anc.; 1900 Census), in Kosse, Tex., and Jake, in 1886, in Corsicana (N.C. Death Cert., 1946, Anc.).

418 *Sun*, Aug. 15, 1917; *CSWL*, July 18, 1922.

419 Over the years, Charlie Simon had various businesses at various locations on Beaton Street.

## 17. The American Jew as Patriot, Soldier, and Rope Walker

420 For example, some six thousand Confederate prisoners, so-called "galvanized Yankees," agreed to serve with the Union to gain their freedom. They served primarily in the West, battling against Native Americans. See, e.g., Wikipedia's "Galvanized Yankees" entry.

421 Civil War Draft Registration Records, 2nd Congressional Dist., Hamilton Cty., Ohio, Vol. 4, Anc.

422 Ancestry.com. The census return itself is not available online.

423 1900 Census.

424 "Perils of an Acrobatic Life," *Cincinnati Enquirer*, Mar. 5, 1883, NP. (Reproduced in Chapter 12.)

425 Additional clippings can be found in Book II of the Rope Walker Series, *One Foot Over Main Street* (projected date of publication, 2021).

426 Jennison's Jayhawkers had a reputation for zealous opposition to slavery, resorting to theft, violence, and arson—all in the name of abolition. Jayhawkers were first known for their pre-Civil War incursions from Kansas into Missouri, one-side of the "bleeding Kansas" attacks which presaged the Civil War.

427 Marker THC-4C-32 is located on State Highway 18 at Enon Lane. The text reads: "BATTLE OF MIDDLEBURG: AUGUST 30, 1862: Ordered to raid Federal supply lines in West Tennessee, Confederate General Frank C. Armstrong rode north from Holly Springs, Mississippi, in August 1862, with a large force of cavalry. Near this spot on August 30, Armstrong engaged a Union brigade commanded by Col. Mortimer Leggett, sent to destroy him. After a fierce day-long battle, the Union troops were forced to retreat, allowing the Confederates to continue their raid north of the Hatchie River" (http://www.lat34north.com/HistoricMarkersTN/ MarkerDetail.cfm?KeyID=035-032 (visited Feb. 1, 2019)). The online transcription has typographical errors; the quote presented here is taken from the plaque itself, from an in-person review.

428 Kansas Historical Society, Research, Genealogy Indexes, Military, *Kansas Adjutant General's Report, 1861-1865*, https://www.kshs.org/p/kansas-adjutant-general-s-report-1861-1865/11175.

429 Hathi Trust Digital Library, *Report of the Adjutant General of the State of Kansas, 1861-'65. Vol. I* (Topeka: The Kansas State Printing Company, 1896), 222, https://www.hathitrust.org/.

## 18. Hebrew Poet Remarks: "O Legs!"

430 Emma Lazarus, "The New Colossus" (1883) (excerpt).

431 "Local News," *Jewish Messenger*, Apr. 28, 1882, p. 2, GB.

432 According to the Roman calendar, the Ides falls on either the thirteenth or fifteenth of the month. In the case of March, it is the fifteenth. Rope Walker did not die on the Ides of March—but close!

433 U.S. National Homes for Disabled Volunteer Soldiers, Dayton, Anc.

434 "Dropped from rolls," i.e., removed from the list of pensioners (U.S. National Homes for Disabled Volunteer Soldiers, Milwaukee, Anc.).

435 Garfield served for less than half of a year, shot by a disgruntled office-seeker.

436 See, e.g., "Official History of Corsicana Red Cross," *Sun*, Sept. 8, 1919 ("Mr. Max London, aged 81 years, made 20 operating gowns in memory of Mrs. Henry Newberg, 204 Helpers' Bed shirts 50, (sic) in memory of Mr. Louis Cerf and 50 in memory of Judge R.S. Neblett.").

437 "To Celebrate 82d Birthday: Max London Has Lived in Corsicana for Forty-Three Years," *Sun*, July 19, 1920.

438 Petition, Oath and Admission papers of Isaac Adams, U.S. Federal Naturalizations, McLennan Cty., Tex., Anc.

439 Max London's arrival in England appears to have been in 1852 and his arrival in the U.S. in 1853. See discussion and sources cited in Chapter 16.

440 Gratiot Street Prison, St. Louis, prisoner's statement by Max H. London, Feb. 12, 1863 (*from* Compiled Confederate Service Records, Max London, www.Fold3.com). Perhaps London's decision not to give up his English citizenship (which citizenship has not been confirmed) has something to do with a remote family ancestor, as discussed in Chapter 16, note 390.

441 1850 Census and later federal censuses list every household member. Earlier censuses counted all household members but only recorded the names of the heads of households.

442 Other Moses Bergs were found, but they were not the correct person, evident because of one data point or another. Searches were made under multiple spellings in the 1870 and 1880 Censuses, when he was known to be living in the U.S. Indexes that include every person listed in those census records have been created by more than one genealogy service.

443 The process is tedious and uncertain and only occasionally successful. Before pursuing this alternate process, all efforts to find the person in the usual way—using name, age, city, relationship to others in their family, etc., should be exhausted. This alternate method is time-consuming and frequently unsuccessful; even when the address is found in the census, the person sought may not be enumerated at that address. The lengthy process starts with the necessary and helpful finding aids at One-Step Webpages, by Stephen P. Morse, "1880-1950 ED Definitions: Obtaining 1880 to 1950 ED definitions" (https://stevemorse.org/).

444 1880 Census, E.D. 370, 37.

# 19. Certifications

445 Wikipedia's disambiguation of the topic "Congregation Shearith Israel" entry.

446 Congregation Shearith Israel, www.Shearithisrael.org.

447 Google Translate.

# 20. Kerrsicana

448 THB.

449 *Memorial*, 525.

450 *Memorial*, 525. Cal Kerr's popularity is attested to by the many articles about him in the *Sun*.

451 *Memorial*, 795. *Memorial* says they married at "Lanesburg, Tennessee." No such place could be found. Their marriage was recorded in Marshall Cty., Tenn., where Lewisburg is the largest town (Tenn. State Marriages, Marshall Cty., for Catherine D. Smith and Samuel H. Kerr, Anc.).

452 *Navarro Express*, Oct. 29, 1859, PTH.

453 *Memorial*, 795-96; *Love*, 71; James Kerr, "Clan Kerr: The Last Thousand Years," *Navarro County Scroll* (1968), 37-54.

454 *Memorial*, 796.

455 Leora, wife of John Duren; William H.; Frank; Mary, wife of Rev. B.M. Taylor, of Ennis; Louisa, wife of Rev. Abe Mulkey; Samuel M.; Fleta, wife of L.P. Keen; and Calvin E.

456 *Love*, 84.

457 Ira Baker Taylor was the first mayor of Corsicana, appointed by Gov. Davis under Reconstruction. He later lived in Weatherford, Tex. and died there in 1920 at the age of eighty-six.

Another of Mayor Taylor's daughters, Elizabeth America "Lizzie" Taylor, married T.P. (Thomas Perkins) Kerr, a son of James Kerr, Sr. T.P. Kerr was cashier of the Corsicana National Bank.

Rev. Benjamin M. Taylor (1833-1904) married as his second wife Mary Elizabeth Kerr, daughter of S.H. Kerr (See RWeb, Obituaries, Mary Kerr). No connection between Rev. Taylor and Mayor Taylor could be established.

458 *Memorial*, 698; Pedigree Resource File database, LDS, citing obituaries in the *Corsicana Daily Sun* & *Courier-Light*, Aug. 10 & 11, 1896.

459 "Interesting Bit of History Related," *Sun*, Aug. 16, 1921; "Confederate Veteran Dies," *HP*, Jan. 24, 1924.

460 They were married on Dec. 1, 1853 (*Memorial*, 699).

461 *Memorial*, 699.

462 "Dr. W.J.W. Kerr," *Sun*, Nov. 21, 1916.

463 *Galveston Daily News*, May 30, 1897, PTH.

464 This is stated in a family tree on Ancestry.com, but could not be verified.

465 1860 Census, Henderson Cty., Tenn., for J.W.J., M.J., and A.A. Kerr; *Memorial*, 698.

466 His biography (*Memorial*, 698) erroneously says that after the war he went to West Texas. He was never in Texas at that earlier time. It should say "West Tennessee."

467 *Memorial*, 698.

468 "Friend Writes of Dr. Kerr: Dallas Citizen Recalls Faithful Deeds of a Former Comrade," *Sun*, Feb. 14, 1927 (letter from Dr. Kerr's friend, Menzies Cumming, to Kerr's brother, published in the *Sun* following Kerr's death). The Odd Fellows Orphans Home is located in Corsicana.

469 See Chapters 14 and 15.

470 *Memorial*, 170.

## 21. Confederate Doctors

471 *Memorial*, 698.

472 See, e.g., Gary Flavion, "Civil War Prison Camps," American Battlefield Trust, https://www.battlefields.org/learn/articles/civil-war-prison-camps. Point Lookout was located at the confluence of the Chesapeake Bay and the Potomac River. It was a large facility with a 1,400-bed hospital ("Point Lookout Prisoner of War Camp," My Civil War, www.MyCivilWar.com).

473 *Confederate Veteran*, Vol. 2 (1917), 31, www.books.google.com.

474 Wikipedia's "Henry Wirz" entry.

475 Some recollections erroneously said he was a surgeon at the camp, but all official records describe him as hospital steward.

476 Over one hundred deaths per day were recorded for most days between mid-August and mid-September, 1864 (Prof. Douglas O. Linde, "Daily Record of Deaths in Andersonville Prison Pen as recorded by Jas. M. Bryant Superintendent of the Cemetery," from Famous Trials, www.law2.umkc.edu/faculty/projects/ftrials/wirz/deathlog.htm).

477 See Chapter 20.

478 "Old Citizen Passes Away: For Four Years a Surgeon in the Confederate Army," *Sun*, Nov. 13, 1916.

479 "Declares it Untrue: Dr. W.J.W. Kerr Says Stedman Was Not President Davis' Captor," *Sun*, Oct. 22, 1915. Dr. Kerr visited the *Sun*'s office "in high dudgeon and when he gets in that mood he calls a spade a spade." The *Sun* had recently printed a national story about the death of the "captor" of President Davis. Kerr insisted the history was inaccurate, and that he, Kerr, was in the vicinity and knew for a fact it was a collection of soldiers who captured Jefferson Davis.

480 "Friend Writes of Dr. Kerr." Cumming references an article in the May 22, 1903 issue of a Corsicana newspaper, the *Light*. The paper is not now accessible, and no copy of the article could be found in any other paper.

It appears that the article was the publication of a talk he had given two days earlier. On May 20, Dr. Kerr, president of the Army and Navy Surgeons of the Confederate States, delivered an hour-long address on the second day of the group's reunion. He defended Wirz, saying his "execution was one of the foulest murders ever known in any country." ("Dr. Wurz [sic] Defended: His execution Not Justified by Facts: Dr. Kerr's Address Throws Light on Occurrence," *Times-Democrat* (New Orleans), May 21, 1903, NP). See also "Facts as to Andersonville Prison," *New Orleans Item*, May 24, 1903, GB.

481 "He was also hospital steward in the noted Andersonville prison in Georgia and served his time as prisoner in the federal prison" ("Tribute of Respect," *Sun*, Mar. 23, 1917 (resolution of Masonic Lodge 174, Corsicana, dated Mar. 5, 1917)). Inquiries to historians and a review of Andersonville histories has not revealed an answer, surprisingly, as to the indictment of Kerr and others who were accused along with Wirz.

482 Library of Congress, Military Legal Resources, "Trial of Captain Henry Wirz," http://www.loc.gov/rr/frd/Military_Law/pdf/Wirz-trial.pdf. The document is 889 pages long.

483 Library of Congress, "Trial of Captain Henry Wirz," 334-35. One of the responsibilities of a hospital steward was to manage the supplies and other needs of the hospital, including the ordering of medicines, food, bedding, etc.

484 Library of Congress, "Trial of Captain Henry Wirz," 679.

485 Library of Congress, "Trial of Captain Henry Wirz," 682.

486 Dilley was one of three prisoners who worked as clerks for Capt. Wirz. His testimony was supportive of Wirz but critical of Kerr. Dilley admitted to accepting privileges because of his favored position, trading illegally in food, and otherwise gaming the system as best he could. His admissions of improprieties make his testimony sound open, honest, and highly credible.

Following the war, Dilley settled in Wilkes Barre, Penn., where he ran a hotel and later a restaurant. According to lengthy obituaries about him he was quite wealthy and gave generously to charities. He had a brusque manner and "biting sarcasm," but beneath his exterior the "kindliest of hearts" ("Benj. F. Dilley Dies Peacefully," *Wilkes-Barre News*, Feb. 25, 1905, NP; "Benjamin F. Dilley Leaves Large Estate to Charity," *Wilkes-Barre Times*, Feb. 25, 1905, GB).

487 *Franklin v. Mooney*, 2 Tex. 452. The primary legal question was whether an oral condition could be used to modify a written contract. The dispute arose over the definition of "served," which either meant joining the militia, which Mooney did, according to the written contract, or actually going to Mexico and fighting, which Franklin alleged was an orally agreed-to modification.

488 Reproduction of marriage record (Silas Starley vertical file, Corsicana Public Library). The Starley vertical file also holds pages from "Transactions of the Texas State Medical Association" and "Transcripts Relating to the Medical History of Texas, Volume XXX: Medical Biographies S-T").

489 Unconditional Certificates issued by the Board of Land Commissioners of the County of Nacogdoches. "Silas F. Starley (became 17 September 5, 1840) emigrated in 1838, 320 acres, issued March 4, 1844; Witnesses: William Roark & Reson Franklin" (Entry 3, Nacogdoches Headrights, Sixth Section 101, [title page is image 5740], by Carolyn Reeves Ericson, Silas Starley vertical file, Corsicana Public Library).

490 "The probate is for May 1858 [...] mentions [Reason Franklin's] will dated 13 Aug 1847 in Cherokee County. In the will he left everything to his stepson Silas F. Starley, with the probate stating he left no wife or kin in the state. His estate consisted of 42 items including: 440 acres of land, 16 head of cattle, a bay horse, a roan horse and other miscellaneous items" (Franklin Family Researchers United, Vol. 62, Jul. 2008, http://freepages.genealogy.rootsweb.ancestry.com/~ffru/Docs/FFRU_back/vol62.pdf; "Cherokee County Texas," http://files.usgwarchives.net/tx/cherokee/land/cherokee.txt).

491 See Joseph H. Raymond, *History of the Long Island College Hospital and its Graduates* (Brooklyn, N.Y.: Association of the Alumni, 1899), 151 (electronic page 195 in image mode), https://archive.org/stream/68140020R.nlm.nih.gov/68140020R_djvu. txt (entry for William Franklin Starley).

492 Navarro Cty. Register of Physicians, Silas F. Starley vertical file, Corsicana Pub. Lib.

493 Compiled Service Records of Confederate General and Staff Officers and Nonregimental Enlisted Men, for Silas F Starley, www.Fold3.com.

494 Mattie Starley and Major Farrar were married in July 1869. Farrar was a leading citizen of Groesbeck where his primary occupation was law. He also organized the Groesbeck National Bank and was its first president, a position he held for many years (*Memorial*, 368-69).

495 Starley's articles appeared in *North American Medico-Chirurgical Review;* the *New Orleans Medical Journal; Daniel's Texas Medical Journal;* and *New York Medical Journal* (Texas Physicians Historical Biographical Database, UT Southwestern Medical Center, Health Sciences Digital Library and Learning Center, http://library.utsouthwestern.edu/doctors/doctors.cfm?DoctorID=16799).

496 *Love*, 152-53.

497 *Austin Weekly Statesman*, April 26, 1883, NP. See Ira Carleton Chase, *Texas State Journal of Medicine Vol. I, July 1905-April 1906* (The State Medical Association of Texas, 1906), 103, www.Googlebooks.com.

498 *Austin Weekly Statesman*, May 24, 1883, NP.

499 Lewis E. Daniell, *Types of Successful Men of Texas* (1890), 464, https://books.google.com.

500 F.E. Daniel, M.D., Ed., *Daniel's Texas Medical Journal: A Monthly Journal of Medicine and Surgery, Vol. III, July, 1887, to June, 1888* (1888), 293-94 (electronic pages 431-32 in image mode), https://archive.org/stream/danielstexasmedi3188dani/danielstexasmedi3188dani_djvu.txt.

501 Daniel, 294-95 (electronic pages 432-33 in image mode).

502 A man with exactly the same name, perhaps his grandfather, was born in 1800 in that county.

503 Confederate Pensions, Texas, for pensioner Mrs. H.F. Witherspoon, file 43271 (1927), Anc.

504 Mattie Hodge "came from an old slave holding southern family. … [Her] father, Capt. Hodges came from Kentucky and purchased the old home at Chatfield and sent back for his family after the house had been built and quarters for his slaves constructed." Her brother, Dink Hodge, "honored and revered the old traditions of the South" ("Prominent Navarro County Citizen is Buried Chatfield," *CSWL*, Nov. 8, 1929 (obituary of R.L. "Dink" Hodge)). Hodge Oaks Plantation is a Chatfield historical landmark.

505 R.L. Hodge, "Chatfield, Texas," in *Navarro County Scroll* (Navarro County Historical Society, 1956).

506 1860 U.S. Census, Slave Schedule, Navarro Cty., Tex., Anc. He owned five of the nearly two thousand enslaved African Americans in Navarro County at that time.

507 *Journal of the American Medical Association* 41:670, https://archive.org/details/journalamericanm41ameruoft.

508 1860 Census; 1870 Census.

509 Tenn. State Marriages, for James Blair and Elizabeth Upton, 1847, Anc.; Tex. Death Cert., Navarro Cty., Oct. 15, 1904, Anc.; 1880 Census, Corsicana, for James M. and Elizabeth Y. Blair and family, Anc.; Tex. Death Cert., El Paso, Martha Blair Goodman, 1955, Anc.

510 1900 Census.

511 1900 Census, Corsicana, for Mattie H. Goodman.

512 1850 Census, 2nd Civil Dist., Monroe Cty., Tenn.; 1860 Census and 1870 Census, Henderson, Rusk Cty., Tex.; 1880 Census and 1900 Census, Corsicana.

513 FAG, Oakwood Cemetery, Corsicana.

514 "Twenty Home Runs: Remarkable Record Made by Corsicana Club Yesterday," *Times-Democrat* (New Orleans), June 16, 1902, NP. Many recent references say the Texarkana team was called the "Casketmakers," but no original source has been found to support this. Corsicana's team was the "Oil Citys." See also Bill Weiss and Marshall Wright, "Top 100 Teams: 51. 1902 Corsicana Oil Citys," MiLB.com, http://www.milb.com/milb/history/top100.jsp?idx=51.

515 March 15, 1883, NP.

516 See, e.g., Wikipedia's "Twenty Negro Law" entry.

517 Enumerated by age, the chattelized humans were listed without names under the names of their owners. The first listed under Blair was a man whose age appeared to be "511," but as they are listed by age, he was probably fifty-one. Other males were aged twenty-eight, twenty-five (two that age), twelve, four, and three. Females were aged twenty-five, twenty-three, eighteen (two that age), eight, six, and four. Nine were listed as "black" and the others as "mulatto" (1860 Census, Slave Schedule, Rusk Cty., Beat 1, p. 1, Anc.). Slaves were included in the census because the U.S. Constitution calculated the number of representatives in Congress per state based on population, and slaves were counted as three-fifths of a person. That fraction was established at the Constitutional Convention of 1787, a compromise between northern and southern states. See, e.g., "The Three-Fifths Clause of the United States Constitution (1787)," www.blackpast.org/aah/three-fifths-clause-united-states-constitution-1787.

518 1850 U.S. Census, Slave Schedule, Monroe Cty., Dist. 2, Tenn., pp. 1-2, Anc.

519 He was not only absent from county histories but also from the Texas Physicians Historical Biographies Database.

520 *Register of Physicians, Navarro County, Texas*, Silas F. Starley vertical file, Corsicana Pubic Library.

521 *Register of Physicians, Navarro County, Texas*.

522 *Memorial*, 503-04. The biographical sketch of Dr. Hugh Sloan includes information about his brother, A.C., and other family members.

523 *Memorial*, 665. His compiled service record contains little information (Service Records of Confederate Soldiers Who Served in Organizations, Alabama, for A.C. Sloan, www.Fold3.com).

524 *Memorial*, 665-66.

525 *Memorial*, 666.

526 Tex. Death Certs., Navarro Cty., Lelia F. Sloan, June 11, 1945, and A.C. Sloan, Nov. 30, 1906, Anc.

527 Stephen Z. Starr, *Jennison's Jayhawkers: A Civil War Cavalry Regiment and its Commander* (Baton Rouge: Louisiana State Univ. Press, 1973).

528 The killers of John Thompson Molloy are unknown. They were probably Northern-sympathizing, anti-slavery proponents because the other Molloy brothers became sympathetic to the confederate cause. J.T. Molloy's story is related in Chapter 15.

## 22. Black Diamond

529 The first U.S. circus appeared in Philadelphia in 1793 (Dominique Jando, "John Bill Ricketts," *Circopedia*, http://www.circopedia.org/John_Bill_Ricketts (retrieved Oct. 8, 2020)).

530 *GDN*, Nov. 9, 1871.

531 "A World's Fair on Wheels!," *GDN*, Apr. 8, 1873 (advertisement). The nearly full-page ad appeared on the paper's first page. Twenty-two performances were scheduled, from April 14 in Galveston through May 10 in Sherman.

532 Mary Miller Affidavit (see note 286).

533 Third Ward School location identified by Ron Maxfield and others.

534 "Robinson's Menagerie and Circus will exhibit in Corsicana next Monday and Tuesday. The Company is considered to be the best in the United States at present time, according to the newspaper reports. A small specimen of the fair sex is the shape of a young girl of 18 years, weighting [sic] 600 pounds net. She is represented as being handsome and can dance as light as a feather. All wishing to see the elephant and Indian can now have the opportunity" ("First Circus to Appear in Corsicana" (transcription), attributed to *Corsicana Times*, June 5, 1857 (RWeb, "Newspaper Extracts Index")).

535 *Trinity Advocate* (Palestine, Tex.), Oct. 6, 1858, GB. Mlle. Durand is advertised with Buckley's Circus in 1858 and 1859. Her name is otherwise not found in historical records. She may have been injured, or died (rope walkers had high mortality rates), or she may have changed her stage name. Other performers in Buckley's circus included horsemen, an acrobatic troupe, and clowns.

536 *Navarro Express*, Apr. 28, 1860, PTH (advertisement); *Navarro Express*, May 5, 1860, PTH (review of performance; performance would be repeated).

537 Previous Black Diamond histories are not clear on this point, only that Hagenbeck was the first known owner. See sources cited in this chapter.

538 Homer C. Walton, "The Story of Black Diamond," *Bandwagon* 3, no. 3 (May-June, 1959): 17-18, http://www.classic.circushistory.org/Bandwagon/bw-1959May.htm (retrieved Feb. 7, 2019); Homer C. Walton, "A.M. Cauble's Wagon Show," *Bandwagon* 6, no. 1 (Jan-Feb, 1962): 20-22, http://www.classic.circushistory.org/Bandwagon/bw-1962\Jan.htm (retrieved Feb. 7, 2019).

539 Walton, "The Story of Black Diamond."

540 R.T. Richards's real name was R.T. Ringling, a son of one of the famed Ringling Brothers, Alf T. Ringling.

541 Walton, "The Story of Black Diamond."

542 Walton, "The Story of Black Diamond."

543 Correspondence, Bill Woodcock to Col. Sturtevant, Mar. 15, 1941, quoted at "William Woodcock's letters #2," Bucklesblog (May 29, 2007), www.bucklesw.blogspot.com.

544 According to Bill Woodcock (Walton, "The Story of Black Diamond").

545 "Posse Helpless as Elephant Wears Path Around Kincaid," *Emporia Gazette* (Emporia, Kan.), Dec. 14, 1926, NP.

546 "Elephant at Large," *Sunday Leader* (Orange, Tex.), Dec. 13, 1925, PTH. Diamond was with the Monroe Bros. at the time. No show called "Morris Bros." is found in historical records.

547 E.g., "Former Trainer Gives Data on Elephant," *CSWL*, Oct. 18, 1929.

548 Ben Sweet handled Diamond when Diamond first arrived there. Bill Woodcock was the bull man, however, and had primary responsibility for Diamond (Walton, "The Story of Black Diamond").

549 "William Woodcock's letters #2"; Walton, "The Story of Black Diamond."

550 Walton, "The Story of Black Diamond." The distance from Sabinal to Oilton, as the crow flies, is 132 miles; as the elephant trods, a bit longer. The time and distance between the incidents make logical sense.

551 Bill Woodcock and others employed at the show when the Ben Sweet/Reed killing occurred were specific about the death, including the date. See Ronald B. Tobias, *Behemoth: The History of the Elephant in America* (New York: Harper Collins, 2013), 114, and other sources cited here.

552 "The Story of Black Diamond" says the sale was to Wilson Fulbright, not indicating they were related. Cauble had a nephew, James Wilson Fulbright, presumably the full name of the referenced buyer. Fulbright was also the brother-in-law of Curley Prickett.

553 Walton, "The Story of Black Diamond."

554 Tobias, *Behemoth*, 103-42.

555 *Behemoth*, 112.

556 *Behemoth*, 115.

557 Walton, "The Story of Black Diamond."

558 A bullhook is a goad used for elephant training.

559 Tobias, *Behemoth*, 117.

560 Walton, "The Story of Black Diamond."

561 "The Story of Black Diamond."

562 "The Story of Black Diamond."

563 Prickett's gravestone says he was born Sept. 10, 1889 (FAG), but his WWI draft registration says Sept 5, 1888 (Draft Reg. Cards, Homer Douglas Prickett, Anc.). The draft registration was more likely to have been self-reported than information on his gravestone. The draft registration was submitted in Medford, Or., June 5, 1917, and says he was then a cook for Foley & Burk Carnival Co., "En Route North."

564 Draft Reg. Cards, Homer Douglas Prickett, Anc.

565 "Former Trainer Gives Data."

566 "Black Diamond #1" (Oct. 19, 2007), www.buckslesw.blogspot.com.

567 Mrs. Fred Hodge, "Black Diamond," *Navarro County Scroll* (Navarro County Historical Society, 1969), 44.

568 "Outlaw Elephant 'Taken for Ride' By His Mates: 'Put on Spot' by Friends," *CSWL*, Oct. 18, 1929.

569 "Former Trainer Gives Data." Prickett's wife, according to the birth record of a son born in 1927, was Ira Fulbright, daughter of Thomas Wilson Fulbright and Lava Eva Cauble. Ira's mother was a half-sister of Albert M. Cauble. Ira's brother was James Wilson Fulbright. In 1931, Ira was presumably divorced and remarried when she gave birth to a child with Paul Ponder. One source said Prickett and Donohoo were married, but it is one, isolated, unverified report.

570 FAG.

571 "Funeral of Victim of Mad Elephant is Buried Here Monday: Mrs. Eva Donohoe [sic] Died Shortly After Attack by Beast Saturday," *CSWL*, Oct. 15, 1929.

572 Eva's father, Lafayette Ebenezer Speed (1848-1914), was a first cousin, once removed, of George Washington Speed (1846-1942). G.W. Speed's father was James Monroe Speed, who was the son of William Wages Speed Sr.; L.E. Speed's father was Felix Washington Speed, son of William Wages Speed, Jr., son of William Wages Speed Sr. Brothers George Washington Speed and Benjamin Franklin Speed made their homes in Navarro County, but other siblings and their parents did not come to Texas. L.E. Speed's father, Felix W. Speed, did immigrate to Texas (Chuck Speed, "Descendants of Descendants of William Speed," http://chuckspeed.com/speed.ged).

573 Wikipedia's "Randall County, Texas" entry; Richard Clarke Randall, "Dr. John Leonard Randal (TX State Senator)," *Bull–Randall Family Genealogy Wiki*, www.bull-randall.com/doku.php?id=john_leonard_randal.

574 Hodge, "Black Diamond," 44. Mrs. Hodge, as she states in the article, was Eva's first cousin. Her husband, Fred Pannill Hodge, was a nephew of Dr. H.F. Witherspoon (Chapter 21) through the doctor's first wife.

575 *HP*, July 7, 1921.

576 "Funeral of Victim of Mad Elephant."

577 *HP*, Oct 30, 1923 (advertisement to rent her Houston house, giving her contact address as Shoestring Plantation); Hodge, "Black Diamond," 44.

578 The Sorosis Club was a popular women's literary club started in 1886 in New York City.

579 "The Sorosis Club," *HP*, Apr. 9, 1922. The original paper (and photographs) presented by Mrs. Donohoo could not be located. The quoted paper was written as a faux press interview of a writer.

580 1850 Census, Covington Cty., Miss., for Ebenezer L. Speed, age two, son of F.W. Speed; 1850 Census, San Augustine Cty., Tex., for Mary Randal, age thirteen, daughter of Leonard Randal. Later census records confirm the age difference (1870 Census, San Augustine Cty.; 1880 Census, Bastrop Cty., Tex.).

581 A military order to enforce and publicize emancipation was issued in Texas by the Union-led state government on June 19, 1865, now celebrated as a Texas state holiday called Juneteenth. The holiday has received increasing recognition in other states.

582 1860 U.S. Federal Census Slave Schedule, East Texas Genealogical Society Computer Interest Group, Harry Thompson, transcriber, from National Archives and Records Administration Roll N, M653-1312, files.usgwarchives.net/tx/smith/census/1860/1860sp31.txt.

583 *Memorial*, 796-97 (identifies the early Speed family as large slave owners); 1860 U.S. Federal Census Slave Schedule, Smith and Covington Counties, Miss., Anc.

584 1900 Census, Hale Cty., Tex.; *Canyon City* (Tex.) *News*, June 10, 1904, NP (Will Donohoo died).

585 1910 Census, Houston, Tex., for D.H. Skinner; "Sixty-first District Court," *HP*, Apr. 5, 1908.

586 Several articles about Donohoo following the mauling state she worked for the *Post*, as does the 1969 *Scroll* article by her cousin, Mrs. Hodge, but no independent confirmation could be located, despite extensive review of archived copies of the *Post*.

587 Tobias, *Behemoth*, 118.

588 Marriage cert., "Black Diamond" vertical file, Corsicana Public Library; "District Clerk's Office," *Sun*, Jan. 18, 1927 (divorce notice). Buck Griffin was a widower with several children when he married Donohoo. A popular and prominent citizen of Navarro County, Griffin was killed in a car accident in 1936, aged seventy ("Prominent Farmer Killed When Auto Crashed Off Road: Woman Companion Also Reported be in [sic] Critical Condition," *Sun*, June 17, 1936).

589 "Elephant is Ordered Killed: Huge Beast That Killed Woman in Corsicana to Die: Mandate of Circus Head to be Carried Out Tuesday or Wednesday," *CSWL*, Oct. 15, 1929.

590 Associated Press, "6 Elephants to Execute Huge Killer: Three on Each End Chain Will Throttle Big Black Diamond," *Eagle* (Bryan, Tex.), Oct. 14, 1929, NP.

591 Tobias, *Behemoth*, 120.

592 References differ on the number of bullets shot into Diamond, e.g. 50 bullets ("Killer Elephant was Killed Near Kenedy Wednesday: Grave for Giant Pachyderm Prepared: Death Parade is Dramatic," *CSWL*, Oct. 18, 1929); 155 shots (Hodge, "Black Diamond," 46); more than 170 rounds (George "Slim" Lewis and Byron Fish, *I Loved Rogues* (Superior Publ. Co., 1978), 47-48). The contemporary newspaper account likely is most accurate.

593 "Killer Elephant was Killed." Jack O'Grady, when informed Diamond would need to be killed, was "broken hearted" (*I Loved Rogues*, 46).

594 "Former Trainer Deeply Affected As Diamond Dies," *CSWL*, Oct. 18, 1929.

595 "Outlaw Elephant 'Taken for Ride' By His Mates: 'Put on Spot' by Friends," *CSWL*, Oct. 18, 1929. The head was displayed for a period of time at the museum (Lewis and Fish, *I Loved Rogues*, 50; Walton, "The Story of Black Diamond"). On its hundredth anniversary, the museum posted a photograph of the head (http://blog.hmns.org/2009/05/100-years-100-objects-black-diamond/).

596 Joe Holley, "88-Year-Old Recalls 1929 Elephant Rampage in Corsicana," *Houston Chronicle*, Sept. 13, 2013, http://www.houstonchronicle.com/news/columnists/native-texan/article/88-year-old-recalls-1929-elephant-rampage-in-4795724.php.

597 Walton, "The Story of Black Diamond." O'Grady was the handler who gave Prickett permission to walk Black Diamond to the fairgrounds. According to Slim Lewis, "after Diamond died, Jack began to change. He became moody and quarreled with others on the show. He broke up with his beautiful equestrian wife, Dixie. After a short time he left the circus, and I didn't see him again until we were thrown together while handling the Mighty Tusko." (Lewis and Fish, *I Loved Rogues*, 47). O'Grady was shot and killed on Oct. 25, 1936 in a bar in Bryan ("Once Handler of Black Diamond is Slain in Bryan," *CSWL*, Oct 27, 1936).

598 "The Story of Black Diamond."

599 One scientist likened it to "a state of elevated testosterone" (Caitlin O'Connell, quoted in Simon Worrall, "Why Elephants are as Ritualistic and Violent as the Mafia," *National Geographic*, Apr. 19, 2015, https://news.nationalgeographic.com/2015/04/150419-ngbooktalk-elephant-behavior-rituals-animals-africa/).

600 Charles Siebert, "An Elephant Crackup?," *New York Times Magazine* (Oct. 6, 2006), www.NYTimes.com.

601 Tobias, *Behemoth*, 112.

602 "Ringling Bros. and Barnum & Bailey Circus," https://www.ringling.com (retrieved Sept. 16, 2017).

## 23. The Real Mystery

603 Even the early chapters and descriptions of the legend in this book repeated this error.

604 There were several newspapers in Corsicana in 1883, but no issues from any of those titles are known to still exist (see Chapter 6).

605 A search of every issue of a year's worth of newspaper in their original, paper format would be a sizeable, but not impossible, undertaking. It would require looking at thousands of pages of newsprint. On microform, either microfilm or microfiche, intermediate media between paper and digital, a review would have been much more difficult because of the reduced legibility of machine-viewed images, the need to manually move viewing machines in order to view different areas of each page, and the manual task of scrolling from each page to the next.

606 The gravestone as it exists must have served as a stern warning for adventurous children, then and even now, and wouldn't have a deterrent effect if it had a normal inscription. An epitaph that included his name, inscribed above his dangerous profession, however, would have provided the same beneficial service for parents.

## 24. Hebrews and Shebrews

607 Additional evidence of Jewish involvement in the town's fraternal organizations, besides the early Masonic records discussed in Chapter 4, is found in the front-page listings of *Morrison & Fourmy's General Directory of Corsicana, 1898-1899*. Rube Freedman, Louis Polasky, and David Deutschner are officers of Masonic lodges; Joseph Levy is "chaplain" of the United Benevolent Association of Texas lodge; Julius W. Friedlander was "dictator" of the Knights of Honor and president of the U.S National Aid Association; and Deutschner was "warden" and Louis Cohen "sentry," Order of Chosen Friends. (City Directories, Waco (sic), Tex., Anc.)

608 The Ennis National Bank was organized April 30, 1883. J. Baldridge (presumably James Baldridge, Pete Freeman's son-in-law) was president in 1893. Among the directors that year were L. Cerf, P. Freeman, I. Cerf, and Baldridge (*A Memorial and Biographical History of Ellis County* (Lewis Publ. Co., 1892), 196).

609 Texas Marriages (indexes), Anc. (abstracted as "Philip Truman").

610 "Conversion and Marriage," *GDN*, Sept. 15, 1874. The same story was also published in the *American Israelite*, Oct. 2, 1874, NP.

611 Bertha Ashberry (she was divorced from her first husband, Sol Lewis), Henrietta Sellers, Lillian Henry, and Genevieve Baldridge (1900 Census, Ellis Cty., Tex.; gravestones at Myrtle Cemetery, Ennis, Tex., visited Oct. 31, 2019).

612 The earliest-dated Jewish gravestone there is Sammie Pizer, died May 31, 1893 (Myrtle Cemetery).

613 "Baby Freeman" was born and died July 1, 1895 (Myrtle Cemetery).

614 Esther maybe lived in Corsicana at the time Rope Walker fell. Although she resided in Flint in 1880, with her brother Alex, her future husband Jacob Blumrosen was single and a boarder with the Freeman family in Ennis at that time (1880 Census). (This is the only known connection between the Freeman and Freedman families, investigated because of the similarity in their names.) Jacob and Esther were married Oct. 14, 1883 in Navarro County (Texas County Marriages, abstracts, LDS).

Alex visited his brother S.S. Freedman in Corsicana in 1885, on his way to New Orleans, so he must have moved to Corsicana sometime after that ("Corsicana Cullings," *DDH*, Feb. 8, 1885, GB).

615 "Appointed Chairman," *DMN*, Mar. 1, 1897.

616 The initial monument committee included Chief R. Freedman as chairman, I.N. Cerf as 2nd assistant chief, and others. Names inscribed on the hexagonal base are those of firemen "called to their final reward" ("Monument Will be Unveiled: Handsome Shaft Dedicated to Chief Freedman, Deceased," *Sun*, July 19, 1918).

617 "Monument Will be Unveiled."

618 From a speech by Judge J.H. Woods ("Fireman's Monument Unveiled Yesterday: Memorial Dedicated to Deceased Chief Rube Freedman and All Deceased Firemen of Corsicana," *Sun*, June 16, 1919).

619 From a speech by Judge Hawkins Scarborough ("Fireman's Monument Unveiled Yesterday").

620 "Firemen Had Great Time: Officers Elected and a Sumptuous Spread Enjoyed," *Sun*, Jan. 17, 1918. Levy was one of Corsicana's Jewish residents at the time Rope Walker fell.

621 "Widow of Advisor to Gov. Hogg Dies," *DMN*, Aug. 6, 1941. The earliest reference to Freedman as "Colonel" was May, 1891 ("The Whirl of Society," *DMN*, May 25, 1891 (Frank family reunion)); see also "Gov. Hogg at Corsicana," *DMN*, Dec. 8, 1893 (Governor's tour of orphanage with Col. Freedman and others). In 1882, Freedman was a Navarro County delegate to the State's Democratic convention ("John Ireland: The Sage of Seguin Nominated for Governor by Acclamation," *GDN* (convention supplement), July 20, 1882, NP).

622 "Corsicana," *Dallas Daily News*, Oct. 24, 1885, GB. Other Finance Committee members were James Garitty and C.W. Jester. A few years later, Freedman was elected a director of the Navarro Fair Association, serving with a dozen leading Corsicana community leaders ("Corsicana Determined That the Fair Shall Go On," *DMN*, Mar. 19, 1889).

623 The land trust was incorporated on May 3, 1888, by S.S. and Rube Freedman, Mayor Neblett, and Judge Simkins ("Governmental," *Austin Weekly Statesman*, May 3, 1888, NP).

624 E.g., *Dallas Weekly Herald*, July 28, 1881, GB. R. Freedman & Co. won a long-running lawsuit of an unspecified nature against Stillman H. Russell for $3,400.

625 "Big Damage Suit on Trial," *DMN*, June 26, 1897. He won $2,250 ("Awarded Damages," *Fort Worth Morning Register*, June 29, 1897, GB).

626 "Corsicana Budget: Sidewalk Ordinance," *DMN*, Sept. 13, 1891; "Decided Against Corsicana," *FWG*, Nov. 29, 1891.

627 "To the Ex-Mayor and Circus Rider," *Corsicana Daily Courier*, July 25, 1888, PTH. The instigating original is from an unavailable issue of the paper. Whatever the source of the discord, it was resolved by 1890 when Neblett, chairman at the County Democratic Convention, appointed Freedman as one of three to escort him to the chair for proceedings ("County Democratic Convention: Enthusiasm, Harmony, Unity," *Corsicana Daily Courier*, July 19, 1890, PTH).

628 According to his fading gravestone, Jacob Blumrosen was born Dec. 28, 1849 and died Jan. 9, 1893. The cemetery record book says he was born in 1840, probably because the gravestone inscription was misread. He is probably the "Jankiel Blumrozen" (Jankel is a common Yiddish variation of Jacob) who was born in Suwalki, Poland in 1849, according to an abstracted birth record (Jewish Records Indexing-Poland, http://jri-poland.org/index.htm).

629 *DMN*, Sept. 26 & 29, 1897.

630 Probate Minutes, Vol. 46, pp. 238-48, in Texas Wills and Probate Records, Navarro Cty., for Alex Freedman (probate dated Mar. 14, 1925), Anc.

631 "Warranty Deeds," *Sun*, May 16, 1928 ("Alex Freedman to Miss Frankie Freedman, Lot 18, Block 33, and Lot 1, Block 60, Corsicana. $10 and other considerations.").

632 See Supplement III. Her birthdate is approximately 1827, based on the 1870 Census (Livingston, Polk Cty., Tex.), which gives her age as forty-two. Her gravestone states she was fifty-one when she died in 1883, which would make her birth date about 1832. Such discrepancies, typical for women, are commonplace. The earliest historical records give her name as Henrietta, and in later records she was Harriett or "Hattie." One grandchild who might have been named for her was Harriett (Barnaby) Moore.

Several online family trees and Navarro County's Rootsweb obituary listings for Harriett and Isaac Rich and their children give Harriett's maiden name as "De Pass." The original source of *De Pass* as her family name may be the death certificate of Harriett's daughter, Barbara (Rich) Barnaby, where the informant was Barbara's daughter, Sally Barnaby, who lived with her mother. The certificate has the exactly correct date and place of birth of Barbara (it agrees with Barbara's New

Orleans birth certificate), evidence that Sally did have accurate knowledge of her mother's family history. The certificate says Barbara Barnaby's mother was "Harriette De Pass," born in France, but this fact is contradicted by several birth record abstracts, for Barbara and her siblings, which state that Harriett's maiden name was Hart, or, in one case, Hardt (see references cited at note 637). It could be that "De Pass," a surname commonly carried by Jewish families, is in some other way a part of the Rich family tree—maybe the maiden name of the mother of Isaac or Harriett, and Sally was mistaken in this particular aspect of the Rich family history.

633 Isaac's birth date is based on the 1870 federal census, which reports him as forty-four years old (1870 Census, Livingston, Polk Cty., Tex.). The 1900 census lists him as born in June, 1830 (1900 Census, Harris Cty., Tex., Precinct 8, for Isaac Rich).

634 New Orleans, La. Birth Records Index, Anc., for Salomon Rich. Parents are listed as Isaac Rich and Rebecca Peizer. See note 636 as to why Charles Rich is believed to be the same as Salomon Rich of New Orleans. His death date is from the Hebrew Cemetery record book. See also Supplement III.

635 1880 Census, Navarro Cty., Enumeration Dist. 129, for "Ivey" (sic) and "Mattie" (sic) Rich. The other children listed on that census, it says, were born in Louisiana.

636 Charles was eighteen when recorded with the family in the 1870 census, on Aug. 30 (1870 Census, Livingston, Polk Cty., Tex.). He was recorded there as "Charles S.," the only one of the seven children in that record showing a middle initial, apparently because he was born as "Salomon." "Salomon Rich" was born June 3, 1852 (making him the correct age to be Charles) to Isaac Rich and Rebecca Peizer (New Orleans, La. Birth Records Index, Anc.). Isaac and Harriett were licensed for marriage on May 18, 1855 (Louisiana Parish Marriages, LDS), so their oldest child in the 1870 census, Charles, at eighteen, was born before they were married, which makes the case that Isaac was previously married, and according to New Orleans records, to "Rebecca Peizer."

"Regina" was also born to Isaac and Rebecca (New Orleans, La. Birth Records Index, born Dec. 30, 1853, Anc. (parents listed as Isaac Retch and Rebecca Pieser)). Notwithstanding some predictable variations in spelling, these appear to be the same parents as those of Salomon (i.e., Charles) Rich.

637 Morris, born May 20, 1857 (New Orleans, La. Birth Record Index, for Moritz Reich, Anc.); Sally, Nov. 1859 (New Orleans, La. Birth Record Index, for Sarah Rich; 1900 Census, Navarro Cty., Precinct 1, for Sally Butler); Caroline "Carrie," Aug. 1861 (1900 Census, Navarro Cty., Precinct 8, for Carrie King); Benjamin R., Oct. 5, 1863 (New Orleans, La. Birth Record Index, for Bernard Reich, Anc.); Barbara, Sept. 30, 1865 (New Orleans, La. Birth Record Index, for Babette Rich, Anc.); Nathan R., Feb. 1868 (1900 Census, Harris Cty., Tex., Precinct 8, for N.R. Rich); and Abraham C., Aug. 9, 1871 (Tex. Death Cert., Houston, died Nov. 27, 1918, for A.C. Rich, Anc.).

638 Sally married Edmund Bradley Lockett, and later Henry Butler. She had one son by Lockett and three daughters by Butler (1900 Census). Carrie was married for the first time in 1881. She had six children of her own, plus stepchildren (1900 Census). See Chapter 28 for more about Carrie. Ben married Mary Barnaby, who had a child from her prior marriage, and no children were born of their union. Barbara married Jefferson Davis Barnaby of Corsicana. They had at least six children who survived to maturity and many descendants who stayed in, or close to, Corsicana (1900 Census and 1910 Census). Mary (Barnaby) Rich and Jefferson Davis Barnaby were the children of John Thompson and Jennette "Nettie" Nancy (Hammond) Barnaby, old-time Navarro County settlers. In other words, two siblings married two siblings.

It's possible that Regina married a Jewish man, but nothing is known about her beyond what is shown on her birth record. Another possible exception is Carrie, who married August Blum, who is presumed to have been Jewish. See Chapter 28 for more information about Carrie and August. Charles, it seems, was never married.

639 Regina's place of burial could not be determined.

640 1880 Census, Navarro Cty., E.D. 129.

641 Charles was in prison from Apr. 8, 1871 until Mar. 15, 1873, when Gov. Davis pardoned him (1873 Register of Convicts, Texas State Penitentiary, Huntsville, Walker Cty., Tex., Anc.). At the start of his sentence he was eighteen years old.

642 *Corsicana Democrat and Truth*, Sept 17, 1908, RWeb (transcribed obituary submitted by Karen Rost).

643 "Bank's Oldest Depositors Recount Lively History," *Sun*, May 13, 1976.

644 The other building is 102 N. Beaton.

645 "Bank's Oldest Depositors."

646 See Chapter 26.

647 Nearly all biographies in these types of books are supplied by the subjects themselves.

648 The Hebrew word, which transliterates to "zedek" or "tzedek," was historically applied to men born into the priestly class, the *Kohens*, and usually takes the form of "Kohen haTZedek" (righteous priest). Those who belong to the group trace their male lineage back to biblical Aaron, the first High Priest of the Israelites and brother of Moses. The contraction of this title, "K'tz," became the common Jewish surname *Katz*. The very common Jewish surname "Cohen" (and variants) also indicates descent from Aaron. Of course, a surname alone is no guarantee a man was a *Kohen*. In recent years, DNA tests have identified genetic markers which confirm Aaronic descent.

649 Not noted in Zadek's 1893 biography is that Butler was a notorious anti-Semite (Wikipedia's "Benjamin Butler" entry).

650 *Memorial*, 714.

651 *Memorial*, 714.

652 *Memorial*, 714.

653 Isaac Baum served as postmaster beginning in 1876, preceding Zadek (Appointments of U.S. Postmasters, Anc.).

654 "Bismark Zadek Has Become Tired of German Cognomen," *Sun*, Dec. 11, 1918.

655 FAG, Oakwood Cemetery. Nothing suggests that the then-trustees of the Hebrew Cemetery refused to have Zadek buried in their cemetery.

656 Oscar Zadek was a Mobile, Alabama jeweler known as Emil Zadek.

## 25. The Jewish Church

657 Most rabbis were in Corsicana for only a year or two. A few of the Agudas Achim rabbis served the congregation for more than a dozen years. Rabbis Joseph and Spear never left; they died in Corsicana and were buried in the Hebrew Cemetery.

658 They also attended meetings of the Corsicana Hebrew Cemetery Association (Compiled minutes, Corsicana Hebrew Cemetery Association (1918-1956), courtesy CHCA ("Minutes")). The Minutes record Rabbi Stolz's attendance at a May 11, 1919 meeting and Rabbi Grey's attendance at a March 25, 1947 meeting.

659 See Chapter 10.

660 Most rabbis had one or more college degrees in addition to their rabbinical training. They were graduates of top European universities, like Zurich and Heidelberg, and many U.S. universities, including Harvard and Columbia. Several of them carried the title of "Dr." See Supplement II.

661 See Supplement II.

662 "The Righteous—In Memoriam," *Jewish Voice* (St. Louis, Mo.), June 10, 1904, NP.

## 26. Till Life Became a Legend of the Dead

663 The final line from Henry Wadsworth Longfellow, "The Jewish Cemetery at Newport" (1858).

664 The International Order of B'nai B'rith is a Jewish-operated charitable and social justice organization. Lodges were established in the earliest years of Jewish communities in Texas, other states, and internationally.

665 Cheryl Kempler, archivist, B'nai B'rith International, email correspondence with author, Mar. 27, 2020.

666 "Some Old Documents: Box Taken from Cornerstone of Old Court House Contains Relics," *Sun*, May 30, 1915. The 1915 article quotes a *Corsicana Daily Sun* article estimated to have been written in 1905. The earlier-referenced article listed the contents of the 1881 courthouse cornerstone, keepsakes which were removed when a newer courthouse was built.

667 Louis Schmier, Ed., *Reflections of Southern Jewry: The Letters of Charles Wessolowsky 1878-1879* (Mercer University Press, 1982) (hereinafter "*Wessolowsky*"), 112-13. Charles Wessolowsky arrived at Corsicana on Tuesday, May 27, 1879, which he noted was Shavuot (the Festival of Weeks, commemorating God's giving the Torah to the Israelites). His previous stop on his travels through Southern Jewish communities was Waco.

See also *American Israelite*, Oct. 12, 1877, listing newly elected lodge officers: D. Cerf, pres.; A. Fan, v.p.; M. Stern, secy.; D. Deut[s]chner, treas.; Jos. Baum, monitor; A. Cahn, ass. monitor; Jos. Aaron, warden; and S.S. Freedman, guardian. Wessolowsky's assessment comes shortly after a May 1, 1879 report from IOBB District Grand Lodge No. 7 (Memphis), published in the *American Israelite* on May 23, "Report of the Secretary of the Endowment," which includes criticism of the Corsicana lodge's egregious failure to remit district dues. Nine of Corsicana Lodge No. 275's twenty-five members had stopped paying their monthly dues, partly the cause of a district-wide fiscal emergency when the need to pay death benefits was highly elevated due to the yellow fever epidemic. The district directed the lodge to remove the nine members, which it did, although one member was reinstated, later. In this context, Wessolowsky's "full of life and debate" seems a euphemistic expression for infighting.

668 Courtesy L. Garner, daughter of James Cerf.

669 The Cemetery Association's founding year of 1875 is also stated in a "Directory of Local Organizations" in Cyrus Adler, Ed., *The American Jewish Year Book: 5661* (Phila: The Jewish Publication Society of America, 1900), 465, www.ajcarchives.org/AJC_Data/files/1900_ 1901_5_LocalOrgas.pdf (retrieved Jan. 30, 2019).

670 "The Trustees were given power to buy a small strip of land now in our possession belonging to the Catholic Cemetery…" (Minutes, 45, undated, ca. 1935-1940).

671 The spelling of *Deutschner* on the founders plaque mistakenly omitted the "S." It is spelled with an "S" on his gravestone and in other records.

672 Navarro Cty. Land Records, Vol. 38, Page 376.

673 RWeb, General History of List of Contents Navarro County Texas, "Navarro County Land Grants."

674 The dead men were buried in an area now marked by a Texas Historical Marker on Highway 31, about one mile west of Dawson (*Memorial*, 90-93).

675 "Deaths," *FWDG*, Oct. 18, 1890.

676 W.M. Love was one of the two men sent back to get a better compass, and thereby avoided the fight. Sources are inconsistent in identifying which white settler built the first house in Navarro County.

677 Should read "R.N. White," the first county court clerk in the county.

678 Mary Miller Affidavit (see note 286).

679 1860 Census, Corsicana, p. 3. Michael is discussed in Chapter 4. Other residents enumerated nearby were Loughridge, Croft, Kerr, etc., meaning that they all lived at the public square, around the courthouse.

680 Problems with cemetery record keeping persisted even after Ivan Rosenberg's 1952 completion of the association's record book. See Chapter 5; note 1089.

681 Minutes, examined courtesy of the CHCA.

682 Hebrew Cemetery chronology:

Dec. 1875 Purchase of cemetery land.

Mar. 19, 1877 First known burial: Leo Fox, son of Alexander and Bertha Fox. The second known death was Anna Wolf, on Apr. 13, 1878.

Oct. 1877 "The first recorded meeting was held in October 1877, when the association was formed, the founders being: Alex Fox, Aaron Shwarts, Dave Cerf, Louis Cerf, Edmond Raphael, Dave Deutchner (sic) and Adolph Zadek" (1951 CHCA Constitution and By-Laws booklet ("1951 CHCA booklet")).

1887 "The next available record is meeting held in 1887 showing membership to be the above founders and Mike O'Bright, Max H. London, M.N. Franks (sic), Louis Polasky, S.S. Freedman, and Louis Cohen" (1951 CHCA booklet). 1887 was considered the date when the CHCA was "organized," e.g., officers elected and rules of some nature established (letterhead on stationary of CHCA secretary, W.B. Levy, bearing a date of Sept. 26, 1951, Minutes, 59).

1887-1918 Max London was secretary of the CHCA starting in 1887, "from the beginning" (1951 CHCA booklet).

July 15, 1891 Ladies' Hebrew Cem. Assn. founded: Mrs. S.S. Freedman, pres.; Mrs. D. Deutschner, v.p.; Mrs. M. Cohen, secy.; Mrs. H.L. Newburgh, treas. A Committee on Cemetery Affairs consisted of: Mrs. L. Hirsch, Mrs. A. Goldman, Mrs. M.A. (sic) London, Mrs. M. Lehman, and Mrs. A. Schwarts (sic) ("Corsicana, Texas," *American Israelite*, July 27, 1891; *Morrison & Fourmy's General Directory of Corsicana, 1898-1899*, City Directories, Waco (sic), Tex., Anc.).

1899 Ladies' Hebrew Cem. Assn.: Mrs. S.S. Freedman, pres.; Mrs. U.P. Levy, v.p.; Mrs. Isaac Levy, treas.; Mrs. Abe Fox, secy. Thirty-six members (*The American Jewish Year Book: 5660*). In the 1900 *Year Book: 5661*, Mrs. Meyer Cohen is the new secretary and there are forty members.

1900 CHCA leaders are: R. Costa, pres.; Louis Cohen, v.p.; Louis Cerf, treas.; Louis Polasky, secy. Trustees are: M.N. Frank; J. Herman; U.P. Levi. Fourteen members (*The American Jewish Year Book: 5660*).

1904 "The next record [after the 1887 meeting] is minutes of meeting held on June 20, 1904, with Mose Levy, as President, M.H. London, Secretary, and Alex Fox, B. Marks, Albert Lustig, M. Hirsch, Trustees. Here it was decided to employ a Civil Engineer to lay out the cemetery in plots. Eighty-seven plots were designated. Prior to this time, spaces were known as Divisions A, B, C, D, E, F, G, and H, which were used as public burial spaces. The records show no private plots until 1904, when Plot #1 was given to M.H. London in recognition for past services… Prior to 1904 no dues were assessed. All finances came from donations and from collections taken up at Yom Kippur services. In 1904, dues were fixed at $.50/month" (1951 CHCA booklet).

May 1905 Shwarts Fountain installed (plaque inscription).

1907-1935 I.N. Cerf, president (1951 Cemetery Association booklet; "Resolution Adopted on Death I.N. Cerf," *CSWL*, June 27, 1935).

1919 Henrietta Newburg bequeaths $250 to the cemetery, which I.N. Cerf and his mother spend to create iron steps (Minutes, 6-9).

1923-1946 Ben Goldsmith, secretary and secretary-treasurer (John Sam Haslam's 1936 Rope Walker article (Chapter 8); 1951 CHCA booklet; "Funeral Rites for Ben Goldsmith Were Held Friday," *CSWL*, July 16, 1946).

1924-1951 In 1924, J.E. Miller hired as sexton with salary of twenty-five dollars per month and use of the dwelling house at the cemetery. "His work is to care for all cemetery grounds also to care for all graves that belonging to cemetery assn." Salary raised to forty dollars per month in 1941 and to ninety dollars in 1948. Shortly after the last raise it was noted that Mr. Miller's "attitude" was a problem, and in 1951 it was decided a new sexton was needed (Minutes, 19-20, 47, 55-58).

1931 Ben Rosenberg bequeaths $500 for care of "lots … in which I or my relations shall have an interest" (Minutes, 34).

1934 Cemetery map created (1951 CHCA booklet).

1940 (approx.) CHCA will "buy a small strip of land now in our possession belonging to the Catholic Cemetery" (Minutes, 45).

1943 Rachel (Flonacher) Cerf, widow of Louis Cerf, bequeaths $1,500 for upkeep of Cerf and Levy family plots ("Temple Beth El and IOOF Receive Bequests in Will," *Sun*, Sept. 7, 1943; Minutes, 51).

1944-1947 Joe Wolens, president ("Resolution," *Sun*, Feb. 8, 1947 (death of Joe Wolens)).

March 25, 1947 Annual dues raised from six dollars to nine dollars (Minutes, 53).

1947-1963 W.B. (Walbert) "Wally" Levy, secretary-treasurer ("Introduction to 1964 Constitution and By-Laws," from "Brief History of Jewish Community: Tour of Temple Beth El" (undated), papers of Sandra Palmer, Texas Jewish Historical Society Collection, Dolph Briscoe Archives, UT Austin, courtesy Goldring/Woldenberg Institute of Southern of Jewish Life).

Nov. 19, 1951 Revised constitution and by-laws are adopted, and together with a history of the CHCA are published in a booklet. A new map is created by Ivan Rosenberg and "work has begun on a Perpetual Internment Book, which will contain a family history record." Association leaders are: Ivan Rosenberg, pres.; M.L. Dreeben, v.p.; Wally Levy, secy.-treas. Trustees are: Ben Miller; Sydney Marks; Morris Ashendorf; and Aaron Samuels (1951 CHCA booklet; Minutes, 61).

1958 Association leaders are: Ivan Rosenberg, pres.; Wally Levy, secy. & perpetual record book keeper (Frank X. Tolbert, "Tragic Saga of a Rope Walker," *DMN*, July 20, 1958 (Chapter 7). Sometime after 1958 the record book was transferred from Wally Levy to his nephew, James Cerf, and subsequently to Irvin and Babbette Samuels.

1962 Mamie (Shwarts) Cerf leaves a bequest of $11,000 to the cemetery ("Local Cemetery Receives Trust," *Sun*, Feb. 7, 1962). Mamie Cerf died Feb. 2, 1962, in Ennis, leaving a $10,000 trust fund for the cemetery and $1,000 for repairs to the Shwarts fountain. A 1965 plaque on the fountain commemorates her love for her husband, Isadore Cerf. She was the daughter of CHCA founding member Aaron Shwarts, sister-in-law of Dave Cerf, Louis Cerf, and Edmond Raphael, also founding members of the association, and aunt of I.N. Cerf, Wally Levy, and James Cerf, longtime officers of the association.

<u>1968</u> Bernard Rosen, pres.; Jay Silverberg, secy. (Frank X. Tolbert, "A Better Memorial for 'Rope Walker'?," *DMN*, Feb. 26, 1968).

<u>2019</u> Babbette Samuels transferred record keeping duties to other CHCA officers.

Many other individuals made substantial contributions to the CHCA, in addition to those whose extraordinary dedication is highlighted in the preceding chronology, their names found throughout the association's compiled minutes, 1918-1956, and remembered here. Their known dates of involvement follow their name: Henry/Harry Kaufman, 1918-ca. 1940; Henry/Harry's brother-in-law, Isaac "Ike" Levy, 1922-1953; Ike and Ike's wife's double-niece's husband, Morris L. Dreeben, 1933-1953; George Daniels, 1941-1951; George's sister-in-law's father, Max L. Levine, 1919-1931; George's brother-in-law's brother, Gabe Goldberg, ca. 1940-1953; George's brother-in-law, Mose M. Miller, 1919-1935 (M.M. Miller's nephew's father-in-law was Ben Goldsmith); H. Rothkopf, 1919-1943; Ivan Rosenberg, 1923-1956; Sam D. Brooks, 1925-1948; and Sydney Marks, 1933-1951. Many others, not mentioned here, also made meaningful contributions, and their absence from this tribute is not meant to lessen their good will and efforts.

# 27. Gone and Forgotten

683 Given time, strength, cash, and patience, there will be a third book about Rope Walker.

684 See Supplement I.

685 See Supplement II.

686 See Supplement II. In 1909, Corsicana's B'nai B'rith lodge was reorganized (Cheryl Kemper, archivist, B'nai B'rith International, email correspondence with author, Mar. 27, 2020).

687 "A Brief History of the Corsicana Jewish Community," *Jewish Monitor*, Dec. 17, 1920, NP.

688 *Wessolowsky*, 112-13.

689 Rabbi Abraham Blum, an early leader in Galveston's Jewish community, travelled throughout Texas to establish Sunday schools (William M. Kramer and Reva Clar, "Rabbi Abraham Blum: From Alsace to New York By Way of Texas and California—Part I," *Western States Jewish Historical Quarterly* 12, no. 1 (Oct. 1979): 63-88). He was the first rabbi of Temple B'nai Israel, where the third rabbi, Henry Cohen, became the most famous and beloved rabbi in Texas history. Blum may have been related to the Galveston mercantile house of Leon & H. Blum (that Jewish family included Leon, Sylvain, and Joseph of Galveston, Hyman of Galveston and New York City, and Alexander also of New York). Rabbi Blum could even have been related to the Blums of Corsicana, but there is no evidence of these family connections. Blum, as previously mentioned, was a common Jewish name. Rabbi Blum was the rabbi who performed the conversion of Theodosio Rushing and her marriage to Philip Freeman (Chapter 24).

690 *Wessolowsky*, 113.

691 Wessolowsky visited Brenham shortly before Corsicana and found, except for the presence of a B'nai B'rith lodge, "matters pertaining to Judaism entirely neglected." He observed Jewish children attending a "'Christian' Sunday School." He railed against the mothers, especially, who he noted were indifferent that Jewish children "receive the most useful instruction that Jesus is the '*Savior of all mankind*'" (*Wessolowsky*, 85).

692 *Wessolowsky*, 112.

693 *Brenham* (Tex.) *Weekly Banner*, May 29, 1890, NP.

694 "Corsicana, Texas," *American Israelite*, July 27, 1891.

695 "Corsicana, Texas," *American Israelite*. According to another article about the event, the money "will be used to beautify the Jewish cemetery here" ("Society in Midsummer," *DMN*, July 27, 1891). The 1891 date is further confirmed in *The American Jewish Year Book: 5661*, 465.

696 See Supplement III.

697 An analysis to determine the extent to which gravestones in other cemeteries are missing key information was contemplated but would be extraordinarily difficult to execute. A preliminary and cursory examination was done using the spreadsheet of Jewish burials available from the Texas Jewish Historical Society's website in combination with searches on Find A Grave to look at selected

gravestones. That limited review did not find other gravestones with essential missing information, like those discussed here, but no conclusions could be drawn from that cursory analysis.

698 Unfortunately, no news story or other information about this child could be found. See Chapter 16; note 380.

699 Chapter 23.

700 Citing the Rope Walker burial as an example, *Pioneer Jews: A New Life in the Far West* noted, "Some funerals also made it clear that the general community expected Jews to be responsible for their destitute or itinerant coreligionists" (Harriet and Fred Rochlin (Boston: Houghton Mifflin Co., 1984), 204). The Rochlins wrote, "The city fathers, believing the man was a Jew, turned over his remains to the leaders of the Jewish Community for burial," a surprisingly accurate statement considering how little the authors would have known about his death. Based on the legend, a safer assumption would have been that the town's Jews had possession of his remains at his time of death. Just the same, the book also says, contrary to all sources available to the authors, that he died "in the early 1900s."

Other examples of the CHCA taking responsibility for the burial of indigents are found in the association's minutes. At a May 11, 1919 meeting, "The trustees were instructed to put headstones and inscriptions on the grave of Sam Gang and Mrs. Zeppora Caplan." At the Oct. 12 meeting, five months later, the trustees were given additional time. Sam Gang's listed date of death was Oct. 24, 1915, and Tsipora Caplan's listed date of death was Feb. 25, 1917. Both received very nice gravestones, properly engraved, but it took at least two-and-a-half years, in one case, and at least four years, in the other case, for them to get their gravestones.

701 "At time of death his father was reported to live in Ennis Texas – but later moved to Chicago."

702 Nothing is known about Morris Rosenbaum's birth or death dates. His designation in the cemetery record book as burial "105" does not pertain to his date of death, although the assigned numerical designations are otherwise used to indicate the chronological order of burials (Babbette Samuels, email correspondence with author, July 10, 2017).

703 Tex. Death Cert., Corsicana, for Louis Niveth, Anc. Niveth was a jeweler who lived in many Texas locations. His first name was misspelled on his gravestone.

## 28. Crushed

704 Chapters 12 and 13.

705 Chapter 13.

706 The Mallory and Allen building was on Beaton Street, near or at the southwest corner with 5th Ave., based on news articles about a fire in early 1884 which burned down the entire block on the west side of Beaton between Collin and White (5th Ave.) Streets ("Corsicana: Another Destructive Fire—Three Stores and Contents Burned," *FWDG*, Feb. 25, 1884; "Fire at Corsicana: Considerable Property Destroyed—Loss Estimated at $50,000," *GDN*, Feb. 25, 1884). One of the other stores burned down was J.P. Vance Drug, known to be located on that block (unpublished, undated photograph, courtesy R. Maxfield). Some articles referred to the building as the "Wilson Building," helping to determine its location ("Corsicana," *DDH*, Mar. 10, 1883, GB; "Corsicana," *DDH*, Mar. 27, 1883, GB; *Times* (Shreveport, La.), Feb. 27, 1884).

707 Marriage Cert., Navarro Cty., for August Blum and Mrs. M.A. Maynard, July 19, 1883 (courtesy S. Finn).

708 August Blum's first wife has not been identified. David King's petition for the guardianship of August's two daughters sheds some light on Blum's background. The older daughter, Matilda, says the petition, was the daughter of August and his first wife. August and his first wife were married in Germany, and she died after emigration. At the time of King's petition, R.B. Molloy was the appointed guardian of August Blum and Matilda had recently received a "substantial inheritance" from her maternal grandparents, who were in Germany. (Navarro County Probate, file G1016).

709 1880 Census, Corsicana.

710 Probate Files, Navarro Cty., Sept. Term, 1883, for Mary Ann Blum, pp. 206-11 (died Aug. 19, 1883), Anc.

711 Marriage Cert., Navarro Cty., of August Blum and Carrie Odaniel, Oct. 5, 1883 (courtesy S. Finn); Marriage Cert., Navarro Cty., of W.L. Odaniel and Carrie Rich, Jan. 12, 1881 (courtesy S. Finn).

712 S. Finn (great-granddaughter of August Blum), email correspondence with author, 2017. At some point, the Maynard children had their mother's body removed from a plot Blum had selected and brought to their family farm for burial. Mary Ann (Maynard) Blum filed a codicil which prevented her estate from going to Blum (Probate Files, for Mary Ann Blum).

713 S. Finn, interview with author, 2017.

714 Marriage Cert., Corsicana, of D. King and Carrie Blum, Aug. 11, 1890 (courtesy S. Finn).

715 Tex. Death Certs., for Mrs. Dave King, Anc.

716 Following business failures, Blum was jailed on four indictments: three counts of "swindling" and one count of perjury. Carrie and her father Isaac were indicted as well ("Corsicana: Work of the Grand Jury—Criminal Notes, Etc.," *Galveston Daily News*, Jan. 10, 1886, PTH). R.P. Goodman alleged that after he bought Blum's bakery, Blum incurred business expenses on the bakery's account ("Dallas: Blum Case," *Galveston Daily News*, Jan. 29, 1886, PTH). Meanwhile, Isaac Baum and M. Cohen foreclosed on certain debt owed by August Blum and sought monetary damages ("Corsicana," *DMN*, Feb. 27, 1886). On appeal, the convictions for swindling were reversed ("Corsicana: Acquitted of a Charge of Swindling," *DMN*, Mar. 31, 1886).

717 Property records show that Louis, August, and Charles Blum all had property interests in the same block in Corsicana's commercial district (courtesy S. Finn).

718 Charles was a saloon keeper in 1873 (*Logan's Railway Business Directory* (A.L. Logan & Co., 1873), 96, Archive.org/stream/logansrailwaybus00loga.) and ran a merchandising house on lower Beaton Street until 1883, when it burned down ("Corsicana," *Austin Weekly Statesman*, Oct. 4, 1883, NP).

719 "Deaths," *FWDG*, Sept. 15, 1889.

720 Navarro Cty. Probate, file no. 976 (1890).

721 FAG, Oakwood Cemetery, Corsicana.

722 See note 717.

723 "German Kills Himself," *Eagle* (Bryan, Tex.), Jan. 29, 1902, NP.

724 "Corsicana Local Occurrences," *DMN*, June 29, 1886. The disposition of the countersuit against Blum is not known.

725 *DMN*, Dec. 26, 1893.

726 "Corsicana," *Austin Weekly Statesman*, Oct. 4, 1883, NP (Oct. 1 fire on Beaton Street).

727 August Blum was buried in an unmarked grave at the asylum (S. Finn, interview). Information about his institutionalization and eventual death were recorded on a page kept by the hospital: he was committed due to an attack of mania, type A, which occurred on Sept. 20, 1889 (the month after Carrie remarried); he was committed by order of the Navarro County Court; the contact for the hospital was David King, Esq. (Carrie's new husband). A note says: "In case of serious illness or death please communicate with James V. Bracken, 2843 Franklin Ave., St. Louis, Mo. [Matilda's first husband] and also [David King] as it is their desire to have his remains taken to Corsicana and buried beside his wife." Another note, dated June 20, 1914, lists another correspondent: Mrs. Mary Bracken, 1932 Washington St., St. Louis, Mo., possibly Matilda except that Matilda had remarried by then to Charles Sturdevant. (Courtesy S. Finn; 1910 Census, Ill., Clark Cty., Casey Ward 1 for Charles and Matilda Sturdevant.)

728 Navarro Cty., Tex. probate records, files G1005; G1016; P653; P976; P1065. The earliest request for a legal guardianship was from Carrie's newest husband for the estate of August Blum, adjudged a lunatic. Not from the House of Israel, David King lived, lived and endured, until 1931.

729 "Miss Eva Britton," *Macon Telegraph*, Sept. 21, 1883, GB. The outcome of the case could not be determined.

730 The American Antiquarian Society holds five issues: Vol. 3, Nos. 6-8 (May, July & Aug., 1882) and Vol. 4, Nos. 5 & 7 (May & Sept., 1883). Issue No. 2 was dated Dec., 1879 ("Personal and Journalistic," *Wilmington* (N.C.) *Morning Star*, Dec. 10, 1879, NP).

731 There was nothing in the May 1883 issue about Berg, or any other news event, and the whereabouts of March and April 1883 issues, if they ever existed, is unknown.

732 "A Giddy Girl: The Career of Eva Britton alias Lillian Markham," *Cleveland Plain Dealer*, Dec. 23, 1884, GB. According to the two articles reproduced here she was eleven in 1880 and

eighteen in 1884–quite a discrepancy. She was born in or near 1868 because on June 7, 1870, she was two years old (1870 Census, Charlotte, N.C., for J. Evans Britton and family). Therefore, she was probably fourteen or fifteen when she visited Corsicana, in 1883.

## 29. The Redemption of Billy Powers

733 *AMB1*, 110-12. Based on the voice of the narrator of the piece, the author is likely Louisa (Kerr) Mulkey.

734 Football is said to be the official religion of Texas, particularly Friday night high school football.

735 See Chapter 21.

736 *Budget*, as used by Mulkey, is an archaic term meaning a collection of varied items.

737 *Budget No. 1* would have been widely read in Corsicana. Sales of Mulkey's first *Budget* raised $3,100 for the orphanage (*AMB2*, "Introduction"). The publication cost was estimated at $600 ("Mulkey at Waxahachie: His Meetings There Resulted in Much Good and Numerous Conversions Were Made," *DMN*, July 13, 1897). If it was priced at fifty cents per copy—the price marked on the cover of *AMB2*—and all proceeds above the book's costs were given to the orphanage, then 7,400 copies of *AMB1* were sold. It probably sold best in Corsicana, Navarro County, and other surrounding areas, certainly in the hundreds, and probably in the thousands.

738 *AMB1*, 178.

739 "Fireman's Monument Unveiled Yesterday," *Sun*, June 16, 1919. See *Love*, 135 & 152-53, discussing the acquisition of a water source for downtown merchants, coordinated by Cerf, Raphael, Fox, and others.

740 *AMB1*, 89.

741 *AMB1*, 53. Mulkey said he would "preach to the colored folks wherever an opportunity presented itself" ("Waxahachie Budget: Evangelist Mulkey's Sermon," *DMN*, July 11, 1897).

## 30. The Good, the Bad, and the Ugly Truth

742 "Missing," *Times-Picayune* (New Orleans), Apr. 12, 1882, NP. No details of the alleged assault beyond this one article are known.

743 "Lost by Fire: A Steamboat Burned and Thirty-Five Lives Reported Lost," *Brooklyn Eagle*, Mar. 30, 1882, NP; "Fire and Death: Burning of the Steamer Golden City," *Cincinnati Enquirer*, Mar. 31, 1882, NP.

744 "Fire and Death" has the most extensive list of passengers and a thorough report of the disaster. The original manifest was lost in the fire.

745 More information about "R. Dietel" could not be located.

746 "Tight Ropers," *Times-Picayune* (New Orleans), Feb. 7, 1882, NP.

747 "First Recorder's Court," *Times-Democrat* (New Orleans), Feb. 12, 1882, NP. Further details are not known, including the connection, if any, between the grand larceny charges and the assault charges.

748 It is almost as if the short newspaper article referring to an assault on C.M. Gilley should have referred instead to the Hackett theft. Unresolved.

749 See Chapter 18.

750 "Professor D. Howse," *Vicksburg Herald*, Mar. 28, 1882, NP. The *Golden City* picked up Stowe's menagerie at Vidalia on March 27 ("Miscellaneous," *Natchez Democrat*, Mar. 28, 1882, NP).

751 See notices of his performances at Fort Worth and Dallas in Chapter 13. News reports of his fall and death which included his name used "De Houne," but that was not, presumably, something he would have had a say in. He had performed for years as Prof. De Houne, not Prof. Berg, so stories written about him at the time he fell would have naturally used "De Houne."

752 See Chapter 28.

753 See Chapter 12.

754 A potential, tantalizing plot twist. If Rope Walker did not actually die in Corsicana, it would require something of a conspiracy. At a minimum, someone would have had to say he died, let's say Mulkey, who ran the hospital, and someone would have had to say he was buried—someone from the Jewish community. If someone had put up a gravestone with Rope Walker's real name, they

could be accused of perpetuating a fraud on the New Orleans authorities. It is a wholly unsubstantiated theory and therefore relegated to a note at the back of this book, but it is a rational explanation for why his well-known name was not put on his gravestone.

755 Corsicana garnered national fame for something else, in 2020, when the Netflix docuseries "Cheer," the deeply emotional saga about Navarro College's championship cheerleading squad's national competition, tumbled into American living rooms.

756 Wikipedia's "Collin Street Bakery" entry.

757 "Collin Street Bakery," https://www.collinstreet.com/about_us; "Corsicana Bakery's Wares Sell Like Fruitcakes," *DMN*, Dec. 5, 1982.

758 Rachel Blidner, "Fruitcake Executive Sentenced to 10 Years for Embezzling $16.7 Million in Texas," *New York Daily News*, Sept. 17, 2015, http://www.nydailynews.com/news/crime/fruitcake-executive-sentenced-embezzling-16-7-million-article-1.2364321.

759 The assets which he then held included "four vehicles, including a 2005 Lexus SC, a 2010 Mercedes Benz CL550, a 2013 GMC Yukon Denali, and a 2013 BMW X53 (having an approximate value of $150,000); 532 luxury items, including forty-one bracelets, fifteen pairs of cufflinks, twenty-one pairs of earrings, sixteen furs, sixty-one handbags, forty-five necklaces, nine sets of pearls, fifty-five rings, and ninety-eight watches (having an approximate value of $3.5 million); $580,754.90 in cash; a wine collection (having an approximate value of $50,000); and a Steinway electronic piano (having a value of $58,500)" ("Update: Sandy Jenkins Gets 10 Years," *Corsicana Daily Sun*, Sept. 16, 2015, http://www.corsicanadailysun.com/news/update-sandy-jenkins-gets-years-prison-probation-for-wife-kay/article_ae1a73b0-5c9d-11e5-a527-9baff4805c5f.html).

760 Katy Vine, "Just Desserts," *Texas Monthly*, Jan. 2016, https://www.texasmonthly.com/articles/just-desserts/, refers to a Mar. 27, 2014 article in the *Corsicana Daily Sun*.

761 From Abe Mulkey's "Restitution" sermon (*AMB2*, 74).

762 Wikipedia's "Barbette (performer)," entry, quoting Francis Steegmuller, "An Angel, A Flower, A Bird," *New Yorker*, Sept. 27, 1969 (quoting Jean Cocteau, "Le Numéro Barbette" (1980)).

# 31. A True Legend

763 *One Foot Over Main Street* follows De Houne's career from his earliest performance through his final curtain call in Corsicana. A sampling of those performances is shown in Chapters 12, 13, and 17 (projected date of publication, 2021).

764 *Semi-Weekly Wisconsin*, July 14, 1869, NP.

765 Regular Army Enlistment Papers, 17981894, National Archives and Records Administration, RG 94, No. 91.

766 "Going as They Please on One Leg," *Paterson Daily Guardian*, May 15, 1880, Fulton History, http://www.fultonhistory.com/Fulton.html. The one-legged men race is covered in more detail in *One Foot Over Main Street*.

767 "The One-Legged Tournament," *Paterson Daily Press*, May 15, 1880, Google News, https://news.google.com/newspapers?nid=aUOtug7Ojf8C.

768 Courtesy Meigs Cty. Hist. Soc., imprinted "Loomis Studios." Loomis Studios was run by photographer Delancey A. Loomis, of Fredonia, Kan., who arrived there in 1878 ("Lost Gallery: Cabinet Card Photographers of the 19th Century - L -," https://lostgallery.blogspot.com/2016/12/cabinet-card-photographers-of-19thl.html (retrieved Dec. 10, 2017); Rootsweb message boards, Loomis, "Re: Loomis Photography," Jan. 4, 2004). De Houne spent two or three months performing in the Kansas City area in the fall of 1878, when Loomis's practice there was getting started. It is extraordinarily unlikely this is a photograph of Moses Berg because it was picked from many hundreds of random nineteenth-century photographs reviewed solely to approximate what Rope Walker might have looked like.

769 See Arika Okrent, "9 Fun Facts About the Schwa," May 20, 2014, www.Mentalfloss.com. Further discussion of orthoepy is beyond the scope of this book, even though the word "orthoepy" appears here five times (see Chapter 15).

# Supplement I: Temple & Synagogue

770 *Love*, opposite 66.

771 Rosh Hashanah, the Jewish New Year, is based on the Hebrew calendar, a modified lunar calendar, and usually occurs in early fall. Ten days later is Yom Kippur, the Jewish Day of Atonement. Jewish business closings were explained to Corsicanans in "Day of Atonement: Yom Kippur Observed by Hebrews in Corsicana," *Sun*, Sept. 15, 1918.

772 B'nai B'rith (literally, children of the covenant) is a benevolent Jewish society founded in New York City in 1843 (Wikipedia's "B'nai B'rith" entry). A table listing Texas's B'nai B'rith lodges, with years founded, is an appendix to Charles Wessolowsky, *Reflections of Southern Jewry*, Louis Schmier, Ed. (Macon: Mercer University Press, 1981).

773 1908 Corsicana City Directory, Anc. (list of Corsicana "churches"). In 1908, the "Hebrew Orthodox Church," met at the Odd Fellows Hall and had twenty-six members. The "Jewish Church," organized in 1900, Beth-El, had thirty members (1908 Corsicana City Directory.)

774 Interview of Rabbi Ernst Joseph transcription, 29 (see note 152). The 1894-95 Corsicana City Directory from the firm of Clarke and Courts, Galveston, stated that Hebrew Services were held at "Freedman's Hall, Rev. Abraham Israel, Rabbi" ("City Directory of 1894-95 Attracts Much Interest Among Library's Patrons," *Sun*, Nov. 5, 1949). In other cities, a "Freedman's Hall" was a building where former slaves and other African Americans would congregate, but here it seems to refer to a space in the store of Alex and/or Rube Freedman. No other reference to a "Freedman Hall" in Corsicana is known.

775 1908 Corsicana City Directory, Anc.; 1913 Corsicana City Directory, Anc.; 1915 Corsicana City Directory, Anc. The WOW Hall was on the second floor of the IOOF building, at 100 W. 3$^{rd}$ Street, aka 406 N. Beaton Street (1910 Corsicana City Directory, Anc.).

776 "Jewish New Year Observed," *DMN*, Sept. 6, 1899.

777 *Morrison & Fourmy's General Directory of Corsicana, 1898-1899*, Anc.

778 *Morrison & Fourmy's General Directory of Corsicana, 1898-1899*.

779. "Jewish New Year Observed." It's possible, perhaps likely, that the City Hall venue was used only for High Holiday services, to accommodate a much larger attendance than what would show up for a weekly Sabbath service.

780 See Supplement II.

781 His wife, Augusta (Hart), was a native of Maryland and had lived in South Carolina (1870 Census) shortly before they met and married. An "infant son" died on May 26, 1874, in Augusta, Ga. (FAG, "Infant son of J.W. Freidlander (sic)"). Another child, William "Will," was born in Augusta Jan. 11, 1876. A third child, who apparently died young, was born in Florida around 1878. In 1880 the family lived in Selma (1880 Census).

782 *DMN*, Aug. 24, 1895 (listed as a Corsicana resident, staying at the St. George Hotel); 1901 Corsicana Business Directory, Anc.

783 Friedlander was twice recognized as WOW's top salesman ("He Won First Prize," *Chickasha* (Okla.) *Express*," July 24, 1903, NP).

784 *DMN*, July 19, 1897. Ida was the oldest child of Rabbi Abraham and Rachel Israel. See Supplement II.

785 "Knights of Honor," *DMN*, Nov. 28, 1897.

786 1870 Census, New York City, for Raphael Costa; Tex. Death Cert., Dallas, Tex., Anc.

787 The 1900 Census says S.S. and Carrie Freedman had been married for twenty-seven years. "Died Yesterday Afternoon," *Sun*, July 27, 1911 (S.S. Freedman resided in Corsicana since 1875).

788 Iowa State Board of Health Return of Marriages, Dubuque Cty., Oct. 15, 1880, Anc.

789 Lillie Polasky's gravestone is shown in Supplement III.

790 Moses Goldsmith was brought to the U.S. in 1858, spent his childhood in Syracuse, N.Y., and moved with his family to Marshall, Texas, where his father, Wolf, established a mercantile.

791 Moses N. and Betsy Frank were born in Poland, he in 1820 and she in 1825. Their oldest child, Abraham, was also born there, in 1850. The other children were all born in Syracuse: Carrie, in 1855; Cornelia, 1857; Nathan, 1859; Daniel, 1861; Ray, 1863; and Minnie, in 1865 (1860 Census, New York; 1865 & 1875 New York State censuses, Anc.). Years of birth could be off by a year because only ages are reported in the aforementioned census records. The 1860 Census reported Polish origins, but other censuses say Germany. In all likelihood it was a border area.

792 "Personals," *Sun*, July 6, 1909; Affidavit of Moses Aaron Goldsmith, appended to Affidavit for Naturalization, S.D.N.Y., dated Dec. 10, 1915, Anc.; 1910 Census, Lincoln, Neb., for Moses A. Goldsmith, his wife, and four Polasky children (staying in a hotel); 1920 Census, New York, for Moses A. and Ray Goldsmith, with two Polasky children; "Louis Pulasky (sic) Dies in New York City," *Des Moines Tribune*, Dec. 14, 1926, NP.

793 Texas County Marriage Records, 1837-1965, LDS. Mose Goldsmith and his Goldsmith family were residents of Marshall at the time.

794 David Nathan, "Costa Fascination: One of England's Oldest Jewish Families," *Avotaynu Online* (Apr. 1, 2007), http://www.avotaynuonline.com/2007/04/costa-fascination-one-of-englands-oldest-jewish-families-by-david-nathan/. A number of online family trees on Ancestry.com and Geni.com show detailed Costa/DaCosta ancestry.

795 *Sun*, Apr. 21, 1924.

796 "New Ladies Ready to Wear Store is Formally Opened," *Sun*, Feb 8, 1923.

797 Corsicana Business Directory, 1898, Anc.

798 Navarro Cty. Land Records, deeds, book 86, p. 603.

799 "Building Operations," *DMN*, July 15, 1899.

800 Lena was twelve in the 1900 federal census (Corsicana; enumeration dated June 12), and according to her gravestone her birthday was September 12 (FAG for Lena Bodenheimer, died Dec. 31, 1924, Shreveport, La.), so she had just turned thirteen.

801 A plaque inside what is now technically the "Corsicana Community Center," but is still called "Temple Beth El," lists the congregation's presidents. Although the congregation was founded in 1898, the list begins in 1913. Ralph Costa, the first president, who held the post for some unknown period of time, and Alexander Fox, elected president in 1909, are not listed on the plaque. There is also a five-year gap between the first two listed presidents on the plaque, reflecting either a gap in known information at the time the plaque was created or a period when there was no leadership.

Congregation Beth El Presidents:

1900-? - Ralph Costa
1909-? - Alexander Fox
1913-1914 - Isaac Cerf
1919-1920 - Mose Miller
1920-1922 - Robert Jarett
1922-1924 - Isaac Cerf
1924-1927 - Sydney Marks
1927-1929 - Sam Brooks
1929-1934 - Isaac Cerf
1934-1936 - Gabe Goldberg
1936-1937 - James H. Cerf
1937-1938 - Morris Dreeben
1938-1940 - Gabe Goldberg
1940-1955 - Sydney Marks
1955-1959 - Alvin Shwarts
1959-1961 - Maurice Rosen

1961-1963 - Gabe Goldberg
1963-1964 - Maurice Rosen
1964-1966 - Irvin Samuels
1966-1968 - Berney Bobkoff
1968-1970 - Gabe Goldberg
1970-1972 - Morris Evans
1972-1974 - Max Rosenbaum
1974-1976 - Irvin Samuels

802 The identity of this Goldberg is not certain. Some articles about the synagogue's dedication say his first initial was "I," but the article in the *Dallas Morning News* said it was "J." ("Dedicated a Synagogue: A Handsome House of Worship Dedicated at Corsicana with Most Impressive Ceremony," *DMN*, Sept. 23, 1900, GB). According to the 1900 federal census, "Isaac Goldberg," born Oct. 1857, and his wife, Maud, born Sept. 1875, resided at a Beaton St. boarding house. They had been married for three years and she had one child who was no longer living. That child would be Jennie Louise, who died at the age of two months in 1899 and is buried in the Hebrew Cemetery. Isaac may have been related to the other Goldbergs in town, but, it seems, not closely. Lena Goldberg, the key bearer at the dedication, was a niece of Ben Rosenberg, whom he adopted as a daughter. Born in Waco, Lena had lost her mother at a young age, lived with the Rosenbergs for many years, and later became Lena (Goldberg) Bodenheimer of Shreveport.

803 "Dedicated a Synagogue." Variations of the news story were found in the records of the Texas Jewish Historical Society's collection at the Briscoe Center, UT, Austin. One is a transcription that has written across the bottom, "Sept. 28, 1900 American Israelite, v. 47, no. 14 (1900)," although the referenced article was not found independently at the citation provided. The other is a photocopy of an article that is a close variation of the purported *American Israelite* transcription, but appears to be written for a Gentile audience, and does not have its source identified.

804 "Dedicated a Synagogue."

805 *The State of Texas by S.S. Freedman v. Kal Shwarts et al.* sought "the enforcement of the charter granted by the state to the 'Jewish Congregation Temple Beth El of Corsicana'" ("Injunction Asked," *Democrat* (McKinney, Tex.), May 9, 1901, NP).

806 "Seek an Injunction: Rival Officers of a Hebrew Congregation Resort to Litigation," *DMN*, May 8, 1901. The four new officers and trustees, whose election in May was challenged, were: Ed Raphael, August Levy, Jacob Herman, and Louis Polasky. The officers and trustees who would have been removed were Costa, Freedman, Abe Levine, Marks, Rosenberg, and Louis Cohen. The litigation was likely settled out of court. Regarding Freedman's propensity for litigation, see Chapter 24.

807 "The Synagogue Movement," *DMN*, Sept. 25, 1898.

808 "Publish List of Donors: Agudas Achem Congregation is Grateful to All Who Aided," *Sun*, Oct. 27, 1917 (reproduced in this supplement); "Orthodox Congregation: Lot Purchased and Plans for Building Now Being Made," *Sun*, Mar. 8, 1915; probated will of Ben Marks (Texas County Wills, Navarro Cty., Anc.).

809 Rabbi Ernest Joseph, "The Jewish Community of Corsicana, Texas," Texas Jewish Historical Society Collection, Dolph Briscoe Center, UT, Austin, Oct. 17, 1988, courtesy ISJL. The IOOF building is now occupied by 100W, an "international residency for artists and writers hosted and furnished by artists and writers" (www.100WestCorsicana.com; Charles Scudder, "An Artists' Haven is Born," www.interactives.DallasNews.com, June 12, 2016 (retrieved Oct. 29, 2016)).

810 1908 and 1913 Corsicana City Directories, Anc. The 1910 directory listed the meeting place for Orthodox Hebrews as WOW (Woodmen of the World) Hall, which was located inside the IOOF Building at 100 N. Beaton Street (alternative address: 100 W. 3rd Street).

811 Joseph, "The Jewish Community of Corsicana, Texas."

812 The Klan emerged in Corsicana in earnest in the early twenties, long after the congregation had moved into its own building.

813 "Orthodox Congregation: Lot Purchased and Plans for Building Now Being Made," *Sun*, Mar. 8, 1915. An advertisement to sell the house on the lot ran for several months (see, e.g., "For Sale," *Sun*, Mar. 8, 1915).

814 "Orthodox Congregation."

815 Joseph, "The Jewish Community of Corsicana, Texas."

816 "K. Wolens Was Leader In Jewish Faith Here," *Sun*, Jan. 25, 1970; "Rabbi Ernest Joseph Serves Three Groups," *Sun*, Apr. 14, 1972.

817 Mrs. Irvin (Babbette) Samuels, "The Final Years of Temple Beth El" (unpublished manuscript), papers of Sandra Palmer (unpublished), Dolph Briscoe archives at UT, Austin, Texas Jewish Historical Society Collection, courtesy ISJL.

818 Forty-three would make more sense, mathematically, to account for the families with dual memberships.

819 RWeb, Religion: Temple Beth-El.

820 Judy Cohen, "Perfect Ecumenicalism as Christians Join Jews to Help Restore Corsicana Historic Synagogue," *Texas Jewish Post* (Hanuka Issue) (Fort Worth, Tex.), Dec. 13, 1984. See also https://changesevenmag.com/2016/11/22/kosher-in-corsicana-by-tom-darin-liskey/; Samuels, "The Final Years"; *Brick Streets and Back Roads* (Navarro Council of the Arts, 2000).

821 Although it is now a community center, the building is still referred to as "Beth El" or "the temple."

822 Frank Joseph, telephone interview with author, Nov. 23, 2016.

823 Eastern Texas Historical Society, www.easttexashistorical.org/v3/programs/terry/terry _1992_temple.html (retrieved Jan. 25, 2016). See East Texas Historical Association, https://etha.wildapricot.org/.

The temple's architect remains unknown. The analysis supporting the Terry Award announcement does not mention Los Angeles's B'nai B'rith Synagogue, completed in 1896, which is also architecturally similar to Beth El. The architect of the L.A. building was Abraham M. Edelman, son of that congregation's first rabbi. There are three links between B'nai B'rith synagogue and Temple Beth El which suggest Edelman may have been Beth El's mystery architect: 1. Rabbi Blum, who established a Sunday school in Corsicana (and other Texas towns) at some time in the 1870s, was rabbi of B'nai B'rith in the 1880s, albeit before they built their new synagogue; 2. Rabbi M.G. Solomon was B'nai B'rith's rabbi at the time the L.A. Jews were planning to build their new synagogue, and later, in 1921, he was Beth El's rabbi, serving for a year or two. Solomon was at Victoria, Texas in 1905. A familial link between M.G. Solomon and Solomon Solomon, Beth El's rabbi at the time Beth El's construction started, would be strong evidence that M.G. Solomon recommended B'nai B'rith's architect to Solomon Solomon to be Beth El's architect, but a family connection between the two Rabbi Solomons has not been found; and 3. Architect Edelman's partner, Leo W. Barnett, who was also Edelman's nephew, was born in Fort Worth (Jun. 3, 1881), a geographic nexus between Edelman and Corsicana (www.jmaw.org/solomon-rabbi-jewish-los-angeles/; various Anc. sources).

Other synagogues also resemble Beth El's architecture, i.e., Wikipedia's "Great Synagogue in Plzen, Czech" entry. The preservation of Temple Beth El was well documented in "Perfect Ecumenicalism." The ETHS analyses of Beth El's architecture (quoted here) echoes observations made in Jane Manaster, "Synagogue Architecture of Corsicana, Texas and Gabin, Poland: Copy or Coincidence?" (1984, thirty-five-page typescript, small collection SC-7691, American Jewish Archives), about possible inspirations for Beth El's architecture, but Manaster's paper, unlike the ETHS announcement of the Terry Award, does not conjecture that one architect was responsible for the Charleston, Butte, and Corsicana synagogues.

# Supplement II: Corsicana Rabbis

824 "City Directory of 1894-95 Attracts Much Interest."

825 The Efrons, like the Corsicana Freedmans, were from Mariampole, Lithuania, and very possibly they were related because Freedman was the maternal family line of the Texas Efron siblings, e.g. Ben Efron (ca. 1842-1913) of Waco (Jim Yarin, "Efron Family History," Vol. II, Chapter 39, http://www.efronfamilyhistory.com/Vol2Chap39.htm). Ben Rosenberg was also from Mariampole and his wife, Ray (Goldberg) Rosenberg, was part of the Efron family as well. ("Pioneer Business Man of Corsicana Died Saturday: Ben Rosenberg Passed Away Early Saturday Following Long Illness," *Sun*, May 4, 1929; "Efron Family History.")

826 Two lengthy articles appeared in the *Dallas Morning News* of Jan. 26, 1891, one describing the wedding and guests, "Society Kaleidoscope: Mexia," and another listing gifts and gift givers, "Efron-Lewis Wedding: The Social Event of the Season at Mexia—List of Presents." In the latter article, "Mr. and Mrs. A. Israel of Corsicana" gave a "plush album" and "B. Rosenberg" of Corsicana gave an "elegant marble clock."

827 The practice of circumcision by biblical patriarch Abraham and his descendants was the result of an agreement Abraham made with God in exchange for God's blessings (Gen. 17), and it is fundamental to the definition of the Jewish people. It is the most ancient and holy of Jewish rituals, familiarly called a "bris." Eight days after a boy's birth, the foreskin of his penis is surgically removed in a ceremony that is sacred, medical, and joyous—all at the same time.

The Sunday referred to in the news item was May 4, 1890. According to Jewish ritual, the Marks boy (unnamed in the article) would have been born eight days prior, on April 26, or the evening of the 25th (the Jewish day starts at sundown). There is only one such birth, that of Louie Marks, who was born April 24, 1890, in Corsicana (WWII draft registration card, Anc.). The one-day difference is immaterial, given the totality of facts. Louie's father, Sam, later moved his family to Waco and had a liquor business there. Louis Marks, who had settled in Chicago, lived to the age of 101 and was buried in Waco.

828 "Enjoyable Event," *Sun*, July 17, 1920. Two rabbis attended the "christening."

829 Bert Eli Israel, a son of the rabbi, was born in Corsicana in May, 1895 (WWII draft reg. card, Anc.). Barnard "Barney" Roy Israel, another, older son, was born in San Antonio, in 1893 (WWII draft reg. card, Anc.). Other, older Israel children were born in the late 1880s in Waco. The youngest child, Ivan, was born on April 16, 1898 in Texas, according to several records, or in New York, according to a few sources. The 1900 census says Ivan was born in Massachusetts. The family likely departed Corsicana in 1897, when a going-away party for daughter Ida was given by the Friedlanders (*DMN*, July 19, 1897).

830 1900 Census, Worcester, Mass., for Abraham Israel and family; "Efron Family History," www.efronfamilyhistory.com/Vol2Chap39.htm.

831 William W. Scott, *History of Passaic and Its Environs, Vol. III* (New York: Lewis Historical Publishing Co., Inc., 1922), 590. The biographical sketch is for Passaic, N.J. glass merchant Charles Elias, husband of Ida, the oldest child in the Israel family. Rabbis without full-time and well-paid rabbinic engagements would by necessity pursue other lines of work.

832 "Corsicana News Notes," *DMN*, Aug. 17, 1897. Ancestry records confirm Louis Levy's birth date was Aug. 2, 1897.

833 ISJL, "San Antonio." Rabbi Solomon was reportedly hired by San Antonio's Temple Beth El in 1899, however, the 1900 Census has him still residing in Corsicana, on June 4, 1900. The first mention of him at San Antonio was on August, 18, 1901, when he circumcised Sylvan, the son of Jefferson Davis Nordhaus (*San Antonio Express*, Aug. 19, 1901); Ancestry.com sources verify Sylvan's date of birth). J.D. Nordhaus was a descendant of the storied Hyams family of Charleston. See Supplement I for more about Rabbi Solomon.

834 Alexander Z. Gurwitz, *Memories of Two Generations: A Yiddish Life in Russia and Texas*, Edward Stone Bryan, Ed., Amram Prero, Trans. (University of Alabama Press, 2016) (portions retrieved from https://books.google.com), 297-98. According to Gurwitz, Solomon was not ordained, and ordination was not necessary to serve in small communities.

835 "Elliott Sullivan, Actor of Stage and the Screen, is Dead at 66," *New York Times*, June 4, 1974, http://www.nytimes.com/1974/06/04/archives/elliott-sullivan-actor-of-stage-and-the-screen-is-dead-at-66.html.

836 "County Notes," *Elkhart Daily Review* (Elkhart, Ind.), Aug. 23, 1900, GB; "A Well Known Rabbi Resigns," *Indianapolis News*, Aug. 23, 1900, NP.

837 1930 Census, 1940 Census, and his 1919 marriage record (Mich. Marriage Records, Anc.) say he was born in Latvia. Other records say he was born in Curland (part of Latvia) or Germany.

838 He is buried in Norton Shores Cemetery in Muskegan Cty., Mich. (FAG).

839 He was responsible for articles related to Spanish-Jewish literature and the biographies of living authors ("Corsicana Rabbi Honored," *Eagle* (Bryan, Tex.), Dec. 1, 1900, NP).

840 "He Says," *Marshall* (Mich.) *Evening Chronicle*, Jan. 10, 1935, NP.

841 "P.O. Employes (sic) See Stamp Worth $7,500," *Janesville* (Wisc.) *Daily Gazette*, Oct. 5, 1945, NP.

842 104 Texas 1 (1908).

843 "Corsicana Cullings," *HP*, Dec. 12, 1903.

844 "Election of a Cantor," *Baltimore Sun*, Aug. 11, 1885, NP.

845 "Two Wives Want Divorces," *Baltimore Sun*, Mar. 13, 1889, NP. Fanny Fleischer and Henry Stollnitz were married in New York on June 24, 1883. "For a year or so he has been engaged in the liquor business, and for the last three weeks has been an inmate of the Hebrew Hospital" ("Two Wives Want Divorces").

846 *Baltimore Sun*, July 28, 1891, NP.

847 "Hannukka Sermon," *San Francisco Call*, Dec. 2, 1899; "Stollnitz Concert: The Tenor Renders Several of His Own Compositions," *San Francisco Call*, Jan. 17, 1900, NP; "An Evening Singing Class" (advertisement), *Chicago Daily Tribune*, Oct. 2, 1892, NP.

848 Census records say he arrived, variously, in 1890, 1893, and 1895; "Two Wives Want Divorces" gives the date of his first marriage, verified as June 24, 1883 (Extracted Marriage Index, New York, for Heyman Stollnitz to Jennie Fleischer, cert. 24654, Anc.). His immigration was in 1881, according to his 1889 passport application (U.S. Passport Applications, for H. Stollnitz, Anc.).

849 Other known positions he held were: cantor at Ulm Wurtemberg and Norfolk St. Cong., both in New York City; Ohabei Shalom, San Francisco; Sharey Tefilo, Orange, N.J.; and Adath Emuno, Hoboken, N.J., in 1904 (*The American Jewish Year Book: 5664*, Cyrus Adler, Ed., 102 (Philadelphia: The Jewish Publication Society of America, 1903), https://www.forgottenbooks.com/en/books/TheAmericanJewishYearBook5664_10703373).

850 Rabbi Stollnitz's grandson heard this from his father (Fred Stollnitz, telephone interview with author, Feb. 16, 2017).

851 Congregation Schaarai Zedek, "Who We Are," http://www.zedek.org/who-we-are/our-history/.

852 Henry Sande Stollnitz (Cambridge, Mass.: printed for the author by the University Press, 1908). A review, written at the time of the book's publication, described it as having sketches (presumably, written sketches) of seven ghettos. A short story by Stollnitz, bearing the same title, was published in *American Jewish Archives* 37 (Apr. 1985): 92-103 (Mark K. Bauman, Compiler, "Articles Relating to Southern Jewish History Published in American Jewish History, American Jewish Archives Journal, Their Predecessors, and Southern Jewish History," *Southern Jewish History* 182).

853 1915 & 1925 N.Y. state censuses, Anc.; 1920 Census; 1930 Census.

854 "The Question Box," *Post Crescent* (Appleton, Wisc.), Nov. 18, 1925, NP. This feat is all the more remarkable because the mechanical typewriters of that era were far more difficult to use than later electric models and today's computer keyboards.

855 The Gilbreths today are remembered not only for their highly celebrated efficiency studies, but also for the depiction of their large, blended family in the hit 1950 movie and 1992 remake, *Cheaper by the Dozen*.

856 Stollnitz, interview.

857 New York, N.Y. Deaths Index, Anc.

858 Activities at the temple had been at a "low ebb" for several years before Rabbi Goldberg's arrival ("A Brief History of the Corsicana Jewish Community," *Jewish Monitor* (Dallas), Dec. 17, 1920, NP).

859 In 1908, Bachrach was in Dubuque (1908 Dubuque City Directory, Anc. see also Arrivals, New York Port, for Elke Bachrach (and children), Mar. 29, 1905, Anc.). By April 1910, he and his family were in Corsicana (1910 Census), and he was listed as Beth El's rabbi (Corsicana City Directory, 1910, pp. 14, 32, Anc.). He had probably left by June, 1910, when Dallas Rabbi Greenburg handled Beth El confirmation exercises. By the Jewish New Year, September 23, 1911, he and his family were living in Wichita where he led services for that city's orthodox Jews at their IOOF Hall (the reform Jews had their services at the Unitarian Church) ("Jewish New Year 5672 to be Celebrated Today," *Wichita Daily Eagle*, Sept. 22, 1911, NP).

860 "After a lapse of eight years the members of Temple Beth-El are bringing out again for confirmation a class of eleven children." A musical program was conducted by Mrs. Huberta Nunn, and the public was invited. ("Class of Eleven will be Confirmed at Temple Beth-El Tomorrow," *Sun*, June 5, 1909.)

861 "Jewish Holidays," *Sun*, Oct. 8, 1910.

862 "Temple Beth El," *Sun*, Dec. 31, 1913.

863 The biblical passage about priestly vestments is appropriate for the installation of a new rabbi, drawing on themes of leadership and power over the congregation by virtue of the "vestments" of leadership.

864 http://www.uniforms-4u.com/p-jewish-chaplain-staff-uniform-collar-device-3699.aspx.

865 "Honored Retiring Rabbi: Congregation of Temple Beth-El has Banquet," *Sun*, Nov. 15, 1917; "Sunshine and Clouds," *Sun*, Nov. 17, 1917.

866 "His Last Sermon," *Sun*, Feb. 16, 1918 (Montaz's final Corsicana sermon informed the congregation that their lack of religious commitment was a dying death, worse than the calming, actual death of a person of faith). Born Aaron Zalmon Monasewitz in Olkeniki (now Valkininkai), Lithuania, Montaz was a rabbi in Spokane, Hazelton, Penn., and Raleigh (various, www.newspapers.com; Ill. Federal Naturalization Records, Petition for Naturalization, Aug. 28, 1926, Anc.), and did not leave a robust biographical record in the dozen years prior to his death in Chicago in 1946. "Will Preach at Temple Beth-El," *Sun*, Feb. 26, 1918 (Barasch). Rumania-born Barasch had a long rabbinic career, serving in Los Angeles; Jamestown, N.Y.; Sedalia, Mo.; Shreveport and Baton Rouge, La.; Florence and Selma, Ala.; Bayonne, N.J.; and military posts (FAG for Nathan Emanuel Barasch) ("Hebrew Union College," *American Israelite*, Dec. 27, 1917, NP (Montaz and other students will serve Corsicana)).

867 "David Goldberg Dead at 91," Jewish Telegraphic Agency, Nov. 17, 1977, https://www.jta.org/1977/11/17/archive/david-goldberg-dead-at-91.

868 "Rabbi Joseph Stolz Goes to Larger Field," *Jewish Monitor* (Dallas), June 11, 1920, NP. His earliest known presence in Corsicana was at Succoth services at Beth El, Sept. 20, 1918 ("The Festival of Succoth: Services in Harmony with Holiday Tonight at Temple Beth-El," *Sun*, Sept. 20, 1918).

869 See, e.g., 1910 Census.

870 Dwight H. Bruce, Ed., *Onondaga's Centennial, Gleanings of a Century, Vol. II: Family Sketches* (Boston, Mass.: The Boston History Company, 1896), 88-89, https://archive.org/details/onondagascentenn02bruc_0). Jacob's brother, David, who married Yetta's sister, Regina, also lived in Syracuse. A brother of Yetta and Regina, Jacob Marshall, likewise a Syracusan, was the father of Louis Marshall, the renowned civil liberties lawyer and founder of the American Jewish Committee. (Matthew Mark Silver, *Louis Marshall and the Rise of Jewish Ethnicity in America: A Biography* (Syracuse, N.Y.: Syracuse U. Press, 2013), 9, portions published at https://books.google.com.) Rabbi Stolz had another well-known cousin, likewise from Syracuse, also a rabbi, and also named Joseph Stolz. The other Rabbi Joseph Stolz was one of the longest-serving reform rabbis in Chicago history.

871 "Rabbi Joseph Stolz."

872 "Marriage Announcement," *Sun*, June 26, 1920.

873 "Rabbi Joseph H. Stolz," *Los Angeles Times*, June 22, 1953, NP.

874 "At Temple Beth-El: Dr. Faber of Tyler will Conduct the Services," *Sun*, Dec. 7, 1917; "At Temple Beth-El Friday Night," *Sun*, Oct. 20, 1920 (Dr. Faber); "Funeral was Largely Attended," *Sun*, Aug. 26, 1918 (funeral of Mrs. L.H. Newburg conducted by Rabbi Greenburg); "Temple Beth-El: Services Tonight Will be Conducted by Dallas Rabbi," *Sun*, Dec. 21, 1917 (Rabbi Greenburg).

875 Samuels, "The Final Years of Temple Beth El" (see note 817).

876 His death information cannot be confirmed. One source, not examined, identified a Michael G. Solomon, 1868-1927 (Susan K. Kinnell, Ed. *People in History. An index to U.S. and Canadian biographies in history journals and dissertations* (Santa Barbara, CA.)). Another source also gives 1927 as his date of death (Reva Clar and William M. Kramer, "Michael G. Solomon, 1868-1927, Rabbi and Lawyer of Los Angeles," *Western States Jewish History* 14/1, 38/3&4 (Los Angeles)). No burial information could be located for him, his ex-wife, Miriam, or their sons, Jacques B. Silverman and Leon A. Silverman.

877 Until age fourteen he attended the Berlin Gymnasium. He entered the College of the City of New York a year later. He entered U. of Cincinnati and Hebrew Union College at the same time in 1886, receiving a B.L. from the former and a rabbinic degree from the latter, in 1893 (*History of the Bench and Bar*. See also "Rabbi M.G. Solomon Will Hold Services Tomorrow Night," *Sun*, Jan. 20, 1921). He also learned under Samuel Adler (father of Felix) and Gustave Gottheil ("Education is Rabbi's Theme").

878 "B'nai B'rith Wants a Rabbi," *Los Angeles Times*, Apr. 14, 1899, NP; "Education is Rabbi's Theme: Dr. M.G. Solomon Lectures Entertainingly: Subject Cleverly Handled," *Los Angeles Herald*, Apr. 16, 1905, N.P. See Jewish Museum of the American West, "Rabbi Michael G. Solomon: The Fourth Rabbi of Congregation B'nai B'rith," http://www.jmaw.org/solomon-rabbi-jewish-los-angeles/.

879 "Victoria to Have Rabbi: Los Angeles Master to Take Charge of Synagogue," *DMN*, Aug. 28, 1905.

880 "Rabbi M.G. Solomon Will Hold Services Tomorrow Night," *Sun*, Jan. 20, 1921; "Celebration of Rosh Hashanah to be Observed Wednesday," *Lexington Herald*, Sept. 5, 1915, GB (Lexington, Kentucky's Maryland Avenue Temple); *History of the Bench and Bar of Southern California* (1909), Anc.; *Jewish Messenger* (New York City), July 21, 1893, GB (Youngstown, Ohio). Additional biographical information may be found at "Michael G. Solomon, 1868-1927."

881 *History of the Bench and Bar.*

882 "Official List of Graduates of the Hebrew Union College Since Its Establishment," *Wisconsin Jewish Chronicle*, Oct. 23, 1925, NP; "Corsicana Rabbi is Honored With Award for Best Sermon," *Sun*, June 3, 1935 (Rabbi Lesser); "Guest Rabbi for Hebrew Holy Days at Temple Beth-El," *Sun*, Sept. 4, 1947 (Rabbi Weiner).

883 Georgia Marriage Records, Chatham Cty., Anc. Her brother, Joseph Silverman, was a Texas rabbi in the mid-1880s, first at Dallas and then at Galveston. In 1888, Rabbi Silverman became the first American-born rabbi of New York City's Congregation Emanu-El, making him one of the most influential reform rabbis in the country (Wikipedia's "Joseph Silverman" entry). Rabbi Silverman's wife was Henrietta (Block), born in Galveston to Jacob and Lena Block (1870 Census; John W. Leonard, Ed., *Who's Who in New York City and State, 3rd Ed.* (New York City: L.R. Hamersly & Company, 1907), https://books.google.com/).

884 "Was No Housewife: Why Mrs. Solomon Went Home," *Los Angeles Times*, Apr. 30, 1904, NP. Ironically, or not, her brother Joseph fought a very public battle against women's suffrage.

885 1920 and 1930 Censuses. The family lived in Cincinnati.

886 "Rabbi M.G. Solomon Will Hold Services Tomorrow Night," *Sun*, Jan. 20, 1921.

887 "Dr. Solomon Re-Elected: Temple Beth-El Was Unanimous in Making Choice," *Sun*, May 9, 1921. At the time, there was no air-conditioning in the temple, so no services were held during the summer.

888 "Class of Five is Confirmed at Temple Beth-El: Special Decorations and Music for the Occasion. Large Audience," *Sun*, May 22, 1923.

889 "Breach Widening in B'nai B'rith Temple," *San Francisco Call*, Apr. 16, 1899, NP.

890 "Rabbi Solomon: Takes Charge at Victoria—Their First Regularly Stationed Rabbi," *GDN*, Sept. 17, 1905, NP.

891 He was listed in the 1930 Census in Monroe, La., but no death record or burial location could be located for him. His wife Lillian died in 1978 in California. His father was buried with other family members in Winnipeg.

892 "Rabbi for Temple Beth-El Has Now Arrived in City," *Sun*, Nov. 15, 1923.

893 "Rabbi Saul Schorr is Dead," *Fort Wayne News*, Aug. 17, 1917, NP. Saul Schorr was also rabbi in Milwaukee (*Sheboygan Press*, May 26, 1915, NP).

894 "Rev. Carl Schorr Succeeds Father: As Pastor of the B'Nair Jacob Congregation, Corner Wayne and Monroe," *Fort Wayne Sentinel*, Sept. 15, 1917, NP.

895 "Rev. Carl Schorr comes to City to Become a Pastor," *Monroe* (La.) *News-Star*, Aug. 28, 1924, NP. The glowing article states that in 1917 he was the youngest ordained rabbi in the country and identifies prior posts at Lima, Ohio, Detroit, Williamsport, and Corsicana. If there was an Edelson Seminary, its name as such was short-lived. More likely Schorr was credentialed by Rabbi I. Edelson, director in 1917 of New York's Rabbinical College of America.

896 *Sheboygan Press*, May 26, 1915, NP.

897 "Dr. Schorr Retained Rabbi Jewish Church," *Sun*, May 19, 1924.

898 "Rabbi Louis Brav Accepts Call to Temple Beth-El," *Sun*, July 8, 1924.

899 *Reading Times*, Aug. 9, 1898, NP.

900 The Reading synagogue's voting became public because of a kerfuffle amongst the congregants. A temple member who had voted in favor of Rabbi Schorr, Mendel Simon, said that Lewis, who had passed the threatening note, had once killed a man in the old country and several in America. Lewis went to a lawyer to sue Simon for slander. An affidavit the lawyer prepared for Lewis, his client, was taken without permission from the lawyer's desk by the office boy, Wolff Fetterman, and shown to Simon, the putative slanderer. Fetterman told Simon that a lawsuit had already been filed, which was not true, so Simon went to the lawyer to settle the (nonexistent) case and paid the lawyer $17.80. The whole matter came before the aldermen of Reading because Fetterman, the office boy, had betrayed the lawyer's confidence by taking the affidavit to Simon, and the lawyer had extracted his fee (and a retraction of the accusation, it seems), under the false pretense that the lawsuit had already been filed. (*Reading Times*, Aug. 9, 1898)

901 Pennsylvania Death Certificates, for Louis Brav, Anc.

902 "Rabbi Louis Brav Accepts Call to Temple Beth-El."

903 *Sun*, June 25, 1926; "The Mother Heart Subject of Sermon Delivered by Brav: Sermon Delivered Mother's Day in Corsicana Printed by Request," *Sun*, July 2, 1926; "New Rabbi Arrives," *Beaumont* (Tex.) *Enterprise*, Aug. 30, 1926, GB.

904 FAG, Adath Jeshurun Cemetery, Phila., Penn. (biography posted there by CemeteryRose (#47195666); Texas County Marriages, Dallas, Aug. 23, 1925, Anc.).

905 See "To Observe Feast of Rosh Hashonah," *Williamsport Sun Gazette*, Oct. 1, 1910, NP; "New Rabbi is Due at Pine Bluff Thursday," *Arkansas Democrat*, Feb. 1, 1922, NP. For additional information, see Stanley R. Brav, "Louis Brav," *Yearbook, Vol. LX* (Cincinnati, Ohio: Central Conference of American Rabbis, 1950), 271-72.

906 "Graduates Get Diplomas," *Philadelphia Inquirer*, June 18, 1906, NP.

907 "Louis Brav Dies, Rabbi was 65," *Philadelphia Inquirer*, May 23, 1950, NP; "Rabbi Louis Brav Called to Raleigh," *News and Observer* (Raleigh, N.C.), Aug. 18, 1915, NP.

908 "To Observe Feast" (Williamsport, Penn.); "Rabbi Louis Brav Installed," *Pittsburgh Gazette Times*, Sept. 15, 1913, NP (indexed as *Pittsburgh Post-Gazette*) (McKeesport temple); "Rabbi Louis Brav Called to Raleigh" (Raleigh, N.C.); *Buffalo Jewish Review*, Mar. 29, 1918, NP (Montefiore Cong., Phila., Penn.); "New Rabbi is Due at Pine Bluff Thursday," *Arkansas Democrat*, Feb. 1, 1922, NP (Temple Israel, Pine Bluff); "Louis Brav Dies" (mentions Natchez and Pensacola, ca. 1912-13).

909 ISJL, Pine Bluff, Ark.; "New Rabbi is Due at Pine Bluff Thursday."

910 Rabbi Louis Brav, "Rathenau—Super—Patriot," *Jewish Chronicle* (Newark, N.J.), Feb. 22, 1929, GB (includes a note that article's author is rabbi of Temple B'nai Israel, Natchez, Miss.).

911 Various *Sun* articles.

912 Various *Sun* articles.

913 "Rabbi Macht Dies; Rites Set Tuesday," *Waco Tribune-Herald*, Feb. 17, 1952, NP; "Waco News," *Jewish Monitor* (Dallas), Sept. 26, 1919, NP.

914 See "Dr. Lefkowitz Will Speak Here Sunday; Jews Urged Attend," *Sun*, June 8, 1929, NP.

915 "Annual Camp Fire Banquet-Business Meeting is Held: Campaign for Funds for Coming Year's Support Opened Wednesday," *CSWL*, Sept. 27, 1929; "Jewish New Year Will be Celebrated on Next Saturday: Rosh Hashanah Opens Friday Evening and Lasts through Saturday," *CSWL*, Oct. 1, 1929.

916 "Former Corsicana Rabbi Married in Cincinnati Sunday," *Sun*, Aug. 22, 1930.

917 Congregation Schaarai Zedek, "Who We Are," http://www.zedek.org/who-we-are/our-history/.

918 Jewish Museum of the American West, "Rabbi Martin Zielonka: the 'Reform Rabbi of the West,' El Paso, Texas," http://www.jmaw.org/rabbi-zielonka-el-paso-texas.

919 Social Security Death Index, for Charles Lesser of Albany, Ga., Jan. 1982, Anc.

920 "11-Ordained Rabbis at Hebrew Union College," Jewish Telegraphic Agency, May 27, 1935, http://www.jta.org/1935/05/27/archive/11-ordained-rabbis-at-hebrew-union-college.

921 "New Rabbi Will Hold Services at Beth-El Tonight," *Sun*, Mar. 22, 1935.

922 "Rabbi Lesser to Deliver Farewell Sermon Tonight," *Sun*, Jan. 29, 1937.

923 "Rabbi to Lead First Seminar," *Augusta* (Ga.) *Chronicle*, Nov. 8, 1964, GB.

924 "Rabbi Lesser Speaker Friday," *Sun*, Nov. 20, 1953.

925 "Rabbi to Lead First Seminar."

926 "Rabbi Lesser Speaker Friday."

927 "Rabbi Lesser Speaker Friday."

928 FAG, Rest-Haven Memorial Park, Eugene, Or., for Rabbi Louis E. Neimand.

929 "Rabbi Neimand to Conduct Closing Services Tonight," *Sun*, May 14, 1937.

930 "Jewish Chaplain at SU to Leave for Oregon Post," *Post-Standard* (Syracuse, N.Y.), Apr. 5, 1963, NP.

931 Wikipedia's "Temple Beth El (Eugene, Oregon)" entry.

932 "Temple Beth-El Services," *Sun*, Aug. 20, 1937.

933 "Services Tonight at Temple Beth-El," *Sun*, June 10, 1938.

934 "Edward Ellenbogen, Rabbi, 76," *New York Times*, Nov. 29, 1988, nytimes.com.

935 Frequently misspelled as "Michaels" or "Michel."

936 FAG, Sunland Memorial Park, Sun City, Ariz., for Rabbi Albert A. Michels.

937 Carolyn Gray LeMaster, *Corner of the Tapestry: A History of the Jewish Experience in AR: 1820s-1990s* (Fayetteville, Ark.: U. of Ark. Press, 1994), 361.

938 American Jewish Archives, "Sun City, Arizona—Temple Beth Shalom Records: Institutional Sketch," http://collections.americanjewisharchives.org/ms/ms0641/ms0641.html; Congregation House of Israel, "Our History," http://www.conghouseofisrael.org/history.html.

939 *Sun*, July 28, 1943; "Rabbi Michels to Speak at Emmanu-El," *Longview* (Tex.) *News Journal*, Aug. 17, 1961, NP (he obtained his doctorate at the "Burton Seminary").

940 New York City Births abstracts, LDS, for Albert Abraham Michels, born 1902; 1910 Census, Bronx, N.Y.; 1920 Census, Lansing, Mich.

941 "Rabbi Michels to Speak," *Longview News Journal*, Aug. 17, 1961.

942 1870 Census, Corry, Penn., for Marx Micalels (sic); *Nelson's Biographical Dictionary and Historical Reference Book of Erie County, Pennsylvania, Part VI* (Erie, Penn.: S.B. Nelson, 1896), Google Books, 769-70; *History of Erie County, Pennsylvania, Part V* (Chicago: Warner, Beers & Co., 1884), 996, Anc. Max suicided at his Corry store in 1895 ("Suicide at Corry: Mr. Michels, a Prosperous Merchant, Hangs Himself to a Window Grating," *Evening Republican* (Meadville, Penn.), Feb. 23, 1895, NP). "Suicide" as a verb was used often—regrettably, too often—in historical newspaper articles. Max's second wife, Rose (Goldschmidt/Goldsmith) Michels, remarried after his death to Simon Rauner. Simon Rauner's mother's maiden name was Regina Michels, presumably a relative of Rose's deceased husband (New York State Marriage Licenses, New Vernon, Westchester Cty., 1914, LDS). Rabbi Michel's father, Moses, was born in 1866 to Max and Max's first wife, Henrietta (Siegel) (1870 Census, Corry, Penn., for Marx Micalels (sic); 1880 Census, New York City, for Moses Michels, grandson of Abraham Siegel). Henrietta died when Moses was a boy. Rosa and Max had a daughter, Augusta (New York City Births abstracts, LDS, for unnamed (female) Michels, born Apr. 12, 1882). In 1900 Rosa (Goldsmith) Michels, widow, lived in Corry with her daughter, Gussie (i.e., Augusta), and her mother, Betty Goldsmith (1900 Census).

943 Texas Naturalization Records, Petition of Erno Szrul Yovics, Anc.; Hollace Ava Weiner, *Beth-El's Congregation Centennial: Fort Worth, Texas, 1902-2002 History*, Chapter 4 (2002), http://www.bethelfw.org/ sites/default/files/media/chapter4.pdf.

944 "Rabbi Ernest Grey Leaving Corsicana," *Sun*, May. 29, 1944. On the evening of June 6, 1945, the congregations of Agudas Achim and Beth El held a joint prayer service in observance of the first anniversary of D-Day. Since both synagogues were then without a rabbi, Sydney Marks conducted the service. ("Jewish Congregations in Joint Services of Prayer Tuesday Night," *Sun*, June 7, 1945).

945 "Dr. Ernest Grey Returns Sept. 1 Temple Beth-El," *Sun*, Aug. 3, 1946.

946 *Sun*, Sept. 3, 1947.

947 *Beth-El's Congregation Centennial*, Chapter 4.

948 Legacy.com, *Denver Post Obituaries*, May 29, 2013, for Alice Seldin Grey, http://www.legacy.com/obituaries/denverpost/obituary.aspx?n=alice-seldin-grey&pid=165032360.

949 Their car left the road on route #401 near London, Ontario on August 28 and rolled over. Alice was severely injured. Grey was then associate professor of Spanish literature at U. of Waterloo. (Report of American Citizens Killed Abroad (with attached death certificate and doctor's report), Anc.).

950 The spelling in some *Sun* articles was "Weiner," i.e., "Morris A. Fox Funeral Services Monday Morning," *Sun*, Jan. 12, 1948.

951 He was born in 1918 in Stettin, Poland, and arrived in the U.S. June 8, 1934 (New York Ship Arrivals, SS *Gerolstein*, for Theodor Wiener, Anc.). He died in 2006 at Arlington, Va. (Social Security Application and Claims Index, Dec. 11, 2006, Anc.).

952 "Dallas Rabbi to Occupy Pulpit at Temple Beth El," *Sun*, Apr. 15, 1948. Contrary to the implication of the article's title, Rabbi Levy was not to be installed as a new rabbi. Levy was a well-established Dallas rabbi.

953 "Guest Rabbi for Hebrew Holy Days at Temple Beth-El," *Sun*, Sep. 5, 1947.

954 "Wiener, Max," https://www.encyclopedia.com/religion/encyclopedias-almanacs-transcripts-and-maps/wiener-max (biographical entry for his father).

955 "Wiener, Max."

956 "Wiener, Max," *Encyclopaedia Judaica*, http://www.encyclopedia.com/.

957 *Sun*, Nov. 21, 1949 ("Rabbi Harvey E. Wessell of Temple Beth-El"); "Thanksgiving Service for Community is Held Here," *Sun*, Nov. 24, 1949 ("rabbi of Congregation Beth-El in Tyler").

958 Gloria Feldt, *Forward*, "No Temple in Temple," Sept. 29, 2010, http://forward.com/articles/131690/no-temple-in-temple/. See Rabbi Lesser biography, above.

959 "New Rabbi Serves Temple Beth-El," *Sun*, July 2, 1952.

960 "Sarasohn Heads Rabbis of Texas," *Sun*, Mar. 12, 1953.

961 "Rabbi Sarasohn Farewell Sermon Temple Beth-El," *Sun*, June 29, 1956.

962 "Rabbi Sarasohn Accepts Post in North Carolina," *Sun*, June 16, 1956.

963 WWI Draft Reg. card, Adams Cty. (Natchez), for Israel Joshua Sarasohn, Anc. Rabbis Brav and Michels also were Natchez rabbis.

964 One source says he was in Augusta from 1919-1922 (Congregation Children of Israel, Augusta Ga., "Past & Present Rabbis," http://cciaugus.rjweb-builder.org/).

965 One source says he went from Augusta to Cumberland ("Augusta, Ga., Rabbi Called to Cumberland Synagogue," *Washington Herald* (Wash., D.C.), Oct. 7, 1920, NP).

966 "Chronicling History: 1943," *Wisconsin Jewish Chronicle* (Milwaukee), Oct. 1, 1993, NP.

967 "Local Jewish Congregation Will Celebrate Rosh Hashana," *Evening Review* (East Liverpool, Ohio) Sept. 16, 1944, NP.

968 WWII Draft Reg. card, Leavenworth Cty., Kan., for Israel Joshua Sarasohn, Anc.

969 N.C. Death Certificates, Anc.

970 "University: To Confer Degrees," *Cincinnati Enquirer*, June 13, 1914, NP (U. of Cincinnati).

971 A number of different birth years are given for Rabbi Spear. His grave has Oct. 25, 1882, but that may not have been from a reliable source, as he had no close family to report his death. The informant on his death certificate was Sydney Marks, who was unable to report Spear's parents' names and was probably uncertain about his birth information as well. The death certificate gives his birth place as Stettin, Germany, but Marks was apparently thinking of Rabbi Wiener, who came from there. In the 1910 federal census, Spear said he was thirty-four (born ca. 1875), but the reliability of that information might be questioned because his wife's age is given as fifty-four, and it is not uncommon in such cases for a husband's age to be exaggerated to narrow an embarrassing gap. In the 1915 New York State census (Anc.), Spear's age is given as thirty-seven (born ca. 1878). His World War I draft registration card gives a birth date of Oct. 25, 1878 (Anc.).

972 "New Rabbi Will Begin Duties at Temple Beth-El," *Sun*, Aug. 30, 1956.

973 "Rabbi Spear Serves Brunswick Temple," *Southern Israelite* (Atlanta, Ga.), Aug. 15, 1952 (Georgia Historic Newspapers), http://israelite.galileo.usg.edu/israelite/search.

974 Her family members appear to have been buried at Union Field Cemetery, N.Y., where Theresa Reinach (her name by her first husband) was also buried, dying May 3, 1921 (FAG). The FAG date of death is at odds with the 1920 date of death given in "$5 Legacy to Husband, 'He Knows Well Why'," *Daily News* (New York), May 19, 1921, NP (estate of $10,000 left to sons from first marriage).

975 "The Jewish Review," *Brooklyn Daily Eagle*, Mar. 10, 1911, NP; "The Jewish Review," *Brooklyn Daily Eagle*, Jan. 17, 1913, NP.

976 WWI Draft Reg. card, Bronx, N.Y., for Joseph David Spear, Anc.; Harry Schneiderman, Ed., *American Jewish Year Book 5680, Vol. 21* (Philadelphia: The Jewish Publication Society of America, 1919), 479, https://books.google.com.

977 "Rabbi Spear Serves Brunswick Temple."

978 "Rabbi Spear Serves Brunswick Temple."

979 "Names in Review," *Jewish Post* (Indianapolis), June 17, 1955 (Hoosier State Chronicles), https://newspapers.library.in.gov/.

980 "Texas Rabbi Dies," *Corpus Christi Caller Times*, Dec. 13, 1958, NP.

981 "Dr. J.D. Spear, Dies Friday; Rites Pending," *Sun*, Dec. 12, 1958; "Dr. J.D. Spear Burial Sunday," *Sun*, Dec. 13, 1958. He was survived by two nephews in West Point, Ga., Sigmund and William Spear.

982 His name in historic records is sometimes misspelled as "Merfield."

983 *Beth El's Centennial History*, Chapter 4.

984 "Rabbi Merfeld Dies Tuesday, Rites Thursday," *Sun*, Jan. 11, 1961.

985 "New Rabbi is Secured for Temple Beth-El," *Sun*, June 26, 1959; "Rabbi Merfeld Dies."

986 "Rabbi Merfeld Dies"; "Merfelds Visit Here," *Fort Worth Star-Telegram*, Aug. 15, 1954, GB.

987 "Rabbi Merfeld Dies."

988 "New Rabbi is Secured."

989 Rabbi Joseph conducted the synagogue's service at 6:15 and the temple's service at 8:00 (Babbette Samuels, "The Final Years of Temple Beth El," (unpublished paper), Texas Jewish Historical Society papers, Dolph Briscoe Center, UT, Austin).

990 "K. Wolens Was Leader in Jewish Faith Here," *Sun*, Jan. 25, 1970. The article identifies only rabbis Ratner, Bachrach, Solomon, and Leibson as Agudas Achim rabbis.

991 1900 Census, Dallas, Tex. His date of death could not be determined. He survived his third wife, Ella, when she died in Chicago, in 1941. When his son David passed away, in 1957, he was already deceased ("Mrs. Ella Ratner," *Chicago Tribune*, Dec. 15, 1941, NP (obituary); "Ratner," *Chicago Tribune*, Jan. 28, 1957 (death notice for Dr. David J. Ratner, son of the late Rabbi Louis Ratner)).

992 Morrison & Fourmy's Corsicana Directory, 1901-1902, Anc.; "Rabbi to Come Here," *Oklahoma News* (Oklahoma City), May 24, 1907, NP.

993 Dallas City Directories, 1891, *et seq.*, Anc.; "Synagogue Plan of Rabbi Ratner: Orthodox Hebrews Start a Campaign to Build Own Temple," *Daily Oklahoman* (Oklahoma City), Oct. 29, 1910, GB.

994 A personal item in the *Corsicana Daily Sun* of May 10, 1909 says, "Rabbi Ratner is here from Oklahoma." One reason necessitating the visit of a rabbi was to perform a circumcision, on a Jewish boy's eighth day of life. Such a boy in Corsicana at that time was Julius Jacobs, son of Jonas and Minnie Jacobs, their seventh child, born on May 3, 1909 (Texas Birth Certificates, Anc.).

995 FAG, Lena Ratner, Dallas, Tex., died 1897.

996 "Rabbi Cruel, is Wife's Charge: Mrs. Dinah Ratner Says That Husband Cursed and Abused Her: Kept in Background: Alleges Preacher Would Not Take Her Into His Society," *Daily Oklahoman* (Oklahoma City), July 16, 1909, NP; "Rabbi's Wife Says She Was Treated Like Dog," *Daily Oklahoman* (Oklahoma City), July 17, 1909, NP.

997 "Rabbi's Wife Asks Divorce," *Chickasha* (Okla.) *Daily Express*, July 29, 1909, NP.

998 1930 Census for Ethel G. Gaberman, L.A., Cal.

999 "Rabbi Ratner Has Release from Wife," *Daily Oklahoman* (Oklahoma City), Nov. 4, 1909, NP.

1000 *Daily Oklahoman* (Oklahoma City), July 29, 1912, NP.

1001 "Ratner," *Chicago Tribune*, June 12, 1929, NP (death notice for Rachel Ratner, wife of Rabbi Louis Ratner).

1002 "Mrs. Ella Ratner," *Chicago Tribune*, Dec. 15, 1941, NP.

1003 Texas Naturalizations, Declaration of Intention for Isaac Mohilner, Aug. 6, 1917, Anc.; JewishGen Online Worldwide Burial Registry for Isaac Mohilner, Miami, Fla.; New York Passenger Arrivals for Isaac Mohilner, arrived June 8, 1904, Anc.; Corsicana City Directory, 1911, Anc.; 1920 Census, Corsicana.

1004 Corsicana City Directory, 1911, Anc.

1005 1910 Census, Topeka, Kan.

1006 New York Passenger Arrivals, for Isaac Mohilner, arrived June 8, 1904, Anc.; 1910 Census, Topeka, Kan.

1007 Declaration of Intention for Naturalization, Kansas City, Mo., Jan. 20, 1909, Anc. His daughter Jean was born in Missouri that year.

1008 Naturalization Records, Texas, Declaration of Intention, for Yidel Dow, 1917, Anc.

1009 "Personals," *Sun*, Jan. 12, 1916. The brief item stated he was travelling to Hillsboro.

1010 Social Security Applications and Claims Index, abstract for Esther Zelda Dow Horwitz/Dreyfus, born Apr. 14, 1914, Anc.

1011 "Services at New Synagogue: Dr. Heller, Man of Many Accomplishments to Make Address," *Sun*, Sept. 21, 1917 (Dow was rabbi; Dr. Nachman Heller was guest speaker) ("dedicatory ceremonies of the new edifice have taken place some two weeks ago…").

1012 "Corsicana District Making Good Progress: Navarro County Little More Than Two Hundred Thousand Below Quota—Victory Today," *Sun*, Oct. 16, 1918 (Dow listed as part of war funding effort).

1013 "Amarillo News," *Jewish Monitor* (Dallas), July 9, 1920, NP (Rev. Y. Dow of Fort Worth performed circumcision at home of D. Rubin).

1014 "Congregation 36 Years Old," *El Paso Herald Post*, June 26, 1936, NP.

1015 "Arizona's Jewish Evolution: Southern Arizona," *Arizona Jewish Life*, Sept. 1, 2013, http://azjewishlife.com/arizonas-jewish-evolution-southern-arizona/.

1016 World War II Draft Reg. card, Maricopa Cty., Ariz., for Ydel Gedolia Dow, Anc.

1017 Rabbi Dow died on Feb. 3, 1956 (Arizona Death Cert., Anc.).

1018 "Many Were Present: Ancient Custom Observed at Home of Mr. and Mrs. M.M. Miller," *Sun*, June 15, 1916 (broad description of ceremony and celebration).

1019 One of the news items under "Corsicana."

1020 Herman (also "Himan") Horowitz did not seem to live in any one place long enough to establish a substantial biographical record. Based on his residences at the times he was listed in censuses, and where his children were born according to those records, he lived in, in this order: Michigan; Texas; Key West, Fla.; Hattiesburg, Miss.; Arkansas; Texas; St. Augustine, Fla.; and Beaumont, Tex. The foregoing assumes the 1900 census (in Key West) enumerates him and his first wife (she died between 1900 and 1910, according to later census records), substantiated by the fact that Anna, Dora, and Rose (of the 1900 census) are living in the New Orleans Jewish Orphans' Home in the 1910 census. Some family members ended up in California. Horowitz was deceased by 1940. No death record for him could be located.

1021 See, e.g., "Tyler," *Jewish Monitor* (Dallas), Apr. 1, 1921 (Purim shpiel (Book of Esther play) produced by Rev. H.J. Horowitz); "Aged Rabbi Dies After Heart Attack," *Mexia Daily News*, July 26, 1951, NP (dateline Houston, for Rabbi Henry Jacob Horowitz, age seventy-two).

1022 Petition for Naturalization, Kansas City, Mo. 1925, Anc.; FAG, Linwood Cemetery, Dubuque, Ia. See www.iowagravestones.org for an image of his gravestone. The date of birth on the gravestone and its Hebrew epitaph, saying he was a rabbi, do not confirm 100 percent that the gravestone is for the Max Bachrach who once lived in Corsicana.

1023 "Rabbi M. Bachrach Accepts Call of Local Synagogue," *Sun*, Aug. 19, 1924.

1024 His Petition for Naturalization to the Federal District Court in Kansas City, Mo., was signed on August 25, 1925 (Naturalizations, for Max Bachrach, Anc.).

1025 According to his naturalization petition, he lived at Dubuque from 1920 to June 1922 and in Kansas City continuously since he left Dubuque.

1026 *Coffeyville* (Kans.) *Daily Journal*, Apr. 8, 1913, NP (Hebrew meat dealer performed Jewish death ritual for his wife in his home); "Rabbi Moves Away," *Wichita Daily Eagle*, June 5, 1913, NP. He later remarried.

1027 "Personal," *Sun*, Apr. 25, 1930.

1028 Records of his year of birth differ. In the 1920, 1930, and 1940 federal censuses he was listed as thirty-six, forty-four, and fifty-five years old, respectively, and with each new decade the number of years he was younger than his wife decreased by one, until in 1940 they were the same age. In 1942 he claimed a birth date of Dec. 19, 1885 (WWII Draft Reg. card for Morris Renov, Bronx, NY, Anc.). No WWI draft registration for him could be found. New York State Death Index for Morris Renov, June 30, 1964, Anc.

1029 There is scant evidence of Rabbi Renov's presence in Corsicana. The primary source is the 1924 Corsicana City Directory (Anc.), which lists him as rabbi of the "Hebrew Orthodox Church," at 109 N. 12th Street and residing at 304 W. 5th Avenue. The nominal date of the directory suggests he was in town prior to Rabbi Bachrach (a news article explicitly stated Bachrach was assuming duties in Sept., 1924), assuming two rabbis were not there simultaneously, but the 1925 *Corsican*, Corsicana High School's yearbook (Anc.), includes freshman Bryna Renov, the rabbi's daughter, suggesting he was there following Bachrach. Morris Renov received a certificate of naturalization on Feb. 16, 1925, from the U.S. Dist. Court at Dallas, Tex., probably while he was still a resident of Corsicana (N. Dist. Tex. Naturalizations, Anc.).

1030 His son Israel won a competition in December of 1928 while enrolled at New York's Central Commercial Continuation School ("Boy, 17, Winner of $180 Prizes for His Poster," *Standard Union* (Brooklyn, NY), Dec. 14, 1928, www.FultonHistory.com (Israel Renov winner of $25 prize)).

1031 Texas Passenger Lists, for Morduch (indexed as "Merduck") Charanowsky, July 23, 1914, Anc.

1032 California Passenger and Crew Lists, for Manasia Haranovoskaja (?) (indexed originally as Mariana Hranowskja) and children, arriving at San Francisco on the SS *Rembrandt* sailing from Surabaya, Indonesia, Dec. 20, 1917, Anc.). Sailing with May, Bryna, and Israel was May's niece, Haya (indexed as Hya), age twenty-six, joining her mother Enid (?) "Renoff" in Shreveport, La.

1033 1920 Census; "Hampden County: Westfield: In Local Churches: Local Notices," *Springfield* (Mass.) *Republican*, Aug. 28, 1920, GB.

1034 "The Latest News from Anderson, S.C.," *Jewish Daily News* (New York, N.Y.), Oct. 31, 1921 ("Dear Aunt Ray:-- …the latest news of Anderson is that we have a shochet and I am going to learn to speak Hebrew…," wrote Gussie Poliakoff to her New York aunt); 1922-1923 City Directory for Anderson, S.C., for Rev. Morice Renov, Rabbi, Anc.

1035 1930 Census, Tannersville, Hunter Township, N.Y.; 1940 Census, The Bronx, N.Y.; WW II Draft Reg. (resides in the Bronx and works in Tannersville for the Talmud Torah Congregation), Anc.

1036 Sometimes spelled Lebovitz.

1037 Declaration of Intention, Supreme Court of N.Y. Cty., N.Y., for Baruch Lebovitz, Anc.; Index to Cal. Deaths, for Baruch Lebovits, Anc.

1038 "Assignments," *Sun*, Feb. 26, 1927.

1039 Passenger Manifest of S.S. Mount Clinton for Baruch, Lea & Israel Lebovitz, 1922, Anc.

1040 U.S. City Directories, Anc.

1041 California Death Index, Anc.

1042 "Palestine Sunday Will be Observed by Corsicana Jews," *Sun*, Mar. 22, 1928.

1043 "Rabbi Leibson to Take Up Duties in Fort Worth," *Sun*, Nov. 11, 1935.

1044 Arrival of SS *Friesland*, June 4, 1906, List M, for Leib Leibson and family, Anc.; 1910, 1920, and 1920 Censuses. He had a total of seven brothers and sisters.

1045 Texas Death Cert., Tarrant County, Mar. 18, 1951, for Rabbi M.J. Leibson, Anc.

1046 "Rev. R.F. Bristol Union Thanksgiving Service Speaker: Event Sponsored by Ministerial Association Held at First Methodist," *Sun*, Nov. 28, 1941.

1047 "Installation Rabbi of Local Synagogue Sunday Afternoon: Rabbi H. Shapiro to be Officially Inducted as Leader Agudas Achim," *Sun*, Feb. 5, 1936.

1048 "Installation of Rabbi for Agudas Achim Synagogue: The Synagogue was also Dedicated at Same Time in Solemn Ceremony," *Sun*, Feb. 10, 1936 (remodeled and repaired United Presbyterian Church building became new home for congregation).

1049 "Kenosha Congregation Appoints New Rabbi," *Wisconsin Jewish Chronicle*, Aug. 31, 1945, NP.

1050 "Fond Du Lac News," *Wisconsin Jewish Chronicle*, Nov. 9, 1928, NP.

1051 "Rabbi Shapiro is Elected Rabbi of Local Synagogue," *Sun*, Nov. 15, 1935; "Kenosha Congregation Appoints."

1052 "Mrs. Harry Shapiro Died in Austin; was Buried on Thursday," *CSWL*, Dec. 15, 1944.

1053 FAG, Beth El Cemetery, Phoenix.

1054 "Rabbi Shapiro Goes to Kenosha, Wis.," *Sun*, May 29, 1945; "Kenosha Congregation Appoints."

1055 WWII Draft Reg. card, Little Rock, Anc. Other records of his birth date vary by several years, e.g., his gravestone gives him a birth date of 1892 (FAG, Whitfield Memorial Gardens, Dalton, Ga.). His wife, Tillie, died in 1980.

1056 "Mrs. Joe Wolens Entertained at Tea Wednesday," *Sun*, May 23, 1946.

1057 "Retiring Rabbi is Honored Wednesday," *Sun*, Oct. 29, 1964; "K. Wolens was Leader in Jewish Faith Here," *Sun*, Jan. 25, 1970. The latter article mistakenly said Shapiro was rabbi for twenty-four years, not eighteen, probably by adding in the years of service of the previous Rabbi Shapiro.

1058 "Retiring Rabbi is Honored Wednesday." At the time of his retirement, special guests from Toronto included two nieces who were daughters of Samuel Meyer Shapiro, a publisher in Toronto ("Retiring Rabbi is Honored Wednesday").

1059 "Rabbi Joseph Shapiro," *Arkansas Gazette* (Little Rock), Dec. 11, 1976, GB (obituary); "Mrs. Joe Wolens Entertained." The number 18 in Jewish numerology is considered good luck. In Hebrew, the number is represented by the same two letters which spell "chai," that is, "life." The number 36 is "double chai," double good luck, and is a frequently preferred amount for charitable contributions (as is single chai, $18).

1060 See, e.g., his son Charles's obituary, "Charles M. Shapiro," *Arkansas Gazette* (Little Rock), Apr. 19, 1988, GB.

1061 "Union Service at St. John's Thanksgiving," *Sun*, Nov. 23, 1965; "K. Wolens was Leader."

1062 Interview by Tommy Stringer, Jan. 10, 1978 (see Chapter 4).

1063 Interview by Tommy Stringer.

1064 Interview by Tommy Stringer. See Supplement I.

1065 Wikipedia's "Haftarah" entry; Wikipedia's "Nevi'im" (Prophets) entry.

# Supplement III: Burials to 1890

1066 See Chapters 2 and 26. The record book is now maintained by other board members of the CHCA.

1067 There are undoubtedly other Jews in Corsicana today, but Babbette is the only one from earlier times, when the population was sufficient enough to support two congregations.

1068 Cleanup efforts at Bayside Cemetery were underway in 2011, when this photo was taken, following decades of neglect. The cemetery has approximately 35,000 burials and dates back to the mid-nineteenth century. See http://www.baysidecemeterylitigation.com/. Cemetery neglect is not restricted to any particular geography or religious denomination.

1069 See Chapter 26. The CHCA record book and a survey of gravestones at the cemetery show Leo Fox was the earliest burial. If there were Jews in Corsicana or nearby who died before the cemetery grounds were purchased (none are known), they would have been buried in Waco's Hebrew Rest Cemetery, established in 1869, or in Dallas, which also had a Jewish cemetery before 1875, both relatively close to Corsicana, or in another Texas Jewish cemetery already in existence, like the Houston and Galveston Jewish cemeteries, which were established before the Civil War. Corsicana's early Jewish dead might also have been buried in a non-Jewish cemetery, like Oakwood, or in a distant Jewish cemetery, i.e. in Louisiana, especially if other family members had already been buried there.

1070 See FAG entries for burials not detailed in this supplement; see Chapter 27 regarding the LHCA.

1071 K. Goldman, personal correspondence with author. Goldman is a distant relative.

1072 See Chapter 27.

1073 Men with the surnames of Morris and Rosenbaum were two of the seven incorporators of the Hillsboro Compress Company in 1887, in nearby Hillsboro. The inclusion of a "Rosenbaum," a typically Jewish surname, suggests this particular Mr. Morris may have been Jewish. ("Hillsboro Roads," *FWDG*, May 17, 1887).

1074 "Texas—Facts and Fancies," *Austin Weekly Statesman*, June 3, 1875, NP.

1075 Tenn. Marriages, Henry Cty., Wm. Wolf and Nancy M. Bufford, Anc.

1076 "Sherman: One more Unfortunate, Weary of Breath, Ends his Earthly Woes," *FWDG*, Jan. 5, 1884. The article says he was buried in the county cemetery (presumably, Grayson County, where Sherman is located), where there are many unmarked, paupers' graves. Nanny's grave is in Corsicana's Oakwood Cemetery (Nancy M. Wolf, b. Jan. 9, 1842, d. Dec. 28, 1903), FAG. Burford Herring Wolf, Nancy's grandson by her son, William C. Wolf, is also buried in Oakwood Cemetery. "Bill" Wolf, Nanny's son, settled in Roswell, N.M.

1077 See Chapter 24.

1078 See Chapter 24.

1079 "S. Fox" is quite possibly Simon Fox of the Corsicana Foxes, brother of Alexander Fox and husband of Lena (Solomon) Fox (see the Simon Fox information accompanying the profile of Michael Hirsch Solomon, below).

1080 Robert L. Harris married to Carrie Shenfeld, Aug. 26, 1883, Kings Cty., New York, Cert. #2510 (Italian Genealogical Group, Record Search: Grooms, http://www.italiangen.org/records-search/grooms.php). Other records indicate her family name was "Schoenfeld." Their three children born in Texas were: Etta (May 1884); Minerva S. (Oct. 1884); and Harry (June 1887) (1900 Census, Paterson, N.J.). One of the girls' recorded birth dates in 1884 apparently must be wrong. Minerva married to Edwin Wolff and was recorded as being born Oct. 6, 1888 in Hillsboro, Texas (Ship Arrivals, Miami, Fla., Sept. 26, 1938, for Minerva and Edwin E. Wolff, Anc.). R.L. Harris of New York may be the Robert Harris of New York City who was the son of Levi and Minnie (Mena/Mina) Harris. Several data points match up. The latter had a sister, Annie Harris, born 1850 in Prussia (1870 Census), who may be the Annie Harris who married Simon Fox's brother, Abraham L. Fox, of New York City, evidence that Robert L. Harris and Simon Fox were the men enumerated at Tyler, Texas in 1880.

1081 *Memorial*, 713. See also Chapter 24.

1082 See Chapter 24.

1083 The handwritten date of death in the cemetery record book was apparently misread as "5/23/1881"; an annotation of her age, added later to the same page, reads "1 mo, 29 da (sic) old."

1084 "Sad Accident: A Babe Killed by a Breakdown on Woodward Avenue," *Detroit Free Press*, July 8, 1875, N.P.

1085 "Roasted Alive: Several Business Houses in the Heart of Ennis Totally Consumed—Loss about $20,000: S. Goldberg, a Prominent Merchant of the Town, Loses His Life while Trying to Save His Money," *FWDG*, Nov. 1, 1886.

1086 "A Fatal Blaze at Ennis: In Which S. Goldsburg Lost His Life," *DMN*, Nov. 1, 1886; "Fatal Fire at Ennis: A Young Man Killed in a Burning Building—Two Large Blazes," *GDN*, Nov. 1, 1886. "A Fatal Blaze" refers to him as "a young man lately from Germany," and the other articles describe him similarly.

1087 The next two earliest Goldberg burials were Jennie Louis Goldberg, a newborn who died in 1899, and Rachel Goldberg, an elderly woman who died in 1925.

A Find-A-Grave entry showing a "S. Goldsburg" buried at Zions Rest Cemetery, a small burial ground in Corsicana, temporarily dampened the theory that Joe Goldberg and S. Goldsburg were the same person. The unusual spelling on the FAG page, *Goldsburg*, and a reference on the page to the news article raised suspicions: was this FAG page based solely on that news article, and not on a visit to the Zion's Rest Cemetery, or was that FAG data supplied by the cemetery or based on an in-person visit—the usual ways memorial pages are created? Contact with the person who posted that FAG memorial confirmed the error: she had mistakenly identified his burial place as Zion's Rest, thinking that was the "Jewish cemetery" mentioned in the news article.

Two feasible hypotheses might explain how the first initial "S." and "Joe" could be mistaken one for the other: 1. the deceased's first initial of "J," for Joe, was misread as an "S;" or 2. the deceased's name was "Sol," and a handwritten note with that name was misread as "Joe."

1088 1880 Census, in Ennis. Amelia Levy's maiden name, Samuels, was determined from the death certificate of her daughter, Sallie Ivy (Levy) Mincer (Tex. Death Certs., Waxahachie, Anc.). Amelia was the sister of Rosa Cohen of Corsicana and Frances Levingston of Ennis.

1089 Isadore Marks's grave location according to the record book is plot G-2. The Cemetery Association's plot map, created by Ivan Rosenberg and dated July 15, 1958, shows the location of section G, grave 2. An in-person visit to the cemetery finds at that location a completely illegible stone accompanied by a newly added footstone commemorating the death of Fannie Freeman. It seems, therefore, that the eroded stone might actually have been a stone for Isadore Marks, not Fannie Freeman, but there's no way to tell because it is so illegible. Fannie Freeman, according to the record book, was buried in plot A-27, which according to the map is not even close to G-2. The gravestone at location G-1, based on the map and a visit to the cemetery, is likewise entirely illegible and also has a newly installed footstone next to it, in this case for "Infant Freeman." According to the record book, however, Infant Freeman was buried in plot A-22, again, not even close.

If Fannie Freeman and Infant Freeman were buried somewhere other than in plots A-27 and A-22, who then was buried in those locations? A thorough analysis was done based on 1) the map; 2) actual gravestone locations; and 3) the record book. The analysis demonstrates a confused mess regarding all burials in sections A and G, with little correspondence between plot locations according to the map, burial locations referenced in the record book, and actual gravestone at those locations.

1090 The Iowa marriage in Dubuque County of their daughter, Rae Brin, to Nathan Novaschelsky in 1897 (LDS) gives Lena's maiden name. Any relation to the Corsicana Freedmans is unknown.

1091 1880 Census, for H. Brin, in Ennis; "Hotel Arrivals," *DDH*, Dec. 31, 1884. ("H. Brin" is from Ennis.)

1092 FAG, Beth Olem Cemetery, Hamtramck, Mich.

1093 David and Josie (Josephine) were married in Detroit in 1879 (Michigan Marriages, Anc.) and lived in Waxahachie in 1880 and in 1900 (Census). The 1900 census states that of the four children born to her, only three then survived.

1094 Sarah's surviving children with William Herman were Joe and Ray (1900 Census, Corsicana). Sarah also gave birth to two stillborn Herman children, Leah and Abraham, and in 1905 to Isaac Herman, who lived for nine days before dying. With Ben Gottlieb, Sarah had given birth to Hayman Gottlieb, who died at the age of ten in 1893 (cemetery record book; gravestone, Hebrew Cemetery). Sarah, who died in 1905, and William Herman, who died in 1918, are also buried in the Hebrew Cemetery.

1095 "Corsicana," *FWDG*, Feb. 11, 1888.

1096 Common Pleas Court, New York City, Sept. 21, 1860, Bundle 253, Record 192, Anc.

1097 "Hotel Arrivals: At the Girardin," *GDN*, Nov. 20, 1888, PTH.

1098 Records, including city directories, list a Michael and a Morris Lissauer in New York at that time (Anc.).

1099 Her common Jewish name, usually spelled "Bluma" in English, was rendered in her case as "Blouma" and she was called "Elizabeth" in the 1900 census (cemetery record book; 1901 Corsicana City Directory, Anc.; 1900 Census, Corsicana).

1100 The 1900 census states that "Elizabeth Solomon" of Corsicana was the mother of seven children, five of them still living, and that she was born in Germany in 1819 (historical records of that type frequently understated a woman's age). A ship manifest listing her and some of her family (Blume, M., Abr. & Line Solomonas) arriving in the U.S. in Oct. 1871 (New Orleans Passenger List Quarterly Abstracts, Anc.) has her age listed as fifty-four, and is likely more accurate than the census record from 1900.

1101 1870 Census, Limestone Cty.; Hebrew Cemetery gravestone.

1102 New Orleans Marriage Licenses, LDS. Bertha's family name, Solomon, is listed on records such as the death certificate of her daughter, Gertrude (Fox) Hickey.

1103 Joe's birth date is from his gravestone in the Hebrew Cemetery (Aug. 4, 1846). The inscribed poem is damaged, but legible enough so that the common funereal verse could be identified. A fully legible copy, possibly with variations from the version on Joe Solomon's stone, was recorded in Find-A-Grave (Waldheim Cemetery, Jewish Graceland section, Forest Hills, Cook Cty., Ill., for Hannah Meyer, died 1888):

> *Tis hard to break the tender cord*
> *When love has bound the heart.*
> *Tis hard, so hard, to speak the words,*
> *Must we forever part?*
> *Dearest loved one, we have laid thee*
> *In the peaceful grave's embrace,*
> *But thy memory will be cherished*
> *Till we see thy heavenly face.*

1104 "Special Spray," *DDH*, June 22, 1884.

1105 "J. Solomon: General Merchandise," *Houston Post*, May 15, 1888, GB. The address given is 101 Beaton, without specifying whether North or South Beaton, but because the street numbering starts with 100 and, on the opposite corner, 101, this puts his store at the intersection with Collin Street, on one of the east-side corners.

1106 "Corsicana Budget," *DMN*, Jan. 27, 1891.

1107 Isadore's birth and death dates are based on his gravestone (FAG, Hebrew Rest Cemetery, Fort Worth, Tex.), although the 1900 Census (Corsicana) says he was born four years earlier, in 1847. The later birth date, from the gravestone, is more likely because more consideration would have been given in that case. The census shows he was two years younger than his wife, but it was very common that inaccurate ages were given to make a husband appear older than the wife, or, as in this case, reduce an age gap; he may have been even older than what was put on his gravestone.

1108 1900 Census, Corsicana.

1109 It is a Jewish tradition to name children after a recently deceased, close relative. Michael died Oct. 31, 1889, and the 1900 census says that Mitchell was born in October, 1889. Presumably, if that naming tradition was followed, Mitchell was born on October 31, later on the same day his namesake, Michael, died. On the other hand, a Jewish boy is named eight days after he's born, so Mitchell would have been named in early November. Or better, based on Mitchell's WWII draft registration card (at San Bernardino, Cal., Anc.), he was born Oct. 31, 1890, not 1889, as reported in the 1900 census. The error may be with the 1900 census: the 1910 census (Fort Worth, Tex.) says he is nineteen years old, indicating a birth date in 1890, exactly a year after his grandfather died.

1110 Abe Solomon's date of death, June 9, 1900, is taken from his gravestone, which is located directly in front of that of M.H. Solomon. Abe was enumerated in the 1880 census in Corsicana as "Abel," a common Jewish nickname for Abraham. Names, ages, and dates of arrivals given in census records were used to find the family's ship arrival record, on the SS *Kohn*, sailing from Bremen via Great Britain. Abe died just prior to the taking of the 1900 census. His birth date is taken from the 1880 census and the ship arrival manifest.

1111 "Failure at Corsicana," *GDN*, Dec. 5, 1892, NP (A. Solomon's clerk, Simon Fox, is the bankruptcy trustee).

1112 1880 Census, Corsicana, for Lena Saliman, age sixteen, boarding with Alx Fox; Texas Death Certs., Fort Worth, for Lena Fox, Anc.; 1900 Census, Corsicana, for Simon and Lena Fox and Simon's mother-in-law, Elizabeth Solomon. Lena's 1925 death certificate mistakenly lists her birth date as Aug. 8, 1860. It says she was born in Mississippi (other records say Prussia) to "Milton Solomon."

1113 1900 Census, Corsicana, for Elizabeth Solomon. Lena's mother, Blouma ("Elizabeth"), was living with Lena and Simon in 1900, listed as Simon's mother-in-law (1900 Census).

1114 Evidence that Alex and Simon Fox were brothers is that they married women who were sisters and that they were enumerated together in the 1870 Census (Eutaw Post Office, Limestone Cty., Texas).

1115 The 1900 Census reported that two of the seven children born to Blouma ("Elizabeth") had died. The date of the census enumeration was June 12, 1900, so it is not clear whether Abe, who died three days earlier, was considered one of her two already deceased children. Her son Joseph clearly had died earlier. Therefore, because only five of her seven children are known, at least one and possibly two of Blouma's unknown children were still living as of 1900.

1116 1901 Corsicana City Directory, Anc.

1117 Many unsuccessful hours were spent attempting to find a connection between the Corsicana and Vicksburg Solomon/Fox families, as the remainder of this note illustrates. It was initially thought that Abraham **Solomon** of Fulshear, Tex. (near Houston) was the same as Abraham **Solomon** of Corsicana. Fulshear Abraham married Mary **Fox**, daughter of Simon and Annetta (maiden name Angle or Augle (Engel?)) **Fox**. Simon **Fox** was a Prussian and Annetta was from Pennsylvania. The 1860 Vicksburg household of Simon and Annetta **Fox** included another married couple, Samuel and Bettie/Bertha **Fox**, and the latter couple's son, Joseph. Based on their four-year age difference, Simon and Samuel Fox were likely brothers. (1860 Census, Vicksburg, pages 18 & 50 (duplicate enumerations).)

In 1870, Simon and Annetta **Fox** and their seven children, including Mary, their oldest, were living in Girard, Richland Parish, La. (1870 Census), while Samuel and Bettie **Fox**, at this point in Houston, had five children (their oldest was also named "Mary"). In 1880, Simon's **Fox** family was back in Vicksburg with Mary's new husband, Abram **Solomon**, living with them (1880 Census). By 1900, Abraham and Mary (**Fox**) **Solomon** and their children had moved to Texas, eventually settling in Fulshear. (1900 Census, Fort Bend Cty., Tex.; "The Death Roll: Mr. H. (sic) Solomon," *HP*, Feb. 19, 1904 (obituary of Abraham Solomon); Tex. Death Cert., Harris Cty., for Mary Solomon, Jan. 21, 1919, Anc.; "Mrs. Mary Solomon," *HP*, Jan. 22, 1919 (obituary); FAG, Beth Israel Cemetery, Houston, for Solomon and Fox family members.)

1118 Texas Death Certs., Dallas, for Abraham Rosenbaum (died 1950) and Eugene Rosenbaum (died 1958) (Anc.) both list their births in Marshall in the 1860s; 1870 Census, Marshall, Tex., for S. Rosenbaum. In 1860, Simon, "Eliza," and Harriet Rosenbaum were in Carthage, Panola County. They had recently arrived there because two-year-old Harriet was born in New York (1860 Census).

1119 The appointment was at Ash Spring (Appointments of U.S. Postmasters, Ash Spring, Harrison Cty., June 19, 1866, Anc.). "Former Resident Dies at Dallas," *Marshall News Messenger*, Jan. 3, 1950, NP (Abraham Rosenbaum obituary).

1120 1880 Census, Wood Cty., Tex., for Ella Rosenbaum.

1121 1900 Census, Dallas, for the Rosenbaum household of A. (Abraham), Minnie, I (Isaac), Hattie, and Ella.

1122 Rosenbaum Bros. was a business in Hillsboro in 1888-1893 ("A Successful Burglary," *DMN*, Feb. 7, 1888; "Hillsboro Budget: Riddled with Bullets," *DMN*, Nov. 9, 1893. See note 1073 regarding Morris and Rosenbaum of Hillsboro.)

1123 Tex. Death Cert. for Eugene Rosenbaum, July 9, 1958, Anc. ("never married"); 1900 Census, Dallas, for I. Rosenbaum (age thirty-eight and single).

1124 It's possible that Morris was Abraham's child by an earlier wife, a conjecture based on the fact that when Abe and Minnie married, in or about 1897, Abe was seventeen years her senior, about thirty-six years old (1900 Census).

1125 In 1900, in Dallas, several relatives of Abraham and Minnie (Marcus) Rosenbaum lived with them, including Herbert and Carrie Marcus, Minnie's siblings (1900 Census). In 1910, Minnie's sister Carrie, who was now married, and Carrie's husband, A.L. Neiman, were the only relatives still living with the Abraham Rosenbaum family. Carrie (Marcus) Neiman, Abraham L. Neiman, and Herbert Marcus founded the nationally known luxury department store chain, Neiman Marcus. (THB, "Carrie Marcus Neiman"; Wikipedia's "Herbert Marcus" entry.)

1126 Many family history mysteries are unresolved due to the absence of records from the 1890 federal census, which was almost entirely destroyed by fire.

# ACKNOWLEDGEMENTS

First and foremost, thank you **Corsicana Hebrew Cemetery Association** for allowing access to association documents and for board members' recollections of Corsicana's Jewish community: Linda Garner; Bob Rosen; and the inimitable Babbette Samuels, a real-life Corsicana legend.

**Everyone** I met in **Corsicana**, in-person and by phone, email, and post, was warm and considerate. Despite my initial hesitancy as an outsider poking his nose into other folks' history, I always felt welcomed. Thank you for sharing your enthusiasm for my project and your knowledge: Mayor Denbow; Navarro District Court Clerk Tackett and his staff; Edward Lynn Williams; Bobbie Young; Dana Stubbs; Verna Bonner; Ines Waggoner; Erica Stubbs; and Dr. Tommy Stringer. I'm most appreciative also to the courtesies extended by Byron Haynie; Jerry Eddins; Michael Kormos and the staff writers at the *Corsicana Daily Sun*; Lowell Olsen Dunn; and Joe McClure. Anyone who knows anything about Corsicana history acknowledges the special brilliance of Ron Maxfield, who knows every pilaster and cornice of historic Corsicana.

**Descendants and other relatives of the Corsicana folk** mentioned in this book kindly shared family fact and lore which helped to develop biographical details of early Corsicanans: Susan Finn; Melodi Amsel-Arieli; Rabbi Frank Joseph; Kina Kay Liland; Wiley and Bill Clarkson; Bo Roberts; Mojavelyn and Lynette Jester; Kay C. Goldman; Melissa Miller Krause; Bud Silverberg; Rabbi Yirmiyahu Ullman; Jennifer Stern; Linda Dow; Lindsey Slott; Fred Stollnitz; Wendy L. Levy; Judy Wolkovitch; Polly Haslam Jamison; and others already mentioned. I benefited from the efforts of **skilled amateur historians and genealogists**: Marilyn Kosanke; Dwight Baker; Dan Wilkes; and Paul Borsellino.

I tapped a host of **experts, researchers, and mavens** to find information on topics as diverse as bull elephant orneriness and gravestone lichen growth rates. I am grateful for the time and attention of: Susan O'Shea; Peter Shrake; Mark Schmitt; Debra J. Hardin; Prof. Helen McLure; Prof. Janet M. Davis; William Marvel; Professor Stjepan Meštrović; explorers Will Ross and Devan Scott; William Groneman; Prof. Louis Schmier; Prof. Lee Shai Weissbach; Sue Morris; Prof. Anne Pringle; Dottie J. Miller; Rosanne Leeson; and Ellen Barbieri. **I'm indebted to** Jonathan Webb Deiss **for his expert research and know-how,** to the enthusiastic efforts of genealogist Sharron Mirikitani, and the photographic skills of Dylan Williams.

I received the assistance of numerous **librarians and archivists** from across the county who fielded questions related to Corsicana, its Jews, and topics hardly related to the Rope Walker legend but which I felt compelled to find out about all the same: Hollace Ava Weiner; Christina Lucas; Lynette Cen; Rachel Myers; Cheryl A. Kempler; Evan Hocker; Abbie H. Weiser; Adrian Morales; Jane McGuigan; Jennifer Reibenspies; Timothy Binkley; Paul Fisher; Sasha Makuka; Shawn Harrington; and Jessy Wheeler.

Gratitude for their time and helpful criticism, and apologies for some—times making them read not-ready-to-be-read manuscripts, **beta readers and other editors**: Dianne West Short; Cathy Silber; Marge Kennedy; Michele Liguori; Jeanie Fallon; Jaclyn Sammis; Paul Davidovich Yarin; Shoshana Yarin; Steve Hoskins; Adam Rosen; and Dana Maclease. Thank you Molly Spain, who has the patience of Job! Prospectively, to BookBaby for getting this thing printed and other publishing support.

I'm grateful to those who pitched in to help **finance** the research and production of this book, for believing I had it in me, and for their patience in waiting, and waiting, and waiting: the Texas Jewish Historical Society for awarding a research grant to a proven researcher but an unproven writer; to my Kickstarter campaign contributors, especially Paul Yarin, Jamie Popkin, and Sharon Efron.

To Suzi, who put up with my puns, which increased inversely pro—portional to how much sleep I got. Even if you are not my target audience, you are the target of my love and affection.

# Illustrations

109 Jim Yarin (Across the Street Diner and Bistro)

109 *Sun*, Sept. 2, 1927

110 *Sun*, Oct. 22, 1927

110 Jim Yarin

111-112 RWeb

114-115 Courtesy Ron Maxfield

116 *Logan's Railway Business Directory* (A.L. Logan & Co., 1873), 96, Archive.org/stream/logansrailwaybus00loga

117 Navarro County Pictorial History, Vol. 1

119 Courtesy Ron Maxfield (map)

119 Jim Yarin (Napoli's Italian Restaurant & Bar)

120 Jim Yarin, by permission of Napoli's Italian Restaurant & Bar

121 "Corsicana," *Navarro Express*, Feb. 25, 1860, PTH

122 *Memorial*, 170

123 Courtesy Ron Maxfield (map)

123 *Corsicana Daily Courier*, Feb. 13, 1888, PTH (Dr. Gulick advertisement)

124 *AMB2*, frontispiece

125 *AMB2*, back matter

126 "Dallas News" (transcribed in *AMB1*, 44).

126 "The Texas Star, Decatur, Texas" (transcribed in *AMB1*, 40)

127 *Sun*, Mar. 1, 1966

128 *AMB1*, 30-31.

129 "Mulkey at Waxahachie," *DMN*, July 5, 1897 (transcribed in *AMB1*, 45-46)

130-131 Courtesy Kay Goldman

132 www.fold3.com

133 "Max H. London Died at Home Here Just After Noon Today," *Sun*, Dec. 24, 1925

134 1860 Census, Springfield, Tex., Sched. 1, Free Inhabitants, p. 2, Anc.

135 *CSWL*, July 18, 1922

136 "Personal," *Pittsburgh Daily Commercial*, Dec.15, 1869, NP

137 "Passengers Sailed," *New York Times*, January 24, 1873, NP

137 Draft list of class II men, June 1863, Cincinnati, Anc.

138 "An Acrobat's Fall," *Chicago Daily Tribune*, Mar. 6, 1883, NP

139 Jim Yarin

141 *The Jewish Messenger*, Apr. 28, 1882, GB

142 Register, National Home for Disabled Volunteer Soldiers, Milwaukee, Anc.

143 Petition for Naturalization, Court of Common Pleas, New York City, Anc.

145 1880 Census, Anc.

146-149 Pension file #19378, National Archives and Records Administration

150-151 *Lippincott's Gazetteer of the World* (1880) (Google Books)

153 *Prairie Blade*, Nov. 17, 1855, PTH

154 Pension file # 19378, National Archives and Records Administration

155 M. Secrist, *Giles County Tennessee: History Revealed Through Biographical and Genealogical Sketches*, 2nd Ed. (2012) (Google Books)

156-157 Pension file #19378, National Archives and Records Administration

162 & 164 Public family tree posted by NavarroCountyGary, Anc.

166 1870 Census, Rusk Cty., Tex., p. 412, Anc.

167 *Memorial*, 665

168 Gail Richards for Find A Grave

172 *Trinity Advocate* (Palestine, Tex.), Oct. 6, 1858, GB

173 Buckles Blog, Buckles.blogspot.com, Dec. 5, 2016

175 "Circus Elephant Running Amuck," *Sun*, Dec. 12, 1925

176 Buckles Blog, Buckles.blogspot.com, Sept. 14, 2017

177 Black Diamond vertical file, Corsicana Public Library

179 Sharon Dodson Sutton for Find A Grave

182 Buckles Blog, Buckles.blogspot.com, Oct. 19, 2007

184-187 Jim Yarin

190 *AMB1*, 99

192 Jim Yarin

193 "Fireman's Monument Unveiled Yesterday," *Sun*, June 16, 1919

197 Courtesy Ron Maxfield

201 Dylan Williams

205 Jim Yarin

206 Sharron Mirikitani

207 Courtesy Linda Garner

212 & 216 Jim Yarin

218 "A Serious Accident—A Fair Journalist," *Waco Daily Examiner*, Mar. 10, 1883, NP

219 *Galveston Daily News*, Oct. 19, 1883, PTH

221 "A Girl Editor," *The Reidsville* (N.C.) *Times*, Nov. 11, 1880, NP

223 Metmuseum.org_art_collection_search_655468

227 "The Religious Revivals," *HP*, Apr. 16, 1906

228 "Mulkey's Epistle," *Sun*, Feb. 27, 1918

232 Jim Yarin; Collin Street Bakery

234 Facebook, "RIP Eli Wallach," still from *The Good, The Bad, and The Ugly*

237 "An Exciting Time," *Semi-Weekly Wisconsin*, July 14, 1869, NP

238 RG 94, File E94, National Archives Records and Administration

239 Courtesy Meigs County (Ohio) Historical Society

242 Jim Yarin

243 *Morrison & Fourmy's General Directory of Corsicana*, 1898-1899, City Directories, Waco (sic), Tex., Anc.

244 "A Synagog for Corsicana, Tex." *American Israelite*, Nov. 3, 1898

245 *Southern Mercury* (Dallas), Nov. 17, 1898, PTH (charter filed)

245 *El Paso Herald*, Nov. 9, 1898, NP (lot to be purchased)

246 "Corsicana, Texas," *American Israelite*, Sept. 20, 1900

247 "Dedicated a Synagogue," *Dallas Daily News*, Sept. 23, 1900, GB

249-250 "Publish List of Donors," *Sun*, Oct. 27, 1917

252 Jim Yarin

253 "Corsicana Cullings," *DMN*, May 7, 1890

255 *Popular Mechanics* (Oct., 1934)

257 Library of Congress Prints & Photographs collection, www.loc.gov/pictures/item/ggb2005023085/

258 *The Sentinel, The American Jewish Weekly*, Nov. 16, 1917, www.idaillinois.org,cdm refcollection p16614coll14id 16191

258 "Dr. Goldberg Making Good," *Sun*, Aug. 8, 1918 (in uniform)

259 *The Jewish Monitor*, Dec. 19, 1919, NP

260 Jewish Museum of the American West, www.jmaw.org

261 *The Sheboygan Press*, May 26, 1915, NP

261 "A Tabernacle Tangle," *Reading Times*, Aug. 9, 1898, NP

263 *The Jewish Monitor* (Dallas), Dec. 19, 1919, NP (Macht)

263 "Rabbis to Debate Jewish Statehood," *The Jewish Floridian*, Jan. 4,1946, University of Florida Digital Collections, www.ufdc.ufl.edu/ (Zielonka)

264 Jewish Welfare Board records, Military Chaplaincy, American Jewish Historical Society, Anc.

265 Courtesy Fort Worth Jewish Archives at Beth-El Congregation, Fort Worth

266 "New Post," *Longview* (Tex.) *News Journal*, June 29, 1952, NP

267 Courtesy Fort Worth Jewish Archives at Beth-El Congregation, Fort Worth

270 Courtesy Linda Dow

271 "Fond Du Lac News," *The Wisconsin Jewish Chronicle*, Nov. 9, 1928, NP

272 "Retiring Rabbi is Honored Wednesday," *Sun*, Oct. 29, 1964

273 "Rabbi Ernest Joseph Serves Three Groups," *Sun*, Apr. 14, 1972

274-279 Jim Yarin

280 Jim Yarin (Elkan London gravestone)

280 Courtesy Babbette Samuels ("Walk Into Oblivion" clipping)

281 Jim Yarin

282 Jim Yarin (Joe Goldberg gravestone)

282 Courtesy Linda Garner (cemetery record book)

282 "A Fatal Blaze at Ennis," *DMN*, Nov. 1, 1886

283 Jim Yarin

284 Jim Yarin (Moses Cerf gravestone)

284 "Infant son of Mr. Henry Cerf," *FWDG*, June 18, 1887

284 Jim Yarin (Brin gravestone)

285-289 Jim Yarin

303 note 202 Helen McLure, "'With the Past Let These Be Buried': The 1873 Mob Massacre of the Hill Family in Springtown, Texas," *Southwestern Historical Quarterly* 105, no. 2 (Oct. 2001): 292, https://texashistory.unt.edu/ark:/67531/meapth101222/m1/322/, PTH

# Subject Index

# Names Index

Page references in **bold** include extended biographical information.

Printed in Great Britain
by Amazon

46652693R00229